AIR CERBERUS, LLC.

Print ISBN 9-7989857284-0-8
EBook ISBN 9-7989857284-1-5
Air Cerberus, LLC.
www.aircerberus.com

Dublin to Vladivostok

John Cody Mosbey

Contents

Part IV

Preface

I became interested in Alexander Dugin when beginning my doctoral studies at Trinity College Dublin. As both a practitioner and student of geopolitics, I attempted to meld my life-long interest in Christian Theology with my career-long involvement with U.S. National Security. The Irish School of Ecumenics at Trinity gave me this opportunity.

My research into Dugin has, so far, resulted in my Ph.D. dissertation, articles, papers, countless discussions, and this subsequent book. My purpose is to examine the development and impact of contemporary Russian geopolitical theologian Alexander Dugin's Eurasianism expressed in his vocal and written explanations of his *Fourth Political Theory*. I peer through political and theological lenses to examine how Dugin and his ideas are perceived in the West. I consider his evolution from a little-known activist to a controversial geopolitical thinker who espouses a political theology critical of Western expressions of Liberal Democracy as I investigate his criticism of the West and its Western Liberalism.

I examine Dugin's critical claims through his words and the words of others questioning his views. I employ two major research strategies to examine and comment on these assertions: first, my study examines Dugin as an interpreter and commentator of the West; second, I compare observations, comments, critiques, and conclusions of selected interpreters and commentators on Dugin and his ideas. Dugin claims to be a Traditionalist and a Eurasianist. I explore these claims using the same approach, Dugin's work and the work of Dugin critics.

I admit bringing the baggage of my experience and education with me, as do all who honestly study and comment on geopolitics and political theology. I do not apologize for this fact. My examination of Dugin intends to provoke thought in the reader about how they interpret him, not to sell my opinions. Although I attach importance to Dugin's self-perception, I am more interested in Western perceptions concerning him.

As I am American—not Russian—I approached my study from an American vantage point and gathered data from a variety of primarily Western sources. These sources included books, interviews, newspapers, journals, published reports, websites, and blogs. This methodology progresses topically, examining each of Dugin's claims by first reviewing the supporting evidence from Dugin's perspective as a prelude to considering the thoughts of his commentators. In this process, I investigate Dugin's development of his Fourth Political Theory, his hermeneutical presuppositions, and their constituent elements.

My conclusions characterize Dugin as a Neo-Traditionalist, a Neo-Eurasianist, and a geopolitical theologian of significant kinetic and potential impact. Elements of Dugin's theory are reflected in Russian governmental policy. His influence likely will, in turn, affect Western reception and reaction—but to a degree as yet unmeasured. While the force of Dugin's exact impact is difficult to predict, it appears to possess the potential to influence World Power conflicts—but, to a level unknown for the present. However, this potential alone is enough to demand attention and consideration.

Acknowledgments

In acknowledging the debt and gratitude to those who have helped me materially, academically, and through encouragement, I find myself humbled and fearful. I am humbled that so many have given so much of their time, effort, and care to help me through this endeavor, and I am fearful that I will leave someone out while offering my public thanks.

I will start by acknowledging several remarkable and influential people who imparted wisdom to me and gave me a seemingly never-ending thirst to learn and to pursue knowledge in formal academics and life lived every day. Among these, my parents and some exceptional teachers, coaches, professors, military, governmental, and other mentors figure prominently.

More pertinent to the creation of this book was Dr. Andrew Pierce. Dr. Pierce was my initial contact with the Irish School of Ecumenics, and I purposefully came to Trinity College to study under him. The subsequent adventure far exceeded my hopes and expectations.

I owe many thanks to the faculty and staff of the Irish School of Ecumenics who taught me, assisted me, corrected me, and just generally put up with me. In addition, I thank the Rev. Dr. Paddy McGlinchey, of the Church of Ireland Theological Institute (CITI) and his wife Helen for help both professionally and in friendship. And I will remember Dr. Charles Russo, of the University of Dayton, for his encouragement and invaluable advice.

To the faculty, staff, and ordinands of the CITI for their incredible hospitality (and marvelous board) during the time I resided with them, I offer my heartfelt admiration and thanks—to the wonderful folks at the Glenside the same for the same.

I owe Ireland's remarkable Ulick McEvaddy special thanks for suggesting, many years ago now, that I consider Trinity College Dublin for my doctoral studies. I acknowledge my debt to my brother, Stewart Mosbey, without whose introductions I would not know Ulick or even Ireland for that matter.

My wife, Melinda, helped me with initial edits and has been unfailing in her support even when it meant time apart. So much of this mission has been both a joint effort and an amazing journey for us. I have also enjoyed the encouragement and support of our children and grandchildren. So many others, college staff, friends, fellow students, and colleagues, unnamed and unrecognized here, I thank in my heart.

Finally, I wish to thank Professor Alexander Dugin, for without him, none of this study would be. I trust he will continue to intrigue and fascinate me for however long my curiosity and lucidity remain.

Soli Deo Gloria

Introduction

Paraphrased to the point of cliché is Carl von Clausewitz's maxim that war is a continuation of politics by other means.[1] Nevertheless, Clausewitz's maxim pointed out the potential at one end of the continuum of the political spectrum where the horror of catastrophic violence becomes reality. While we may turn to various philosophies of politics and examine the more passive end of the spectrum, undoubtedly a worthwhile endeavor, it is toward the active end where my present gaze is focused.

Politics should never be considered a closed system. Correctly observed, politics must, for example, include the interactive elements of economics and the physical and cultural constituents of geography. Considering the active end, the area where politics incorporates physical violence, and modifying Clausewitz's definition slightly, war should be seen as a continuation of *geopolitics* by other means.[2] Still, there is a vital ingredient often poorly considered. As this is a study in geopolitical theology, there should be no mystery as to what this ingredient must be.

The Oxford English Dictionary (OED) states that politics is associated with "the debate between parties having power."[3] I would add that it also involves parties *striving* for power. Politics is competitive. Anyone engaged in politics, at any level, may readily admit that politics is either a stylized form of combat, like many sports, or the real thing. Alexander Dugin is a contemporary Russian scholar, sociologist, philosopher, and political theologian.[4] He is deeply engaged in geopolitics, that is, according to the OED, "international relations, as influenced by geographical factors." This study demonstrates Dugin's geopolitics and considers the Clausewitzian extension of conflict as a part of the geopolitical continuum.

To Dugin's geopolitics his theology must be added. Central to this contemplation is the idea that the political milieu is inextricably infused with elements of theological praxis, concepts, analogies, and allusions. Because my observations and interpretations involve Dugin's inclusion of

xi

his theologically related considerations within his overall geopolitical outlook, I concur that politics and theology are inseparable. Here, I agree with many others but contradict many as well. Lastly, I believe we must give attention to the reception, especially in the West, afforded to Dugin and his ideas.[5] I aim to present a systematic examination of Dugin's geopolitical theology and remark on its reception.

I acknowledge two broad descriptive geopolitical classifications—unipolar and multipolar. The embedded strife in these two political concepts is apparent in the obvious conflict evident in their respective desire for either a singular pole or plural ones. The stress is intense. If more than one geopolitical power strives for unipolar hegemony, war (as the continuation of geopolitics) is a real threat. If a multipolar actor opposes a unipolar actor, war (by the same Clausewitzian conclusion) is a risk as well.

Dugin argues that the United States, intends to remain the world's unipolar power—the single dominant hegemon.[6] He advocates opposition to U.S. intentions by Russia becoming *the* Eurasian power, a regional power in a multipolar world.[7] Conflict, perhaps catastrophic, between adversaries that are multipolar and unipolar proponents is a real risk. Studying how Dugin and his ideology contribute to this risk is prudent; additionally, I submit that it is necessary.

Dugin's introduction of significant metaphysical material into the geopolitical conversation highlights a dimension not widely appreciated in current Western European and United States politics.[8] My study centers on Dugin's geopolitical stance, political theology application, and the reactions his combination of these two elements elicit in Western academic and political arenas. It examines how he constructs and describes his Fourth Political Theory and the response it provokes. Dugin's stance contains the substance of his geopolitics with its embedded theologically related material. This tripartite topology (geography, politics, and theology) requires that I closely attend to how Dugin adapts Traditionalism, Sacred Space, and other theological and metaphysical elements into Fourth Political Theory.[9]

Dugin interprets the West, and the West interprets Dugin.[10] There are two often counter-directional movements involved here. One is the vector of Dugin's frequently encountered interpretation of the West—its character, motives, and goals—all ascribed by him. The second vector involves the West's reception of Dugin—the impressions of Dugin formed by interpreters and commentators and their perceptions of Dugin's influence on current and future Russian geopolitical actions. I maintain that it is not merely the ideas contained within Dugin's geopolitical theology that matter; the acceptance of his ideas portends far more significant consequences.

Conclusions derived from this study depend, in large part, on how expressions of Dugin's ideas are encountered in the West, that often means their clarity when rendered in English. More than this is how Dugin's explanations, reactions, and critiques, also often rendered in English, are perceived and interpreted in the West. If Dugin's Fourth Political Theory contributes to his goal of a multipolar world, with Eurasia representing one of the dominant poles, how the West—especially the Anglosphere—responds to it bears upon its ultimate realization. The main question is this: how does Dugin propose to counter the perceived evils of Western Liberalism, its secular worldview, efforts toward globalization, and goal of unipolar hegemony, and how does his approach to geopolitical theology propose to thwart these perceived evils and maintain a multipolar world?

Dugin's Fourth Political Theory vision of a future Russian-led Eurasian constituent of a multipolar world reflects a political theology soaked in Traditionalism. He saturates his geopolitical Eurasian intentions with an acknowledged messianically inspired Manifest Destiny. Dugin's Eurasia champions direct opposition to Western global and unipolar aspirations. I suggest that systematically exposing Dugin's geopolitical theology will allow for more accurate reception, response, and engagement in proportion to the extent that Russian national policy incorporates Dugin's ideas.

I must stipulate some positions and presuppositions that I determined to be instrumental in explaining Dugin in the complexity of his geopolitical theology. Especially here and in Part One, I attempt to acknowledge my positions, opinions, assumptions, and presuppositions. I know that my geopolitical education and experience come from a decidedly American perspective. Additionally, I freely acknowledge that I advocate increasing awareness, consideration, and application of religious and theological discussion in the public forum.

Notes

1. Cf. One of the many editions and translations, e.g., Carl von Clausewitz, *On War* (London: K. Paul, Trench, Teubner, 1918).

2. On the use of italics: throughout, italics will be used to note standard publication titles where appropriate (as in *On War* above). Italics will also be used to note various non-English words (e.g., *raison d'être*). Italics will be favored over inverted commas (quotation markings) for introducing and/or emphasizing certain words and short phrases (as in *geopolitics*, in this case).

3. OED. I generally adopt the Oxford Dictionaries' (OED) definitions and connotations. I will not normally footnote OED references, instead noting the reference in the text. Cf. OED, en.oxforddictionaries.com.

4. Aleksandr Gelyevichn Dugin (Александр Гельевич Дугин). Hereafter, Alexander Dugin, unless his name is given a different spelling in quoted material. Throughout, I attempt to maintain the exact spelling in the source reference as spelling anomalies are relatively common in translations. Translations of Dugin's work (and others cited herein) frequently omit the uppercase capitalization and articles usually present in English. Although I address theological subject matter from several aspects in this study, I will not assume that Dugin is an academic or ecclesial theologian in any sense that would satisfy members of either of these two categories. Dugin indeed uses abundant theologically related material in his speaking and writing. His employment of such supports viewing him as a practitioner of political theology. Unless applying broad definitional latitude to the term theologian, I will limit my endorsement of Dugin's theological credentials within the area of political theology and no farther.

5. When referring to the *West* and *Western*, The OED states that historically, "the non-Communist states of Europe and North America, contrasted with the former Communist states of eastern Europe." Currently, "Europe and North America seen in contrast to other civilizations." Alsd, include the countries formerly colonized by Great Britain, where English is the common language, referred to as the *Anglosphere*. Cf. Daniel Hannan, *Inventing Freedom: How the English-speaking Peoples Made the Modern World* (New York: Broadside Books, 2014). I will capitalize West and Western when derived from the definitions above.

6. In most cases, I apply the term *West* (as does Dugin) primarily to the United States and its geopolitics, especially when addressing a Western point or counterpoint to Dugin's Russian and/or Eurasian multipolar or anti-Western rhetoric. When addressing the West in more general terms, I am referring to the Anglosphere, NATO, and European and other countries (post-Soviet Union) historically aligned with the Western powers—as in the case of Israel. Herein, the terms *Soviet Union* and *USSR* (*Union of Soviet Socialist Republics*) will be used interchangeably. Dealing with capitalization (Eurasian in this case) throughout this study is a constant issue—and appears, at times, to be a bit inconsistent. Because I am dealing with political, theological, religious, and philosophical beliefs, practices, movements, and theories, I capitalize terms such as *Liberal*, *Modern*, and *Traditional*, etc., when I am addressing these and similar terms as characterizing a more-or-less definable idea or ideology—hence, *Dugin's Neo-Eurasianism* or *Western Liberalism*. I capitalize Liberalism when it is mentioned as a specific ideology or contrasted with the attributes of Fourth Political Theory. I use lowercase first letters when dealing with more general characterizations—e.g., *modernity*, *postmodern*, and *liberalism*. The spelling of these types of terms within quotations, titles, etc., will not usually be altered. The use of italics or uppercase letters (e.g., Pivot Area) are employed instead of inverted commas and will appear throughout for words or terms often found within inverted commas elsewhere. Inverted commas (quotation marks) are reserved for specific quotations.

7. Eurasia and its derivatives (Eurasian, Eurasianism, etc.) is a familiar term combining sometimes all and sometimes only parts of the European and Asian continents. It sometimes refers to physical geography and, sometimes, to political and cultural characteristics—often to all three at once. Herein, it is heavily

saturated with geopolitical meaning, which will become evident as I progress through this study.

8. This argument is developed in detail by Mark Lilla. Cf. Mark Lilla, *The Stillborn God: Religion, Politics, and the Modern West* (New York: Vintage Books, 2008). While counterarguments supporting religious factors contributing to modern liberal democracy are made, the evidence that theological discourse is largely absent in current venues of academe and governmental institutions throughout contemporary Western liberal democracies is commonly accepted. Cf. e.g., Daniel Philpott, "Political Theology and Liberal Democracy," Review of *The Stillborn God: Religion, Politics, and the Modern West*, by Mark Lilla, *The Immanent Frame*, January 23, 2008, tif.ssrc.org/2008/01/23/political-theology-liberal-democracy/. While this may be a trend, it is by no means a *fait acomplii*. There are efforts by commentators and scholars to reverse this trend. Cf. e.g., Richard John Neuhaus, "Politics and Religion: 'the Great Separation,'" *First Things*, January 2008, firstthings.com/article/2008/01/religion-and-politicsthe-great-separation#print.

9. *Traditionalism* refers to the metaphysical "theory that all moral and religious truth comes from divine revelation passed on by tradition, human reason being incapable of attaining it," according to the OED. The terms *Sacred Space* and *Sacred Geography* are used interchangeably throughout. Within quotes or specific references to quotes and/or certain other references, the terms may or may not be capitalized depending on the spelling in the source employed; otherwise, both will be capitalized in the text. Dugin seems to prefer Sacred Geography, but I conducted no thorough survey of his works to determine this. Study involving Traditionalism encounters definitional overlaps between Traditionalism, usually expressed with the uppercase T, and traditionalism often expressed with the lowercase t. This holds true for the variants of both—Traditionalist/traditionalist, Traditional/traditional, etc. While traditionalism, with its adherence to custom and historical practice, is discernible within Traditionalism, the two concepts are not identical. Traditionalism claims unbroken links to eternal Truth and is often accessible only through gnostic pathways, while traditionalism is much more the recognition of associated practices closely akin to custom. Paradoxically, it is accurate to state that Traditionalism contains traditionalism, but traditionalism does not contain Traditionalism.

10. Although the term *West* lacks specificity, Dugin seems to refer to West and the West (including derivatives e.g., Western, etc.), applying the same, or very similar, meaning as does the OED. Considering Dugin's attention to The New World Order, for example, Dugin appears to focus on the United States at the top of a Western geopolitical hierarchy. Except for the United States, Dugin does not tend to specifically identify Western countries, preferring to group them collectively under the Western designator.

Part I

Chapter One: Recognizing Dugin

Essential Recognitions

Proceeding systematically through this study requires what I think are four essential recognitions:

- **Dugin is a geopolitical theologian**
- **Liberal Democracy--Dugin portrays the West, with its secular and individualistic worldviews, as the geopolitical and metaphysical opponent of a Traditional and Russian led Eurasia**
- **Traditionalism—Dugin applies this metaphysical element of his geopolitical theology as a foil to Liberal Democracy**
- **Eurasianism—Dugin's adaptation of this element of his geopolitical theology is presented as a divinely inspired Manifest Destiny**

Who and What is Dugin?

Dugin was born on January 7, 1962, in Moscow to Galina Viktorovna Dugina, a medical doctor, and Gelij Alexandrovich Dugin, a senior officer in the KGB.[1] His baptism at the age of six was overseen by his great-grandmother (likely to avoid issues with his father's military and political superiors).[2] Dugin was awarded a PhD in Sociology in 2004.[3] Dugin's wife also holds a doctoral-level degree, and they have two children.[4]

Dugin is indeed a complex subject. But, while his geopolitics are reasonably accessible and open to examination and debate in the West, not so his theological outlook. Thus, his complexity is obscured.[5] In Western circles, much of the academic conversation of Dugin's geopolitics lacks the necessary inclusion of his political theology and its metaphysical implications. This lack is especially evident where an organized or systematic treatment of

Dugin's political theology is desired. Yet, to call Dugin a theologian, one who engages primarily from a purely theological perspective in a strict sense, is too broad a stretch.

Andrey Tolstoy and Edmund McCaffray claimed, "Dugin's rise has been partly camouflaged by an intellectual biography that is complex and at times contradictory."[6] Despite his rather recent appearance in the more mainstream American media, Dugin is no overnight sensation. His status as a current Russian geopolitical figure has developed from the 1980s. Marlene Laruelle identified four main vectors of Dugin's "intellectual tendencies."[7] These she listed as political theory inspired by Traditionalism, Orthodox religious philosophy, Aryanist and occultist theories, and geopolitical and Eurasianist conceptions.[8] Contrary to what one might expect, Laruelle commented that Dugin's range of "ideological diversity" went through a relatively short evolutionary stage and "did not emerge in succession but have co-existed in Dugin's writings since the beginning of the 1990s."[9]

Dugin's recognition as a geopolitician, philosopher, and finally, geopolitical theologian evolved from those days when he initially gained Western recognition. The early Dugin was outwardly esoteric, even mystical, in his expressions of Russian history's trajectory and its projected future flight. Today, though remaining staunchly conservative, traditional, and controversial, Dugin projects a more consistent and defined image.

Tolstoy and McCaffray portrayed Dugin's anti-communist stance in the 1980s in contradistinction to his work "with the remnants of the Communist Party after the fall of the Soviet Union."[10] They noted Dugin's association with the National Bolshevik Party (NBP), implying an association with Eduard Limonov, and remarked that Dugin "praised Joseph Stalin and the Soviet Union while also supporting family and religious values."[11] Dugin has since distanced himself from the NBP. Moreover, he appears to have taken a much more mainstream approach to politics than Limonov and his associations, with their various revivals and Frankenstein's Monster-like constructions and reconstructions of neo-Bolshevik parties and their spinoffs.

Perhaps there was a desire on Dugin's part to avoid being associated with the anti-Vladimir Putin activities exhibited by Limonov and his various confederates. There may have been other reasons. Dugin may have decided not to accompany Limonov in his activist role as Limonov headed in a direction leading to a destination Dugin did not want to explore. Separation proved fortuitous for Dugin because afterward, Limonov served prison time on charges of weapons dealings.[12]

The NBP and other neo-Bolshevik groups created various coalitions that formed, broke up, and re-formed over time. Factions within the NBP, not satisfied with Limonov, split off in 2006, and the government eventually banned the NBP. Limonov published *Limonka*, a counterculture newspaper that was also banned but has continued to reappear in various guises, and he continues to be involved in politics.[13]

The roles played by Dugin and Limonov in creating the NBP can be reviewed in Charles Clover's *Black Wind, White Snow: The Rise of Russia's New Nationalism*, and Thomas Parland's, *The Extreme Nationalist Threat in Russia*.[14] "Putin's Brain: Alexander Dugin and the Philosophy Behind Putin's Invasion of Crimea," by Anton Barbashin and Hannah Thoburn, is also valuable for insight into Dugin's NBP history[15]

The increase in Dugin's popularity in Russia has been relatively gradual. Andreas Umland, chronicling Dugin's development, commented that "in the late 1980s and early 1990s, Dugin's activities resembled those of other politically active intellectuals of this period."[16] At this time in his life, Dugin "was building up his research and publication center," according to Umland, "and trying to propagate his ideas among ultranationalist political organizations, and further potential supporters in such spheres."[17] In the period between 1980-1990, Dugin made various organizational and literary attempts to gain a toehold among the myriad of late Soviet-era dissidents, skeptics, and aspiring academics and critics. Then, in the early 1990s, Dugin gained traction. Umland remarked on two of Dugin's benchmark successes. The first is the historical-religious association, Arktogeya (Northern Country), a publishing house. The second, the Center for Special Meta-Strategic Studies, Umland described as a think-tank that later became the Center for Geopolitical Expertise.[18]

Umland attributed the increase in Dugin's traction to such things as his "frequent contributions by, or references to, inter-

and post-war Western authors in Dugin's journals and books."[19] Umland recognized that Dugin's incorporation of "esotericism might have also contributed to his growing popularity in some Russian sub-cultures devoted to various brands of Russian and international occultism, Traditionalism, [and] paganism."[20] Barbashin and Thoburn stated that Dugin's 1991 pamphlet, "The War of the Continents," was his earliest claim to fame.[21]

Regarding Dugin's reception with the European New Right (ENR), political journalist Roman Horbyk wrote that Mark Bassin, studying Putin-Eurasian connections, noted that "the links between Russian and Eurasian radical conservatism" have been long established.[22] Horbyk credited Umland with observing that Dugin hosted popular ENR figure, Alain de Benoist, on visits to Moscow State University, while Dugin reciprocated by visiting Paris at Benoist's invitation.[23]

In the early 1900s, various right-wing groups, often characterized as fascist and known as the Black Hundred, emerged in Russia. Walter Laqueur's in-depth study of these groups, captured in his work, *Black Hundred: The Rise of the Extreme Right in Russia*, focused on the comeback of these groups following the fall of the Soviet Union, especially Pamyat, the People's National-Patriotic Orthodox Christian Movement.[24] Dugin was an active participant in Pamyat in the late 1990s and sought acceptance for his historical and prophetic views of Russia and its future manifestations.[25] Eventually, Pamyat and Dugin parted ways. Perhaps Dugin was unwilling to adopt Pamyat's brand of conspiracy theory with its overt anti-Semitism and Nazi expressions and symbolism.[26] After splitting with Pamyat, Dugin became involved in various projects, including his instrumental efforts with the Arctogaia publishing house.[27]

Umland traced Dugin's emerging recognition milestones by identifying some notable developments and events, such as Dugin's socio-political movement, *Evraziya*, and its later international transmutation through its derivative Eurasian Youth Movement.[28] Dugin's momentum increased in an energetic flurry of projects and publications in the last decade of the twentieth century.[29] Frequent contributions to *Den'* and other newspapers and the 1992 launch of what would become the journal, *Elementy*, helped establish Dugin's reputation in Russia and abroad, Umland reported.[30]

Dugin gained additional exposure through various radio and television programs and other media. For example, Dugin was featured on the 1997 radio presentation, *Finis Mundi*, and the weekly television broadcast, *Vekhi* (Landmarks), beginning in 2005, and frequent print, radio, television interviews, and guest appearances.[31] Even so, as recently as 2009, Umland, though acknowledging that Dugin had "been mentioned in a number of influential Western outlets," was still of the opinion that he, at that time, remained "an obscure figure" to Russia watchers.[32] Over time, Dugin's Western exposure has substantially increased thanks to numerous publications in French, English, and other languages and through web-based blogs and sites and the ubiquitous social media, Twitter and Facebook.

Geoffrey Hosking addressed Dugin's more recent reception and growing acceptance in his review of Clover's *Black Wind, White Snow*.[33] Also, a more academic source, the Risk Management Lab of the New Bulgarian University, reported on the Russian government's reception of Dugin through his personal and professional links and contacts.[34] The report provided detail with an example of Dugin's relationship with the highly controversial Igor Girkin, who also uses the name Ivanovich Strelkov, and his connection to Putin associate, Konstantin Malofeev.[35] While the strength of these connections may be questionable, the implication of a Dugin-Putin link deserves mention.

Dugin's development has not come without criticism. Umland did not hesitate to pin the label "obscurantist pseudo-scholar" onto Dugin in 2011, claiming that Dugin "uses 'conservatism' as a cover for the spread of a revolutionary ultranationalist and neo-imperialist ideology."[36] To charge that Dugin is a controversial figure is to engage in a remarkable understatement. He appears to have existed in an ethereal world where he at once wielded power through his influence while at the same time being politically out of favor. Dugin was once listed as Head of the Department of Sociology of International Relations at Moscow State University.[37] Then, he was reportedly dismissed from the faculty in mid-2014, for reasons unclear, only to become later the subject of conflicting reports from the University (and other sources) regarding his actual employment status.[38] Given the various contradictions, controversy can be counted on to be a constant with Dugin.

Dugin's Religious Path

By applying metaphysics, Dugin engages with theological and religious terms that support his geopolitical endeavor. In keeping with the multipolar world anticipated by Fourth Political Theory, Dugin does not advocate a world where a single hegemon determines religious belief or practice. Favoring a multipolar world that negates the dominance of Western Liberalism, Fourth Political Theory rejects the civil religion of post-revolutionary France and the civil religion that arose from it in its modern and postmodern manifestations. Dugin's theory dismisses civil religion and coalesces around more complex theological and metaphysical notions. Avoiding the shallow trappings of civil religion, Dugin began constructing his Fourth Political Theory on the deeper foundation of Carl Schmitt's explanation of the state's theological origins.[39]

Dugin claims that he is a Traditionalist. Traditionalists believe that many religions contain elements of Truth but hold that all religious traditions have become, to some degree, corrupted. Also believed is that only a relative few, Traditionalism's enlightened Adepts, possess Truth in its pure and original forms. Dugin displays a Traditional view, rather than a doctrinally orthodox Christian one, in his pronouncement that, "Judeo-Christian Christianity is not the real 'perennial Christianity' associated with the grand Tradition."[40] Dugin did not continue by going into detail about what the Perennial Christianity he mentioned entails. Still, it appears likely to be a version of Christianity marked by strong Traditional influences.

Dugin's Christianity

Dugin credited Traditionalist René Guénon with the notion that a dual structure consisting of two essential elements is necessary for a mature or "complete" society.[41] The esoteric is one

6

essential element with the exoteric social and legal systems comprising the other. Dugin suggested that Guénon looked at Judaism and Islam as complete societies. Both developed to an esoteric and initiatic level, taking the further step of fully realizing a social and legal dimension.[42] Dugin added that Christian society was an exception where this dual structure is a reasonable expectation. Christianity developed esoteric and initiatic characteristics, as did Judaism and Islam, but did not continue to evolve to internal completeness.[43]

Guénon stated his belief that Christianity, "unlike Judaism and Islam, was originally incomplete."[44] Guénon claimed Christianity was forced to import pagan Roman Law rather than waiting for the internal maturation of its own indigenous social and legal structures.[45] Supporting his claim, Dugin offered the lack of "consideration in the New Testament of any legal or social dimension which constitutes the essence of any exotericism."[46] "Only in later eras did Christianity 'descend' to the exoteric level in adopting the socio-religious basis of a revised code of Roman law," according to Dugin.[47]

Dugin wrote that, for Guénon, "the existence of precisely such a dual structure in traditional society is a necessary condition" that allows it "to be considered normal and fully-fledged."[48] Whereas Judaism and Islam both contain much exoteric material within their sacred texts, it was only in the first few Christian centuries that Canon Law and other exoteric fixtures were appended to Christianity. Hence, Guénon believed Christianity to be incomplete. Christianity, with its esotericism, is accepted by Dugin, but not so in its exotericism.

Dugin is drawn to the "esoteric underpinnings of Orthodoxy."[49] He noted these foundational elements "can be clearly traced and are evident in the sacred architecture of churches, initiatic iconography, and a widespread apophatic theology as well as in the monastic contemplative practices in Hesychasm, the Old Believers," and, for example, "the traditions of the Holy Fools."[50] Dugin's attraction to Russian Orthodoxy is part of his Russian heritage. Given his proclivity to mysticism, the orthopraxis of Russian Orthodoxy adds to its appeal.

Dugin identifies with the post-schismatic confines of the Old Believers. This faction did not accept the reforms instituted by the

Orthodox Church under Patriarch Nikon of Moscow in a synod convened in 1666. The Old Believers (or Old Ritualists)—due to their holding to the pre-1666 reforms and the old liturgical forms—split from the Orthodox Church. Old Believers were held to be schismatic until Anathema was lifted in 1971. Cancelation of Anathema allowed for Old Believer restoration within the Orthodox communion, and this has, at least partially, occurred.

Mikhail Epstein asserted that Dugin contended that the Old Believer form of Orthodoxy more closely resembles the original Christian expression than does either Roman Catholicism or Protestantism.[51] There is a mystical element in Dugin's Traditionalism that displays an affinity to Orthodox Christianity. A similar relationship with Protestantism and Roman Catholicism is mostly absent. Not only this, Dugin's claims that the Old Believer position is sympathetic to Traditionalism should also be considered as part of its attraction.

> I came to the conclusion that there is an ideal form, which actually is our "national guenonism." It's the Old Believers, of old Christianity, which, since the second half of the seventeenth century, actually is in the ontological, eschatological and apocalyptic state, where it is crystal-clear and easy to understand the positions expressed by Guenon. There is not just the proximity or similarity of the positions (at the level of discourses), but almost complete identity. Adequately internalized Guenonism (i.e. postguenonism) in Russia and in the framework of Orthodoxy is an extremely old reality which preserves the paradigmatic traditionalist language, upon which rests the entire Christian tradition. Cycloplegia (or historical "ecclesiology") of Christianity is adequately represented in this sector of Orthodoxy.[52]

An illustrative example of the depth of Dugin's mystical intimacy with the "esoteric specificity of Orthodoxy" is evidenced in his observations of the proper separation of the altar from the laity.[53]

> The sacrament of the altar is genuinely exoteric and "descends" to the outer level. In Orthodoxy, however, the gates of Iconostasis—the Royal Gates—are open only for a short period during the key moments of the liturgy (the exception being on certain holidays). This symbolizes the unique revelation of the apophatic, unknowable Principle on the other side of the cataphatic vision of the sacred world which in a normal state is presented only by symbols.[54]

Of the factors contributing to Dugin's affinity for Orthodoxy, including its inseparable bonds to Russian culture, Russian Orthodoxy's accommodation of Old Believer doctrine affording Christian approaches to Traditionalism is not the least. I believe Dugin can be more easily understood considering his identification with Old Believer/Old Ritual theology. Vladimir Moss noted that 1990 was the year "Dugin became an Old Ritualist; whether he actually joined the schism or only the yedinoverie (Old Ritualist) section of the official Moscow Patriarchate is not clear."[55] "What is clear," Moss elaborated, "is that the Old Ritualist understanding of Russian and world history has deeply influenced his thought."[56]

Vadim Joseph Rossman wrote that Dugin believes the Old believers preserved the most authentic aspects of Orthodox tradition.[57] Moss suggested a way to capture an essential element for understanding Dugin is to consider him in light of his being an Old Believer; or at least in light of his positive reception of Old Rite doctrine.[58] In Moss' view, "it is more fruitful and accurate to see his thought as a product of a kind of modernized Old Ritualism than as a species of right- or left-wing politics."[59] While I agree with Moss to some degree, I would submit that it is "more fruitful and accurate" to consider Dugin's affinity to Old Rite doctrine as an agreeable expression of his geopolitical theology. Considered in this way, Moss provides insight into how the combined geopolitics and theology of Dugin arranges itself.

9

Epstein maintained that Traditionalists, and he would include Dugin here, are much more eclectic than other conservatives regarding their Orthodox Christianity:

> The range of their mystical interest is as 'cosmopolitan' as their political strategy. Although they praise Orthodoxy, they see in it only a external manifestation of a much deeper esoteric tradition, which unites paganists, Muslims, gnostics, Christian heretics and Indian holy men.[60]

Epstein suggested that Dugin's affinity to the Orthodox Church arises in large part "because of its closeness to an ancient, paganist worldview," which Dugin believes "is more faithful to original Christianity" than is the belief and practice of the "Western churches."[61] Some expected measure of disagreement from the Orthodox community regarding the accusation of its inclusion of things pagan notwithstanding, there is ample evidence supporting the contention that Dugin identifies with pagan concepts in his Traditionally influenced worldview.

In Paris, after his exile from the Soviet Union, Orthodox theologian Vladimir Lossky published *The Mystical Theology of the Eastern Church*.[62] In this work, Lossky provided insights into mystical elements of Orthodoxy that help explain the foundations of Dugin's geopolitical theology. Lossky's views are helpful to a Western audience that, with its Protestant heritage, lacks experience in the degree of mystical fusion found within Eastern Christianity.[63] While I believe that many factors contribute to Dugin's acceptance of Russian Orthodoxy, it is likely one of the main drivers is that Russian Orthodoxy, as Lossky put it, "has never made a sharp distinction between mysticism and theology; between personal experience of the divine mysteries and the dogma affirmed by the Church."[64]

Old Believer doctrine holds that Moscow is the *Third Rome*, and they, the Old Believers, authentically and faithfully represent the truth of this doctrine. If Moss is correct, then Dugin accepts that until the fall of Constantinople "true piety was preserved," in that the Byzantine emperors were the *de facto* Restrainers that "held back the appearance of the Antichrist."[65] Here it is important to emphasize, as Rossman did, "Dugin's appeal to the replacement theology suggested by the seventeenth-century schismatics and abandoned by the Orthodox Church."[66] The theology that Dugin appeals to refers to his belief that the Millennium, the Thousand-year Reign of Christ, was realized through Byzantium.[67] According to Dugin, Russia has inherited the "divine presence" that had belonged to Byzantium.[68] The "divine presence" is expressed for Dugin through the sequential acceptance of Constantinople as the Second Rome and Moscow as its divine successor.

Symphonia's Attraction

In addition to the mystical attraction of the Orthodox Church, I suggest that Dugin is drawn to the potential for synchrony and symbiosis in the church and state relationship evident within Eastern Orthodoxy. The "Bases of the Social Concept of the Russian Orthodox Church," states that humans, not God, introduced temporal rule in Israel.[69] Given the human demand for the Hebrew monarchy in Israel, Orthodox Christianity recognizes that kingship was not a substitute for, or subordination of, the divinely created priesthood.[70] Accepting that neither church nor state should maintain the superior position and recognizing that there is no proscription regarding a working relationship between the two resonates throughout Dugin's geopolitical theology.

Symphonia Theory, close interdependence, but without subordination of either church or state, emerged from the Orthodoxy of Byzantium. "One way of explaining the Byzantine political ideal of symphonia is to say that, under its auspices, Byzantine society sought a 'balance' between church and state," wrote David J. Dunn.[71] There is little evidence of this concept in Christianity today outside of Eastern Orthodoxy, and its presence there may account for Dugin's own symphonia-like leanings and subsequent rejection of contemporary Western ideas of church and state separation. Dugin rejects the severe Western practice of isolating religion and proposes rediscovering, advocating, and entwining theological elements in his geopolitical constructions.

11

Although Islam does not embrace Symphonia Theory, *per se*, it does not recognize anything like the distinction present between Western political and religious practice. Dugin's positive attitude towards Orthodox Symphonia and even a more syncretistic relationship between governance and faith bears a remarkable similarity with what is evident in much Islamic political expression. This similarity likely contributes to Dugin's attitude regarding the religious pervasiveness and inclusiveness evident throughout his Eurasian ideas.[72]

Comparing Eastern Orthodoxy with Roman Catholicism, Dugin explained that, "the Orthodox Patriarch, unlike the Pope, is first and foremost the spiritual center of the Church," yet he "does not directly influence public and political life."[73] Also of interest is Dugin's notion of the *Ghibelline Archetype* and his claim that this concept "was embodied in the sacred attitude towards the Russian Tsars," where it was the Tsar who occupied "the sacred center of the Russian imperial ecumene."[74] According to Dugin, the Tsar was the focus of all the "immanent religious energies" of the population of the Empire.[75]

Dugin related that "this 'Ghibelline' aspect is typologically close to the Shiite understanding of the sacred nature of authority," in that, "Shiite doctrine (unlike Sunni) insists on the rule of only the Aliites, the holy invested descendants of the first of the Imams."[76] The Shiites believe that no-one outside of this line has any "sacred" or "initiatic" right to rule.[77] Here, we can witness Dugin expressing the syncretism of Shiite doctrinal propositions within the Traditionalist approach of Fourth Political Theory. Dugin acknowledges the so-called separation of church and state position, that, in effect, attempts to place a wall between governmental and religious expressions in much of Western political practice. He rejects this proposition.[78]

Church historian Bernard Reardon provided analysis of Hugues-Félicité-Robert de Lamennais that sheds historical illumination on Church and State relationships.[79] Thomas Bokenkotter, a Catholic historian, has also presented material useful in evaluating Dugin's theological infusion into the geopolitical sphere with his commentary on Gabriel-Ambroise de Bonald and Lamennais.[80] Advocating stronger inclusion of spiritual power within the divinely imbued power of state sovereignty, Bonald, and Lamennais also deserve attention.[81] Taking positions mainly supportive of the Vatican, and, thus, differing from Orthodox Symphonia, Bonald and Lamennais were voices that argued the superior political authority of the Church and Pope over temporal powers. In a political theology pre-dating Schmitt by about a century, Lamennais, a supporter of the Restoration in France, favored spiritual input—Roman Catholic in this case—in state matters. He believed that religion is a necessary element in governance, especially in its contribution to public order.[82]

Both Bonald and Lamennais are noteworthy for their assertions of faith and state inseparability, but Lamennais is of special interest because of his support for a return to traditional authority and his firm belief that "political havoc" was the result of "the anarchy of reason."[83] Lamennais' conclusion finds expression in Fourth Political Theory.[84] The reality of Political theology in both Orthodox Symphonia and the inseparable Islamic expression, is abundantly evident. Dugin unreservedly condemns the Western concept of separation expressed in contemporary Western practice.

Dugin's religious path, his distinctive take on Christianity, and his attraction to Symphonia all contribute to determinations of just who and what Dugin is. There is more. Proceeding from here, I shall present the main ideas of Dugin's Fourth Political Theory systematically in an attempt to further address the *who* and *what* questions about Dugin.

Notes

1. "Alexander Dugin," Geopolitica.ru, accessed September 17, 2018, geopolitica.ru/en/person/alexander-dugin?page=2. Cf. Stephen D. Shenfield, *Russian Fascism: Traditions, Tendencies, Movements* (Armonk, NY: M.E. Sharpe, 2001), 191. Here Shenfield wrote that Dugin's father, grandfather, and great-grandfather were military officers. Stephen D. Shenfield, independent scholar, specializing in Russian/Eurasian studies.

2. "Alexander Dugin," Geopolitica.ru.

3. Ibid. "[Dugin] has defended his post-graduate degree in Philosophy in Rostov-Na-Donu with the dissertation 'The Evolution of the

Paradigmatic Foundations of Science' in 2000 and the PhD in the Faculty of Sociology in the same University in 2004; theme: 'The Transformation of the Political Structures and Institutions in the Process of Modernization of the Civil Society.'"

4. Mark Sedgwick, "Occult Dissident Culture: The Case of Aleksandr Dugin," in *The New Age of Russia: Occult and Esoteric Dimension*, ed. Michael Hagemeister, Birgit Menzel, and Bernice Glatzer Rosenthal (München: Sagner, 2012), 278 for mentions of Dugin's first wife, Evgeniia Debrianskaia. Also, Cf. Masha Gessen, *The Future Is History: How Totalitarianism Retook Russia* (New York: Riverhead Books, 2017).

5. Andrey Tolstoy and Edmund McCaffray claimed, "Dugin's rise has been partly camouflaged by an intellectual biography that is complex and at times contradictory." Cf. Andrey Tolstoy and Edmund McCaffray, "Mind Games: Alexander Dugin and Russia's War of Ideas," *World Affairs* 177, no. 6 (2015): 25.

6. Tolstoy and McCaffray, "Mind Games," 25.

7. Marlene Laruelle, *Aleksandr Dugin: A Russian Version of the European Radical Right?*, Kennan Institute Occasional Papers Series #294 (Washington, DC: Woodrow Wilson International Center for Scholars, 2006), 1. Cf. wilsoncenter.org/publication/aleksandr-dugin-russian-version-the-european-radical-right-2006#sthash.zRsQiV92.dpuf and 4pt.su/en/content/aleksadr-dugin-russian-version-european-radical-right.

8. Laruelle, *Russian Version of European Radical Right*, 1.

9. Ibid.

10. Tolstoy and McCaffray, "Mind Games," 25.

11. Ibid., 25-26. Limonov is the nom de plume of Eduard Veniaminovich Savenko, a poet and political dissident. For a more in-depth look at the unusual history of Limonov, Cf. Gessen, "The Weird and Instructive Story of Eduard Limonov," review of *Limonov: The Outrageous Adventures of the Radical, Soviet Poet Who Became a Bum in New York, a Sensation in France, and a Political Antihero in Russia*, by Emmanuel Carrère, New York Review of Books, May 15, 2015, nybooks.com/articles/2015/05/21/weird-and-instructive-story-eduard-limonov/.

12. Gessen, "Weird and Instructive Story." Cf. Anton Barbashin and Hanna Thoburn, "Putin's Brain: Alexander Dugin and the Philosophy Behind Putin's Invasion of Crimea," *Foreign Affairs*, March 31, 2014,

237-52. A transcript may be accessed at foreignaffairs.com/articles/russia-fsu/2014-03-31/putins-brain.

13. Barbashin and Thoburn, "Putin's Brain." Cf. Fabrizio Fenghi, "Making post-Soviet counterpublics: the aesthetics of Limonka and the National-Bolshevik Party," *Nationalities Papers*, 45:2, 2017, 182-205.

14. Charles Clover, *Black Wind, White Snow: The Rise of Russia's New Nationalism* (New Haven: Yale University Press, 2016), and Thomas Parland, *The Extreme Nationalist Threat in Russia: The Growing Influence of Western Rightist Ideas* (New York: RoutledgeCurzon, 2005).

15. Barbashin and Thoburn, "Putin's Brain."

16. Andreas Umland, "Aleksandr Dugin's Transformation from a Lunatic Fringe Figure into a Mainstream Political Publicist, 1980 – 1998: A Case Study in the Rise of Late and Post-Soviet Russian Fascism," *Journal of Eurasian Studies* 1, no. 2 (May 21, 2010): 148. This article is also available online at, sciencedirect.com/science/article/pii/S1879366510000242. Umland's outline of Dugin's geopolitical life in this article is valuable and probably the most concise and comprehensive encountered in my research. Also, Cf. arctogaia, arctogaia.com/public/eng/, and cge.evrazia.org/. Andreas Umland, Research Fellow, Stockholm Centre for Eastern European Studies, Swedish Institute of International Affairs.

17. Umland, "Dugin's transformation," 148.

18. Ibid., 149. Cf. arctogaia, arctogaia.com/public/eng/, and cge.evrazia.org/.

19. Ibid.

20. Ibid. Brackets added.

21. Barbashin and Thoburn, "Putin's Brain." There is confusion as to the exact title of Dugin's "The War of the Continents" (as cited by Barbashin and Thoburn). This is likely a translation issue. The publication date, and the source (pamphlet or some other medium) are also unclear. Cf. e.g., tfmetalsreport.com/blog/6670/eurasianism-dugin-and-ukraine-part-1?page=2, where the title is cited as "The Great War of Continents" and the date of the subsequent "notoriety" of Dugin as 1992. Perhaps the best source to cut through this confusion is Dugin himself. Cf. "Alexander Dugin: The Great War of Continents," Open Revolt, February 3, 2013, openrevolt.info/2013/02/03/alexanderdugin-the-great-war-of-continents/. Here, Dugin states that "this text was

originally published as Part III of 'Konspirologya' Arktogeya, Moscow 1992."

22. Roman Horbyk, "The Right Model for the Right Europeans," under, Putin a "new rightist"?, *The Ukrainian Week*, February 12, 2014, ukrainianweek.com/World/101730. Horbyk also spells Bassin as "Bessin" in this article. Roman Horbyk, Senior Lecturer, Örebro University. Mark Bassin, Professor, Södertörn University.

23. Horbyk, "The Right Model," under, Putin a "new rightist"? Alain de Benoist de Gentissart, who has also gone by Robert de Herte, Fabrice Laroche and other names, is a well-known figure in the ENR and founder of the *Nouvelle Droite*.

24. Walter Laqueur, *Black Hundred: The Rise of the Extreme Right in Russia* (New York: Harper Collins, 1993), 204-21. Walter Laqueur, 1921-2018.

25. Laqueur, *Black Hundred*, 204ff.

26. Ibid., Cf. e.g., 210, 213.

27. Cf. arctogaia.com/public/eng/. Also rendered herein as, *Arktogeya*.

28. Umland, "Dugin's transformation," 145. *Evraziya* is translated as *Eurasia*.

29. Ibid., 149. Umland notes Dugin's "first larger and widely noted books," with beginnings in 1991. Umland lists examples: *The Mysteries of Eurasia and The Paths of the Absolute*, and the first issues of the *almanakh Milyy Angel* (Enchanting Angel). Cf. Umland's footnote 57 for a more extensive listing of Dugin's 1991-2003 publications. Cf. Laruelle, *Russian Version of European Radical Right*.

30. Ibid.

31. Cf. Umland's and Laruelle's articles cited above.

32. Umland, "Dugin's transformation," 145.

33. Geoffrey Hosking, "How a Theory of Russian History That Rejects the West Came to Inspire Putin's Kremlin," review of *Black Wind, White Snow: The Rise of Russia's New Nationalism*, by Charles Clover, *Financial Times*, April 22, 2016. Geoffrey Hosking, Emeritus Professor of Russian History, School of Slavonic and East European Studies, University College, London.

34. *Hypotheses, Propaganda and Forecasts Following the Murder of Nemtsov*, technical paper (Sofia: Risk Management Lab, New Bulgarian University, 2015).

35. Management Lab, *Hypotheses, Propaganda and Forecasts*. Cf. euromaidanpress.com/2015/01/24/ex-terrorist-leader-referendum-in-crimea-was-a-farce/ and bellingcat.com/news/uk-and-europe/2019/06/19/identifying-the-separatists-linked-to-the-downing-of-mh17/ for views of Igor Girkin (aka: Strelkov). For a look at Konstantin Malofeev, Cf. ft.com/content/84481538-1103-11e4-94f3-00144feabdc0. Igor Girkin, Former Minister of Defence, Donetsk Peoples Republic. Konstantin Malofeev, Russian businessman under U.S. Sanctions.

36. Umland, "Fascist Tendencies in Russian Higher Education: The Rise of Aleksandr Dugin and Moscow University's Sociology Faculty," Opednews.com, August 24, 2011, opednews.com/articles/Fascist-Tendencies-in-Russ-by-Andreas-Umland-110823-348.html. Cf. Umland's note that this article appeared in the web edition of *Demokratizatsiya: The Journal of Post-Soviet Democratization*, Spring (2011).

37. Cf. "Biography," Alexander Dugin, dugin.ru/biography. When accessed on July 1, 2017, this site contained Dugin's posted CV. This Website is in Russian and was translated with Chrome. The CV showed that from September 2009 to June 2014 Dugin was "Head of Department of Sociology of International Relations, Sociology Department of Moscow State University."

38. Cf. e.g., Catherine A. Fitzpatrick, "Russia This Week: Dugin Dismissed from Moscow State University?" The Interpreter, June 29, 2014, interpretermag.com/russia-this-week-what-will-be-twitters-fate-in-russia/. Apparently, the original posting was June 27, and it was updated on June 29. Catherine A. Fitzpatrick, writer and translator, *The Interpreter* online news site. Cf. "Biography," Alexander Dugin, accessed July 1, 2017, dugin.ru/biography, contains Dugin's posted CV. This Website is in Russian and was translated with Chrome. This CV showed that from September 2009 to June 2014 Dugin was "Head of Department of Sociology of International Relations, Sociology Department of Moscow State University."

39. Cf. Dugin, *The Fourth Political Theory*, trans. Michael Millerman and Mark Sleboda, ed. John B. Morgan (London: Arktos, 2012), 39-40. Cf. Carl Schmitt, "Political Theology," in *Studies in Contemporary German Social Thought*, ed. Thomas McCarthy, trans. George Schwab (Cambridge, Massachusetts: MIT Press, 1985), 36. Originally published as *Politische Theologie: Vier Kapitel zur Lehre uon der Souveriinitat,* 1922, and in a revised edition 1934 by Duncker & Humblot, Berlin. Carl Schmitt, 1888-1985. The 2012 edition of *The*

Fourth Political Theory, (Arktos, 2012) will be used as the primary source throughout. There are other editions available in the body of literature. It is often confusing as to which edition is being referred to or quoted as pagination may be different, and some material may be markedly different from the edition I use herein. For example, there is a 2012 online edition published by the "Eurasian Movement," redacted by Sleboda and translated by Nina Kurpianova, *et al* that is different in some wording and pagination. *The Fourth Political Theory* (*Четвертая политическая теория, Chetvertaia politicheskaia teoriia*) was originally published in Russian in 2009. Translations of these editions (and others—or excerpts from them) often appear online and in other publication media.

40. Vadim Rossman, "Anti-Semitism in Eurasian Historiography: The Case of Lev Gumilev," ed. Dmitry Shlapentokh, in *Russia between East and West Scholarly Debates on Eurasianism* (Boston: Brill, 2007), 174. Here Rossman is paraphrasing Dugin. Cf. Rossman's note 1995a: 11. Vadim Rossman, Economist and Educator.

41. Dugin, "Russian Orthodoxy and Initiation," The Fourth Political Theory, accessed June 24, 2017, 4pt.su/en/content/russian-orthodoxy-and-initiation, under, Religion and Initiation according to René Guénon (1886–1951).

42. Dugin, "Russian Orthodoxy and Initiation," under, The uniqueness of Christianity.

43. Ibid.

44. Ibid.

45. Ibid.

46. Ibid.

47. Ibid.

48. Ibid., under, Religion and Initiation according to Guenon.

49. Ibid., under, Orthodoxy and the East.

50. Ibid. Cf. *Encyclopædia Britannica,* s.v. "Hesychasm (Eastern Orthodoxy)," February 15, 2007, britannica.com/topic/Hesychasm; "in Eastern Christianity, type of monastic life in which practitioners seek divine quietness (Greek *hēsychia*) through the contemplation of God in uninterrupted prayer. Such prayer, involving the entire human being— soul, mind, and body—is often called 'pure,' or 'intellectual,' prayer or the Jesus prayer." Cf. Eugene Vodolazkin, "Russian 'Umberto Eco' demystifies the Holy Fool," Russia Beyond, June 6, 2013,

rbth.com/literature/2013/06/06/russian_umberto_eco_demystifies_the_
holy_fool_26401.html. "The fool for Christ, or Holy Fool, is similar to
a biblical prophet, prescient, but more importantly able to reveal truths.
As one church hymn has it, the yurodivy (*holy fool* in Russian) strives
'with imaginary insanity to reveal the insanity of the world.'" Kiev
born Eugene Vodolazkin, expert in medieval history, is an award-
winning fiction writer.

51. Mikhail Epstein, *The Russian Philosophy of National Spirit:
Conservatism and Traditionalism*, report (Washington: National
Council for Soviet and East European Research, 1994), 20. Mikhail
Epstein, Professor, Emory University.

52. Dugin, "Traditionalism as Language," under, Traditionalism and
Russia, The Fourth Revolutionary War, September 8, 2015,
4threvolutionarywar.wordpress.com/2015/09/08/traditionalism-as-a-
language-alexander-dugin/. This information is posted just prior to the
body of the text: "A. G. Dugin The Philosophy Of Traditionalism, M.,
2002 Lecture 1. Rene Guenon: Traditionalism as a language." This
essay carries the date notation 09.09.1998 following the body of the
text, however, several footnotes are dated post-1998. The word
seventeenth was written entirely in uppercase in the original.

53. Dugin, "Russian Orthodoxy and Initiation," under, Orthodoxy and
the East.

54. Ibid.

55. Vladimir Moss, "Alexander Dugin and the Meaning of Russian
History," *Vladimir Moss - Orthodox Christian Author*, accessed April
19, 2014, orthodoxchristianbooks.com/articles/517/alexander-dugin-
meaning-russian-history/. Vladimir Moss (born Anthony Moss in
London—baptized Vladimir in the Orthodox Church), Researcher in
Orthodox Church history.

56. Moss, "Meaning of Russian History."

57. Rossman, "Anti-Semitism in Eurasian Historiography," 165.

58. Moss, "Meaning of Russian History."

59. Ibid.

60. Epstein, *Conservatism and Traditionalism*, 21.

61. Ibid., 20.

62. Vladimir Lossky, "Theology and Mysticism in the Tradition of the
Eastern Church," in *The Mystical Theology of the Eastern*

Church (Crestwood, NY: St. Vladimir's Seminary Press, 1976), 7. Vladimir Lossky, 1903-1958.

63. Lossky, "Theology and Mysticism," 7.

64. Ibid., 8.

65. Moss, "Meaning of Russian History," under, Dugin's Eschatological Ecclesiology.

66. Rossman, "Anti-Semitism in Eurasian Historiography," 165. Cf. Rossman's footnote 37.

67. Ibid.

68. Ibid.

69. "Bases of the Social Concept of the Russian Orthodox Church," Orthodox Europe, under, III Church and State, accessed June 24, 2017, orthodoxeurope.org/print/3/14.aspx.

70. Social Concept of the Russian Orthodox Church, under, III Church and State. Cf. 1 Samuel 8.

71. David J. Dunn, "Symphonia in the Secular: An Ecclesiology for the Narthex" (PhD diss., Vanderbilt University, 2011), 110. Cf. Stanley S. Harakas, *Living the Faith: The Praxis of Eastern Orthodox Ethics* (Minneapolis, MN: Light and Life Pub, 1993), 259-93. Here Harakas explains his view that there are four possible categories of Church/State relationships: Separation of church and state—in this case, the state can be neutral, friendly, or antagonistic to the church; Papocaesarism (theocracy)—the church, or religious authority, is the government; Caesaropapism—the church is governed by the state; and Symphonia theory—where the church and state are complementary and exhibit mutual respect. David J. Dunn, Theologian, Writer, and Commentator.

72. Cf. Dugin, "Russian Orthodoxy and Initiation," under, Orthodoxy and the East

73. Ibid.

74. Ibid. In twelfth and thirteenth century Italy, the Guelph family and their faction sided with the Papacy, the Ghibelline family and their faction sided with the Empire. These designations are used by many writers to distinguish a conflict between Church or other religious attempts to control the State and the State to attempt to control the religious institution(s).

75. Ibid.

76. Ibid.

77. Ibid.

78. Interestingly, *Separation of Church and State* phraseology appears nowhere in the U.S. founding documents. The phrase is traced to an 1802 letter of Thomas Jefferson to a group of concerned churchmen in which he assures them that the Constitution forbids the creation of a *State* religion (Christian denomination, in this case). Cf. Charles J. Russo, "Does the Free Exercise of Religion Have a Future in the Marketplace of Public Education in the United States?," *International Perspectives on Education, Religion and Law*, ed. Charles J. Russo (New York: Routledge, 2014), 3. Cf. Russo's endnote 9: (excerpt) "The metaphor of the 'wall of separation' was popularized by Thomas Jefferson's letter of January 1, 1802, to Nehemiah Dodge, Ephraim Robbins, and Stephen S. Nelson, A Committee of the Danbury Baptist Association: Jefferson wrote…their legislature should 'make no law respecting an establishment of religion, or prohibiting the free exercise thereof' thus building a wall of separation between church and state.'" Cf. Russo's note: Andrew Adgate Lipscomb & Albert Ellery Bergh, (eds.), 16 Writings of Thomas Jefferson (1903) 281. The date of this volume may be 1905. Charles J. Russo, Professor, Dayton University. David Martin suggested that influences of monopoly may have a bearing on secularization. Martin looked at degree of religious (especially denominational in his illustration) pluralism versus the degree of monopoly. His conclusion was that "thus in England and Holland there was some degree of pluralism, and in the USA an even greater pluralism that led to the separation of Church and State." Cf. David Martin, *On Secularization: towards a Revised General Theory* (Burlington, VT: Ashgate Publishing, 2005), 20-21. David Martin, 1929-2019.

79. Bernard M. G. Reardon, *Liberalism and Tradition: Aspects of Catholic Thought in Nineteenth-century France* (Cambridge: Cambridge University Press, 2010). In this work, Reardon devoted two chapters on Lamennais that are useful regarding the Church/State discussion. Reardon related that Bonald's influence on Lamennais was substantial. Cf. Reardon, *Liberalism and Tradition*, 64. Bernard M. G. Reardon, 1913-2006.

80. Thomas Bokenkotter, *Church and Revolution: Catholics and the Struggle for Democracy and Social Justice,* (NY: Doubleday, 1998). Thomas Bokenkotter, 1924-2021.

81. Cf. Bokenkotter, *Church and Revolution*. Cf. W. Jay Reedy, "The Historical Imaginary of Social Science in Post-Revolutionary France:

21

Bonald, Saint-Simon, Comte," *History of the Human Sciences* 7, no. 1 (February 01, 1994): 1-26. Jay Reedy, Emeritus Professor, Bryant University.

82. Ibid.

83. Reardon, *Liberalism and Tradition*, 86.

84. Cf. e.g., Dugin, *Fourth Theory*, 53.

Chapter Two: Dugin Through his own Words

Systemizing Dugin's Work

Attempts to define Dugin, his impact on Western action, and the West's reaction to Russian political policy and practice are more difficult because of the work-in-progress reality of his endeavors. Due to the seemingly universal availability of the World Wide Web and the ubiquitous presence of social media, it is necessary to tap material from the range of online sources to more fully consider Dugin. Attempting to balance the rapidly growing mass of Dugin's work currently available online and in electronic formats, with books, journals, and other print media, is both a goal and a challenge.

Dugin's works cover a broad range of geopolitics and political commentary, theologically and metaphysically related material, conspirology, philosophy, and sociology engaged in no particular or chronological sequence. My attempt to systemize the wide range of Dugin's work proceeds with a topical approach to literature produced by Dugin, literature presented about Dugin, and literature providing an understanding of his wide-ranging interests.

Awareness of Dugin continues to increase in the Western news and commentary media. Dugin's geopolitical and, though to a lesser degree, theologically and metaphysically related works, are the subject of various literary reviews, news media features, journal and magazine articles, blogs, and other online sources. His views are increasingly the subject of books of both academic and more general audience appeal. Dugin related material is available from these same sources but is also found through media not previously considered proper for comprehensive academic examinations. Studying Dugin in depth requires at least some venturing into esoteric metaphysical material. I, and any other serious Dugin scholar, must occasionally go there as well.

Dugin's earlier work, from the 1980s until around the mid-1990s, were not widely available to the West in English translations. However, because of European interest in Dugin's work, initially fueled mainly by adherents and observers of the ENR, a significant amount of his early work was published or otherwise made available in French, Spanish, and other European languages. Dugin is a prolific writer, lecturer, and blogger and is increasingly proficient in English. His publications and website postings in English are now readily accessible. Since 2000 many of Dugin's writings, transcripts of his lectures and addresses, and audio/video of his speaking engagements and podcasts are also available in English.

The Main Pillars of Dugin's Writing

Dugin's book, *The Fourth Political Theory*, provides a supporting structural column of his opus as it offers an overview of the thrust of his geopolitical theology.[1] My comparatively less reliance upon his book, *Foundations of Geopolitics*, is in no way meant to diminish it. I certainly did not ignore this work, but Dugin's subsequent writing is more pertinent to his current and near-term Western reception. John B. Dunlop stated that Dugin produced *Foundations of Geopolitics* for Russian consumption—specifically for "Russian military, police, and statist foreign policy elites."[2] Today, I find Dugin interested in a much broader audience.

Dunlop emphasized Dugin's upturn in notoriety after publication of *Foundations of Geopolitics*. I believe Dunlop was correct some years ago when he wrote:

> There has probably not been another book published in Russia during the post-communist period which has exerted an influence on Russian military, police, and statist foreign policy elites comparable to that of Aleksandr Dugin's 1997 *Foundations of Geopolitics*.[3]

The Fourth Political Theory was edited and published for Western readership, it is available in several languages, and it is reinforced by any number of Dugin-related and inspired blogs and websites. The style of *The Fourth Political Theory* is accessible and conducive to reception from Western audiences. It is fairly concise and readable. It suffers from the lack of an index but provides ample material, albeit controversial, that is conducive to Western consumption.

Development of Dugin's Writing

Umland covered Dugin's early recognition within Russia, and he continues following him to the present day. A review of Umland's Dugin material yields a trove of comprehensive quantitative and qualitative historical research of Dugin's works.[4] Laruelle also collected and commented on Dugin's work in meaningful ways.[5] Anton Shekhovtsov's writing, along with the established work of Rossman and Epstein, also provides a good deal of background material concerning Dugin's earlier work and rise to prominence.[6]

Dugin began editing *Elementy*, in 1992. Dunlop pointed out that much of each edition of the once or twice-yearly release contained articles of a geopolitical nature.[7] In *Aleksandr Dugin: A Russian Version of the European Radical Right?*, Laruelle listed Dugin's editorial development commenting on *Elementy* (9 issues between 1992 and 1998), *Milyi Angel* (4 issues between 1991 and 1999), *Evraziiskoe vtorzhenie* (published as a supplement to the weekly *Zavtra*, with six special issues in 2000), and *Evraziiskoe obozrenie* (11 issues from 2001 to 2004).[8]

Dugin's Self-placement as a Vertical Platonist

Dugin's Platonism is evident as he contrasts the Platonic and Atomistic worlds. "Platonism is a philosophy essentially vertical," he wrote explaining that "Platonism is built around the vertical axis."[9] He continued, stating that ideas are above are the phenomena below—the Platonic world is the hierarchical, vertically organized world.[10] Dugin contrasted "essentially vertical" Platonism with "horizontal" Atomism, the philosophy of Democritus, Epicurus, and Lucretius.[11] Dugin claimed that modernity is built on Atomism.[12] In modernity, Atomism became "scientific orthodoxy," and Platonism was marginalized.[13] Atomism, in Dugin's view, is a democratic philosophy, "it begins from below, by the material particles," and "doesn't know the ideas, the platonic lights."[14] Democritus then is proto-modern; he "can be understood as a representative of the counter-initiation in the world of Tradition."[15] Plato is said to have set fire to the writing of Democritus, regarding Atomism as "the world upside down," an impossible world, contrary to the natural order of things.[16]

Aversion to governance from below—the world upside down—is evident throughout Dugin's geopolitical theology. Dugin's assertion that Atomism "doesn't know hierarchy," is critically important.[17] Dugin is telling us that the Platonic vertical demonstrates a hierarchical characteristic where enrichment and understanding are monarchical—knowledge and light come down from above as from a sovereign.[18]

Furthermore, Dugin presents modernity as a choice; "we can choose to be modern—atomists, materialists, liberal democrats," he said.[19] We can also choose not to be modern, opting to be Platonic; thus, understanding eternity as the "present" and rejecting the supposed linear progressivism of modernity.[20] Atomism "goes against verticality," Dugin claimed, supposing that, from above, events are viewed with the perspective of all eternity, not limited by the obscured visibility of Atomism's horizontal and linear world.[21]

Building on Heidegger

"At the dawn of philosophical thought," Dugin wrote in *The Fourth Political Theory*, "people (more specifically, Europeans, even more specifically, the Greeks), raised the question of Being as the focal point of their thinking."[22] Although praising Platonism in several respects, Dugin contends that Plato and other Greek philosophers erred in their attempts to categorize Being. He concluded that the Greek philosophers became "confused by the nuances."[23] Commenting on the Greek philosophers' discussions of Being and employing the terminology of Martin Heidegger, Dugin stated that, by thematizing Being,

> they risked getting confused by the nuances of the complicated relationship between Being and thought, between pure Being (*Seyn*) and its expression in existence—a being (*Seiende*),

26

between human Being-in-the-world (*Dasein*—being-there) and Being-in-itself (*Sein*).[24]

Avoiding the confusion of Plato and adopting the concepts of Being fostered by Heidegger, Dugin proclaimed that Fourth Political Theory is "a fundamental ontological theory which contains the awareness of the truth of Being at its core."[25] Emphasizing his reliance on Heidegger, Dugin wrote:

> Here, we should pay attention not only to theologies and mythologies, but also to the reflective philosophical experience of one particular thinker who had made a unique attempt of constructing a fundamental ontology—the most summarizing, paradoxical, profound, and penetrating study of Being. I am talking about Martin Heidegger.[26]

Dugin contemplates Being, borrows heavily from Heidegger, and acknowledges the debt. Dugin relates Being, using Heideggerian terms, *Sein*—being in itself—and *Dasein*—being there, being present. Dugin credits Heidegger for the significant development of *Sein* and *Dasein*.[27] Relying on Heidegger's consideration of Being, Dugin purposely placed Fourth Political Theory into the current postmodern milieu.[28] Fourth Political Theory is concerned with Being (which Dugin equates with *Sein*) and with Being-there (being in the existential moment, which Dugin relates with *Dasein*).[29]

Also noteworthy is his treatment of the relationship between *Sein* and the development of technology. Hence, Fourth Political Theory contends that Heidegger related that modernity's increasing reliance on and embrace of technology resulted in a corresponding decreasing awareness of *Sein*—technology replaces Being, and this replacement produces an ever-increasing nihilism.[30] Dugin places much of the blame for the increased embrace of *Dasein*, with its corresponding love of the moment, and the corresponding decrease of *Sein*, on Western Liberalism.

Dugin bluntly stated that Heidegger "bitterly hated liberalism, considering it an expression 'of the calculative

27

thinking' which lies at the heart of 'Western nihilism.'"[31] In postmodernity, *Sein* suffers a terrible nihilistic fate. "Postmodernity," Dugin wrote, "is in every sense, the ultimate oblivion of Being."[32] "Little by little, man lost sight of pure Being," with the advent of postmodernity.[33] As nihilism progresses in this "New Era," technical development "displaces Being and crowns 'nothingness.'"[34]

Even with the recognition of "the midnight" resulting when nihilism "begins to seep from all the cracks," Dugin entertains none of the opinions that Heidegger's philosophy was "hopelessly pessimistic."[35] Rejecting pessimistic interpretations, Dugin emphasized Heidegger's paradoxical "flip side of pure Being."[36] Although Heidegger would view postmodernity as the ultimate destroyer of Being, Dugin suggested that the flip-side of that opinion allows "thinking mankind" the chance to "save itself with lightning speed at the very moment of its greatest risk."[37]

The lightning speed of "this sudden return of Being" is identified by Heidegger as *Ereignis*—the "event."[38] *Ereignis* occurs "exactly at midnight of the world's night—at the darkest moment in history."[39] Heidegger vacillated on whether *Ereignis* is upon us or is somewhere in the "not quite yet," according to Dugin.[40]

Affirming the "not quite yet" places *Ereignis* in an almost here but still approaching future.[41]

> Thus, at the heart of the Fourth Political Theory, as its magnetic centre, lies the trajectory of the approaching *Ereignis* (the 'Event'), which will embody the triumphant return of Being, at the exact moment when mankind forgets about it, once and for all, to the point that the last traces of it disappear.[42]

Similar to his acceptance of *Ereignis* is Dugin's acknowledgment of Heidegger's *inzwischen*.

> Heidegger mentioned *inzwischen*, or the "between" while talking about existence of *Dasein*. The principal nature of *Dasein* is being

"between." *Dasein* is *inzwischen*. We should not use the system of classical political dualism, the scientific topography of both modernity and Aristotle's time while talking about the Fourth Political Theory, and presume the fact that the subject and the core, the basis of the Fourth Political Theory pole, is *Dasein*.[43]

"What is the subject of the Fourth Political Theory?" Dugin asked. "The subject of the Fourth Political Theory is *Dasein* or *Zwischen*, the 'between' in the space between the subject and object."[44] "*Zwischen*, on the border between the internal and external," is where Heidegger placed *Dasein* and where Dugin consigns Fourth Political Theory to dwell.[45] These interwoven and identifiably esoteric elements found throughout Dugin's geopolitical thinking are evident in this folding of Heidegger into a metaphysically rich construction.

Consider Dugin's assertion that Traditionalism has never known, nor would it accept Cartesian or Kantian Dualism involving any strict separation of "the 'subjective' from the 'objective' ('phenomenal' and 'noumenal')."[46] Expanding on his concepts of Sacred Geography, Dugin explained that "the sacred determinism of North or South is nor [sic] just a physical, natural, landscape-climatic factor (i.e., something 'objective').[47] Not being objective, it would seem to follow that it must be an idea or concept generated in the mind, therefore, it is something subjective.[48]

Placing it in this unfamiliar between space, Dugin claimed that sacred determinism is neither objective nor subjective, "but something of a third kind, exceeding both the objective and subjective poles."[49] Hence, we can see that Dugin, like Heidegger, acknowledges that *Zwischen* is a location or condition that is neither wholly objective nor subjective.[50] Heidegger's between must be recognized, not as a definitive border beginning at the edge of something—rather, as space at the end of one subject and the beginning of another. Sacred determinism, as Dugin relates it, lies in this between.

Dugin's builds on the philosophy of Heidegger. With the acknowledged centrality of Heidegger's concepts of *Sein* and

Dasein through his adoption of corollaries like Heidegger's *Ereignis* and between, Dugin made it clear that it is Heidegger who provided the proximate philosophical framework of Fourth Political Theory. He stated, "Heidegger's philosophy may prove to be that central axis threading everything around it—ranging from the reconceived second and third political theories to the return of theology and mythology."[51]

The Radical Subject

Dugin, as a *Radical Subject*, embraces "the concept of *Gottesnacht*, 'the night of God,'" in which there is darkness—a dark age.[52] Dugin also characterized *Gottesnacht* as "the Iron Age," where the "organized world," the world as it should be, is replaced by chaos.[53] As Dugin expounds on the Radical Subject, a glimpse at the proximity of esotericism to the surface of his thinking is possible. In his treatment of the Radical Subject, Dugin demonstrates the extent of his elevated view of Traditionalism. Radical Subjects occupy the upper echelons of genuine understanding.

Comparatively, the progressive liberal rush to advance reveals a headlong fall into decay. Dugin applies the identity of "the Antichrist Collective" to the progressive proponents engaged in this race to corruption.[54] In the non-Traditional world, the sacred things of Traditionalism, such as initiation into the mysteries of perennial Truth, have disappeared, and humankind is left occupying a vacuum.[55]

For Traditionalists agreeing with Dugin's understandings, this vacuum is a starting point; it is where they find themselves in *Gottesnacht*.[56] "The Radical Subject goes with the world without being of this world;" not afraid of modernity, the Radical Subject "is in the modern world and wants to be here, not beyond this world."[57] The Radical Subject realizes the transitory nature of the present world and wishes to remain temporarily in its chaos to actively help end it.[58] Dugin characterized Julius Evola and similarly inclined Traditionalists it terms of the Radical Subject, and there can be little doubt that here he includes himself.[59]

As Dugin expounded on the Radical Subject, he employed Heidegger's comparison of the four types of men.[60] Dugin's Neo-

Traditionalists occupy the position of the New Philosophers in Heidegger's four-types model. They are Radical Subjects in the terminology Dugin used to describe those Traditionalists who desire to be in the epicenter of the postmodern world.[61] Placement within *Gottesnacht* proves the nature of the Radical Subject's soul.[62] *Gottesnacht* is the dark place of the present, the center of the night, the center of hell as Dugin described it, using the words of Yevgeny Golovin, the Traditionalist poet.[63]

Notes

1. Dugin, *Fourth Theory*. Cf. Part I, Chapter One, footnote 39.

2. John B. Dunlop, "Aleksandr Dugin's Foundations of Geopolitics," *Demokratizatsiya* 12, no. 1 (January 31, 2004): 41. Cf. tec.fsi.stanford.edu/docs/aleksandr-dugins-foundations-geopolitics for a transcript of this article. Cf. "Aleksandr Dugin's Foundations of Geopolitics," 4pt.su/en/content/aleksandr-dugin%E2%80%99s-foundations-geopolitics. Cf. Dugin, *Osnovy Geopolitiki: Geopoliticheskoe Budushchee Rossii*. John B. Dunlop, Emeritus Senior Fellow, Hoover Institution, Stanford University.

3. Dunlop, "Dugin's Foundations of Geopolitics," 41.

4. Cf. Umland, "Dugin's transformation," 148.

5. Cf. Laruelle, *Russian Version of the European Radical Right*.

6. Cf. Anton Shekhovtsov, "Aleksandr Dugin's Neo-Eurasianism: The New Right à La Russe," *Religion Compass* 3, no. 4 (2009): 697-716, Rossman, *Russian Intellectual Antisemitism in the Post-Communist Era* (Lincoln, NE: University of Nebraska Press, 2002), and Epstein, *Conservatism and Traditionalism*. Epstein's work cited here was written relatively early in Dugin's geopolitical career but is detailed and insightful—perhaps the best of early Dugin examinations in English. Anton Shekhovtsov, Political Researcher and Commentator of the European Right.

7. Dunlop, "Dugin's Foundations of Geopolitics," footnote 11. Cf. Aleksandr Verkhovskii and Vladimir Pribylovskii, *Natsional-patrioticheskie organizatsii v Rossii* (Moscow: Izdatel'stvo 'Institut eksperimental'noi sotsiologii,' 1996), 50.

8. Laruelle, *Russian Version of the European Radical Right*. 1.

9. Dugin, "The Figure of the Radical Subject," under, Part 1, Traditionalism and Sociology—The Modern and the Eternal. I reference Dugin's treatment of the Radical Subject repeatedly because of the emphasis I feel required to place on the kinetics of Dugin's applied Neo-Traditionalism. For other of Dugin's treatments of the Radical Subject, Cf. Dugin, "The Radical Subject and the Metaphysics of Pain," The Fourth Revolutionary War, September 17, 2016, 4threvolutionarywar.wordpress.com/2016/09/17/the-radical-subject-and-the-metaphysics-of-pain-alexander-dugin/. For treatments from other than Dugin on the Radical Subject, Cf. e.g., Joy James and Edmund T. Gordon, "Activist Scholars or Radical Subjects?," Afterword, in *Engaging Contradictions: Theory, Politics, and Methods of Activist Scholarship*, ed. Charles Adams Hale (Berkeley: University of California Press, 2008), 267-73 and Laura Gray-Rosendale and Steven Rosendale, eds., *Radical Relevance: Toward a Scholarship of the Whole Left* (Albany: State University of New York Press, 2005).

10. Ibid.

11. Ibid.

12. Ibid.

13. Ibid., under, Part 2, The Figure of the Radical Subject and the Traditionalist without Tradition

14. Ibid., under, Part 1, Traditionalism and Sociology—The Modern and the Eternal.

15. Ibid.

16. Ibid.

17. Ibid.

18. Cf. Schmitt, "Political Theology," and other Schmitt references herein.

19. Dugin, "The Figure of the Radical Subject," under, Part 1, Traditionalism and Sociology—The Modern and the Eternal.

20. Ibid.

21. Ibid.

22. Dugin, *Fourth Theory*, 28. Parentheses in original.

23. Ibid.

24. Ibid., "This failure already occurred in the teaching of Heraclitus regarding the *phusis* and the *logos*," according to Dugin. Emphasis in

32

original. John B. Morgan makes the editorial footnote that *phusis* refers to *nature*, that which exists, and *logos* refers to that which orders the universe. Cf. Morgan, in *Fourth Theory*, 28, footnote 29.

25. Ibid., 54.

26. Ibid., 28.

27. Ibid., 28-29.

28. Ibid., 28. For additional explorations into Heidegger's treatment of Being, Cf. e.g., John Macquarrie, *Martin Heidegger* (Richmond: John Knox Press, 1968). John Macquarrie, 1919-2007, was Lady Margaret Professor of Divinity in the University of Oxford from 1970 until 1986.

29. Ibid.

30. Ibid.

31. Ibid., 29.

32. Ibid. The OED states that postmodernity is "a period or movement representing a departure from modernism and characterized by the self-conscious use of earlier styles and conventions, a mixing of different artistic styles and media, and a general distrust of theories." *Britannica* states, in part that, "postmodernism is largely a reaction against the intellectual assumptions and values of the modern period in the history of Western philosophy (roughly, the 17th through the 19th century). Indeed, many of the doctrines characteristically associated with postmodernism can fairly be described as the straightforward denial of general philosophical viewpoints that were taken for granted during the 18th-century Enlightenment, though they were not unique to that period." Cf. britannica.com/topic/postmodernism-philosophy.

33. Ibid., 28-29.

34. Ibid., 29.

35. Ibid. Here Dugin is referring to Friedrich Hölderlin's poem "Bread and Wine." Johann Christian Friedrich Hölderlin is a favorite of Dugin. Friedrich Hölderlin, 1770-1843.

36. Ibid.

37. Ibid. Dugin states that Heidegger quoted Hölderlin, "But wherever the danger lies, there also grows that which saves." Cf. Morgan's editorial footnote 32. Cf. Martin Heidegger, *Off the Beaten Path*, ed. Julian Young and Kenneth Hayes, trans. Julian Young and Kenneth Hayes (Cambridge: Cambridge University Press, 2002).

38. Ibid.

39. Ibid.

40. Ibid.

41. Ibid.

42. Ibid.

43. Ibid., 179.

44. Ibid., 189.

45. Ibid., 190.

46. Dugin, "From Sacred Geography," under, Sacred North and Sacred South. Parentheses in original.

47. Ibid. Parentheses in original. Brackets added. Sacred Geography is addressed in more detail in Part III, Chapter Three.

48. Ibid.

49. Ibid.

50. Ibid. Cf. Michael Millerman, "Heidegger, Left and Right: Differential Political Ontology and Fundamental Political Ontology Compared," *Journal of Eurasian Affairs* 2, no. 1 (2014): 94ff. Michael Millerman, Political Philosophy Scholar, Writer, and Translator.

51. Dugin, *Fourth Theory*, 29. In Dugin's opinion, Heidegger's work on Being was not anecdotal or incomplete. Quite the contrary, "Many researchers have lost sight of the fact that Heidegger, especially, in his middle period between 1936 and 1945, developed a complete history of philosophy centered around *Dasein*, which, apparent in retrospect, can form the basis of a full-fledged and a well-developed political philosophy," Dugin wrote in Dugin, *Fourth Theory*, 41.

52. Dugin, "The Figure of the Radical Subject," under, Part 2, The Figure of the Radical Subject and the Traditionalist without Tradition. Emphasis added. Cf. footnote 9 above.

53. Ibid. Cf. Part IV, Chapter Two where I give specific attention to assigning Identity.

54. Ibid. The OED identifies three major categories of Antichrist interpretation: "A personal opponent of Christ expected to appear before the end of the world." "A person or force seen as opposing Christ or the Christian Church." "A person or thing regarded as

supremely evil or as a fundamental enemy or opponent." Dugin mostly employs the term within the third definition.

55. Ibid.

56. Ibid.

57. Ibid.

58. Ibid. Here Dugin is directly alluding to Christian Scripture. Cf. John 17:14 NASB: "I have given them Your word; and the world has hated them, because they are not of the world, even as I am not of the world." Cf. Romans 12:2 and others, e.g., Hebrews 13:14.

59. Ibid. I apply the descriptor of Neo-Traditionalism to Dugin, Evola, and others of similar active Traditionalist characteristics (as opposed to the more passive attributes of Guénon and the Integral Traditionalists). This application is discussed in more detail herein.

60. Ibid. The four types being (adapted from: "The Figure of the Radical Subject," under, Part 2, The Figure of the Radical Subject and the Traditionalist without Tradition): The Simple and Ignorant—people who cannot choose anything and change with the world and society; Conservatives—people afraid of *Gottesnacht*, of decadence who want to conserve what exists against time, but time devours everything; Progressives—people who want to go in the direction of decay faster and faster still, the ones responsible for the current situation—liberals, the World Government, together can be called "The Antichrist Collective;" The New Philosophers—those not afraid of *Gottesnacht* rather they seek it—Heidegger said of them: these philosophers are faced with the "hard knowledge of nihilism" *(schwere Wissen des Nihilismus)*.

61. Ibid.

62. Ibid.

63. Ibid. Here, Dugin also refers to Hölderlin and stresses poetic allusions. Sedgwick discusses the Dugin-Golovin connection and the influence of George Ivanovich Gurdjieff on Golovin via Vladimir Stepanov. Cf. traditionalistblog.blogspot.com/2007/03/russian-traditionalism-started-with.html.

Chapter Three: Dugin's Metaphysical, Esoteric, and Conspirological Mindset

The Esoteric and the Existential

Grasping just how tightly Dugin binds esoteric metaphysics to his day-to-day thinking is probably difficult for Western geopoliticians. With his Cartesian comparisons and Traditionalism, Dugin illustrates the distance between the esoteric realm and the perceived reality of the West.[1] Because Dugin tends to place mystical narratives to the fore, he often ignores contrary empirical evidence—this tendency often proves a vexation to Western observers and commentators.

Consider Dugin's treatment of the Arthurian Narrative, Charlemagne, and Apollo, as he looks to the future of Russia and Europe in one short paragraph.[2] First, Dugin claimed that the basis of what he terms the "Russian vision" is found in Russian Orthodoxy and Russia's past Eurasian empire.[3] He then supposed, "that the future of Europe lies in the restoration of the Charlemagne heritage and of the eschatological anticipation of the return of King Arthur."[4] Dugin added that some may even "hope for the new Roman Empire professed by Virgil, who thought that Apollo would return and this time for eternity."[5] Dugin was in no way attempting to argue the historicity of his examples; he was purposefully presenting them in mythological and heroic terms.

Considering Dugin's Metaphysics

When expanded into worldviews, there are three major "global-metaphysical systems" into which "the variety of the world's political ideologies" can be divided, wrote Epstein of Dugin's perspective.[6] Epstein's consideration of Dugin's metaphysical worldview included an interpretation of these three concepts under the headings of *Absolute Unity*, *Transcendental*, and *Magical Materialism*.[7] A brief explanation of these three placements provides a starting point for consideration of Dugin's metaphysical outlook.

Absolute Unity

Absolute Unity is the condition of humankind like it was before the Fall, where there was a closeness with God now unknown except to the Traditionalist Adepts.[8] In his 1994 analysis of Dugin, Epstein concluded that by fully embracing the "esoteric doctrine of immanence," Dugin accepts Absolute Unity as achievable.[9] Relevant to interpreting Dugin is the realization that he identifies Absolute Unity as the gnostic "noblest of all worldviews."[10]

Furthermore, Dugin believes that Absolute Unity is witnessed in the historical manifestations of the sacred imperialism of the Ghibellines, the beliefs of Cathars and Albigenses, in the teachings of Rosicrucianism, and in German National Socialism.[11] While accepting that the esoteric doctrine of immanence was characteristic of the Ghibelline supporters of the Holy Roman Empire in its quarrels with the Popes may be arguable, it was nonetheless familiar to the Cathars and Albigenses. Rosicrucian acceptance of immanence, expressed similarly to Dugin's Absolute Unity, is no doubt present in its gnostic approach to religion in general and Christianity in particular.[12]

Dugin associates specific archetypes personified within the state of Absolute Unity; here, the personalities of the *Divine Subject*, the *Hero*, the *Angelic Leader*, and the *Sacred Emperor* are recognizable.[13] For Dugin, there is "no higher metaphysical principle" than that embodied in the Divine Subject within Absolute Unity.[14] Herein is the pinnacle of Dugin's metaphysical fusion with politics—in Absolute Unity, man "is absolutely free and inseparable from God."[15]

This total inseparability—absolute immanence, God's complete indwelling—"is personified in the figure of a 'Divine Subject, Hero, Angelic Leader, Sacred Emperor,'" in Dugin's hermeneutic.[16] While it seems that the personification of this relationship is individualized, Dugin's examples of their manifestation appear to demonstrate some decidedly community relationship aspects.[17]

Metaphysical Transcendentalism

Metaphysical Transcendentalism follows Absolute Unity in Dugin's formulation. According to Epstein's understanding, Dugin believes Transcendentalism is the position that mainstream Christianity attempts to maintain.[18] However, leveling a charge of heresy, Dugin claims that the Roman Church departed from the Orthodox purity of original Christianity, a purity now preserved only by its gnostic remnant.[19] Moreover, both Roman Catholicism and Protestantism fail to maintain a place in Transcendentalism today.[20]

Transcendentalism expresses adherence somewhat between the "Paradise Principle" of Absolute Unity of Traditionalism and the irreconcilable transcendence of Judaism.[21] While Christianity doctrinally recognizes Christ as the mediator, the intercessor, that is a bridge across the otherwise irreconcilable separation of human existence from Paradise after the Fall, Christianity largely failed to restore the order of Paradise through "God and man in the figure of Christ."[22]

Christianity failed to achieve the immanence present in Paradise because Christianity "surrendered to Jewish transcendentalism," and became a religion consumed by the depravity of sin and a need to constantly seek repentance.[23] The Roman Church abandoned its true mission, restoration of the order of Paradise through Absolute Unity, and settled for control of Christianity by the rationing of forgiveness.[24] Therefore, the Roman Church stands condemned in gnostic teachings, and is henceforth viewed "as Satanic and Luciferian."[25] Epstein wrote that Dugin accepts the gnostic teaching condemning the Roman Catholic Church for corrupting the notion of Absolute Unity representing "the true manifestations of original Christianity."[26] What Dugin is advocating, as Epstein expressed it, "is the struggle of authentic Christianity against its Judaic distortions."[27]

Magical Materialism

Magical Materialism occupies the lowest rung on Dugin's Metaphysical Systems ladder. Materialism, in Dugin's opinion, has been falsely endowed with near-magical properties to solve the world's ills without resorting to monotheistic religion.[28] The technological power of humanistic evolution is thought to be all that is required to address any, and all, issues.[29] The materialistic element in Magical Materialism is easy to identify, and Dugin's anti-Western, anti-globalist scorn is easily detected.

Dugin accuses the Magical Materialism of the West as being a false religion where super-technology supplants the supernatural. Magical Materialism, as a practical matter, elevates Scientism into the realm of authentic religion "where paradise is identified with purely material comfort and technological progress."[30] Interestingly endowed with a diverse membership, Magical Materialism is also the category where Dugin deposits Soviet Communism, Western consumer-oriented globalism, Roman Catholicism and Protestantism.

Unpacking Magical Materialism, readily identifies its materialistic element. The "magical" modifier may seem almost flippant but is understandable in the sense of trusting in the seemingly magical ability of evolutionary Humanism to solve all problems. "Where there is the necessary technical skill to *move mountains*, there is no need for the *faith that moves mountains,*" quipped Eric Hoffer.[31] Because, for Dugin, the degree of faith required to move mountains through technology imitates, albeit poorly, supernatural faith; he, therefore, accuses Western materialism of being a false religion.[32]

Magical Materialism is the category where one may expect to find atheistic and totalitarian communism. At the same time, paradoxically, it is where the American and other Western models of consumer-oriented societies are found. In places were Enlightenment-inspired humanistic consumerism and consumption is the model, "paradise is identified with purely material comfort and technological progress."[33] Dugin readers in the West may find it somewhat shocking that he so readily relegates Protestantism within the same category where he places Soviet Marxism and American Liberalism but Dugin does it with no apparent compulsion.[34]

Metaphysics occupies a prominent place in Dugin's conception of Russia's relationship with the West. In a future Russia/Eurasia highly infused with Traditionalism, he believes that Absolute Unity is approachable. Western globalism, with its inherent materialism, is relegated to a place where technological magic becomes the dominant, but none-the-less false religion of Scientism.[35]

Turbo-Capitalism and the Cosmic Egg

There are myriad illustrations of Dugin's esoteric mindset and how he incorporates it into standard mainstream dialog. I have selected two examples to make this point.

Consider Dugin's writing on "The problematic ontology of turbo-capitalism."[36] Dugin unhesitatingly inserts traditionally recognizable allusions and illustrations into his discourse on any number of subject areas he is discussing—in this case, economics. First, Dugin wrote of how Turbo-Capitalism is "eroding the system of things and invoking a system of signs."[37] Dugin addressed the move from an economy based on exchanges in material things to a "new economy" based on "contemplation and sensorial stimulation."[38]

> In turbo-capitalism we reach not simply the borders of ontology, as the borders of the ontology of the third state, the limits of the bourgeois system of measures. And the "new economy" itself is not yet a new era—it is an ambiguous and pluri-significant [sic] challenge to say goodbye to the old, but not offering at the same time anything new.[39]

Second, he addressed the move from material accumulation to sensorial stimulation, "in which the essential element is not so much possession," but one where there is a "proliferation of narcotics, television networks and computer games."[40] Then, Dugin abruptly made a leap into the esoteric realm:

> True, the extreme conservatives (R. Guénon) say that the present phase of post-materialism corresponds to the "opening of the cosmic egg from below," while in the epoch of the traditional societies it was opened from above, and later

(during classic capitalism) it was closed from all sides.[41]

The Cosmic Egg, Dugin's Egg of the World in his 2011 Paris lecture, refers to the representation of the creation of the world (the Cosmos) in the creation narratives of various sacred and esoteric texts.[42]

> In Paris, in 2011 I gave a lecture under the title: "René Guénon as a sociologist." René Guénon in his book "The Reign of Quantity and the Signs of the Times" used the traditional and sacred symbol of the Egg of the World. In Guénon's perspective, the pre-modern world corresponds to the Egg of the World open on the top and closed on the bottom. The spiritual rays enter the world and so the cosmic and material things receive the sacred qualities.[43]

"Modern society corresponds to the Egg of the World closed on the top and on the bottom," Dugin explained.[44] He went on to say that the Cosmic Egg, closed at both ends, "is the materialistic, atheistic, consumerist civilization," it comprises "the scientific, mechanical and atomistic worldview."[45] Perhaps even worse, "Postmodern society corresponds to the Egg of the World open on the bottom and closed on the top."[46] Dugin added that this "demonic post-human and post-social civilization," happens to be "the reality in which we live."[47]

These excerpts are not intended to examine the validity of Dugin's economic ideas and observations but to emphasize the rapid change of direction he took in his otherwise economic discourse. Dugin moved from the economics of material accumulation to the Cosmic Egg without missing a beat. Dugin's deviations from a dialog that is understood, or at least that engages with familiar words and phrases, to the esoteric realm of mystical symbolism are likely disconcerting to most Western audiences. For Dugin, such leaps are commonplace and show the esoteric bend of his Neo-Traditionalism.

The Serpent

Recalling the enmity proclaimed in the Book of Genesis, Dugin understated, "there is a bad attitude towards the serpent."[48] Snakes, to memorialize "the temptation of Eve in Paradise," are penalized by being "deprived of legs" and having to "creep on their bellies upon damp, crude ground."[49] But what of the Serpent, blamed by some for all snakes bearing the hipless and shoulderless curse? Most certainly, through the Serpent described in Genesis, Satan is seen acting out his role as the Deceiver. Satan possesses an inherent dualism—he is angelic yet demonic. Though in his fallen state, he is no longer an angel of light, he attempts to appear so.[50] He is not of this world, yet he is its prince for a time. Contributing to his success as the Deceiver, serpents are not always synonymous with Satan. Sometimes a serpent (in snake form) is depicted as a symbol of Goodness—even analogous to Christ Himself.

> The early Christians were aware of an amazing symbol, the Anfisbena, a two-headed serpent consisting of two halves, one black and one white, the two participants of the last struggle with a common body.[51]

Here, intertwined snakes of the Anfisbena represent Evil and Goodness, not in a dualism of personality, but in a close struggle of Darkness and Light, of Antichrist and Christ. It is the appearance of goodness that camouflages the Deceiver's evil. The more truth the Dark Serpent can mix with his lies, the more like the Serpent of Light he appears to be.

A much more mundane symbol is that of the mole. Not eliciting the same degree of visceral repugnance as does the snake, the mole is seemingly cast poorly and out-of-character as an evil and sinister actor on the world stage. Dugin related that "Marx named the mole as a symbol of capitalism."[52]

> Like a blind mole Capitalism digs gloomy holes
> in the hearts of the blotto people, rushing around
> in the vampiric labyrinths with increasing value

for the benefit of the meanest minority and for the uncountable sufferings of the silliest majority.[53]

For a time, the mole dominated the stage, but the time of the mole has passed. Dugin claimed that French philosopher, Gilles Deleuze, was correct in saying that we have now come to the "phase of the serpent."[54] It is not that the serpent replaced the mole—capitalism replaced by an entirely different ideology—instead, the mole has morphed into the snake. The serpent is the symbol of capitalism gone to the extreme. "The old monetary mole is the animal of the space of enclosure, but the serpent is that of the societies of control," wrote Deleuze, adding, "we have passed from one animal to the other, from the mole to the serpent."[55]

> In the modern globalist world the distinction between dominating and dominated, between men and women, full and hungry, doctors and patients, teachers and scholars is erasing itself. An open society is constructed in accordance with the serpent principle. Everything merges into everything else, the continuous social surfing penetrates the strata of global society. Capitalism no longer bribes Labour, but creates Labour in the form of entertainment.[56]

Extending his metaphysical thinking, Dugin recalled the Copper Serpent, the serpent on a cross found in Orthodox churches. It is this other serpent, the not-Satan serpent, the Copper Serpent, "whose image was erected in the desert by Moses."[57] The Copper Serpent, Dugin reminded us, is "considered to be a prototype of the Redeemer," to whom Traditionalists turn to defeat the Dark Serpent symbol-bearing capitalism of the West.[58] Dugin believes that the Serpent of Light will emerge victorious in its struggles against the Serpent of Darkness—triumphant Traditionalism will overcome postmodernity.

Adapted by Mud Pie Graphics from
clker.com/clipart-bronze-serpent.html

Dugin as Conspirologist

On January 6, 2020, the United States' Capitol Building witnessed the manifestation of either a protest gone extreme or a real or imagined conspiracy. If a conspiracy it was either evidence of a real, focused, and specific event or proof of a ridiculous conspiracy theory—a conspiracy theory promoted by none other than the President of the United States. The explanation one deems to be accurate depends on the amount of credibility afforded to one side or the other in the nearly 50/50 political split in America evidenced in the November 3, 2020, presidential election.

From a conspiracy theory vantage point, Nina Jankowicz, whom the AP identified as an expert in explaining disinformation, referred to the pro-President Donald Trump demonstrators' very presence being due to disinformation, conspiracy theories, and extremism displayed to the world.[59] From the alleged conspiracy quarter, bloggers, politicians, commentators, and others, cited as experts by various sources have repeatedly expressed views supporting President Trump's position of a real and present conspiracy contrived to deprive him of a second term of office.

While conspiracy theories are usually considered products of extreme fringe players, if the depth and magnitude of President Trump's accusations of coordinated election fraud were proven substantially correct, the impact of recognizing real conspiracy in

44

the 2020 election would be unprecedented. On the other hand, if Jankowicz and others sharing her opinion are correct, the sitting President of the United States engaged in a conspiracy against the Constitution he was sworn to defend. Against this background of a head-on collision between alleged conspiracy and alleged conspiracy theory, I suggest a review of some aspects of conspirology may prove useful.

A criminal conspiracy is "an agreement between two or more people to commit an illegal act, along with an intent to achieve the agreement's goal," according to Cornell University Law School's Legal Information Institute.[60] Unlike a criminal conspiracy, Conspirology, which considers conspiracy theories' belief in the manipulation and control of events for the benefit of an elite group of purposely obscured transcendent puppet-masters, requires only an individual or collective belief that events are being controlled, Oz-like, by a person, or persons behind the curtain. In this case, the allegations assume elections, finance, wars, and culture, for example are being manipulated in a secret, hidden, and devious fashion.

Conspirology, though by itself not a theology, often involves religious and theological subjects and issues. The religious appearance is evident in numerous examples and seems to enjoy public popularity across the media spectrum. It is also prevalent in individually held beliefs, considering my altogether noncomprehensive view of several social media sites' comments sections.

Conspirology mega-narratives tend toward universal control or one-world government outcomes. Recognizing this, I highlight the expressed views of Dugin, who claims the Traditionalist heritage of Guénon and Evola. Traditionalism claims that there is an Absolute Truth, revealed through divine revelation, known, passed down, and maintained unaltered from the time of Creation by a small and secretive group of adept adherents. Dugin advocates Traditionalism in direct opposition to the relativism and progressivism of Western Liberalism.

As Dugin saw Western Liberalism as political philosophy's victory over the vanquished ideologies of Fascism and Communism, he developed his Traditionally based Fourth Political Theory as an alternative. He promotes his theory as a competitor to Western visions of unipolar political, economic, and cultural domination often portrayed as a One World conspiracy. Dugin is becoming more widely known in the West for his geopolitical influence in Russia and among rightist elements in Europe. Additionally, Dugin has gained recognition in the U.S. for his views and commentary on the 2016 presidential election and subsequent events. It is becoming increasingly interesting to follow Dugin's anti-progressive rhetoric when attempting to gauge its effect on the conservative movements in Europe and the U.S.

Given Dugin's growing reach in Europe and the U.S. over the past decade or so, some examination of Dugin's associations to various perceived conspiracies is in order. This course is warranted because, according to Rossman, Dugin has introduced himself, simultaneously, as a metaphysician and conspirologist.[61] Dugin's 1991 book, *Konspirologija*, is the product of a well-educated and meticulous author, according to its reviewer, Branko Malić.[62]

Malić wrote that Dugin is interested in conspiracy theories dwelling at the academic margins. This placement of Dugin's focus notwithstanding, Dugin highlighted that conspirological notions of both history and everyday life are quite common in the public mind.[63] Demonstrated interest in conspiracies, real or imagined is certainly not confined to Dugin.t

Groups, organizations, and associations that are secretive or exclusive become magnets creating a pull that often attracts an incredible amount of attention. The many and varied Masonic Orders, the Illuminati, the Trilateral Commission, Opus De, The Bilderberg Group, and countless other shrouded individuals and supposed cabals draw widespread attention ranging from serious conspirology scholars in the Academy to strange but equally serious conspiracy theory groupies dwelling on the fringes of paranoia.

The field is at once graced with limited amounts of serious scholarship and strewn with diatribes posing as scholarship. Into this muddy water, I now venture. Many find voyages into the deterministic and persecution-complex filled regions of conspirology to be alluring. I will make a brief excursion as I am no exception.

Conspiracy Theory

Umberto Eco offered John Chadwick's example that "even the least curious mind is roused by the promise of sharing knowledge withheld from others."[64] Eco noted Chadwick's observation that "the urge to discover secrets is deeply ingrained in human nature."[65] Eco thought that conspiracies gain traction "because they purport to offer explanations in ways that appeal to people who feel they've been denied important information."[66]

Karl Popper expounded on conspiracy theory at some length. His work, *The Open Society and Its Enemies*, anti-totalitarian and widely lauded for its defense of Liberal Democracy, also examines conspiracy theory.[67] Popper explained that conspiracy theory is a social phenomenon where many of society's events, especially the negative ones, are believed to be contrived by members of an enormously influential group.[68] Epstein explained it as "the notion of conspiracy," which "presupposes that history is designed according to some initial plan, so that all particular events—wars, revolutions, natural disasters—can be explained as part and parcel of a grand scheme."[69]

Epstein stated that, for Dugin, "Tradition is a totality, subordinating all aspects of culture and establishing strict rules and rituals of everyday conduct for all members of society."[70] Dugin envisions that "the connection between metaphysics and politics is dictated by the very essence of total traditionalism, which denies the liberal principle of the separation of powers and specialization of knowledge."[71] Epstein observed that within Traditionalism, there is an identifiable mistrust of history that he identified as the *Hermeneutic of Suspicion of Historical Reality.*[72]

Epstein's observation suggests that both liberal and Traditionalist perspectives of things spiritual, political, professional, and economic point to a similar hermeneutic.[73] For the liberal, each of these areas noted by Epstein is "governed by their own particular laws."[74] For the Traditionalist, "even the most concrete and seemingly arbitrary facts" within the same subject areas "are conditioned by some underlying principles and therefore testify to an all-comprehensive determinism."[75] The grand scheme referred to by Epstein, as part of this all-comprehensive determinism, allows conspiracy theory to find nurture in Traditionalism.

Conspiracy Theory as Literature

There is an entire literary genre devoted to conspiracy theory.[76] Conspiracy-spawned fictions are frequently read works in popular literature. Often these fictional works center on religious groups, gnostic intrigues, and secret societies. Here dwell speculations and conjectures yet unproven, and more often unprovable. Conspiracy theory finds ample expression in literature, as Eco illustrates in various of his books, using well-researched elements of conspiracy theory to support his storyline's structure.[77] However, many popular treatments of conspiracy-related topics, such as Dan Brown's *The Da Vinci Code,* do nothing to dispel the aversion to more serious study within the Academy.[78]

Although an acknowledged work of fiction, Brown presents his work within a well populated category where historical fiction poses as fact. Unlike Eco, who weaves fiction around a framework of carefully researched historical events, Brown adopts a faux-historical approach whereby he creates pseudo-historical events and then twists his tale around them. As a result, *The Da Vinci Code* becomes a conspiracy theory based on a contrived narrative rather than a conspiracy theory based on an alternate interpretation of actual evidence.

The Academy's current aversion to Traditionalism and other metaphysical subjects may be exacerbated due to the proliferation of pseudo-academic works more disguised than *The Da Vinci Code.* Works such as *The Holy Blood and The Holy Grail*, for example, present popularized esoteric literature as a serious study.[79] Works of this kind have attracted sufficient literary and academic criticism to pause researchers when ventures onto the esoteric and gnostic ground of Traditionalism and other metaphysical subjects are contemplated. *Observer* Literary Editor Robert McCrum addressed the issue directly:

> There is something called historical evidence—
> there is something called the historical method—

and if you look around the shelves of bookshops there is a lot of history being published, and people mistake this type of history for the real thing. These kinds of books do appeal to an enormous audience who believe them to be 'history,' but actually they aren't history, they are a kind of parody of history. Alas, though, I think that one has to say that this is the direction that history is going today.[80]

Conspiracy Theories as Social Constructs

Popper wrote at length on conspiracies as social constructs and identified his *Conspiracy Theory of Society* as:

The view that an explanation of a social phenomenon consists in the discovery of the men or groups who are interested in the occurrence of this phenomenon (sometimes it is a hidden interest which has first to be revealed), and who have planned and conspired to bring it about.[81]

Popper then insisted this view arises from the "mistaken theory" that societal evils, such as wars and economic disparities, are "the result of direct design by some powerful individuals and groups."[82] Popper maintained that part of the blame for societal inequity rests in historicism—the belief that natural laws determine societal and cultural events.[83] In thinking similar to that of Schmitt, Popper explained that the attitude of modernity toward natural laws is the "typical result of the secularization of a religious superstition."[84]

Popper concluded that historicism is a derivative of conspiracy theory. Thus, conspiracy theory is the older of the two.[85] In conspiracy theory, the human determinism of the conspirators replaces supernatural determinism. In Popper's theory, belief in supernatural determinism is replaced through a very human substitution wherein the gods "are abandoned" and replaced "by powerful men or groups—sinister pressure groups whose wickedness is responsible for all the evils we suffer from—

49

such as the Learned Elders of Zion, or the monopolists, or the capitalists, or the imperialists."[86]

The New World Order as a Conspiracy

Dugin, as might be expected, rejects Popper's overall position out of hand. "The neuroses and fears located at the pathogenic core of liberal philosophy are clearly seen in *The Open Society and its Enemies*," says Dugin.[87] Far from seeing his reading of history from Popper's viewpoint as being historicism derived from conspiracy theory, Dugin embraces history as a realization and understanding of divine revelation. Dugin's historical approach does not quarrel with determinism.

Dugin, and those like-minded, link the New World Order with commonly mentioned conspiracy theory actors: the Trilateral Commission, the Bilderberg Group, and the cabal of "occult" international bankers.[88] Dugin suspects the entire New World Order enterprise to be part of a broad conspiracy. The seriousness of the implications Dugin and his colleagues of the journalistic magazine *Elements* placed on President George H.W. Bush's repeated use of New World Order phraseology immediately took on conspirological tones with statements such as:

> The New World Order, based on the establishment of One World Government, as has been candidly admitted by odeologists [sic] of the Trilateral Commission and Bildenburg [sic], is not simply a question of politico-economic domination of a certain "occult" ruling clique of international bankers. This "Order" bases itself on the victory on a global scale of a certain special ideology, and so the concept concerns not only instruments of power, but also "ideological revolution," a "coup d'état" consciousness, "new thinking."[89]

In addition to the New World Order, Dugin displays other conspiratorial projections. Dugin remarked on a "deep, sacred, and well-grounded mystical and theological hostility of Russian nationalism" directed toward the Jews.[90] There is a substantial amount of past Dugin material that links Dugin with Jewish conspiracy themes.[91] Some of these connections appear to be associated, at least in part, toward Dugin's eschatologically focused associations of the Jewish Messiah with Antichrist.[92]

Epstein identified and explored five conspiratorial themes that he claimed surface in Dugin's thinking: foremost was the Jewish conspiracy followed by the popular conspiracies ascribed to the Masons and Bankers.[93] Epstein also observed those to whom "the idea that capitalism and communism are two strategies of a single conspiracy, conceived by Zionists and Masons and designed to crush Russia as the world's last bastion of true Christian spirituality."[94] Here, one can see evidence, from Epstein's perspective, of Dugin's Jewish and Masonic conspiracies.

> In a popular version of conspirology, the plot can be traced to an ancient Jewish and Masonic attempt to take over the world, and both Soviet Communism and American Capitalism are seen as participants in this conspiracy, whose antagonism is merely a simulation concealing their basic collaboration.[95]

Rossman also claimed that the basis for Dugin's conspiracy theory is anti-Semitic.[96] He expressed the opinion that of Dugin's five conspiracies, the Jewish conspiracy is the overarching and permeating one, as Dugin's description of each conspiracy has "more or less pronounced anti-Semitic implications."[97] Rossman stated that with Dugin's adoption of the Jewish conspiracy, it "is discerned as a central and most basic one."[98]

> The idea of Jewish conspiracy, undoubtedly, corresponds to deep unconscious arche-types of very remote and diverse human communities. It is most likely that this theory is the activation of unconscious energies, which constitute the 'conspirological instinct' at its source.[99]

51

Dugin appears conflicted and inconsistent when considering the validity of the anti-Semitism accusations aimed at him. Victor Shnirelman offered a somewhat similar view to Rossman's but with reservations. "After Dugin read a book by the Eurasian Yaakov Bromberg (1931) in the mid-1990s, he stopped considering all the Jews the 'enemies of humanity,'" Shnirelman wrote.[100] Dugin may now view the Hasidim orthodox sect of Jews as conservatives and "allies of the Eurasians," and "secular assimilated Jews" as "Westernisers" and enemies.[101]

According to Benjamin Parker, while enthusiastic about pressing on his ideas of New World Order conspiracies, Dugin may have stepped back from the outright Jewish conspiracy theory.

> He may easily be called a Russian supremacist and would probably agree that he is a nationalist, but he is not necessarily an anti-Semite because he does not reserve for Jews special fear, hatred, or discrimination. If the Kremlin—or at least one part of it—is truly are [sic] enamored of Dugin's theories, it is possible that they could share his imperialist Russian supremacism without anti-Semitism. The problem, however, is how they could so easily accept Dugin while rejecting his influences and intellectual ancestors.[102]

One facet of Dugin's background and development culminates in his perception of the New World Order, expanded to its universalist and globalist extremes. This culmination positions Fourth Political Theory within a conspiracy theory framework. Keeping in mind that Dugin claims that Western Liberalism is attempting to create a unipolar hegemony—materialistic and universal in its globalism—it is evident that Dugin believes the New World Order is active in furtherance of this goal.

"Ideology attempts to mobilize the collective will of society for the construction of a deferred paradise," wrote Epstein.[103] In line with Epstein's idea, Dugin's accusations of the New World Order conspiracy are an attempt to mobilize his Fourth Political

Theory adherents to "oppose the demonic plots which destroyed the original paradise."[104] Dugin then rallies support for creating a Eurasian barrier to foil the Western plot aimed at world domination.

Epstein presented conspirological constituents of Dugin's theory in his discussion of the *Hermeneutic of Suspicion of Historical Reality*.[105] This concept suggests that Dugin's Traditionalism yields to conspiratorial influences—Dugin is conditioned to read history from a conspiratorial perspective. Not only that, he also purposefully assigns a collective identity to the Antichrist through decidedly conspiratorial conclusions aimed at the West and the New World Order.

Epstein's example comparing Marxism with Traditionalism allows for a better understanding of how both are affected by the Hermeneutic of Suspicion of Historical Reality. "Where Marxism, with its materialist assumptions, speaks about 'laws,'" Epstein observed, "traditionalism, with its spiritual bias, identifies concealed 'volitions' and 'intentions.'"[106]

Thus, both subscribe to a recognizable Hermeneutic of Suspicion of Historical Reality—laws are suspect in the former, and volitions and intentions are suspect in the latter. In this hermeneutic, there is a realization that something beyond events themselves is pulling at the strings.[107] In Epstein's view, this hermeneutic compels Dugin and many Traditionalists to read and interpret history "in terms of 'conspirology.'"[108]

Dugin's conspirology is both a cause and a symptom of his stance against Western Liberalism and its historical development. If the New World Order is a real conspiracy directed at a unipolar world endgame, it is natural to realize Dugin's opposition to Western hegemony. On the other hand, if a unipolar world goal is only a misguided perception of Dugin's interpretation of Western intentions, this supposed conspiracy may be symptomatic of a potentially dangerous conspiracy theory. If Dugin's insistence on Western Liberalism's world domination goal is not correct, it is based on a conspiracy theory with distinctive paranoid characteristics.

Paranoid Elements in Conspiracy Theory

Eco also produced valuable non-fictional examinations of conspiracy theory, exposing trails into its paranoid elements. In his article, "A Theory of Conspiracies," Eco demonstrated the considerable research power evident in his fiction writing.[109] Eco notes that historian Richard Hofstadter's 1964 *Harper's* article, "The Paranoid Style in American Politics," employs the psychiatric term *paranoid* applied to conspiracy theorists.[110]

If Dugin's conspirology culminates with a Jewish conspiracy or the New World Order striving for the goal of unipolar globalism, symptoms of a kind of paranoia are visible. Likewise, in Trump's conspiracy accusations, demonstrated in his belief in the *Deep State*, a network of embedded governmental officials dedicated to achieving goals contrary to his stated policies, and a purposeful web of coordinated voter fraud, similar symptoms have been suggested.

Hofstadter's research led him to Norman Cohn's work and the remarkable association of pre-seventeenth century European Millennial Sects with their psychological "preoccupations and fantasies."[111] Hofstadter's adoption of Cohn's conclusions that the paranoid conspiracy theorist views the ultimate result of conspiracy apocalyptically is directly applicable to Dugin's eschatological thinking.[112] Hofstadter noted that the paranoid "sees the fate of conspiracy in apocalyptic terms—he traffics in the birth and death of whole worlds, whole political orders, whole systems of human values."[113]

Given this interpretation, Hofstadter could be imagined to be writing with Dugin specifically in mind because as Eco explained, "Hofstadter used the word 'paranoid' not in a clinical sense, but as a rhetorical device."[114] "The clinically paranoid person," Eco continued, "thinks that others are plotting against him personally, whereas the socially paranoid person believes that occult powers are persecuting his class, his nation, his religion.[115]

Eco advanced this especially pertinent observation that should be considered in Dugin's case: "I would argue that the latter is more dangerous, because he sees his plight as one that's shared—perhaps by millions of other people."[116] This perspective, as perceived by the conspiracy theory adherent, "validates his paranoia and seems to him to explain current as well as historical events."[117]

Hofstadter was clear that conspiracy theory is not a recent phenomenon. Remarking on research that studied "the millennial sects of Europe from the eleventh to the sixteenth century," Hofstadter wrote that "Norman Cohn believed he found a persistent psychic complex that corresponds broadly with" what Cohn considered, "a style made up of certain preoccupations and fantasies."[118] Cohn described these "preoccupations and fantasies" as:

> The megalomaniac view of oneself as the Elect, wholly good, abominably persecuted, yet assured of ultimate triumph; the attribution of gigantic and demonic powers to the adversary; the refusal to accept the ineluctable limitations and imperfections of human existence, such as transience, dissention [sic], conflict, fallibility whether intellectual or moral; the obsession with inerrable prophecies.[119]

Cohn stated that "these attitudes are symptoms which together constitute the unmistakable syndrome of paranoia."[120] He then observed two points that should be given weight in Dugin's case. First, "a paranoid delusion does not cease to be so because it is shared by many individuals," and second, it does not cease to be paranoia "because those individuals have real and ample grounds for regarding themselves as victims of oppression."[121] Dugin may be somewhat paranoid, a not uncommon condition. In-and-of-itself, however, this does not mean his Fourth Political Theory and the conspiracy of a New World Order is not supportable. Conspiracies proven are, of course, no longer theories; they exit the genre to take up residence elsewhere.

Dugin attributed the goal of unipolar globalism to the New World Order. Given the Trumpian idea that the Deep State, the imbedded opposition of unelected career government bureaucrats, is a major actor protecting a conspiracy of leftist elites with universalist goals, a question that needs to be asked now is to what extent, if any, does the Deep State mirror Dugin's conception of

55

the New World Order? To what extent are Trump and Dugin of like mind? Keeping in mind that Dugin perceives that Western Liberalism is attempting to create a global materialistic unipolar hegemony, he wants a multipolar oriented Eurasian barrier erected against this Western plot. A similar cause and effect model could perhaps be applied to Trump in his perception and resistance to the Deep State.

Adherents of Deep State and QAnon, an ultra-conservative fringe group to its detractors, conspiracies and self-styled counter-conspiracy theory participants collide in the current rush to occupy the political center stage. When considering a Deep State conspiracy theory projected from the Right, it is essential to acknowledge that accusations that it is Trump who promotes paranoid conspiracy theories that guide his behavior can also become a conspiracy theory in itself. That is to say, attributing and attempting to align Trump's behavior with, for instance, the QAnon conspiracy theory, "which holds that President Trump is secretly working to save the world from a satanic cult of pedophiles and cannibals," according to Brian Krebs, may reflect its own conspiracy theory related paranoia.[122]

Although I believe there are valid grounds to do so, in this brief forum I will leave detailed comparisons of Dugin with Trump to the reader for the present. None-the-less, note that former Trump adviser, Steve Bannon, has been linked with Dugin for several years, even reportedly meeting with Dugin in November 2018.[123] Additional examinations and comparisons into the extent of Dugin's influence on Trump are warranted, especially given speculation on Dugin's influence on Putin.[124]

Properly studying conspirology involves accepting that, at their foundational heart, conspiracy theories spring from the fact that conspiracies do exist. Additionally, it is germane to recognize a level of paranoia present in most, if not all, people. Furthermore, these two facts are not mutually exclusive. The existence of real conspiracies does not preclude some level of paranoia in those that acknowledge them. Conversely, the presence of paranoia, by itself, does not negate the reality of a proven, or provable, plot.

The question the serious conspirologist must ask is if an alleged conspiracy contains factually based suspicions? The answer must be derived regardless of a recognized presence of some degree of paranoia. To make this point, suppose Dugin is paranoid when considering the New World Order. Does this supposition, of itself, mean that there is no truth to specific claims of New World Order objectives? The same thinking must be applied to accusations directed at the Deep State and Trump's (or any) alleged conspiracy theory manifestations. For any scholarly or credible journalistic examination, the principles of a valid historical method must prevail.

Considering Dugin's conspirological mindset is part of understanding the whole of his thinking. Keep in mind that "Dugin introduced himself as a 'metaphysician, conspirologist, and expert in sacred geography.'"[125] Dugin's conspirology is either a cause or a symptom of his stance against Western Liberalism and its historical development. If the New World Order is a real conspiracy directed at a unipolar world endgame, it is natural to realize Dugin's opposition to Western hegemony. On the other hand, if a unipolar world goal is only a manifestation of Dugin's misunderstanding of Western intentions, conspiratorial ideas may only be a symptom of his misperception.

Notes

1. Dugin, "Cure You With Poison," under, Serpents against Serpents. Dugin, "We Are Going to Cure You With Poison," under, Serpents against Serpents, ARCTOGAIA, 2001, arctogaia.com/public/eng/serpent.html. This article can also be found at openrevolt.info/2011/10/23/we-are-going-to-cure-you-with-poison/, where it is given a posting date of October 23, 2011. Cf. my.arcto.ru/public/eng/serpent.html.

2. Dugin, "An Interview with Alexander Dugin: Against Universalism," interview by Rémi Tremblay, Affirmative Right, May 21, 2015, affirmativeright.blogspot.com/2015/05/an-interview-with-alexander-dugin.html.

3. Dugin, "Against Universalism."

4. Ibid.

5. Ibid.

6. Epstein, *Conservatism and Traditionalism*, 14.

7. Ibid.

8. Ibid. Here Epstein cites Dugin, "Metafizicheskie Korni Politicheskikh Ideologii," *Milyi Angel, Ezotericheskoe Reviu* 1 (1991): 84.

9. Ibid.

10. Ibid.

11. Ibid. Interestingly, Epstein includes German National Socialism in his list of Absolute Unity manifestations. Epstein's suggestion that Dugin maintains a "sacred imperialism" linked to National Socialism is interesting given fascist accusations directed toward Dugin.

12. "God, the Great Spirit, in Whom we actually and in fact 'live and move and have our being,' is the Power that permeates and sustains the whole Universe with Its Life; but while that Life flows into and is immanent in every atom of the six lower Worlds and all contained therein." This quotation is from "The Sevenfold Constitution of Man." Cf. rosicrucian.com/rcc/rcceng03.htm.

13. Epstein, *Conservatism and Traditionalism*, 14. Epstein cites Dugin, "Metafizicheskie Korni Politicheskikh Ideologii," 84ff.

14. Ibid. Cf. Epstein's note 33, where Epstein cites Dugin as above.

15. Ibid.

16. Ibid.

17. Ibid. Dugin claims examples were present within Ghibelline imperialism, the Cathar and Albigensian heresies, Rosicrucian teachings, and German National Socialism.

18. Ibid., 14-15.

19. Ibid., 15. Dugin repeatedly makes the claim that Roman Catholicism and Protestantism lack authenticity. Authentic Christianity is realized in Traditionalism, and is, therefore, gnostic in nature. Furthermore, Dugin holds that Old Believer/Old Ritualist Orthodox Christianity preserves the major *Original*, *Authentic,* and, therefore, *eternal* essences of True Christianity.

20. Ibid., 14ff.

21. Ibid., 15.

22. Ibid.

23. Ibid.

24. Ibid.

25. Ibid.

26. Ibid., 14.

27. Ibid., 15.

28. Ibid.

29. Ibid.

30. Ibid.

31. Eric Hoffer, *The Passionate State of Mind* (Cutchogue, NY: Buccaneer Books, 1996), 7. Arthur C. Clarke's statement that "any sufficiently advanced technology is indistinguishable from magic," comes to mind. Cf. Arthur C. Clarke, *Profiles of the Future: An Inquiry into the Limits of the Possible* (Revised Edition) (New York: Harper and Row, 1933), 36. Eric Hoffer, 1898-1983.

32. Cf. e.g., Dugin, *Fourth Theory*, 196.

33. Epstein, *Conservatism and Traditionalism*, 15.

34. Perhaps relating it to the Protestant work ethic that produced much of Western capitalism.

35. Dugin, *Fourth Theory*, 196.

36. Dugin, "The Evaporation of Fundamentals in the 'New Economy'," Evrazia, November 2001, under, The problematic ontology of turbo-capitalism, evrazia.org/modules.php?name=News&file=print&sid=414.

37. Dugin, "Evaporation of Fundamentals," under, The problematic ontology of turbo-capitalism.

38. Ibid.

39. Ibid. Brackets added.

40. Ibid.

41. Ibid.

42. Dugin, "The Figure of the Radical Subject," under, Part 1, Traditionalism and Sociology—The Modern and the Eternal. Creation narratives involving the Cosmic Egg idea are widespread; Cf. e.g., the *Upanishads*, the *Brahmanda Purana*, the Orphic Egg of Ancient Greek narrative, etc.

43. Ibid.

44. Ibid.

45. Ibid.

46. Ibid.

47. Ibid.

48. Dugin, "Cure you with Poison," under, The Evolution of Capitalist Animals.

49. Ibid.

50. Cf. 2 Corinthians 11:14 NASB.

51. Dugin, "Cure you with Poison," under, Serpents against Serpents.

52. Ibid., under, The Evolution of Capitalist Animals.

53. Ibid.

54. Ibid. Gilles Deleuze, 1925-1995.

55. Gilles Deleuze, "Postscript on the Societies of Control," *October* 59 (Winter 1992): 5.

56. Dugin, "Cure you with Poison," under, The Evolution of Capitalist Animals.

57. Ibid., under, Serpents against Serpents. This serpent is described in various renditions as made of brass, bronze, or generally that it was "brazen."

58. Ibid.

59. Amanda Seitz, "Mob at U.S. Capitol Encouraged by Online Conspiracy Theories," AP NEWS (Associated Press, January 7, 2021), apnews.com/article/donald-trump-conspiracy-theories-michael-pence-media-social-media-daba3f5dd16a431abc627a5cfc922b87.

60. "Conspiracy," Legal Information Institute (Legal Information Institute), accessed January 16, 2021, law.cornell.edu/wex/conspiracy. The entry adds that "most U.S. jurisdictions also require an overt act toward furthering the agreement."

61. Rossman, *Russian Intellectual Antisemitism in the Post-Communist Era*, 38.

62. Branko Malić, "Leviathan and Behemoth—Alexander Dugin's Geopolitical Conspirology," Kali Tribune, December 12, 2014, en.kalitribune.com/leviathan-and-behemoth-geopolitical-conspirology-of-alexander-dugin/. Branko Malić, Publisher and Commentator, Kali Tribune.

63. Malić, "Leviathan and Behemoth."

64. Umberto Eco, "A Theory of Conspiracies," trans. Alastair McEwen, Live Mint, October 6, 2014, livemint.com/Opinion/5lhODHqqZHUCqwOZcw2liL/Umberto-Eco--A-theory-of-conspiracies.html?facet=print. Here Eco is quoting John Chadwick, *The Decipherment of Linear B* (Cambridge: Cambridge University Press, 1958), 1. Eco notes that Chadwick was one of those who deciphered Linear B, an ancient Greek (Mycenaean) script. Umberto Eco, 1932-2016.

65. Eco, "A Theory of Conspiracies."

66. Ibid.

67. Cf. Karl Popper, "The Autonomy of Sociology," in *Mill, a Collection of Critical Essays*, ed. J. B. Schneewind (London: Palgrave Macmillan, 1968), 426-42. Also, Cf. Popper, "The Autonomy of Sociology," in *The Open Society and Its Enemies*, 5th ed., vol. II (Princeton, NJ: Princeton University Press, 1966). Dugin, although not directly addressing Popper's ideas on conspiracy theory, rejects many of Popper's liberal hypotheses. Cf. Dugin, *Fourth Theory*, 51. Karl Popper, 1902-1994.

68. Popper, "Autonomy of Sociology," 435.

69. Epstein, *Conservatism and Traditionalism*, 13.

70. Ibid.

71. Ibid.

72. Ibid.

73. Ibid.

74. Ibid.

75. Ibid.

76. The genre contains literature that ranges from trivial and fringe to academically, politically, and socially serious. Cf. e.g., Svetlana Boym, "Conspiracy Theories and Literary Ethics: Umberto Eco, Danilo Kis and The Protocols of Zion," *Comparative Literature* 51, no. 2 (1999): 97-122.

77. Cf. *In the Name of the Rose, Foucault's Pendulum*, and *The Prague Cemetery*. Eco, *In the Name of the Rose*, trans. William Weaver (Orlando: Harcourt, 1983), Eco, *Foucault's Pendulum*, trans. William

Weaver (Orlando: Harcourt, 1989), and Eco, *The Prague Cemetery*, trans. Richard Dixon (Boston: Houghton Mifflin Harcourt, 2010).

78. Dan Brown, *The Da Vinci Code* (New York: Doubleday, 2003). Dan Brown, Novelist.

79. Michael Baigent, Richard Leigh, and Henry Lincoln, *The Holy Blood and the Holy Grail* (London: Jonathan Cape, 1982). Michael Baigent, 1948-2013. Richard Leigh, 1943-2007, Henry Lincoln, Born Henry Soskin, 1930-2022.

80. "The History of a Mystery," *Timewatch* (BBC, 1996).

81. Popper, "Autonomy of Sociology," 435.

82. Ibid., 435-36.

83. Ibid., 436.

84. Ibid.

85. Ibid.

86. Ibid.

87. Dugin, *Fourth Theory*, 51.

88. Dugin, "Ideology of the World Government," The Fourth Political Theory, September 28, 2012, 4pt.su/en/content/ideology-world-government. Note: this article appeared as, Dugin, "Ideology of the World Government," ELEMENTS-8, trans. Victor Olevich, December 20, 1998, arctogaia.com/public/eng-ed2.htm. This article was here sub-titled "Editorial" and indicated that it was originally published in *Elements*, #2. The website noted that this page (or perhaps the article) was updated on December 20, 1998. The article itself bore a date of 1991. This site is no longer adding new material; a search here in July 2019 failed to locate this article. Cf. Dugin, "Russian Orthodoxy and Initiation." Dugin, "Ideology of World Government."

89. Dugin, "Ideology of World Government."

90. Rossman, *Russian Intellectual Antisemitism in the Post-Communist Era,* 55. Cf. His footnote 89. Cf. Rossman, "Anti-Semitism in Eurasian Historiography," 181 and Rossman's note: 1993a: 149; "Apologiia natsionalisma." Den' 38.

91. Cf. e.g., Victor Shnirelman, "Alexander Dugin: Between Eschatology, Esotericism, and Conspiracy Theory," in *Handbook of Conspiracy Theory and Contemporary Religion*, ed. Asbjørn Dyrendal, David G. Robertson, and Egil Asprem (Leiden: Brill, 2018), 443-460.

92. Cf. e.g., Rossman, "Anti-Semitism in Eurasian Historiography," 175. Also, consider Dugin's associations of America with Antichrist. Victor Shnirelman, Russian Historian and Ethnologist.

93. Adapted from Epstein, *Conservatism and Traditionalism.*

94. Epstein, *Conservatism and Traditionalism*, 22.

95. Ibid., 13.

96. Rossman, "Anti-Semitism in Eurasian Historiography," 181.

97. Epstein, *Conservatism and Traditionalism*, 13.

98. Rossman, "Anti-Semitism in Eurasian Historiography," 181.

99. Ibid. Cf. Rossman's note: 1993c: 20; i.e., Dugin, *Konspirologiia*, Moscow, 20.

100. Shnirelman, "Between Eschatology, Esotericism, and Conspiracy," 450. Cf. Shnirelman's note: Dugin, A.G. 1997d "Evrei i Evrazia." Zavtra 47: 4. For similar material, Cf. Shnirelman, "The esotericis of Alexander Dugin: Building a bridge between eschatology and conspiracy," *Государство, религия, церковь в России и за рубежом* 34, no. 4 (2016), pp. 194–221. Shnirelman's note (Bromberg (1931) refers to Yaakov [Yakov] Bromberg, "Evreiskoe vostochnichestvo v proshlom i buduschem," *Mir Rossiii—Evraziia*, ed. L. Novikova and I. Sizemskaiia. Moscow, 1995.

101. Ibid.

102. Benjamin Parker, "Putin's Chosen People: Theories of Russian Jewish Policy, 2000-2017," Master's thesis, University of Pennsylvania, 2017, 25. Brackets added. Benjamin Parker, Senior Editor, The Bulwark.

103. Epstein, *Conservatism and Traditionalism*, 14.

104. Ibid.

105. Ibid., 13.

106. Ibid.

107. Cf. Karen M. Douglas et al., "Someone Is Pulling the Strings: Hypersensitive Agency Detection and Belief in Conspiracy Theories," *Thinking & Reasoning* 22, no. 1 (2015): 57-77.

108. Epstein, *Conservatism and Traditionalism*, 13.

109. Cf. Eco, "A Theory of Conspiracies."

110. Richard Hofstadter, "The Paranoid Style in American Politics," *Harpers*, November 1964, 82. Cf. Eco, "A Theory of Conspiracies." Richard Hofstadter, 1916-1970.

111. Norman Cohn, *Pursuit of the Millennium* (London: Secker & Warburg, 1957). Cited in Hofstadter, Paranoid Style, 86. Norman Cohn, 1915-2007.

112. Hofstadter, "Paranoid Style," 82.

113. Ibid.

114. Eco, "A Theory of Conspiracies."

115. Ibid.

116. Ibid.

117. Ibid.

118. Hofstadter, "The Paranoid Style," 86.

119. Cohn, *Pursuit of the Millennium*, 52. Brackets added.

120. Ibid.

121. Ibid.

122. Brian Krebs," All Aboard the Pequod!," under, A Little Sunshine, Ne'er-Do-Well News, January 7, 2021. Brian Krebs, Journalists and Blogger.

123. "The Rise of the Traditionalists: How a Mystical Doctrine Is Reshaping the Right," Katehon, November 30, 2020, katehon.com/en/article/rise-traditionalists-how-mystical-doctrine-reshaping-right. Cf. e.g., Sedgwick, "Bannon, Traditionalism, Dugin, and Olavo," Traditionalists, April 21, 2020, traditionalistblog.blogspot.com/2020/04/bannon-traditionalism-dugin-and-olavo.html., Erasmus, "Russian Anti-Liberals Love Donald Trump but It May Not Be Entirely Mutual," The Economist (blog) (The Economist, November 20, 2016), economist.com/erasmus/2016/11/20/russian-anti-liberals-love-donald-trump-but-it-may-not-be-entirely-mutual, and James J. O'Meara, "Hook, Line, & Sinker: Steve Bannon & the Usual Suspects: Counter-Currents," Counter-Currents, October 14, 2020, counter-currents.com/2020/10/hook-line-and-sinker/.

124. Cf. e.g., Ilan Berman, "Slouching Toward Eurasia," Perspective, Volume 12, Number 1 (September - October 2001), 1. Cf. a copy of this article may be accessed at:

dcommon.bu.edu/bitstream/handle/2144/3589/perspective_12_1_berma n.pdf?sequence=1. Ilan Berman, Senior Vice President of the American Foreign Policy Council.

125. Rossman, *Russian Intellectual Antisemitism in the Post-Communist Era,* 38.

Part II

Chapter One: Geopolitics

Capturing a Definition

Guénon considered modern chemistry to be the progeny of alchemy.[1] Adopting Guénon's genealogical suggestion, physics may be regarded as the offspring of magic. Dugin, following Guénon, characterized geopolitics as occupying the position "in an intermediate place between traditional science (sacred geography) and profane science," thus ascribing an origin close to the metaphysical and esoteric realm.[2] For Dugin, the Schmittian derivative of politics from theology applies to physical sciences as well. Dugin's metaphysics and esotericism are always close at hand.

Speaking to the crucial place of geography in politics, Dugin wrote:

> In contrast to "economical ideologies" it is founded on the thesis: "geographical conditions as destiny." Geography and space in geopolitics serve the same function that money and means of production serve in Marxism and Liberalism—all fundamental aspects of human being are reduced to them, they are the main method of explaining the past, the main factors of human being, around which all other aspects of existence are being organized.[3]

"What is geopolitics?" queried Colin Flint.[4] Then, answering his own question, he summarized, "it is about how the powerful have created worlds."[5] He went on to say that it is about geography, and actions—specifically about how those actions have been portrayed or represented.[6] Moreover, it involves "connected actions and actors and the geographies they make, change, destroy, and maintain."[7] I believe this sentence captures the essence of Dugin's geopolitical thinking—the Eurasian world he wishes to make, the present world he wishes to change, the

66

unipolar world he wishes to thwart, and the traditional worldview he wishes to maintain.

The study of geopolitics involves the "analysis of the geographic influences on power relationships in international relations," according to Daniel H. Deudney.[8] The OED states that it is "politics, especially international relations, as influenced by geographical factors." Use of the term *geopolitics* has been employed for slightly over a century since being coined by Swedish political scientist, Rudolf Kjellén.[9] Near the end of the nineteenth century came the "'classical' theories" of geopolitics; those of "Sir Halford Mackinder, Alfred Thayer Mahan, and General Karl Haushofer," wrote Flint.[10]

Remarking on temporal placement, Flint wrote that classical geopolitics "should not be interpreted as historic, past, and hence redundant," instead as something "alive and well."[11] Notably, the classical approach to geopolitics is still an active factor to and through Dugin, evident in various manifestations to be explored within Fourth Political Theory. Dugin, realizing the importance of classical geopolitics to his developing ideas, built on the work of previous geopoliticians in his book, *Foundations of Geopolitics*. Doing so, he did much to keep their theories alive and well in Russia.[12] Indeed, a prevalent approach to geopolitics today is of the classical variety—and it is the starting point for Dugin. However, Dugin's treatment of geopolitics developed somewhat differently, as will be seen.

Clover stated that the influence of *Foundations of Geopolitics* "was profound if measured by book sales."[13] This influence was "even more profound if measured by the true yardstick of the scribbler—plagiarism," he added.[14] Dugin's ideas "were reprinted in dozens of similar manuals and textbooks, all of which devoted themselves to the theories of Mackinder, Haushofer and others."[15] In a 1999 article, Clover prophetically stated that "victory is now to be found in geography rather than history; in space rather than time."[16] Astutely and succinctly, Clover identified an essential essence of Dugin's geopolitical Eurasianist thinking—giving geography star billing alongside history.

Notes

1. Guénon is recognized as one of the most (perhaps *the* most) prominent figures of Integral (or Classical) Traditionalism. His influence on Traditionalism and Dugin is addressed in greater detail herein.

2. Dugin, "From Sacred Geography to Geopolitics," *The Fourth Political Theory*, under, Geopolitics as "Intermediate" Science, accessed June 12, 2017, 4pt.su/en/content/sacred-geography-geopolitics. A note on the manuscript states that this text appeared under the title "Ot sakral'noy geografii k geopolitike" in *Elementy*, 4, and as Chapter 7 of *Misterii Evrazii* [the Mysteries of Eurasia], Moscow: 1996, Cf. evrazia.org/modules.php?name=News&sid=416. Note: There is potential for confusion in this (and similar footnotes) because of the obvious similarity of the title of Dugin's book (*The Fourth Political Theory*) and the Website (*The Fourth Political Theory* - 4pt.su). Also, recall discussion of Heidegger's Between.

3. For the translation of this, and other, quotations from Dugin's *Foundations of Geopolitics*, I rely on that provided in Malić, "The Invisible Empire: Introduction to Alexandr Dugin's 'Foundations of Geopolitics,' Part 1," *Kali Tribune*, May 7, 2017, en.kalitribune.com/the-invisible-empire-introduction-to-alexander-dugins-foundations-of-geopolitics-pt-1/, and Malić, "The Invisible Empire: Introduction to Alexandr Dugin's 'Foundations of Geopolitics,' Part 2," *Kali Tribune*, July 1, 2017, en.kalitribune.com/the-invisible-empire-introduction-to-alexander-dugins-foundations-of-geopolitics-pt-2/. Malić notes that he made his translation from a Serbian edition of *Foundations of Geopolitics*. Throughout, I will mainly rely on Malić's translation when citing *Foundations of Geopolitics*.

4. Colin Flint, *An Introduction to Geopolitics*, 2nd ed. (New York: Routledge, 2011), 2.

5. Flint, *Introduction to Geopolitics*, 2.

6. Ibid.

7. Ibid.

8. Daniel H. Deudney, "Geopolitics (Political Science)," *Encyclopædia Britannica*, June 12, 2013, britannica.com/topic/geopolitics. Daniel H. Deudney, Professor of Political Science, Johns Hopkins University.

9. Deudney, "Geopolitics." Deudney states that, "in contemporary discourse, *geopolitics* has been widely employed as a loose synonym for international politics." Italics in original.

10. Flint, *Introduction to Geopolitics*, 2. Karl Haushofer, 1869-1946.

11. Ibid., 3.

12. Cf. e.g., Flint's citation of Dugin, *Osnovy Geopolitiki: Geopoliticheskoe Budushchee Rossii* (Moscow: Arktogeya, 199), the Russian citation of Dugin's work, *The Foundations of Geopolitics*.

13. Clover, *Black Wind, White Snow*, 356.

14. Ibid.

15. Ibid.

16. Clover, "Dreams of the Eurasian Heartland: The Reemergence of Geopolitics," *Foreign Affairs* 78, no. 2 (1999): 9.

Chapter Two: Dugin's Geography

Geopolitics of the Heartland

Long recognized are the seven continents of Asia, Africa, North America, South America, Antarctica, Europe, and Australia. Combining Asia and Europe into Eurasia, a single continent, reduces the number from seven to six.[1] A six continent world is envisioned by Dugin as he imagines Eurasia stretching from Dublin to Vladivostok.[2]

As a U.S. Air Force officer, hailing from the Air National Guard, and advancing in the ranks, I hoped to be one of those relatively few selected to attend one of the nation's war colleges in residence, as selection is often a harbinger of future advancement into the senior officer cadre. If I was so fortunate, I expected appointment to the Air War College at Maxwell, AFB in Alabama. I was completely surprised when receiving an assignment to the Naval War College in Newport, Rhode Island.

Although familiar with air and land battle concepts, I confess that even suggesting a strategic understanding of anything located out of sight of land was completely foreign to me. I marveled at the ever-present recognition of sea-power when traversing the halls of the college where Albert Thayer Mahan had been president and remains prominent after many years. Suffice it to say, that, during my time at the Naval War College, I became much more acquainted with Mahan and the importance of ocean dominance.

Dugin maintains that the conflict between land-power and sea-power is a fundamental divider of the Eurasianists and the West. This conflict can be readily observed in the opinions of Mackinder and Mahan, two of the greatest nineteenth century geopolitical strategists. Mackinder, the British geopolitical academician, famously stated, "whoever rules East Europe commands the Heartland; whoever rules the Heartland commands the World-Island; whoever rules the World-island commands the World."[3] Mahan, whose precepts I was initiated into at war college and whom John Keegan tagged "the most important American strategist of the nineteenth century," believed that "control of the sea, by maritime commerce and naval supremacy, means predominant influence in the world."[4]

Mackinder's opinion is recognized in geopolitical circles as *Heartland Theory*. The Heartland Mackinder referred to geographically corresponds to Eurasia, a region that, in a 1904 paper, he termed the *Pivot Area*.[5] Nicholas Spykman, a Dutch-born American who became head of Yale's Institute of International Studies, developed a similar, but somewhat challenging theory to Mackinder's ideas. Visualizing Eurasia as the Heartland, Spykman argued that controlling the periphery of Eurasia was tantamount to controlling Eurasia itself—hence, the destiny of the world.[6] The Eurasian periphery was dubbed the *Rimland* in Spykman's theory.

Resonance of Spykman's Rimland Theory is recognizable in the Cold War containment ideas advanced by George Kennan.[7] It is said that "at his dacha, standing before a map of the newly expanded Soviet Union shortly after Germany's surrender in May 1945, Josef Stalin nodded with approval" because "the vast buffer he'd carved out of Soviet-occupied Eastern Europe would now protect his empire against future Napoleons and Hitlers."[8] The Rimland provides this buffer—it also can act as a barrier to Russian expansion if controlled by Russia's adversaries.

The Pivot Area and the Rimland

Dugin does not fail to grasp the significance of Heartland and Rimland Theories. One of the keys to unlocking Fourth Political Theory involves engaging the views of Mackinder and Spykman. Dugin's deliberate-expansion argument derives underlying support from these two geopolitical pioneers. In 1904 Mackinder presented his paper, "The Geographical Pivot of History," to the Royal Geographic Society. Mackinder knew that "the core area of Eurasia" was protected from attack by the maritime powers of his day.[9]

Stephen Mladineo related that with this paper, Mackinder "first offered the theory of the 'Pivot Area,' a designation for the core area of Eurasia," reasoning "that the development of the potential power of this area could enable the continental power that controlled it to dominate the world."[10] Mackinder's main concern at the time of his paper and subsequent book was with the threat Germany presented to Europe and the world. Mladineo stated that Mackinder realized that Russia represented little danger at the time.[11] However, Mackinder also recognized that in the future, a buffer would be required between the two Eurasian powers of Germany and Russia.[12] Mackinder designated the buffer areas partially surrounding Eurasia, the *Inner Crescent* and the *Outer Crescent*.[13]

Adapted by Mud Pie Graphics from: H.J. Mackinder, "The Geographical Pivot of History," *The Geographical Journal*, avril 1904, drawn by Bernard Vernon Darbishire.

In Spykman's somewhat competing theory, attention focused on the nations "on the periphery of the World Island."[14] Mladineo wrote that "Spykman renamed the inner crescent the Rimland, and argued based on his analysis of power politics that Mackinder's slogan should be recast as 'Who controls the rimland rules Eurasia; who rules Eurasia controls the destinies of the world.'"[15]

Controlling the Rimland indeed proved to be a significant element of the Western policy during the Cold War. The ensuing *Containment Policy* incorporated aspects of both the Inner and Outer Crescents identified by Mackinder, and the control of the Rimland. According to the U.S. Department of State Historian's Office:

Despite all the criticisms and the various policy defeats that Kennan suffered in the early 1950's, containment in the more general sense of blocking the expansion of Soviet influence remained the basic strategy of the United States throughout the cold war. On the one hand, the United States did not withdraw into isolationism; on the other, it did not move to "roll back" Soviet power, as John Foster Dulles briefly advocated. It is possible to say that each succeeding administration after Truman's, until the collapse of communism in 1989, adopted a variation of Kennan's containment policy and made it their own.[16]

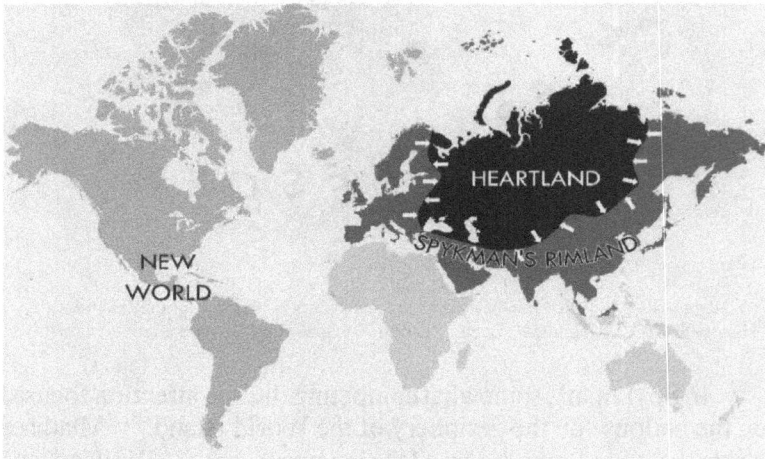

Adapted by Mud Pie Graphics from: vahineblog.over-blog.com/2016/03/geopolitique-le-grand-jeu-et-le-pipelineistan-ou-la-guerre-des-tubes.html

The importance attached to both Mackinder's and Spykman's concepts to Dugin's Neo-Eurasianism must be contemplated considering the combined elements of Heartland Theory, Rimland Theory, Containment Policy, and the historical references and inferences of Fourth Political Theory. Dugin's Neo-Eurasianist proposal exhibits characteristics that reflect both

Heartland and Rimland Theories, and tacitly acknowledges and opposes Containment Policy.

Contemporary scholars, Eldar Ismailov and Vladimer Papava elaborated on Russian expansion and its connections with the ideas of Mackinder and Spykman.[17] Ismailov and Papava recognized that a nineteenth century expanding Russian Empire "conquered the strategically important littoral strips in the west (the Baltic states and Finland), in the east (Kamchatka, Sakhalin, the Maritime Area, and Alaska), and in the north (the littoral part of the Arctic Ocean)."[18] The result of this expansion was Russian-gained access to three oceans, allowing it to become a combined "land and sea power able to function as a geopolitical actor in the Heartland and Rimland simultaneously."[19] Ismailov and Papava note that "the Russian Empire began moving into all segments of the Pivot Area" by the mid-1800s. Russia had "conquered the entire Central Caucasian region by the 19th century and was looking westward at Central Europe and eastward at Central Asia."[20]

"Initially, the ethnic Russians lived mainly in the East European segment of the Heartland," Ismailov and Papava observed.[21] In the nineteenth century, Russia "gained domination over all the key segments of the Pivot Area," including Central Europe, Central Caucasia, and Central Asia, "in the form of the Russian Empire."[22] Expressing inclusion, but with a decided nod toward primacy, Petr Savitsky, in *Exodus to the East*, articulates the Eurasian position with his emphatic, "we do not want to confine it within the narrow bounds of national chauvinism."[23] Savitsky added, "we direct our nationalism not merely toward 'Slavs,' but toward a whole circle of peoples of the 'Eurasian' world, among whom the Russian people has the central position."[24] Doing so, he affirmed his inclusive attitude but made it clear that Russia should be first among equals.

Notes

1. Cf. *Encyclopædia Britannica*, s.v. "Continent (Geography)," January 23, 2019. *Britannica* lists seven continents but notes that "Europe and Asia are sometimes considered a single continent, Eurasia."britannica.com/science/continentwww.britannica.com/place/Asia.

2. Cf. Dunlop, "Dugin's Foundations of Geopolitics," 41. Cf. Markku Siira, "Dugin's Image of Finland," Geopolitica.ru, February 28, 2018, geopolitica.ru/en/article/dugins-image-finland. Here Siira, the Finnish traditional journalist, writes, "Dugin has also been influenced by the Belgian politician Jean-François Thiriart, who already in the 1950s envisioned a symbiotic European-Russian empire from Dublin to Vladivostok." Cf. Jean Thiriart, "Europe as far as Vladivostok," *Niekisch Translation Project*, October 30, 2015, niekischtranslationproject.wordpress.com/2015/10/30/europe-as-far-as-vladivostok-jean-thiriart-1992/. Thiriart wrote, "I am known as the messenger of the united Europe, from Dublin to Vladivostok. But this united Europe, that I describe and invoke, is bound to the domain of the Imperium. And my opinion is that such an Imperium must be a power, dynamic, merciless—to be effective." Cf. Thiriart, "L'Europe jusqu'à Vladivostok," *Nationalisme et. République*, no. 9 (1992). Jean-François Thiriart, 1922-1992.

3. Halford J. Mackinder, *Democratic Ideals and Reality: A Study in the Politics of Reconstruction* (Washington, DC: National Defense University Press, 1996), 113. This work was first published by Henry Holt and Company, 1919. The *World Island* refers to the continents of Europe, Asia, and Africa. The *Offshore Islands* refer mainly to the British Isles and the Japanese islands. The *Outlying Islands* refer to the continents of North America, South America, and Australia. Halford J. Mackinder, 1861-1947.

4. This quote is taken from David Morgan-Owen and Louis Halewood, "Economic Warfare and the Sea, 1650-1945," Liverpool University Press Blog (Liverpool University, April 23, 2020), liverpooluniversitypress.blog/2020/04/23/economic-warfare-and-the-sea-1650-1945/. The authors cite Alfred Thayer Mahan, *The Interest of America in Sea Power, Present and Future* (Port Washington, 1897), 124. Also, Cf. Alfred Thayer Mahan, *The Influence of Sea Power upon History, 1660-1783* (Lexington, KY: Emereo Publishing, 2013). Alfred Thayer Mahan, 1840-1914.

5. Stephen V. Mladineo, "Introduction," in *Democratic Ideals and Reality: A Study in the Politics of Reconstruction*, by Halford J. Mackinder (Washington, DC: National Defense University Press, 1996), xviii. Mackinder presented *Democratic Ideals and Reality* to the Royal Geographic Society. Cf. Mackinder, "The Geographical Pivot of History," *The Geographical Journal* 23, no. 4 (1904): 421-37. Stephen V. Mladineo, Pacific Northwest National Laboratory.

6. Nicholas John Spykman, *The Geography of the Peace*, ed. Helen R. Nicholl (Hamden, CT: Archon Books, 1969), 43. Cf. Mladineo, "Introduction," xx. Nicholas John Spykman, 1893-1943.

7. "Kennan and Containment, 1947," *The U.S. State Department Office of the Historian*, accessed June 11, 2017, history.state.gov/milestones/1945-1952/kennan. George Kennan, 1904-2005. In 1946 Kennan was Deputy Chief of Mission (*chargé d'affaires*) in the U.S. Embassy, Moscow. In a lengthy telegram (the co-called Long Telegram), Kennan explained his reasons for advocating a policy of containing the territorial expansion of the Soviet Union. A derivative article was published by Kennan using a pseudonym. Cf. X, "The Sources of Soviet Conduct," *Foreign Affairs* 25, no. 4 (1947): 566–82.

8. Benn Steil, "Russia's Clash With the West Is About Geography, Not Ideology," *Foreign Policy*, February 12, 2018, foreignpolicy.com/2018/02/12/russias-clash-with-the-west-is-about-geography-not-ideology/. The article was adapted from Benn Steil, *The Marshall Plan: Dawn of the Cold War* (New York: Simon & Schuster, 2018). Benn Steil, Senior Fellow, Council on Foreign Relations.

9. Mladineo, "Introduction," xviii.

10. Ibid.

11. Ibid., xix. The "two great historical organizers" refer to Germany and Russia.

12. Ibid.

13. Ibid.

14. Ibid. As previously mentioned, the "World Island" can be understood as Europe, Asia, and Africa (or at least the northern portion) around the heartland. The "offshore" islands are mainly composed of the UK, Ireland, and Japan. The "outlying" islands are the Americas and Australia.

15. Ibid., xx, footnote 7. Mladineo is quoting Spykman.

16. U.S. State Department, "Kennan and Containment."

17. Eldar Ismailov and Vladimer Papava, "The Heartland Theory and the Present-Day Geopolitical Structure of Central Eurasia," in *Rethinking Central Asia* (Washington: Johns Hopkins University/Central Asia-Caucasus Institute & Silk Road Studies Program, 2010), 95. Eldar Ismailov, Institute of Strategic Studies of the Caucasus. Vladimer Papava, Professor, Tbilisi State University, former Minister of Economics, Georgia.

18. Ismailov and Papava, "Heartland Theory," 95.

19. Ibid.

20. Ibid., 94.

21. Ibid., 95.

22. Ibid.

23. Petr Savitskii, *Exodus to the East: Forebodings and Events: An Affirmation of the Eurasians*, trans. Ilya Vinkovetsky (Idyllwild, CA: Schlacks, 1996), 4. Quoted in Stephan Wiederkehr, "Eurasianism as a Reaction to Pan-Turkism," in *Russia between East and West Scholarly Debates on Eurasianism*, ed. Dmitry Shlapentokh (Boston: Brill, 2007), 49. Savitsky and others (including Nikolai Trubetskoi and other Eurasianists) apparently published *Exodus to the East* originally as an anthology in Sophia in 1921. [Pyotr Nikolaevich] Savitsky is sometimes rendered *Savitskii* or *Savitskiy* in English. Dugin renders the spelling *Savitsky* in the edition of *The Fourth Political Theory* preferred herein. I will use this spelling except in quoted material or citations. Cf. Darina Grigorova Grigorova, "Towards the Sun: Eurasian Historiosophy," trans. Roumen Genov, *Almanach Via Evrasia* 2013, no. 2, 14ff. Petr Savitskii, 1895-1968.

24. Savitskii, *Exodus to the East*, 4.

Chapter Three: The Geopolitics of Culture and Theology

Dugin Mirrors Huntington

Added to the centrality of geography in Dugin's geopolitics is the influence of culture—of civilization, if you will. Speaking of the world after the collapse of the Soviet Union, Samuel Huntington wrote that "the fundamental source of conflict in this new world will not be primarily ideological or primarily economic."[1] Huntington's hypothesis was that it would primarily be cultural. There can be little doubt that Dugin reflects Huntington's ideas around a perceived "clash of civilizations."[2] One need go no farther than Dugin's statement that "Samuel Huntington described in a realistic manner the obstacles which inevitably face the supporters of a Unipolar World and the fanatics of the *End of History*" to verify this assertion.[3]

As part of his campaign against Western Liberalism, Dugin attacked the hubris of Francis Fukuyama's bold 1990s pronouncement that, with the triumph of Western Liberalism, the world experienced the End of History.[4] From this vantage point Dugin asserted the accuracy of Huntington's thesis contradicting Fukuyama's proclamation. By analyzing the phenomena of the situation of geopolitics after the fall of the Soviet Union, Huntington correctly "arrived at the conclusion that they could be included under a single denomination: civilizations." Dugin emphatically illustrated this belief.[5]

> Huntington formulated a new political-scientific concept...a new dimension of international politics which was born after the demise of the USSR...the Atlanticist milieus discovered that they would face an enemy which, unlike the Soviet Union, is not based on an explicitly formalized ideology, but which nonetheless has begun to question and undermine the foundations of the liberal and Americano-centric "New World Order." The enemy is now the civilizations, and no longer only countries or states.[6]

Directly opposing End of History claims, Dugin stated that in considering "all civilizations, only the Western civilization has presented itself as universal, pretending to be in this way 'the civilization' (singular)."[7] "In reality," according to Dugin in his interpretation of Huntington, "the great majority of men and women who live outside of the European or American space reject this dominion, and continue to be rooted in different historical-cultural types."[8] The correct view, where Dugin agrees with Huntington, is that there is a "resurgence of civilizations" not any broad striving for globalization on the American model.[9]

Fukuyama is globalism's optimist and Huntington its pessimist in Dugin's opinion.[10] It was Huntington "who analyzed the risks and measured the dangers."[11] Dugin clarified Huntington's conclusion that a clash of civilizations is real by identifying the participants. There are only two—if "there must be a 'clash' of civilizations, it has to be a clash between the West and the 'rest of the world.'"[12] At the end of the Cold War, Huntington opined, international politics moved from the conflict between two superpowers toward one of Western and non-Western civilizational interaction and actions from within the non-Western world itself.[13]

Dugin is attempting to assist this move by diminishing internal hostile actions in the non-Western world.[14] Diminishment is a task of "reorienting the hostility," not eliminating it, then redirecting it "against the United States and Western Civilization, instead of against neighboring civilizations."[15]

> We must organize the common front of civilizations against one civilization which pretends to be the civilization in singular. This priority [sic] common enemy is globalism and the United States, which is now its principal vector. The more the peoples of the Earth will be convinced of that, the more the confrontations between non-Western civilizations can be reduced. And Eurasianism is the political formula which suits this "rest."[16]

There are points of disagreement between Huntington and Dugin to be sure. An obvious point of departure is Huntington's call "for the strengthening of transatlantic relations between Europe and the United States."[17] In a siren call to Europe, Dugin first claimed that "the destiny of Europe is not on the other side of the Atlantic."[18] Then, harkening a future fracturing of the West, Dugin becomes tempter. "Europe must clearly establish itself as a distinct civilization, free and independent."[19] "It has to be a European Europe, not American and Atlanticist," Dugin wrote.[20]

> It must construct itself as a postmodern democratic empire, through the reclaiming of its cultural and sacred roots, as a part of its future as well as something residing in its past. A Europe which does not also rise up against the United States would betray its roots at the same time that it would condemn itself to not having a future.[21]

The Sacred Geo in Geopolitics

Dugin develops his geopolitical theology as a remarkable blend of politics, geography, culture, and political theology. This blending is nowhere more evident than in Dugin's embrace of Sacred Geography. Bassin, addressing the observation of a fellow Russian political observer, remarked that "Eurasianism, as Stephen Shenfield reminds us, means many things."[22] Foremost of these things for Dugin is the sacred nature of Eurasia's geography. To Dugin, Eurasia is not just a classification of continental geography, it is a divine combination of geopolitics with history, the metaphysical and spiritual manifestation of Sacred Geography.

Dugin does not place Sacred Geography tangential to human development; instead, he ascribes it an essential place. "According to the given logics of natural cosmic symbolism," wrote Dugin,

> the ancient traditions organized their "sacred space," founded their cultic centers, burial places, temples, and edifices, and interpreted the natural

80

and "civilizational" features of geographical, cultural and political territories of the planet.[23]

Dugin stated that the very structure "of migrations, wars, campaigns, demographic waves, building of empires etc. was defined by the original, pragmatic logics of sacred geography."[24]

Epstein, noting Dugin's opinion that "the upheavals in the contemporary world are derived from the competition between two prehistoric civilizations—Atlantis and Hyperborea," indicated that this view arises from Dugin's "more esoteric level."[25] Epstein also wrote that Dugin affirms an ancient Atlantis-Hyperborean War and associates it with "conventional 'meta-geographical' terms in theosophy and other occult sciences," to connect his ancient analogy to the current geopolitical situation.[26]

Dugin displayed a Manichaean understanding of the metaphysical elements of his geopolitics and his characteristic fusion of the two when he stated that "the affirmation of primordial duality displayed by geographical structure of the planet and historical typology of civilizations is the basic law of geopolitics."[27] The "primordial duality" refers to his consistent expressions of a long and enduring conflict between land-power and sea-power—*Tellurocracy* and *Thalassocracy*.

> This duality is being expressed in the opposition between "Telurocracy" (land power) and "Talasocracy" (sea power). The character of this opposition is being reduced to a conflict between mercantile civilization (Carthage, Athens) and military authoritarian civilization (Rome, Sparta) or, in other words, to a duality between "democracy" and "ideocracy." Fundamentally, this duality possesses the character of enmity of its constitutional poles.[28]

Dugin commented that the one, associated with water, is more fluid—therefore unstable, while the other, associated with land, is more solid—consequently more stable.[29] Dugin wrote:

81

[the] Geopolitical outlook on history is a model of the development of planetary duality to its final extremes. The Land and the Sea expand their primordial conflict onto the whole world. The history of the human kind is nothing else but the expression of this struggle and the path towards making it absolute.[30]

Developing Geopolitical Theology in Fourth Political Theory

Dugin combines classical geopolitics with his metaphysical illustrations of Sacred Geography to create his vision of a future Eurasia. Geopolitical theology applied to his vision for a future multipolar world is laid out in Dugin's *The Fourth Political Theory*.[31] Its contents represent an accumulation of Dugin's political thought regarding the trajectory of Russia's political future and the demise of Western political power in the world arena.[32] Fourth Political Theory incorporates Dugin's ideas of Traditionalism and Eurasianism as it articulates a competitive alternative to Western Liberalism.

On Dugin's multipolar global political landscape, liberalism, already severely damaged by postmodernity, is curtailed to be supplanted by Fourth Political Theory.[33] The nascent theory has been sketched out, although Dugin admits it lacks the detail or experiential elements needed to thoroughly compare its viability with that of its long extant rival.[34] Dugin characterizes his introduction to this fourth way as an "invitation" to participate in the full development of a new political paradigm.[35] The specific invitees of this invitation are not clearly identified, but Dugin's ideas have gained traction with the more right-leaning political groups and politicians, first in Russia, then Europe, and, increasingly, in the United States.[36] How much more traction Fourth Political Theory earns and where it is obtained is a matter of immediate interest.

In his Fourth Political Theory, Dugin posits that modernity produced three major political movements: Liberalism, Communism, and Fascism. Of the three, Liberalism prevailed and was the only viable survivor, although Dugin maintains that it too has fallen—a victim of postmodernity.[37] Dugin claims that liberalism, spawned by the Enlightenment, is a product of the West. Furthermore, it is evident that he utterly rejects the assumption that Western Liberalism is either positive or desirable to the East in general and Russia in particular.

Notes

1. Samuel P. Huntington, "The Clash of Civilizations?" *Foreign Affairs*, 72, 3, Summer 1993, 22. Samuel P. Huntington, 1927-2008.

2. Huntington, "Clash of Civilizations?"

3. Dugin, "Huntington, Fukuyama, and Eurasianism," trans. Lucian Tudor, Translated from: "Huntington, Fukuyama y el Eurasismo," Página Transversal, January 6, 2015. Cf. Lucian Tudor, "'Huntington, Fukuyama, and Eurasianism' by Alexander Dugin," Academia.edu, accessed April 1, 2021, academia.edu/11789976/_Huntington_Fukuyama_and_Eurasianism_by_Alexander_Dugin. Also, Cf. Dugin, "Huntington, Fukuyama, and Eurasianism," Tankesmedjan Motpol, 4 April 4, 2015, motpol.nu/lucian/2015/04/04/huntington-fukuyama-and-eurasianism/. Italics added. Francis Fukuyama, Senior Fellow, Freeman Spogli Institute for International Studies, Stanford University.

4. Dugin, *Fourth Theory*, 19ff and Francis Fukuyama, "The End of History?," *National Interest*, Summer 1989, 3. Cf. Fukuyama, *The End of History and the Last Man* (London: Hamish Hamilton, 1992). Dugin notes that Alexandre Kojeve, 1902-1968, preceded Fukuyama with ideas, later characterized by Fukuyama, as the End of History. Cf. Dugin, *Fourth Theory*, 22. Here Dugin cites, Alexandre Kojève, *Introduction to the Reading of Hegel: Lectures on the Phenomenology of the Spirit* (New York: Basic Books, 1969).

5. Dugin, "Huntington, Fukuyama, and Eurasianism."

6. Ibid.

7. Ibid.

8. Ibid.

9. Ibid.

10. Ibid.

11. Ibid.

12. Ibid. The expression of a unipolar, or at least of a cohesive West, in opposition to the rest of the world is not by any means a Dugin exclusive. Cf. e.g., Roger Scruton, *The West and the Rest: Globalization and the Terrorist Threat* (London: Continuum, 2003) and Niall Ferguson, *Civilization: the West and the Rest* (London: Allen Lane, 2011) as just two examples. Roger Scruton, 1944-2020. Niall Ferguson, Senior Fellow, Hoover Institution, Stanford University.

13. Huntington, "Clash of Civilizations?" 38.

14. Dugin, "Huntington, Fukuyama, and Eurasianism."

15. Ibid.

16. Ibid. Brackets added.

17. Ibid.

18. Ibid.

19. Ibid. Contrast this position with Dugin's Dublin to Vladivostok desires. Dugin appears to be self-contradictory in his assertion of a Europe for Europeans given his desire to include Europe in his Eurasian construct. I suggest he really means Europe for Eurasians, not Europe for Europeans.

20. Ibid.

21. Ibid.

22. Mark Bassin, "Eurasianism 'Classical' and 'Neo': The Lines of Continuity," in *Beyond the Empire: Images of Russia in the Eurasian Cultural Context*, ed. Tetsuo Mochizuki (Sapporo: Slavic Research Center, Hokkaido University, 2008), 279. Cf. Bassin's footnote 1 where he cites: "Shenfield, 'Official Eurasianism in Orenburg Province,' *Johnson's Russia List: Research and Analytical Supplement*, no. 10, (July 12, 2002).

23. Dugin, "From Sacred Geography," under, East and West in Sacred Geography.

24. Ibid.

25. Epstein, *Conservatism and Traditionalism*, 18. Dugin suggests an ongoing strife between the West and Eurasia. He depicts the West as Atlantis, the maritime power, and Eurasia as Hyperborea, the land power. Hyperborea was a mythical and idyllic Northland that Dugin implies has sacred associations within his Eurasian construct.

26. Ibid.

27. Ibid., 26. OED: Manichaean in the sense of "Religious or philosophical dualism."

28. Ibid. Tellurocracy is a combination of the Latin (*tellus*) for land and the Ancient Greek word κράτος (power), hence, to rule by power on the land. Thallassocracy is the counterforce, the rule of sea-power. Cf. e.g., Christy Constantakopoulou, "Thalassocracy," *The Encyclopedia of Ancient History*, ed. R. S. Bagnall (Blackwell Publishing Ltd, October 26, 2012), onlinelibrary.wiley.com/doi/abs/10.1002/9781444338386.wbeah04305. Constantakopoulou wrote that "'Thalassocracy' is the phonetic adaptation of a noun meaning 'sea power' in Greek. Ancient Greek historians, and particularly Thucydides, used the concept of 'thalassocracy' as an analytical tool in investigating the past." Within this quote can be seen a conflict of spelling alternatives encountered herein. Again, I have attempted to be consistent in my spelling choices except when offering direct quotations and citations where I will endeavor to provide the spelling in the quoted or cited material. Christy Constantakopoulou, Professor of Classics and Ancient History, Birkeck College, University of London.

29. Epstein, *Conservatism and Traditionalism,* 26.

30. Dugin, *Foundations*, 29. Brackets added.

31. Dugin, *Fourth Theory*.

32. Morgan, "A Note From the Editor," in Dugin, *Fourth Theory*, 7. Here, Morgan wrote that the "bulk of the text in this book was published as *Chetvertaia politicheskaia teoriia,* which was published in St. Petersburg in 2009 by Amphora. The text has been revised by the author, and additional chapters have been added to this edition from other writings by Professor Dugin which were published later, dealing with the same theme."

33. Dugin, *Fourth Theory*, 19.

34. Dugin, *Fourth Theory*, 35ff.

35. Dugin, *Fourth Theory*, 35.

36. E.g., the Russian New Right (RNR) and the European New Right (ENR).

37. Dugin, *Fourth Theory*, 19.

Part III

Chapter One: Eurasianism

Genesis

As geopolitical awareness and concepts developed independently in the East after the Western portion of the Roman Empire's disintegration, a slow-growing perception of continental Eurasia began to develop.[1] This perception originated as the East looked westward, not as a Western European enterprise looking eastward. This development constituted "a formative period of classical Eurasianism," according to Dugin.[2] Laruelle stated that sometime later, Vladimir I. Lamanskii proffered a theory possessing distinctly identifiable Eurasian elements before the end of the nineteenth century:[3]

> Russia did not exist in two continents, European and Asiatic, but in one unique Eurasiatic continent in which three radically different worlds confronted each other: the Romano-Germanic world, the Greek-Slavic world of the middle, and a non-Christian world, Asia. Russia at the same time encompassed the whole and was encompassed by the whole, an empire inside the Greek-Slavic world.[4]

Bassin presents pre- or proto-Eurasian evidence in his observation that "external sources have been particularly important for the development of Russian nationalist thought, from at least the early 18th century."[5]

Laruelle wrote that several scholars developed doctrines that would justify the Russian presence in Asia.[6] For example, Vasilii V. Barthold, an official historian under both the Tsars and Soviets, "advocated for a cultural rapprochement between people from different origins," suggested that "worldwide empires" represent a "historical necessity," and welcomed a Russian move into Central Asia.[7] Laruelle stated that "according to N. M. Przheval'skii, peoples of Mongolia and Sing-Kiang were waiting to be under the domination of the 'White Czar.'"[8] Going a step further, Lamanskii and Vasilii V. Dokuchaev offered theories postulating a "third continent" situated between Europe and Asia.[9] Joining Lamanskii and Dokuchaev in this suggestion was the economist Peter B. Struve, who went on to become Savitsky's professor.[10]

Rémi Tremblay credited Trubetskoi with being the founder of a distinguishable Eurasian movement and identified Trubetskoi's friend, Claude Lévi-Strauss, as the source of the movement's pluralistic ideas.[11] Reflecting Lévi-Strauss' pluralistic thinking, Tremblay characterized universalism as an outgrowth of the Enlightenment and proclaimed that Eurasianism is directly opposed to its development.[12] Eurasianism supposes a multipolar world. Tremblay identified the "first and most important position of the Eurasian philosophy" as "its idea of a pluralistic world" and, correspondingly, "as the rejection of Western universalism."[13]

While he undoubtedly would admit to significant historical antecedents, with an academic certainty rarely encountered, Dmitry Shlapentokh precisely pinpointed that "Eurasianism as an intellectual and political trend emerged in 1921 when a group of Russian émigrés published the brochure, 'Turn to the East.'"[14] The movement grew, and well before WWII, a bifurcation yielded a leftist version in contrast to the much more rightist and monarchist leanings of the Russian Diaspora. Bassin emphasized that "important aspects of the thinking of the Eurasian movement of the 1920s and 1930s—which, we can surely all agree, was nothing if not nationalist"—were influenced by inputs from outside Russia, "specifically from Western Europe."[15]

Yigal Liverant suggested that Eurasianism inspired and largely established by Trubetskoi began to wane "as early as the 1930s, and its fate was sealed in 1938," with his death.[16] Trubetskoi was gone, but a seed of the Eurasian concept survived, to be revived by Lev Nikolayevich Gumilev. "By the end of World War II, Eurasianism had become known in the USSR, with Lev Gumilev as one of the major representatives," a point highlighted by both Shlapentokh and Laruelle.[17] Gumilev's theories are widely acknowledged in Russia and throughout the Eurasian region. Gumilyov National University's creation and its officially stated mission are tangible evidence of this, but his theories find no similarly widespread reception in the West.[18]

Russia's historical movements into Ukraine, the Baltics, Poland, all the countries that came to make up the Warsaw Pact, combined with expansion both eastward and southward, appears to support the Russian desire to control the Heartland and Rimland of Eurasia. However, there is a less deliberate explanation to be considered: "Russian policies can be explained not by ideologies but by the circumstances surrounding Russia."[19] Eric Shiraev explained:

> These circumstances were unique. For example, Russia grew in size and expanded because it could: there were only a few natural barriers holding its Eurasian expansion. Although Russia could be viewed as an aggressive and imperialist state, its policies were determined by Russia's unique geographic position, under which the policy of expansionism was a natural one.[20]

While this may be the argument articulated by Shiraev and supported by the writings of Jared Diamond, Dugin presents the much more metaphysical imperative of Sacred Geography embedded in his ideas of messianic Manifest Destiny in the Neo-Eurasian construction of Fourth Political Theory.[21]

Movement to the East and South

Russian expansionist desires are nothing new, and historical Russian expansion may be viewed as a precursor to any developed concept of Eurasianism. For example, in 1903, Sergei M. Seredonin developed notions of a more eastward-looking Russia "to justify the 'need for space' of Russia and its natural orientality."[22] Laruelle wrote:

> More than a millennium of cohabitation and interpenetration between Russians and Asians, the inheritance of Byzantine empire—antechamber of Asia—and the Mongol yoke, as

well as the easy conquest of the cold spaces, caused [Seredonin] to conceive an Asian Russia, oriented toward [the] Orient but not Europe, which was considered as too insular and too populated.[23]

While the eastward leanings expressed by Seredonin were decidedly pre-Eurasian insofar as any geopolitical movement was concerned, they do present a recognizable historical foundation on which later more discernible concepts of the Eurasian movement were erected. Acknowledging the bridge, and therefore the debt owed by Eurasianists to earlier more Slavic-centered exponents, Laruelle astutely observed that while Eurasianists may have drawn "their intellectual knowledge from the inheritance of Pan-Slavists and [Vladimir] Soloviev, they were also heirs of geopolitical currents turned toward [the] Orient."[24]

Pan-Slavic elements, Oriental leanings, and Russian mystical messianic ideas of Sacred Geography were all at play in the pre-Eurasian milieu. Evidence of Eurasianism as the beneficiary of these ingredients is found in Bassin's observation that Trubetskoi grafted the "old belief" of Russia's messianic mission into his Eurasian project.[25]

Practical expansion took "the shape of a pacific [sic] colonization by Russians that would follow the construction of the Trans-Siberian railway."[26] The Trans-Siberian and its associated tributary lines were the existential manifestations preceding from both the geopolitical competition, the so-called *Great Game*, between the Empires of Russia and Great Britain and Eurasian development in the nineteenth and into the twentieth century. However, hundreds of years before the Great Game was played out and railroads were contemplated, other historical events provided some of the early foundations that would later contribute to Russia's Orientalism.

In 1279 the vast Mongol Empire of Genghis Khan, significantly expanded by his scions—notably, Kublai Khan— extended from the Sea of Japan in the East to present-day Turkey and Ukraine in the West before it receded and faded in history. The empire of the Khans ended, although residual elements of culture, genetics, received myth, and legend paled but remained.

Reza Parchizadeh stated that just over 300 years after the Mongol Empire, the Romanovs ascended in Russia and "developed major tendencies for expansionism towards the east and the south."[27]

Parchizadeh reported that eastward "lay the powerful Tartar khanates whose lords were the descendants of the great medieval Mongol conqueror, Genghis Khan."[28] It took more than three centuries to subdue the Tartars, but the Russian Empire's efforts and later the Soviets gradually succeeded.[29] Historical and cultural attractions are evident in Russia's eastern expansionist efforts. Looking to its historical past and adopting ingredients from it is also a Russian characteristic. "The role of the heritage of Gengis-Khan, trustee of the Tatar statehood assimilated by Moscow in the XVI century, was seen as a decisive turn of Russia to the East, to its origins, to its own values," Dugin remarked.[30]

Turning his gaze southward, Parchizadeh related that the Russo-Persian Wars effectively established Russian military supremacy over Persia.[31] This southward expansion "led to the imposing of two humiliating 'Accords' on Persia," said Parchizadeh. The Golestān and Turkmanchay agreements ceded sizable Persian territories to the Russian Empire.[32] Parchizadeh wrote that, as a result, "the Tsar acquired the title of Protector of the Persian Crown, effectively making Persia a protectorate of the Tsar."[33]

Persian developments have exerted tremendous influence on Russian regional policy, political actions, and military strategy from Czarist times, through Soviet times, and into the present day. Parchizadeh reminded that from the time of the Russo-Persian Wars, through successive iterations, "Russia/Soviet Union/Russia has been one of the most influential players on the Persian/Iranian stage."[34]

The Ottomans were much more successful than the Persians in resisting outright Russian absorption and domination as they "put up a heavy resistance to the Russian encroachment for around two centuries."[35] Ottoman resistance was not without its setbacks, however. Parchizadeh remarked that "along the way," the Ottoman Empire "would be forced to concede many obligations and cede vast tracts of lands to the expanding Tsarist Empire."[36] The Treaty of Küçük Kaynarca concluded between Tsarist Russia and the Ottoman Empire in 1774 is noteworthy because "after decades of tension, struggle and war between the Russians and the Turks in the proximity of the Black Sea basin," it "ceded de facto control over the strategic lands around the Sea of Azov, like the Crimean Peninsula, to the Russians."[37]

The significance of this diplomacy resonates to this day. Peter Alexeyevich—Tsar Peter I, Peter the Great—frequently castigated by Dugin and the Neo-Eurasianists for displaying Europhile leanings, was nonetheless instrumental in giving clear access to long-sought-after, ice-free southern ports and oceans.[38] Despite setbacks and improved Russian naval avenues to the south, the Ottoman Empire still represented a real barrier to Russian access to the present-day Middle East, and, for over 200 years, the Ottomans obstructed "full-throttle expansion southwards."[39] Parchizadeh correctly pointed out that this covers a period when "the British Empire was also at the height of its power, and would lend a hand to the old Ottoman Empire if necessary, as it did in the case of the Crimean War."[40]

Movement to the West

Like using tree trunk rings to mark growth over time, Russian history may be viewed by considering periods of territorial expansion and contraction. Reckoning just from the Romanov period beginning in 1613, Russia expanded, then contracted when previously gained territory was subsequently lost, only to have the cycle begin again. In 1682, Tsar Peter I began an expansion period that included territorial acquisition and cultural development. An increasingly European, therefore Western, perspective was encouraged and embraced—at least at Court and among the Russian wealthy and aristocratic elite. With the increased attention toward Europe also came a period of westward expansion.

Andreas Kappeler examined the expansion-contraction characteristic as he considered Russian attempts to move westward into the Baltic region in 1558.[41] He found that during the Livonian War, "which lasted for twenty-five years, large parts of Livonia and the Grand Duchy of Lithuania were temporarily under Russian rule."[42] Then contraction occurred with "the defeat of Russia and the partitioning of Livonia between Poland-

Lithuania and Sweden."[43] The westward expansion phase was initiated again in the Northern Wars commencing in 1654 and again in 1700. With its increased territory, Russia also acquired problems of integration of European populations into its governmental scheme. Centralist and autocratic Russia "was confronted with the task of integrating societies which possessed a corporate organization, different estates and regional traditions," observed Kappeler.[44]

Russian access to the Baltic Sea and the acquisition of Baltic territory were vividly underscored with the founding and building of St. Petersburg and the relocation of the Capital in 1703. In 1721 Peter I declared that Russia had become the Russian Empire. The practical result of acquisition and integration is especially pertinent to Dugin's somewhat simplified assumption of Eurasian cohesiveness. For with the Baltic and Polish additions,

> The basic dilemma of Russian policy on nationalities became clearly evident for the first time, since Russia, which was superior in military and political terms, was annexing areas whose socio-political organization, economy and culture were more advanced than those of the metropolis.[45]

Nancy Shields Kollmann, acknowledging the dilemma Kappeler identified, wrote that, as a result, "these lands were allowed to maintain their well-articulated political systems and social elites."[46] The Ukrainian expansions reverberate still. From the mid-seventeenth century, "the ensuing gradual integration of a part of Ukraine into the Russian empire have been and continue to be the subject of controversial debates" was Kappeler's understated observation.[47]

Movement to the North

Ivan Groznyy, known today as "Ivan the Terrible," gained access to the Caspian Sea and subdued the Volga River's Tartar Khanate territories. The Britannica notes that Russian occupation and colonization of Siberia followed to the point where Russian commerce was established to the Taz River fur-trading regions of

Mangazeya using an Arctic route from the mouth of the Dvina River along the coast and the Yugorsky Shar Strait to the coast of Yamal. The Romanovs continued Russian expansion northward after they ascended to power in the early 1600s.

While the Western European powers looked across the Atlantic to acquire new territories, the Romanov Tsars expanded their territory in Eurasia. Russian Eurasian expansion continued so that before the twentieth century the Romanov Empire stretched from the Pacific to the Black Sea and included Alaska and even other colonies in North America. Northward movement was merely a result of the historical Russian multi-purposed reason for expansion. Arctic explorer Artur Chilingarov left no doubt of the reasoning behind Russian's current moves northward with his pointed statement that "the Arctic has always been Russian."[48]

Suggesting the supporting reasoning behind his beliefs, Shane Tayloe suggests that Russians have demanded

> a restoration of the greatness of the Soviet era (though not the failed aspects of its communist system). Nationalist sentiment has been compounded as recent economic challenges have triggered fears of a repetition of the depravation of the 1990s. Russian leaders have responded by demonstrating the state's emergence from its period of weakness following the collapse of the Soviet Union and have undertaken an unprecedented program of energy extraction to swell social spending.[49]

Guglielmo Migliori traced "the first effective document" aimed at clarification of the "status of the Arctic territories" to "a note issued on September 20, 1916, by the Ministry of Foreign Affairs of the Russian Empire."[50] "This source," reported Migliori, "stated a provisional inclusion into the official map of the Tsar's lands of all those territories representing a (generic and ambiguously defined) 'continuation' of imperial borders northwards."[51]

Expansion of the northern borders continued under the Bolsheviks. In 1921, the Soviets "defined an exclusive exploitation area extending from Cape Svyatoy Nos (Murmansk) to Kanin Nos peninsula (Arkhangelsk) and the archipelago Novaya Zemlya."[52] This action was taken to include territorial waters of the USSR out to twelve miles. The Soviet Union confirmed many of the former provisions of the Russian Empire "and proclaimed its sovereignty over all the lands and islands included between the North Pole and its Eastern and Western extremities."[53]

"The geopolitics of the twenty-first century will be different from the days of empire and conflict of the nineteenth and twentieth," wrote Caitlyn Antrim, going on to state that

> The increased accessibility of the Arctic, with its energy and mineral resources, new fisheries, shortened sea routes, and access to rivers flowing north to the Arctic, is pushing Russia to become a maritime state.[54]

Time will tell if climate change proves to be a significant strategic benefactor in Russia's breakout from the West's long-time Rimland containment efforts. NOAA's 2021 Artic Report Card said "The substantial decline in Arctic sea ice extent since 1979 is one of the most iconic indicators of climate change."[55] It went on to state that "Summer 2021 saw the second-lowest amount of older, multi-year ice since 1985, and the post-winter sea ice volume in April 2021 was the lowest since records began in 2010."[56] Tayloe, remarking on this change, suggests that "the thaw makes way for new sea routes, expansive, untouched fishing grounds, and provides unprecedented access to deposits of oil, gas, and minerals—most of which are concentrated within US and Russian territory."[57] Consider that "Arctic-wide ice loss is expected to continue through the 21st century, *very likely* resulting in nearly sea ice-free late summers by the 2040s"[58]

As remarkable and potentially world changing as the physical and commercial effects influenced by the climate may be, Tayloe underscored that "perhaps the most substantial change is of a geopolitical nature."[59] A useful derivative of Tayloe's prescience is one that examines just how the climate-affected changes are affording geopolitical challenges.

The Emergence of Eurasian Ideas

Tremblay, in his article, "Thoughts of Dugin's Eurasian Mission," credited Trubetskoi and anthropologist Lévi-Strauss for their establishment of baselines on Eurasianism as a geopolitical concept—Trubetskoi for the cohesive formulation and Lévi-Strauss as the source of Trubetskoi's pluralistic adaptations.[60] Even so, proto-Eurasian ideas are identifiable before the twentieth century, preceding those of Trubetskoi.[61]

Laruelle wrote that Lamanskii identified recognizable Eurasian structure and identity in his 1892 book, *Tri mira evroaziatskogo materika*.[62] As I previously noted, Lamanskii recognized that Eurasia is a continent in itself encompassing the "three radically different worlds"—the Romano-German, the Greco-Slavic, and non-Christian Asia.[63]

Eurasianism matured significantly from the 1920s onward, although many other pre- and non-Eurasian sources contributed significant elements to its development. The debt Eurasianism owes to Pan-Slavic thinkers is not insignificant. Laruelle, for example, acknowledges the debt Eurasianism owes to Nikolai Danilevskii and others.[64] Identifying the pan-Slavic theme, Laruelle stated that "Eurasianism borrowed many of its historical and philosophical patterns from Danilevskii and other conservative pan-Slavists."[65]

Among the borrowed items are cyclic history concepts, ongoing European and Russian opposition, philosophy of territory, and "a Platonic existence of a hidden reality 'truer' than material appearance."[66] While Danilevskii's theories characterized Russia as only Slavic, "Eurasianism took the assumptions of Danilevskii but let the Turco-Mongols enter the stage," resulting in an integrated creation—Slavic and oriental combined with inputs from the Russian Steppes.[67] Neo-Eurasianism inherits its pan-Slavic nature mainly from its Eurasianist past, though it inherits its expansionist nature from a time long before defined Eurasianist ideas developed.

Parchizadeh identified historical antecedents of Russian expansion detectible in the southward and eastward movement evident after the Romanov ascension in the early seventeenth century.[68] It should be acknowledged, however, that Russia's Westward movement experienced periods of expansion and contraction beginning in the sixteenth century, even before the reign of Peter the Great beginning in 1682. Kappeler commented on the mid-1500s Russian attempts to expand into the Baltics.[69]

As noted, the westward expansion phase rekindled in 1654 and again in 1700, building of St. Petersburg commenced in 1703, and in 1721 Russia was declared an empire. Ismailov and Papava wrote that after the declaration of the Empire, Russian expansion was evident in "all segments of the Pivot Area."[70] Additionally, Kappeler emphasized that from the mid-1600s, Russia attempted to integrate parts of Ukraine into the Empire.[71]

Russia's current expressions of its national interests, anticipated through history, were recognized in remarks made by Andrew Wood:

> Putin's Russia has sought a renewed claim to eminence whether by virtue of Moscow's victory in 1945, or by at various times asserting its guardianship of traditional morals and/or its geo-political position at the center of Eurasia. All these claims rest on Russia's effectiveness as a centralized and militarily powerful state covering a major part of the world's land mass.[72]

Especially noteworthy in this context are Wood's observations regarding Russia's interpretation of guardianship responsibilities and its Eurasian geopolitical situation when considered as elements of Russia's Historic National Interests.[73] And what are these Russian Historic National Interests? Julia Gurganus and Eugene Rumer provided an examination of this subject from the contemporary look-back vantage point:

> Continuity with the Soviet era and even earlier periods of Russian history is a hallmark of the Kremlin's current foreign policy and the toolkit it

relies on to advance its goals. It is therefore essential to review the foreign policy legacy of the Soviet Union. Core components of the current Russian toolkit have withstood the test of time, and there is every indication that Moscow will continue to rely on them, even in a post-Putin era.[74]

"Contemporary Russian foreign policy displays the unmistakable presence of three centuries-old drivers of Moscow's posture on the world stage," wrote Gurangus and Rumer, remarking on Russia's Historic National Interests.[75] Summarizing and, at the same time, reiterating these consistent interests, they stated:

> Chief among these drivers is Russia's quest for strategic depth and secure buffers against external threats, which, considering the country's geography and absence of natural protective barriers between it and neighboring powers, has guided its geographic expansion. Along with physical insecurity and expansion, the second key driver of Russian foreign policy has been its ambition for recognition as a great power, which the Kremlin has long seen as necessary for legitimizing its geographic conquests and geopolitical ambitions. The third driver, related to the first two, is Russia's complicated relationship with the West, which combines rivalry with the need for cooperation.[76]

Bassin examined Eurasianism in pursuit of points of comparison to Dugin's Neo-Eurasianist proposal.[77] Dugin is an innovator; his modifications to classical Eurasianism follow his pattern of mining earlier projects for salvageable material that can support new construction. Dugin suggested that "the Eurasian theory went through two stages," the first being "a formative period of classical Eurasianism at the beginning of the 20th century by Russian emigrant intellectuals."[78] Dugin then listed Trubetskoi,

Savitsky, Gumilev, and others as the Russian intellectuals responsible for the formulation of classical Eurasianism.[79] The second stage involves the development of Neo-Eurasianism from the 1980s to the present.[80]

If there was one requirement Dugin had to move from the established expressions of Eurasianism espoused by Trubetskoi, Savitsky, and Gumilev, it was their demand to isolate Eurasia from Europe. Andrei P. Tsygankov wrote that "following Savitskiy and Gumilev, [Gennadiy] Zyuganov emphasized that, as a unique civilization with a unique geographic location, Russia must be isolated from the West to survive and preserve its uniqueness."[81] Because of the need for European integration in Dugin's Neo-Eurasian conception, Tsygankov's mention of Gumilev's rejection of Russian/European mixing cannot be squared with the Dublin to Vladivostok ambitions Dugin expresses.

Tsygankov pointed out that "Europe, in Gumilev's racist writings, represents an alien Supraethnic group and can never be mixed with Russia," a claim that has resonance in the contemporary debates on Muslim migration and the merits of effective integration.[82] This claim brought Eurasianism to a boundary—on one side, Eurasianism before Dugin; on the other, Dugin's Neo-Eurasianism. Pre-Dugin Eurasianists subscribed to the opinion that, as Gumilev warned, "adaptation to the West would mean nothing less for the Russian people than the loss of their own 'ethnos and soul.'"[83] Therefore,

> as has been noted, Eurasianism in both its classic prewar and later "Gumilevian" interpretations basically saw Russia/Eurasia as a self-contained unity. Russia/Eurasia was constrained by geographical, cultural, and "bio-cosmical" limits—at least in Gumilevia interpretations—and had no desire to spread outside this geopolitical niche to the outside world.[84]

Stephan Wiederkehr thought that Trubetskoi took a broad view of what constitutes "Russianness."[85] Through Wiederkehr, Eurasian themes emerging in Trubetskoi are exposed, including

Slavic and Thracian elements that both became incorporated into Russia's "historical mission" in Trubetskoi's scheme.[86] Trubetskoi also made the point that Russian culture must have ecumenical characteristics and not be based solely on Eastern Orthodoxy.[87]

The refrain of inclusion is a prominent characteristic of Eurasian thought from its beginning. Wiederkehr observed that this feature even predates Eurasianism when pointing to the fact that Russians living together with Turanians "is a recurring motif throughout Russian history."[88] Reminiscent of Francis X. Clooney's ideas of deep learning across borders, Trubetskoi remarked that "for a correct national self-knowledge we, Russians, have to take into account the presence of the Turanian element in ourselves, we have to study our Turanian brothers."[89] Eurasian (hence Neo-Eurasian) movements evolved from being Slavic-oriented to much more multicultural and multinational inclusiveness. "Eurasianism, rather than pan-Slavism for Russians, Pan-Turanianism for Eurasian Turanians, or Pan-Islamism for Eurasian Muslims, should become predominant," suggested Trubetskoi.[90]

Zbigniew Brzezinski, National Security Advisor to President Jimmy Carter, wrote that "Eurasianism was given an academic gloss in the much-quoted writings of Lev Gumilev, a historian, geographer, and ethnographer."[91] Brzezinski believed that Gumilev's books, *Medieval Russia and the Great Steppe*, *The Rhythms of Eurasia,* and *The Geography of Ethnos in Historical Time*, "make a powerful case for the proposition that Eurasia is the natural geographic setting for the Russian people's distinctive 'ethnos.'"[92] Ethnos, as Brzezinski read Gumilev, is "the consequence of a historic symbiosis between them [the Russian people], and the non-Russian inhabitants of the open steppes, creating thereby a unique Eurasian cultural and spiritual identity."[93]

Savitsky also clearly articulated the essential multinational and multicultural nature of Eurasianism that Dugin picked up in his Neo-Eurasian doctrine. "Russians and those who belong to the peoples of 'the Russian world,'" quoting Savitsky, "are neither Europeans nor Asians."[94] Savitsky summed up the feeling, now shared by Dugin, by proclaiming, "we are not ashamed to declare ourselves Eurasians."[95] Savitsky alluded to a "secret affinity of souls," which allows Russian culture to be comprehensible to East Europeans and Asians.[96]

Savitsky's affinity-of-souls helps make Russian culture understandable. It also contributes to a high degree of closeness to Russian culture among the East European and Asian populations.[97] Related to affinity-of-souls is *Passionarost*. In his review of *Black Wind, White Snow*, Hosking commented on Clover's interpretation of Gumilev's concept of *Passionarost*— social solidarity characterized by "creative energy, lust for expansion and ruthlessness combined with a capacity for suffering and endurance in pursuing the common cause."[98]

Without the benefit of Savitsky's affinity-of-souls, Trubetskoi believed that ethnic nationalism creates a "one-sided link" in an attempt to realize a Eurasian reality.[99] This belief led to the fear that "the centrifugal energies of particular ethnic nationalisms" would prevent ties of "brotherhood" from coalescing within the Eurasian construct.[100] Trubetskoi suggested that with true Eurasian brotherhood, Eurasianism would not rely on any single link of ethnic nationalism but on multi-linked criteria bound up in a common historical destiny.[101] Gumilev maintained, *Passionarost* "not technological or moral progress," provides the key to world history.[102] *Passionarost* is a saturated and abiding grit bound up in deep, ancient, and persistent loyalties and allegiances that contribute so meaningfully to the Russian persona—to Russianness.

Thus, *Passionarnost* provides the real key to understanding the Soviet tenacity and sacrifice in its WWII victory over Germany.[103] *Passionarnost* is an Eastern characteristic and understanding. The Russians possess *Passionarnost,* wrote Hosking, claiming that with this commonality with the Central Asia peoples, "they formed a civilisation quite distinct from that of Europe."[104]

Passionarnost explains much that makes Russia resistant to Western globalism. Laruelle drew on Lev P. Karsavin's views of Western culture in explaining the Eurasianists aversion to Western Democracy.[105] Dugin is not alone; rejecting not just Eurocentrism, Karsavin "discarded Western culture because of its stress on the individual and particular."[106] Laruelle emphatically stated,

100

"Karsavin and in fact all Eurasianists implicitly discarded the notion of Western democracy," suggesting, that for them, Western democracy constituted "the dictatorship of the elite which manipulated the electorate."[107]

Providing a pointer to Dugin, in his 1920 manifesto, *Europe and Mankind*, Trubetskoi suggested that the concept of Russian opposition to the West could be concentrated into a coalescence of outliers in opposition to Europe.[108] Referring to Europe, Trubetskoi mainly alluded to those countries engaged in colonial rule. He identified the outliers in this instance to include "Slavs, Chinese, Indians, Arabs, Negroes and other peoples, all of whom, regardless of color, are groaning under the heavy Romano-Germanic yoke and squandering their national energies on the production of raw materials for European factories."[109]

Trubetskoi was emphatic in his calls for a Eurasian creation, saying it "is not only pragmatically valuable; it is nothing less than a vital necessity."[110] Trubetskoi may have been prophetically speaking about the collapse of the Soviet Union in its failure to provide "the awakening of self-awareness as a single, multiethnic Eurasian nation."[111] Trubetskoi wrote that "the destinies of the Eurasian peoples have become interwoven with one another, tied in a massive tangle that can no longer be unraveled."[112] He posited that a proper Russian-Eurasian creation would be able to provide "the ethnic substratum of statehood without which it will eventually fall to pieces."[113]

Bassin surmised that Trubetskoi believed that the Russian revolutions of 1917 spelled the end of any formal existence of the Russian Empire.[114] Therefore, henceforth, any distinctly "Russian element" could not "legitimately claim its traditional hegemonic position within the larger geographical-political realm of Eurasia."[115]

Trubetskoi recognized the "true and properly homogenizing element of the Eurasian culture zone, however, was not Russian but a more general and comprehensive Eurasian culture."[116] The success of the Bolsheviks forever altered the Eurasian concept to a much less Russia-centric construct. Trubetskoi realized that "with the revolution, the old situation had undergone a fundamental transformation that was not to be undone."[117]

The Soviet Union was unable to create the Eurasia Trubetskoi envisioned and Dugin proposes. Even so, lessons were gleaned from the emerging and resulting reality. Among the lessons learned, Trubetskoi recognized that a "critical impetus" could be realized from Russian resistance to European hegemony.[118] This critical impetus, this "mankind against Europe" idea, could be used by Russia to secure the emancipation of colonial empires produced by "Romano-Germanic oppression."[119] Although after the 1917 Russian Revolution Trubetskoi believed that Russia could provide impetus, Bassin recognized the formulation of Trubetskoi's opinion was based on the understanding that the "homogenizing element" required for Eurasian cohesion must be Eurasian, not merely Russian.[120]

Trubetskoi acknowledged the importance of Russia's Historic National Interests. Still, he was also astute enough to realize that Russia alone, Russia as a specific national and cultural entity, could not accomplish the establishment and maintenance of a Eurasian conglomerate—a new creation was required.

> By virtue of its imperial legacy, it was obviously quite out of the question that the Russian element could supply the unifying basis for national cohesiveness, and thus an entirely new identity had to be supplied, which could assemble and unify the different parts of the former state.[121]

Trubetskoi believed in "the superiority of cultural over anthropological or racial criteria."[122] Bassin appreciated the significance of Trubetskoi's insistence that a new creation replace Imperial Russia. Trubetskoi's then yet unrealized new alternative would be Eurasia.[123]

> To replace imperial Russia, Trubetskoi offered the alternative of Eurasia: a cultural edifice as yet "under construction," as he conceded with admirable frankness, but which he nonetheless quite sincerely believed to correspond to historical, cultural, and political reality.[124]

Trubetskoi's Eurasia could not embrace a "return to the situation in which Russians were the sole owner of the state territory."[125] The Russian Empire and subsequently the Soviet Union consisted of a multiethnic mix with several separate nationalisms. Trubetskoi's solution was to advocate for the creation of Eurasia—a nation called Eurasia, *"its territory Eurasia, and its nationalism Eurasianism."*[126] Nationhood is justified, in Trubetskoi's mind, for "Eurasia constitutes a geographical, economic, and historical whole."[127] Laruelle expressed the opinion that twentieth century "Eurasianism provided the opportunity for a variety of geopolitical arrangements."[128]

Gumilev proposed one of the most influential arrangements before Dugin's Neo-Eurasian introduction. Like Dugin, Gumilev was concerned with the rise, decline, and fall of peoples and civilizations.[129] Hosking noted that Gumilev's Eurasianist theories were anti-Marxist.[130] Being the son of well-known poets and a poet, literary character, and critic in his own right, Gumilev ran afoul of the Stalinist authorities and became familiar with the Gulag system on more than one occasion.

Gumilev, personally acquainted with Savitsky, engaged in regular correspondence with him.[131] Gumilev's official biography on the L.N. Gumilyov Eurasian National University website notes this fact.[132] While in the Gulag, he met Savitsky, who was to prove a vital link between Trubetskoi and the later Eurasianists. Notably, Gumilev was also part of that link himself.[133] WWII intervened, and when Gumilev was out of the Gulag system, he was into the Red Army.

After the war, Gumilev's academic career was somewhat checkered as his anti-Stalinist labeling, Gulag experiences, and associates may have contributed to his academic inconsistencies. Gumilev began postgraduate work at the USSR Institute of Oriental Studies but was not allowed to continue. In 1948 he was accepted into the postgraduate program at Leningrad State University and eventually earned a doctoral degree with a thesis on the ancient Turks.[134] In 1976, it appears he was refused a second doctoral degree with his dissertation "Ethnogeny and Earth's biosphere."[135] Even within the prevailing repressive atmosphere, Gumilev developed a sizable following in ethnology, although much, or even most, of his writing was suppressed and left unpublished until pre-collapse Soviet reforms relaxed the restrictions on his work.[136]

Gumilev suggested that one ingredient of Eurasianism is a biological determinant, and Dugin's Eurasian modification, his Neo-Eurasianism, is composed of more than just geopolitical elements.[137] Akin to the manipulation of perceived reality in Guy Debord's *Spectacle*, Dugin acknowledges the manipulation by biopolitics described by Michel Foucault in *The History of Sexuality*.[138] Morgan characterizes biopolitics as the "means by which a political system regulates the actual physical, biological lives of the people it governs, such as through health and medicine, sexuality and reproduction, and family life."[139]

Gumilev's deterministic suggestion that history is predictable contains the intriguing idea of cultural DNA. Gumilev advanced the notion of ethnicities formed over centuries, perhaps millennia, through a geographical association with the very soil and terrain they have inhabited.[140] Jonathan Rushbrook offered a critique of Gumilev's applications:

> While the Eurasianists posited a largely religious and cultural definition of Russianness, the ethnic theories of Lev Gumilev are an example a purely biological and pseudo-scientific understanding of the Russian nation that is defined purely by a biological determinism and social Darwinism.[141]

Dugin agrees with Gumilev's explanation that the attraction of soil is a powerful determinant of Eurasian cohesiveness.

The Revival of Eurasian Ideas

A resurgence of Eurasianist ideas occurred in the latter decades of the twentieth century. "At the national level," Bassin observed, "a variety of very different Eurasian perspectives and doctrines have been articulated," and he pointedly acknowledged those of Evgenii Primakov and Zyuganov along with Dugin.[142] Of these, "the best known and most important representative of post-Soviet neo-Eurasianism is Alexander Dugin," according to

104

Bassin.[143] However, "Yevgeny Primakov was the architect of Moscow's geopolitical reorientation from the West to the Eurasiatic space," in Emanuel Copilaş' concise opinion.[144]

Primakov, a Soviet and later Russian Federation official, served as Foreign Minister beginning in 1996 and as Prime Minister under Boris Yeltsin for a short time from 1998 to 1999. Copilaş acknowledged that "the neo-Eurasianist inspiration of Primakov's geopolitical concept is undeniable."[145] Copilaş recognized the mantel, "the Primakov Doctrine," attached to Primakov's geopolitical prescriptions and claimed it to be "the political articulation of Neo-Eurasianism."[146]

Dugin addressed the Eurasian portion of the Primakov Doctrine, stressing the emphasis on creating a robust Eurasian pole to oppose the Western unipolar objective:

> The multipolar vision recognizes the integration on the basis of the common civilization. So we speak of Eurasian civilization common not only to Russians and slaves [Slavs] and/or Orthodox peoples but also to the Turkish and aboriginal peoples of Central Asia, Siberia and the Caucasus. Putin's foreign policy is centered around multipolarity and Eurasian integration that is necessary to create the full standing pole.[147]

The arrival of the Primakov Doctrine and Dugin's Neo-Eurasianism brings us to the state of Eurasianism today but, the rise of Neo-Eurasianism notwithstanding, much Russia-centered nationalism remains. Zyuganov, the ardent Communist Party leader, set a confrontational tack toward a Neo-Eurasian cultural and geopolitical future. Quoting James Gregor regarding Zyuganov's placement of Russia at "the core and foundation of the main Eurasiatic block," claiming the Murmansk to Vladivostok "Big Space," Copilaş pointed out that Gregor highlighted Zyuganov's concept of a Russia serving "as a defense line against Western hegemony."[148]

Zyuganov has opposed the unipolar inclined West, placing Russia, not a Eurasian creation, as the bulwark against Western postmodern globalism. So, we see that Russian-centric thinkers may also share the Eurasian geopolitics of Dugin regarding macro-political applications and defense against Western power projections without opting a larger Eurasian goal.

Doubting the depth of culture in a society, the predominant Western view, based on the assumption that the entire world is striving for government constructed on the Western model, is that societies' multicultural aspects are mostly superficial differences.[149] Shlapentokh challenged this assumption and criticized the notion that multiculturalism has any such universal appeal.[150] Extrapolating Shlapentokh's criticism, one can conclude that assuming multiculturalism as a merely superficial characteristic is mistaken, as it is fundamentally a civilizational difference.[151] This interpretation is consistent and evident within Dugin's Neo-Eurasian model.

Development of Dugin's Neo-Eurasianism

Dugin acknowledges the heritage of his Neo-Eurasianism and is careful to give it an identifiable and credible genealogy. Dugin remarked that it was two Eurasianist pioneers of phonology and structural linguistics, Roman Jakobson and Trubetskoi, who "were the mentors of Levi-Strauss and had taught him the skills of structural analysis."[152] With this in mind, Dugin extrapolated the chain of Neo-Eurasian intellectual heritage from Eurasianism to Structuralism to Neo-Eurasianism.[153]

Laruelle observed that as Eurasianism developed politically and ideologically, it changed and became more diverse.[154] To be sure, Dugin has deviated from previous visions of Eurasianism, but essential consistencies remain. What has not changed is that most Eurasianists, and this includes Dugin, "assumed that Russia-Eurasia is a distinct civilizational unit, different from both Asia and Europe."[155] Summarizing his views on the development of Eurasianism, Dugin explained:

> The Eurasian Idea represents a fundamental
> revision of the political, ideological, ethnic, and
> religious history of mankind, and it offers a new

106

system of classification and categories that will overcome standard clichés.[156]

And,

> The Eurasian theory went through two stages—a formative period of classical Eurasianism at the beginning of the 20th century by Russian emigrant intellectuals (Trubeckoy, Savickiy, Alekseev, Suvchinckiy, Iljin, Bromberg, Hara-Davan, *et al.*) followed by the historical works of Lev Gumilev and, finally, the constitution of neo-Eurasianism (second half of the 1980s to the present).[157]

The Russian Revolution stymied late nineteenth century and early twentieth century attempts to stimulate Russia's Eurasian desires as the Soviet Union was more interested in creating a western buffer between the USSR and Europe than expanding its physical boundaries. Dugin lamented the demise of the early Eurasian pioneering efforts.

> Alas, historically, this remarkable movement was not appreciated in due measure. The impressing successes of Marxist ideology made the refined conservative-revolutionary perspective of the eurasist [sic] ineffective, superfluous. By the end of the '30s, the original impulse of the eurasist [sic] movement, both in Russia and among the Russian emigration, had definitively died away.[158]

Neo-Eurasianism involves more than physical considerations. "Classical Eurasianism might have passed," but Dugin surmised that "neo-Eurasianism has given it a second birth, a new sense, scale, and meaning."[159] The Neo-Eurasian view of the Eurasian movement's key doctrinal positions includes accepting the idea of the West in opposition to the rest of the world, "the West against mankind."[160] Dugin claimed this Western position forms a pattern of unipolar totalitarianism.[161] Comprehending this pattern, he accuses the West of attempting "economic, political and cultural domination."[162] Dugin believes that the West's view is grounded in a deep-seated belief that all people constantly desire to pursue Western ideals culminating in globalization. Dugin, disagreeing, suggested that,

> Adherents of globalization deny any alternative plan of the future, but today we are experiencing a large-scale phenomenon—contra-globalism, and the Eurasian Idea coordinates all opponents of unipolar globalization in a constructive way. Moreover, it offers the competing idea of multipolar globalization (or alter-globalization).[163]

Dugin emphasized his point that Neo-Eurasianism, "does not see the creation of a world government on the basis of the liberal-democratic values as the one and only path for mankind."[164] Agreeing with the earlier Eurasianists in opposition to the Western quest for domination, Dugin concurred that effective opposition is available through a credible geopolitical rival to the West. The worthy rival, in the minds of the Classical Eurasianists, was Eurasia itself. Unfortunately for this option, Eurasia does not exist as a distinct geopolitical reality. To achieve Eurasian reality, Dugin concluded that "Russia needs not simply to go back to its roots," it needs to combine "a conservative and a revolutionary new start."[165]

Writing of his Eurasianist forebears, Dugin emphasized the deeply seeded anti-Westernism embedded in Eurasian geopolitical thought. He downplayed Western influence on Russia, yet he also suggested that a degree of purposeful Eurasian reasoning has allowed some specific Westernization reception. Dugin was careful to note that Western experience, techniques, and methods are employed, "with the only purpose" being "to confront the West with its own weapons."[166] Dugin styled Russia's adoption of the desired Western imports with the rejection of any accompanying cultural replacement as "modernisation without westernization."[167] He claimed that by following this practice, "Russia also managed longer than other traditional societies to effectively counter the pressure of the West."[168]

Dugin does not eschew all technological advancement, even if it means cherry-picking technologies and other useful advances from the West. Neo-Eurasianism can be selectively anti-Western as long as it avoids absorption into Western globalism. This selective borrowing technique allows Dugin to visualize that Russia can actively modernize, develop, and open somewhat to the surrounding world but still save and harden its own identity.[169] Dugin carefully and methodically cataloged Russia's strengths and motivations while noting its primacy among other Eurasian counterparts.

- **Previous Eurasianists purposely conceived Russia as the avant-garde of the East against the West**
- **Russia is the forward defense of traditional society against modern, secular, ordinary, rationalized society**
- **Russia is different from other Eastern societies**
  - In the centuries-old struggle for preserving a cultural ego, Russia actively acquired experience from the West
  - Russia selectively adopted techniques applied by the West and borrowed some Western methods [170]

In a seeming contradiction, Dugin declared that Neo-Eurasianism is postmodern. It is undoubtedly postmodern in that it is a player remaining on the field after modernity's demise. But Dugin's declaration was more than a proclamation of survival, for it addressed a postmodernism that is radically different from the current state of postmodernism in the West. Compared to the Western version, Neo-Eurasianism is postmodernism "with [a] radically different inner substance."[171]

Notes

1. Dugin, "The Eurasian Idea," under, Eurasianism as a Philosophical Struggle, Counter-Currents, November 8, 2013, counter-

109

currents.com/2013/11/the-eurasian-idea/. A note at the end of this article credits *Ab Aeterno* no. 1, November 2009.

2. Dugin, "The Eurasian Idea," under, Eurasianism as a Philosophical Struggle.

3. Laruelle, "The Orient in Russian Thought at the Turn of the Century," in *Russia between East and West Scholarly Debates on Eurasianism*, ed. Dmitry Shlapentokh (Boston: Brill, 2007), 24

4. Laruelle, "Orient in Russian Thought," 24.

5. Bassin, "'Classical' Eurasianism and Russian Identity," *Ab Imperio* 2003, no. 2 (2003): 257. A transcript of this article may be accessed at: scribd.com/document/103155000/Mark-Bassin-Classical-Eurasianism-and-the-Geopolitics-of-Russian-Identity.

6. Laruelle, "Orient in Russian Thought," 24.

7. Ibid.

8. Ibid. Also often rendered as, "Przhevalsky."

9. Ibid.

10. Ibid.

11. Rémi Tremblay, "Thoughts of Dugin's 'Eurasian Mission,'" Alternative Right, May 7, 2015, alternative-right.blogspot.com/2015/05/thoughts-on-dugins-eurasian-mission_7.html. This site is apparently no longer viable. Instead, Cf. 4pt.su/en/content/thoughts-dugins-eurasian-mission. Cf. e.g., Nikolai S. Trubetzkoy, *Principles of Phonology* (Berkeley, CA: University of California Press, 1969). Trubetzkoy is often rendered as *Trubetskoi* or *Trubezkoy* in English. Dugin uses Trubetskoi in my preferred edition of *The Fourth Political Theory*. Rémi Tremblay, Journalist.

12. Tremblay, "Thoughts of Dugin's 'Eurasian Mission.'"

13. Ibid.

14. Dmitry Shlapentokh, "Introduction: Eurasianism and Soviet/Post-Soviet Studies," in *Russia between East and West Scholarly Debates on Eurasianism*, ed. Dmitry Shlapentokh (Boston: Brill, 2007), 6. Cf. Laruelle, "Orient in Russian Thought," 10. Dmitry Shlapentokh, Professor of History, Indiana University-South Bend.

15. Bassin, "Eurasianism and Russian Identity," 257. Brackets added.

16. Yigal Liverant, "The Prophet of the New Russian Empire," *Azure* 35, no. Winter 2009, azure.org.il/article.php?id=483.

Yigal Liverant, Israeli/Ukranian historian and Russian and political writer and commentator.

17. Shlapentokh, "Eurasianism and Soviet/Post-Soviet Studies," 6 and Laruelle, "Orient in Russian Thought," 10. Cf. Liverant, "The Prophet of New Russian Empire."

18. As the University's name so clearly indicates, Gumilev's popularity and fame are such that the University, founded in 1996 and located in Astana, Kazakhstan, was named for him. The official university website states the main purpose of the university is found in the "idea of Eurasian Union."

19. Eric Shiraev, *Russian Government and Politics, 2nd Ed.* (London: Palgrave MacMillan, 2013), 61. Cf. Andrew Kuchins and Anders Åslund, *The Russia Balance Sheet* (Washington, DC: Peterson Institute for International Economics Center for Strategic and International Studies, 2009). Eric Shiraev, Professor, George Mason University.

20. Shiraev, *Russian Government and Politics*, 61.

21. Cf. Jared M. Diamond, *Guns, Germs, and Steel: The Fates of Human Societies* (New York: W.W. Norton & Company, 1997). In this work, the popular geographer and anthropologist examines migration patterns across Eurasia in consideration of geographical and environmental factors. Cf. Dugin, "The Eurasian Idea," under, The New World as Messiah. Jared Diamond, Geographer.

22. Laruelle, "Orient in Russian Thought," 24.

23. Ibid. Brackets added.

24. Ibid., 23. Brackets added. Solovyov, also spelled Soloviev. According to Laruelle, Solovyov, "uniting orthodoxy and neoplatonism and calling for ecumenism of all Christian churches," believed "Russia had to give up religious and political nationalism and accomplish the mission that neither Constantine nor Charlemagne could achieve." His ideas "provoked a deep interest for the Eurasianists in their search for an original unit, a totality that would form the cosmos and humanity." Cf. Laruelle, "Orient in Russian Thought," 21.

25. Bassin, "Eurasianism and Russian Identity," 265.

26. Laruelle, "Orient in Russian Thought," 24. Brackets added.

27. Reza Parchizadeh, "The Historic Roots of Russian Expansionism in the Middle East," American Thinker, October 18, 2015, americanthinker.com/articles/. Reza Parchizadeh, Iranian-born political

theorist, Researcher in Middle Eastern and English literature and politics.

28. Ibid.

29. Ibid.

30. Dugin, "Eurasia Above All."

31. Parchizadeh, "Historic Roots of Russian Expansionism."

32. Cf. e.g., Vahid Rashidvash, "History of Iran: The Circumstances of Signing Golestan and Turkmanchy Treaties and Its Contents," *International Review of Social Sciences and Humanities* 3, no. 1 (March 2, 2012): 246–61. Golestān (Golestan) is also found rendered as *Gulistan*. For an English translation of the Treaty of Golestan, Cf. mfa.gov.az/en/content/809. For an English translation of the Treaty of Turkmenchay, Cf. mfa.gov.az/en/content/810. Vahid Rashidvash, Iranian Studies Scholar.

33. Parchizadeh, "Historic Roots of Russian Expansionism."

34. Ibid.

35. Ibid.

36. Ibid.

37. Ibid. For an English translation of this treaty, Cf. fas.nus.edu.sg/hist/eia/documents_archive/kucuk-kaynarca.php.

38. Ibid. Parchizadeh claims that this fulfilled the "foremost desire" of Peter I in contrast to those who claim Europeanization of Russia was primary. Perhaps the two are complementary; at the least, acquisition of ports to support a modern fleet could help place Russia in a more balanced political position *vis-a-vis* the powers of Europe. Cf. Jardar Østbø, *The New Third Rome: Readings of a Russian Nationalist Myth* (Stuttgart: Ibidem, 2016), 135ff.

39. Ibid.

40. Ibid.

41. Andreas Kappeler, *The Russian Empire: A Multi-ethnic History*, trans. Alfred Clayton (London & New York: Routledge, 2013), 60. Andreas Kappeler, Emeritus Professor of Eastern European History, University of Vienna.

42. Ibid.

43. Ibid.

44. Ibid.

45. Ibid., 60-61.

46. Nancy Shields Kollmann, *The Russian Empire 1450-1801* (Oxford: Oxford University Press, 2017), 103. Nancy Shields Kollmann, William H. Bonsall Professor of History, Stanford University.

47. Kappeler, *Russian Empire*, 61.

48. Artur Chilingarov quoted in Nicholas Breyfogle and Jeffrey Dunifon, "Russia and the Race for the Arctic," *Origins*, August 2012, origins.osu.edu/article/russia-and-race-arctic.

49. Shane C. Tayloe, "Projecting Power In The Arctic: The Russian Scramble for Energy, Power, and Prestige In The High North," *Pepperdine Policy Review*: Vol. 8, Article 4, June 4, 2015, 1. Available at: digitalcommons.pepperdine.edu/ppr/vol8/iss1/4." Shane C. Tayloe, Pepperdine University.

50. Guglielmo Migliori, "On Thin Ice: Russia's Arctic Geopolitics in the Age of Climate Change," Master's thesis, University of Bologna, March, 2020, 27.

51. Migliori, "On Thin Ice," 27. Parentheses in original.

52. Ibid. Cf. Migliori's citation of Dekret SNK ob Ohrane Rybnyh i Zverinyh Ugodij v Severnom Ledovitom Okeane i Belom More, retrieved from: docs.historyrussia.org/ru/nodes/12076-24-maya-dekret-snk-obohrane-rybnyh-i-zverinyh-ugodiy-v-severnom-ledovitom-okeane-i-belom-more. Parentheses in Migliori's text.

53. Ibid. Cf. Migliori's footnote 6.

54. Caitlyn Antrim, "The Next Geographical Pivot," *Naval War College Review*, 63, 3, (Summer 2010), 15-16. Quoted in Tayloe, "Projecting Power in the Arctic," 5. Caitlyn Antrim, 1949-2018.

55. arctic.noaa.gov/Report-Card/Report-Card-2021.

56. Ibid.

57. Tayloe, "Projecting Power in the Arctic," 1. Cf. his reference to the US Geological Survey. (2008) Circum-Arctic resource appraisal: Estimates of undiscovered oil and gas north of the Arctic Circle, pubs.usgs.gov/fs/2008/3049/fs2008-3049.pdf.

58. P.C. Taylor, W. Maslowksi, J. Perlwitz, and D.J. Wuebbles, "Arctic changes and their effects on Alaska and the rest of the United States," Key Finding 3, in D.J. Wuebbles, D.W. Fahey, K.A. Hibbard, D.J.

Dokken, B.C. Stewart, and T.K. Maycock (eds.), *Climate Science Special Report: FourthNational Climate Assessment*, Volume I, U.S. Global Change Research Program, Washington, DC, 2017. Italics in original. Near-term and long-term melting conditions in the Arctic are currently receiving a great deal of attention. For more detail addressing the anomalies of Arctic ice and melting Cf. e.g., Renato R. Colucci's December 31, 2021 article at severe-weather.eu/global-weather/arctic-sea-ice-second-highest-18-years-end-2021-rrc/.

59. Tayloe, "Projecting Power in the Arctic," 1.

60. Tremblay, "Thoughts of Dugin's 'Eurasian Mission.'"

61. Cf. e.g., Laruelle, "Orient in Russian Thought," 24.

62. Ibid.

63. Ibid.

64. Ibid.

65. Ibid., 23.

66. Ibid.

67. Ibid.

68. Cf. Parchizadeh, "Historic Roots of Russian Expansionism."

69. Kappeler, *Russian Empire*, 60.

70. Ismailov and Papava, "The Heartland Theory," 95.

71. Kappeler, *Russian Empire*, 61. According to Vladimir Sazonov, Putin is greatly influenced by the concept of *Russkiy Mir* (Russian World) that expresses the nostalgic desire for the supposed glories of Russia-past and the duty to protect Russian speakers throughout Eurasia. Cf. Vladimir Sazonov, "The Ideology of Putin's Russia and Its Historical Roots," in Vladimir Sazonov, Holger Mölder, Kristiina Müür (ed.). Russian Information Warfare against the Ukrainian State and Defense Forces: April-December 2014, *Russian Information Warfare against the Ukrainian State and Defense Forces*, report, April-December (Riga: NATO Strategic Communications Center for Excellence, 2014), 20ff. *Russkiy Mir* is also visible in Moscow's expansionist efforts directed toward Ukraine and elsewhere.

72. Andrew Wood, "Cold War II?," *The American Interest*, July 18, 2018, the-american-interest.com/2018/07/18/cold-war-ii/. *OED: Raison d'état:* French, literally "reason of state." Andrew Wood, Associate

Fellow of the think tank, Chatham House, former British Ambassador to Belgrade and Moscow.

73. There is an obvious underlying thread of recognition of Russia's Historic National Interests running throughout Dugin's works. My use of Historic National Interests attempts to categorize Russia's long-standing efforts to accomplish identifiable national goals across Empire, USSR, and current Russian Federation history. Cf. Bassin, "Eurasianism and Russian Identity." Cf. references to Russia's Historic National Interests throughout.

74. Julia Gurganus and Eugene Rumer, "Russia's Global Ambitions in Perspective," February 20, 2019, carnegieendowment.org/2019/02/20/russia-s-global-ambitions-in-perspective-pub-78067. Julia Gurganus, Russian and Eurasian scholar of the American intelligence community. Eugene Rumer, Senior Fellow and Director, Russia and Eurasia Program, Carnegie Endowment for International Peace.

75. Gurganus and Rumer, "Russia's Global Ambitions in Perspective."

76. Ibid.

77. Cf. e.g., Bassin, "Eurasianism and Russian Identity" and Bassin, "Eurasianism 'Classical' and 'Neo.'"

78. Dugin, "The Eurasian Idea," under, Eurasianism as a Philosophical Struggle.

79. Ibid.

80. Ibid.

81. Andrei P. Tsygankov, "Mastering Space in Eurasia: Russia's Geopolitical Thinking after the Soviet Break-up," *Communist and Post-Communist Studies* 36, no. 1 (2003): 108. Andrei P. Tsygankov, Professor of Political Science and International Relations, San Francisco State University. Gennady Zyuganov became First Secretary of the Communist Party of the Russian Federation (found referred to as either CPRF or KPRF). He has made repeated unsuccessful bids for the presidency of the Russian Federation. Cf. John H. Mathews, "Gennady Andreyevich Zyuganov," *Encyclopædia Britannica*, updated June 22, 2919, britannica.com/biography/Gennady-Andreyevich-Zyuganov.

82. Tsygankov, "Mastering Space in Eurasia," 110.

83. Zbigniew Brzezinski, *The Grand Chessboard: American Primacy and Its Geostrategic Imperatives* (New York: Basic Books, 2016), 111. Cf. Laruelle, *Russian Eurasianism: An Ideology of*

Empire (Washington, DC: Woodrow Wilson Center Press, 2008), 69. Zbigniew Brzezinski, 1928- 2017.

84. Shlapentokh, *Russian Elite Image of Iran: From the Late Soviet Era to the Present* (Carlisle: Strategic Studies Institute, Army War College, 2009), 18. Cf. ssi.armywarcollege.edu/pdffiles/PUB936.pdf.

85. Wiederkehr, "Eurasianism as a Reaction to Pan-Turkism," 51.

86. Ibid., 51, 55. Cf. Wiederkehr's footnote 7. Here the ideas of Russian "historical mission" and Russia's Historic National Interest share common ground.

87. Ibid., 51. Cf. Wiederkehr's note, 1921a: 102–3; trans. slightly modified 1991: 99. Here Wiederkehr quoted Trubetskoi. Cf. *The Legacy of Genghis Khan and Other Essays on Russia's Identity*, ed. A. Liberman (Ann Arbor: Michigan Slavic Publications, 1991).

88. Ibid. Cf. Wiederkehr's note, 1925a: 351–52. Here Wiederkehr quoted Trubetskoi, "O turanskom èlemente v russkoi kul'ture." *Evraziiskii vremennik* 4: 351–77.

89. Ibid. Cf. Francis X. Clooney, *Comparative Theology: Deep Learning across Religious Borders* (Chichester: Wiley-Blackwell, 2010). Francis X. Clooney, Jesuit priest and scholar, professor, Harvard Divinity School.

90. Ibid., 52. Cf. Wiederkehr's note, 1991: 242. Here Wiederkehr quoted Trubetskoi, "Pan-Eurasian Nationalism," 29-30, translated from its original 1927 publication. Wiederkehr noted that the translation was slightly modified in Trubetzkoy, "Pan-Eurasian Nationalism," in *The Legacy of Genghis Khan and Other Essays on Russia's Identity*, 242.

91. Brzezinski, *The Grand Chessboard*, 110-111.

92. Ibid., 111. Cf. Eurasian National University, "Gumilev Biography," (in English): gumilevica.kulichki.net/English/bibliography.htm; (in Russian): gumilevica.kulichki.net/matter/Article15.htm.

93. Ibid. Brackets added.

94. Savitskii, *Exodus to the East*, 4. Cited in Wiederkehr, "Eurasianism Reaction to Pan-Turkism," 49-50.

95. Ibid. Cf. "Wiederkehr, Eurasianism Reaction to Pan-Turkism," 50.

96. Ibid. Cf. "Wiederkehr, Eurasianism Reaction to Pan-Turkism," 49.

97. Ibid. Cf. "Wiederkehr, Eurasianism Reaction to Pan-Turkism," 49-50.

98. Hosking, "Theory of Russian History." Often rendered as *Passionarnost*. Both spellings will be used herein depending on the spelling employed in the reference.

99. Wiederkehr, "Eurasianism Reaction to Pan-Turkism," 52. Here Wiederkehr is quoting Trubetskoi. Cf. Wiederkehr's note: 1927: 29–30; trans. slightly modified 1991: 242.

100. Ibid. Again, quoting Trubetskoi as above.

101. Ibid.

102. Hosking, "Theory of Russian History." Here Hosking interpreted Gumilev via Clover.

103. Ibid.

104. Ibid.

105. Laruelle, "Orient in Russian Thought," 11. Lev P. Karsavin, 1882-1952, historian, religious philosopher and medievalist. His complex religious philosophy contains elements of Eurasianism, anti-Westernism, unifying concepts, and resistance to Soviet intrusion into exercise of communal religious activities.

106. Ibid., 10.

107. Ibid., 11.

108. Trubetzkoy, "Europe and Mankind," in *The Legacy of Genghis Khan and Other Essays on Russia's Identity*, 59.

109. Cf. Trubetzkoy, "Europe and Mankind." Cf. Bassin, "Eurasianism and Russian Identity," 264. Here Bassin wrote that "Russia in other words was part of the colonial realm, of what some decades later we would become accustomed to call the 3rd World, and the stigma associated with this colonial status was particularly apposite at the moment he was writing, in the immediate aftermath of the revolution, for a weakened and defenseless Russia would be utterly powerless to resist European efforts to subjugate and exploit her even more fully."

110. Wiederkehr, "Eurasianism Reaction to Pan-Turkism," 52. Here Wiederkehr is quoting Trubetskoi. Cf. Wiederkehr's note: 1927: 29–30; trans. slightly modified 1991: 242.

111. Ibid.

112. Ibid.

113. Ibid.

114. Bassin, "Eurasianism and Russian Identity," 260.

115. Ibid.

116. Ibid.

117. Ibid.

118. Ibid., 265. Here Bassin is discussing Trubetskoi. Cf. Trubetzkoy, "The Russian Problem," in *The Legacy of Genghis Khan and Other Essays on Russia's Identity*, 107-108.

119. Trubetskoi, "The Russian Problem," 107.

120. Bassin, "Eurasianism and Russian Identity," 260.

121. Ibid., 266.

122. Ibid.

123. Ibid.

124. Ibid.

125. Ibid. Here Bassin is quoting Trubetskoi. Cf. Bassin's note 13. Cf. Trubetzkoy, "Pan-Eurasian Nationalism," 239.

126. Ibid., 267. Here Bassin is quoting Trubetskoi, as above. Bassin notes that this portion of the quote was given emphasis in the original.

127. Wiederkehr, "Eurasianism Reaction to Pan-Turkism," 52. Here quoting Trubetskoi.

128. Laruelle, "Orient in Russian Thought," 14.

129. Hosking, "Theory of Russian History."

130. Ibid.

131. Eurasian National University, "Gumilev Biography."

132. Ibid. Despite the awkward English evident in this biography, the gist is clear. Brackets added.

133. Ibid.

134. Ibid.

135. Ibid.

136. Hosking, "Theory of Russian History."

137. Cf. Laruelle, *Russian Eurasianism*, 116, for an examination considering biological determination. Cf. Jamil Brownson, "Landscape

& Ethnos: Reading L. N. Gumilev," Preface, accessed April 14, 2021, academia.edu/9179626/Landscape_and_Ethnos_Reading_Gumilev_Preface.

138. Dugin, *Fourth Theory*, 12, and footnote 5. Cf. Guy Debord, *Society of the Spectacle* (Detroit: Black and Red, 1977). Originally published in French in 1967, this work of Marxist Critical Theory and philosophy has been published several times in English and is also available in various translations from online sources. Cited in Alain Soral, "Why We Should Read Alexander Dugin," Foreword, in *The Fourth Political Theory*, trans. Sergio Knipe, 9. Also, Cf. Morgan, in *Fourth Theory*, 9, footnote 1. The *Spectacle*, as described, could apply as well to Communism, Fascism, and other forms of governance. Cf. e.g., Hoffer's descriptions and explanations of the power of propaganda in *The True Believer* and other of his works. Guy Debord, 1931-1994. Alain Soral, aka Alain Bonnet or Alain Bonnet de Soral, is a Franco-Swiss conspiracy theorist who was sentenced to a year in prison in France for denying the Holocaust. Cf. Michel Foucault, *The History of Sexuality* (Vancouver: Crane Library at the University of British Columbia, 2009). Michel Foucault, 1926-1984.

139. Morgan, in *Fourth Theory*, 12, footnote 5.

140. Cf. Laruelle, *Russian Eurasianism*, 116.

141. Jonathan Rushbrook, "Against the Thallassocracy: Fascism and Traditionalism in Alexander Dugin's Neo-Eurasianist Philosophy," Master's thesis, University of Tartu, 2015, 36. Note: Often found as *Thalassocracy*. Cf. e.g., Wiley Online Library, accessed January 8 2016, onlinelibrary.wiley.com/doi/10.1002/9781444338386.wbeah04305: "'Thalassocracy' is the phonetic adaptation of a noun meaning "sea power" in Greek. Ancient Greek historians, and particularly Thucydides, used the concept of "thalassocracy" as an analytical tool in investigating the past." Jonathan Rushbrook,

142. Bassin, "Eurasianism 'Classical' and 'Neo,'" 279-280.

143. Ibid.

144. Emanuel Copilaş, "Cultural Ideal or Geopolitical Project? Eurasianism's Paradoxes," *Strategic Impact* 3, no. 2009, 74. Cf. This article may be accessed at scribd.com/doc/47787411/Cultural-Ideal-or-Geopolitical-Project-Eurasianism-s-Paradoxes. Emanuel Copilaş, Professor, West University of Timosoara.

145. Copilaş, "Cultural Ideal or Geopolitical Project," 74.

119

146. Ibid. Applying Copilaş, the Primakov Doctrine can be summed up as: the U.S. refuses to accept a multipolar world; NATO's aspirations eastward intended to weaken one of the major multipolar actors—the Russian Federation. For a more detailed explanation of the Primakov Doctrine, Cf. e.g., Ariel Cohen, "The Primakov Doctrine: Russia's Zero-Sum Game with the United States," *Heritage Foundation, F.Y.I.* (Heritage Foundation, December 15, 1997), heritage.org/report/the-primakov-doctrine-russias-zero-sum-game-the-united-states. Ariel Cohen, Senior Fellow, Atlantic Council.

147. Dugin, "The Long Path: An Interview with Alexander Dugin," as part of his response to the first question, Open Revolt, May 17, 2014, openrevolt.info/2014/05/17/alexander-dugin-interview/. This interview is posted in English. *Open Revolt* does not state if this interview was originally conducted in Russian or English, nor make any notes on its translation. Brackets added in the assumption that "Slavs" corrects a typographical error.

148. Copilaş, "Cultural Ideal or Geopolitical Project?" 71. Cf. Copilaş' footnote 48.

149. Shlapentokh, "Eurasianism and Soviet/Post Soviet Studies," 4.

150. Ibid., 4ff.

151. Ibid., 4.

152. Dugin, *Fourth Theory*, 100. Similar to Muhammad Legenhausen's accusation aimed at Traditionalism, it may be that Neo-Eurasianism is largely a reaction to Westernism rather than an independent geopolitical formulation. Cf. Muhammad Legenhausen, "Why I Am Not a Traditionalist," Religioscope, March 31, 2002, religioscope.com/pdf/esotrad/legenhausen.pdf. Muhammad Legenhausen, Philosopher.

153. Dugin, *Fourth Theory*, 100. Cf. Terry Eagleton, *Literary Theory: an Introduction* (Oxford: Basil Blackwell, 1983), 97ff. Eagleton goes into some detail on Roman Jakobson and Claude Levi-Strauss and their involvement with the formulation of Structuralism. Terry Eagleton, Literary Theorist.

154. Laruelle, "Orient in Russian Thought," 10.

155. Ibid.

156. Dugin, "The Eurasian Idea," under, Eurasianism as a Philosophical Struggle.

157. Ibid.

158. Dugin, "Eurasia Above All," under, The Founding-Fathers of Eurasism. The term *Eurasist* occurs in this translation. Brackets added.

159. Dugin, "The Eurasian Idea," under, Towards Neo-Eurasianism, counter-currents.com/2013/11/the-eurasian/idea/

160. Dugin, "Eurasia Above All," under, The Founding Fathers of Eurasism. For comparison with Dugin's interpretation of Huntington in this regard, Cf. Part Two, under, The Geopolitics of Culture and Theology.

161. Ibid.

162. Ibid.

163. Dugin, "The Eurasian Idea," under, Unipolar globalization has an alternative.

164. Ibid., under, Eurasianism as Pluriversum.

165. Dugin, "Eurasia Above All," under, The Founding Fathers of Eurasism.

166. Ibid.

167. Ibid.

168. Ibid.

169. Ibid.

170. Bullets adapted from Dugin, "Eurasia Above All," under, The Founding Fathers of Eurasism.

171. Dugin, "Eurasian Idea and Postmodernism," under, Alternative Eurasian net in post modernistic world, accessed April 12, 2015, 4pt.su/en/content/eurasian-idea-and-postmodernism. Dugin addressed the Constitutive Conference of Eurasian International Movement in Moscow on April 21, 2001. This reference is a link to a transcript of Dugin's address. Brackets added.

Chapter Two: Confronting a Neo-Eurasian Reality

Concern with Putin's Russia occupies a significant amount of current attention in the West, but an increasing focus in a broader Eurasian context is needed. Fortunately, some increased attention is discernable. Brzezinski gave notable Western, especially American, attention to a Eurasian geopolitical reality as a potential threat to continuing American superpower supremacy. Echoing Mackinder, Brzezinski observed:

> How America "manages" Eurasia is critical. A power that dominates Eurasia would control two of the world's three most advanced and economically productive regions. A mere glance at the map also suggests that control over Eurasia would almost automatically entail Africa's subordination, rendering the Western Hemisphere and Oceania geopolitically peripheral to the world's central continent.[1]

These are strategically significant points. Brzezinski pointed out another with his observation that approximately three-quarters of the world's people live in Eurasia, and most of the world's physical wealth is located there as well.[2] The combined potential of Eurasia is unprecedented compared to most of the world.

Although decades have intervened, Brzezinski's concern over managing Eurasia is still recognizable in the West today. Not confining himself to a narrow economic focus, Brzezinski warned of the overall threat of rising Eurasian power exemplified in his imperative that no Eurasian challenger be allowed to emerge with the capability of dominating Eurasia, thus also able to challenge America.[3]

> America is now the only global superpower, and Eurasia is the globe's central arena. Hence, what happens to the distribution of power on the Eurasian continent will be of decisive importance

122

to America's global primacy and to America's historical legacy.[4]

While much Neo-Eurasian rhetoric appears to be defensive – providing a bulwark against the juggernaut of U.S.-led Western global domination—voices in the West have expressed similar conclusions. Brzezinski, for example, stated his case clearly and concluded prophetically:

> In the long run, global politics are bound to become increasingly uncongenial to the concentration of hegemonic power in the hands of a single state. Hence, America is not only the first, as well as the only, truly global superpower, but it is also likely to be the very last.[5]

Dugin would agree with Brzezinski concerning Eurasia's potential importance. The agreement appears to stop there. Taking up the Eurasian standard, Dugin not only opposes Brzezinski's doctrinal pronouncements implying the desirability of American hegemony, he also directly challenges them. When overlaid on today's geopolitical situation, Brzezinski's goal was to forestall a potentially overly powerful Eurasian political creation. In contrast, Dugin's goal is to limit America's power—in his eyes, the world monster.[6] "It follows that America's primary interest is to help ensure that no single power comes to control this geopolitical space and that the global community has unhindered financial and economic access to it," as Brzezinski expressed the American view.[7] Dugin's ambition is to see the creation of a multipolar world featuring a Russia-centric Eurasia. Thus, the lines are drawn.

To deny that Russia is casting a longing gaze on all of Ukraine, Poland, the Balkans, and Scandinavia is to engage in a naiveté that disregards Russia's Historic National Interests. Richard M. Langworth asked if Russia would "one day seek to reclaim the conquests of Peter the Great, regaining her ice-free Baltic coastline, which the Czars had dominated for centuries?"[8] "In the early 1930s," Langworth wrote, "the small republics could only hope that the Soviet treaties would hold, or that Germany would insist on preserving Baltic integrity for its own security interests."[9] At the time, others, including Winston Churchill, "were less optimistic."[10]

Ignoring Dugin's desires for Russia to continue beyond mere reclamation of the old Warsaw Pact territory—to the point of geographically expanding from Dublin to Vladivostok— disregards Dugin's repeated assertions. Recall that "Trubetskoi did not miss the opportunity to translate the old belief in Russia's messianic mission of salvation into terms appropriate to the early 20th century."[11] Neither does Dugin. He consciously and unflinchingly invests Eurasia with Tradition and a theologically based messianic and prophetic legacy.

Modeling Neo-Eurasianism

Instead of viewing the various religious expressions present in Europe and Asia as a hindrance to geopolitical cohesiveness, Dugin projects an ecumenical outreach. Neo-Eurasianism involves "integration of civil societies and its key institutions," considering "cultural, ethnic and confessional features," in Dugin's thinking.[12] Dugin's ecumenism allows for a "constructive solid dialogue between the creeds traditional for Russia— Orthodoxy, Islam, Judaism, Buddhism."[13] Dugin suggests that there are similar spiritual views within the religious Eurasian confines. This element of spiritual kinship "does not eliminate at all differences and originality of tenets," but it is "a serious and positive basis for rapprochement, mutual respect, mutual understanding."[14]

Dugin envisions an idealistic Russia; he establishes it as the keystone in the central arch of his Neo-Eurasian construct. The Russian keystone "gives the integration of Europe a Eurasian dimension in both the symbolic and geographic senses."[15] Russia and Turkey, related Dugin, are both ancestors of the Europeans, "and Russia is historically connected with the Turkic, Mongolian, and Caucasus nations."[16] This connection and similar historical and civilizational perspectives are part of the mortar that Dugin uses to cement his Neo-Eurasian construction. Though not original with Dugin, emphasis on the Slavic, Turkic, Mongolian, and Caucasus lash-up and their ultimate intertwined historical destiny is astute, and he boldly proclaims it.[17]

Dugin presents his Neo-Eurasianism as part of a construct wherein the nation-state declines in importance and power as the world becomes much more geopolitically focused. In Dugin's scheme, multipolar powers appear to emerge more as geographically and culturally centered zones and less as defined nation-states. Despite this, Dugin's commitment to the decline of nation-states is doubtful, at least as it applies to Russia. Dugin's Eurasia will comprise one of these zones, and it will be recognizably Russian in many respects. The long-term outcome may be a non-Russia-centric Eurasia, but Dugin's preferred near-term technique to achieve this result appears to be Russian expansion.

Dugin's argument is evident in a single paragraph wherein he concisely articulates his basic geopolitical trajectory.

> The Eurasian model is a contemplation of our current situation on the basis of a qualitative civilisational space. We must preserve the main impulse (geographical, historical, cultural, civilisational) of the previous stages in the development of our state and develop a brand new and unique mentality for twenty-first century Russia. We must move forward: not just go back into the past, but create a new synthesis.[18]

Creating a new synthesis is not an easy task, however. Dugin cannot merely fill in an outline on the map and call it Eurasia. In Dugin's thinking, even a peaceful multipolar world is undesirable to the unipolar-minded West. The particulars of a world where political theology is a featured characteristic appear to be beyond the pale of current Western acceptance. Dugin rejects any notion of a *Pax Americana* founded on unipolar globalization. Although a peaceful multipolar world may be possible, a mere glance at history and current widespread conflicts presents a stark and contrasting reality.

Defining a foundational block of Neo-Eurasianism, Dugin wrote that instead of following the Western path to its unipolar worldview, "the Eurasian Idea suggests that the planet consists of a constellation of autonomous living spaces partially open to each other."[19]

> These areas are not nation-states but a coalition of states, reorganized into continental federations or "democratic empires" with a large degree of inner self-government. Each of these areas is multipolar, including a complicated system of ethnic, cultural, religious and administrative factors.[20]

Dugin's Four-Zone Neo-Eurasian Model[21]

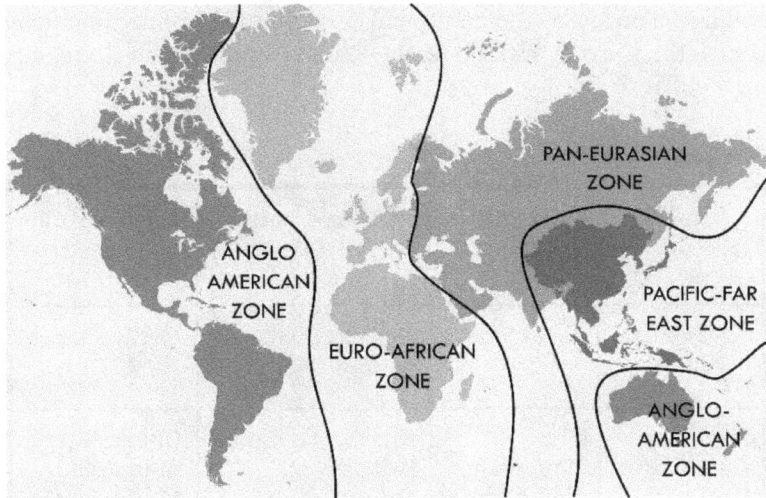

Mud Pie Graphics

Dugin envisions the globe divided into zones where "Eurasian plans for the future presume the division of the planet into four vertical geographical belts (meridian zones) from North to South."[22] Surprisingly, perhaps especially to those who believe that Dugin aspires to world domination for the future Eurasia, one of the planned zones, the Atlantic, contains both North and South America. This Atlantic Zone (Anglo-American Zone) "will form one common space oriented on and controlled by the USA within the framework of the Monroe Doctrine."[23]

Dugin's Neo-Eurasian model contains four poles, and their associated four zones are:[24]

- **Atlantic (Anglo-American)**
- **Euro-Africa (with the European Union as its center)**
- **Russian-Central Asian**
- **Pacific**

Realization of Dugin's concept depends on a multipolar counterbalance where each zone interacts with the others. For example, the significant global outreach of the Atlantic Zone is counterbalanced by the combined strength of the remaining three zones, the Euro-Africa Zone, the Russia-Central Asia Zone, and the Pacific Zone.[25]

The Great Spaces [29]

Atlantic Zone	Euro-Africa Zone	Russia-Central Asia Zone	Pacific Zone
Great Spaces	Great Spaces	Great Spaces	Great Spaces
American-Canadian, Central and South America, Australia*	The European Union, the Arab, Trans-Saharan Africa, the Middle East	Russian Federation (with several countries - the Eurasian Union), Continental Islamic countries, Asian countries of the CIS, Hindustan	China, Japan, Indonesia, Malaysia, the Philippines, and Australia*

The Great Spaces in Dugin's model are applied to correspond to the boundaries of the predominant civilizations with minimal regard for included nation-states or their current diplomatic or military agreements with one another.[26] According to Dugin, "the

Meridian zones of the Eurasian project consist of several 'Great Spaces' or 'democratic empires.'"[27] Each of these Great Spaces "possesses relative freedom and independence but are strategically integrated into a corresponding meridian zone."[28]

The inclusionary reach of the expansion minded Eurasianists was, according to Dugin, a much broader effort than it was in the days of the Russian Empire. "The founding-fathers of Eurasism for the first time gave the highest possible estimation to the multi-national (imperial) nature of the Russian State," in Dugin's assessment.[30] Dugin's division of the globe recalls the vision of a Eurasian expanse from Dublin to Vladivostok.

Almost pondering, Dugin wrote that "if we consider the alliance of the USA and Western Europe as the Atlantic vector of European development, European integration under the aegis of the continental countries (Germany, France) may be called European Eurasianism." [31] Then, as if to complete his thought, he added that his speculation "becomes more and more obvious" if a theory of Europe from the Atlantic Ocean to Vladivostok is considered.[32] Dugin then stated the obvious and underscored the massive geography involved with his understated conclusion that, "the integration of the Old World includes the vast territory of the Russian Federation."[33]

"Eurasianism is based on the multipolar vision," not a continuation of the unipolar hegemony of American globalism, Dugin explained.[34] Dugin believes that world events of recent decades in Russia and elsewhere have created an urgent and essential need for continuing development of the Neo-Eurasian model. Marxism has lost its appeal, but there is yet to appear a fully developed alternative to American-led Westernism, "a monster" about which "even the Europeans, the grandparents of the world monster, begin to feel nervous."[35]

Dugin's Eurasian model, "protects not only anti-Atlantic value systems, but the diversity of value structures."[36] Dugin's Eurasian construct "provides living space for everyone, including the USA and Atlantism, along with other civilizations, because Eurasianism also defends the civilizations of Africa, both American continents, and the Pacific area parallel to the Eurasian Motherland."[37]

Notes

1. Brzezinski, *The Grand Chessboard*, 31. Cf. Mackinder, "Geographical Pivot of History."

2. Ibid.

3. Ibid., xiv.

4. Ibid., 194. We must, of course, consider this statement from the perspective of the elapsed time since Brzezinski wrote it.

5. Ibid., 209. Today, China is challenging Brzezinski's notion.

6. Dugin, "Eurasia Above All," under, Neo-Eurasism.

7. Brzezinski, *The Grand Chessboard*, 148.

8. Richard M. Langworth, "Churchill and the Baltic," April 28, 2017, winstonchurchill.hillsdale.edu/churchill-baltic-part-2/. Richard M. Langworth, Senior Fellow, Churchill Project, Hillsdale College.

9. Langworth, "Churchill and the Baltic."

10. Ibid.

11. Bassin, "Eurasianism and Russian Identity," 265.

12. Dugin, "Eurasian Idea and Postmodernism," under, Actuality of Movement to current politics.

13. Dugin, "Eurasia Above All," under, Priorities of the Eurasia movement.

14. Ibid.

15. Dugin, "The Eurasian Idea," under, Integration of the Eurasian Continent.

16. Ibid.

17. Ibid. This line of thinking is evident throughout his article. Dugin acknowledges Eurasian pioneers and endorses the mutual commonality of the Eurasian destiny of the various ethnic groups involved.

18. Dugin, *Putin vs Putin*, 134.

19. Dugin, "The Eurasian Idea," under, Eurasianism as Pluriversum.

20. Ibid.

21. Adapted from: Dugin, "Eurasian Idea." Some researchers connect Australia with the Atlantic (Anglo-American) Meridian zone. Cf.

4pt.su/en/content/eurasia-above-all for an example of another map rendition of Dugin's Zones and Great Spaces. Dugin's Four-Zone Neo-Eurasian Model has been illustrated in several different iterations; this figure is based on conceptions current at the time of this writing.

22. Dugin, "The Eurasian Idea," under, Three Eurasian belts (Meridian Zones).

23. Ibid.

24. Adapted from: Dugin, "Eurasian Idea." There appears to be some contradiction here; assuming a Dublin to Vladivostok reality, the European Union would have to become a Eurasian subset.

25. Dugin, "The Eurasian Idea," under, Three Eurasian belts (Meridian Zones).

26. Ibid.

27. Ibid.

28. Ibid.

29. Adapted from: Dugin, "Eurasian Idea." Again, whether the placement of Australia and New Zealand, for example is included in the Atlantic (Anglo-American) Zone or the Pacific Zone is somewhat unclear.

30. Dugin, "Eurasia Above All," under, The Founding-Fathers of Eurasism. Parentheses in original.

31. Ibid., under, Integration of the Eurasian Continent.

32. Ibid.

33. Ibid.

34. Dugin, "The Long Path," as part of his response to the second question.

35. Dugin, "Eurasia Above All," under, Neo-Eurasism.

36. Ibid., under, Atlantism is not Universal.

37. Ibid.

Chapter Three: Sacred Geography/ Sacred Space

Accepting Russia as Sacred Geography

Dugin's understanding of Russia as *the* nation with a divinely given messianic mission includes his accepting that it occupies Sacred Space. The very geography of Russia, Dugin believes, contains specific holy features. Acknowledging the underlying Fourth Political Theory idea of Russia's messianic Manifest Destiny is also necessary when exploring his concept of Eurasia. Essential to Fourth Political Theory is Dugin's development of Neo-Eurasianism that depends on a Eurasian reality constructed within Sacred Space, Russia's, hence Eurasia's, messianic mission, and its Manifest Destiny.

Paul Coyer noted the impact of *Duginsque* thinking by highlighting the spiritual importance Putin attached to Russia's claims in Ukraine.[1] Coyer connected Russia's annexation of Crimea in 2014 with its "sacred" links to the "birthplace of the Russian nation" by quoting Putin saying that Crimea is "spiritual soil" where Russian "ancestors first and forever recognized their nationhood."[2] Dugin imagines Eurasia as much more than a classification of physical geography. He realizes Eurasia as Sacred Geography/Sacred Space.[3] Dugin further anticipates Eurasia as a combined spiritual and geopolitical reality stretching from the boundaries of Europe on the west to those of Asia on the east—in the familiar Dublin to Vladivostok refrain.

In Dugin's perception, Eurasia contains a spiritual dimension that is inextricably melded with its physical reality. Sacred Geography is compatible with ideas of Sacred Space—recognizing that various land and water locations contain significant and persistent metaphysical properties. Dugin has written in some depth concerning his ideas of Sacred Geography. His article, "From Sacred Geography to Geopolitics," for example, is comprehensive and provides a helpful window into Dugin's thinking.[4] Evident in this work, Dugin's conception is compatible with a range of Sacred Geography/Sacred Space literature and other research focused on indigenous peoples and their concepts of the spiritual aspects of land and water.

131

Reviewing Rossman's treatment of Sacred Geography/Sacred Space, in his "Anti-Semitism in Eurasian Historiography: The Case of Lev Gumilev," preparatory to overlaying more overtly geopolitical layers on Dugin's Neo-Eurasian model is useful.[5] Rossman's claim that Russians, more than others, place critical importance on geography is necessary to understanding Dugin. Lacking depth of metaphysical awareness, the contemporary West cannot adequately grasp Rossman's extensive evidence that "Russians regard space as sacred."[6] Dugin displays multiple awarenesses of Sacred Geography, and this fact sheds light on his perceptions and conclusions. Dugin accepts, as reality, sacred characteristics of geography that the West holds as largely imaginary or superstitious. This Western interpretation of geographical reality is the product of a materialistic-centered misunderstanding, in Dugin's opinion.[7]

Judaism, Christianity, and Islam are replete with examples of Sacred Geography. Stephen R. Burge wrote that Mircea Eliade pioneered "religious theories of sacred space in the 1950s and 1960s."[8] Eliade's works, *Sacred and the Profane* and *Myth of the Eternal Return*, provide foundational understandings of Dugin's later conceptualization of Sacred Geography.[9] Illustratively, Geoffrey Simmins, in his book *Sacred Spaces and Sacred Places,* displayed his comprehensive research into Native American perceptions of Sacred Space and the importance attached to cardinal compass directions.[10] Simmins' work bears interesting parallels to the considerable treatment Dugin gives to the cardinal points and their metaphysical connections.[11] Hui-Chih Yu's commentary on color associations in their geographical context can also be linked to Dugin's Sacred Geography conclusions.[12]

When examining Dugin's Neo-Eurasianism, John Fiske's notions of *Imperializing Power* and *Localizing Power* are applicable.[13] Bill Kirkpatrick said that these two powers represent "a powerful framework for thinking through different kinds and directionalities of power, resistance, governmentality, and agency."[14] "Imperializing power seeks to extend its reach as far as possible over physical reality, society, and consciousness," said Kirkpatrick.[15] Fiske's notion is pertinent and vital when assessing the impact of Dugin within both Russian and Western academic and political circles because of Dugin's Fourth Political Theory expansionist and imperialist leanings.

Dugin's critique of the West incorporates elements of Imperializing Power as he disparages Western globalist desires. Interestingly, Imperializing Power concepts can offer insights into both Eurasian expansionism and Western globalism. Dugin suggests that Eurasian expansion is limited to defined geographic ambitions, whereas Western global desires describe a universal imperialistic undertaking.

Physical features figure prominently in concepts of Sacred Space when recognizing that Imperializing Power desires to affect physical reality. Dugin emphasized that "varieties of landscape in sacred geography are understood as symbolical [sic] complexes linked to the specificity of state, religious and ethical ideology of the different peoples."[16] These linkages are more than mere longings or recognitions. Physical geography is deeply connected with "'spirit,' 'contemplation,'" and "resignation to superhuman force" in sacred civilizations.[17] These connections have been, and remain as positives, "for the Eastern peoples at the level of [the] 'collective unconscious.'"[18]

Dugin, however, is individually conscious of sacral geometrical constituents within Sacred Geography. He believes in a world situated along various axes of power.[19] Alignment of the axes connecting Sacred Poles governs the location and recognition of areas or territories of geography possessing a sacred nature.[20] Dugin does not describe the cardinal points as Sacred Geometry, associated with celestial and seasonal changes, as do many allegorical renditions, but draws axes of power by connecting the Sacred Poles.[21] In a similar vein, Philip Sheldrake remarked, "For Eliade, every sacred place was thought of as an *axis mundi*, the center of the world, with boundaries separating it from surrounding secular or profane space."[22] Sheldrake clarified that "Such places were a kind of Jacob's ladder linking heaven and earth."[23]

Following this perception, the characteristics and attributes of the cardinal points supporting Sacred Geography in Dugin's theory may be examined:

Along the East-West axis were drawn peoples and civilizations, possessing hierarchical characters—closer to the East were those closer to Sacral, to Tradition, to spiritual wealth. Closer to West, those of a more decayed, degraded and dying Spirit.[24]

Similarly, Dugin related that "in sacred geography the West is the side of death, darkness, and decline, the East of life, bloom, and light."[25] Dugin's claim that "the West and the Jewish tradition are associated with Atlantis," whereas "the pure primordial tradition" is associated "with Hyperborea," demonstrates his persistent co-mingling of spiritual and geographical elements.[26]

Metaphorically, the "South is a civilization of the Moon receiving the light from the Sun" associated with a North civilization.[27] The moon reflects the sun's light, "preserving and diffusing it for some time, but periodically losing contact with it," waning until it becomes a new moon.[28] It would be unperceptive not to associate the solar and lunar symbolism used here with the symbolic language of many indigenous and pagan religious traditions. Dugin holds that Nordic-type persons better recognize the persistence of awe and other pointers toward perennial Truth.[29]

In contrast, those belonging to the South worship life as the highest authority. Southern people relate to *carpe diem*, instead of being in the world but not of it—those belonging to the South worship life as the highest attainment.[30] People of the South live "by passions and rushes," putting "the psychic above the spiritual" that they do not understand.[31] "The cult of the Great Mother" defines their worship, however unconscious they are of it.[32] Therefore, the South's focus is materialistic; matter-generating-matter is the shallow extent of its existential awareness.[33]

"The man of the South is a Mondmensch," according to Dugin.[34] Dugin's conception of Mondmensch seems close to José Ortega's explanation of the "mass-man."[35] The mass-man is surrounded by marvelous instruments, effective medicines, comfort, and "watchful governments."[36] But, despite the environment, "he is ignorant how difficult it is to invent those medicines and those instruments and to assure their production in the future."[37] Additionally, mass-man does not realize the

134

instability of the state organization nor recognize any personal obligations to it.[38]

In stark contrast to Mondmensch—the Moon Man of the South—stands *Sonnenmensch*—Sun Man of the North.[39] "The man of North is a particular kind of being possessing a straight intuition of the Sacred," wrote Dugin, and Sonnenmensch well understands that "the cosmos is a texture of symbols, each of them called out of secret by the eye of the Spiritual First Principle."[40] "The man of North" is the "solar man," and is not Mondmensch— the mass-man described by Ortega.[41] Sonnenmensch is "not absorbing energy, as black holes do;" he is not an existential materialist, but a source of light, force, and wisdom flowing from creation.[42]

Dugin espouses Northern superiority, "the sacred North, the archetype of North," half immersed in history derived from the natural landscape and half immersed in Nordism—the concept of being Northern.[43] Nordism can still be found, according to Dugin, wherever "true spirituality, supra-rational Mind, divine Logos," and the capacity to see the "secret Soul" of the world is present.[44] Dugin stated that "Northness" may be perceived across a wide range of references and offers the example of "ancient Iranic and Zoroastrian texts."[45] These texts mention "the northern country of '*Aryiana Vaeijao*' and its capital '*Vara*,' from where the ancient arians [sic] were expelled by glaciation."[46]

Dugin's examples also include the Veda, where ancient texts "speak about the Northern country as the ancestral home of the Hindu, about a *Sveta-dipa*, White Land laying [sic] in the far north."[47] Examples extend throughout the cyclic concept of space-time with Dugin associations of a Nordic Race of Teachers with the Sacred North.[48] He will have us accept that these Nordic Teachers carry on today, although the pure Nordic civilization was lost with the disappearance of the ancient paleocontinent of Hyperborea.[49] Nonetheless, trace evidence of a "Hyperborean Cult" remains among the North American Indians, ancient Slavs, founders of the Chinese civilization, and natives of the Pacific.[50] Dugin also maintained that residual evidence could be detected in blond Germans, black shamans of Western Africa, red-skinned Aztecs, and "among the Mongols with wide cheek-bones."[51]

We must take care not to assign overt racism to Dugin's characterization of Nordism. The ancient Nordics, "the race of the 'white teachers'" associated with the North "in the primordial epoch, does not coincide at all" with the "white race" of today, Dugin explained.[52] True Nordism today is not based on physical characteristics or skin color, according to Dugin.[53] However, to the discerning, evidence for the Sonnenmensch can be detected even in the world's diversity. "There is no such people on the planet, which would not have a myth about the 'solar man,'" Dugin wrote.[54] "Wherever there is Sacred Purity and Wisdom, there invisibly is the North," in Dugin's view.[55.]

The Great War of North Versus South

The Preacher of Ecclesiastes tells that there is nothing new or original in this world.

> That which has been is that which will be, and that which has been done is that which will be done. So there is nothing new under the sun. Already it has existed for ages which were before us.[56]

As part of this continuous recurrence, Dugin tells that a great war has been raging in cyclic space-time—it rages now, and it will continue to rage until the end-times. In what Dugin referred to as "'antidiluvian' times," the time before the flood described in Genesis and elsewhere, there were two "ancient paleo-continents," Hyperborea and Gondvana.[57]

Dugin associated North and South attributes, both geographically, spiritually, and allegorically with these two now-lost continents. In the axial shift that occurred sometime in deep pre-history, the qualities of the sacred North and South have become correspondingly attributed to East and West. The symbolic, metaphorical, and allegorical attributes of East and West remain but they are now invested with the sacred qualities heretofore respectively assigned to North and South.

The great war of North and South, Hyperborea
and Gondvana refers to "antidiluvian" times. In
the last phases of the cycle it becomes more
hidden, veiled. The paleo-continents of North and
South themselves disappear. The testimonial sign
of opposition is passed to East and West.[58]

The East inherits tradition and origin and is sacred.[59] The
West inherits decay and is profane.[60] A direct link is detectable
from the esoteric "testimonial sign of opposition," inherited by the
East, to the style of anti-Westernism so vividly displayed in Fourth
Political Theory and throughout Dugin's other offerings.[61] Dugin
believes that "Modern geopolitics understands the terms 'North'
and 'South' as wholly different categories than sacred geography
does."[62] Sacred Geography understands that "the symbolical
North univocally corresponds to positive aspects, and the South to
negative," wrote Dugin.[63] But, "in an exclusively modern
geopolitical picture of the world everything is much more
complex, and to some extent even turned upside down."[64]

Earth and Ocean

In his explanation of Sacred Geography, Dugin radically
reduced the four ancient elements of Earth, Water, Air, and Fire
to only two—Earth and Water—saying that Earth and Sea

are in essence the major categories of earthly
existence, and for mankind it is impossible not to
see in them some basic attributes of the universe.
As the two basic terms of geopolitics, they
preserve their significance both for civilizations
of a traditional kind and for exclusively modern
states, peoples and ideological blocks.[65]

These two broad categories connect to the two related terms,
Tellurocracy and Thalassocracy.[66] In these definitions, it is not
difficult to detect discernable links to Dugin's Atlantis
associations with oceans and sea-power.[67] Dugin noted that
historically, "thalassocracy is linked to the West and the Atlantic

137

Ocean."[68] Thalassocratia is the geopolitical territory characterized by its close association with the sea, and as it is able, primarily projects sea-power. Thalassocratic states often have or had an active colonial component, and their territory is often not contiguous.

Dugin implied that this non-contiguous characteristic "creates an element of discontinuity" within Thalassocratic states.[69] Tellurocratia is the geopolitical territory characterized by its close association with the land and primarily projects land-power. Tellurocratic states usually locate their capitals and provinces contiguously—there is territorial continuity. Dugin associates Tellurocratia with the East and Eurasia.[70]

Dugin claims that empires do not settle themselves in mountain regions. Expansionist impulse is not initiated from the mountains. Instead, there are found sanctuaries, fortresses, and retreats where "the victims of the geopolitical expansion of other tellurocratic forces" are concentrated.[71] "No empire has its centre in mountain regions," according to Dugin.[72] This observation led Dugin to suggest that the expression "mountains are populated by demons" may reflect the historical dearth of mountain-centered states.[73] Nonetheless, mountains remain the habitat of things spiritual.

Dugin stated that "it is even possible to say that in tellurocracies a mountain corresponds to some spiritual power."[74] "On the mountains the sacred centres of tradition are placed," said Dugin.[75] Consider Mount Olympus or Mount Sinai as examples of the sacred attachment to geographical features. Some biblical scholars believe Jesus' Sermon on the Mount to have occurred at a site where its divine importance may be associated with symbolic similarity to the transmission of the Law to Moses on Sinai.[76]

Although Dugin rejects the mountain as a tellurocratic political center, he does recognize the authority and power bestowed by elevation. Dugin suffuses the development of physical elevation symbolism into his geopolitical theology, where hills are located between the elevated spiritual power of the mountain and the "secular level of the steppe."[77] "The hill," not the mountain, "is a symbol of imperial might," Dugin stated.[78] The hill is "above the secular level of the steppe, but not reaching the

138

limit of supreme power," the mountain—the dwelling place of the gods.[79] Mountains are the abode of divine beings, the lesser high ground being associated with temporal authority and power. "A hill is a dwelling place for a king, a count, an emperor," Dugin wrote, adding that "capitals of large tellurocratic empires are placed on a hill or on hills."[80]

Dugin does not consider forests as the location for the capital of a Tellurocracy. Dugin explained, "the forest in sacred geography is close to the mountains in a definite sense."[81] That is to say, "the symbolism of the tree is related to the symbolism of the mountain."[82] "Therefore," Dugin elaborated, "in tellurocracies the forest also plays a peripheral function"—also being the "'place of the priests' (druids, magi, hermits), but also at the same time," as a residual of the ancient past, it is the "place of demons."[83]

Portraying the West as Atlantis

Dugin connects Fourth Political Theory through symbolism, allegory, and metaphor to Greek and Platonic thought. Perhaps the most familiar of these connections is Dugin's frequent references equating the West with Atlantis. Casting Proclus in the role of a prototype Neo-Platonist, Dugin commented that, "in his commentary on the dialogue 'Critias' of Plato," Proclus described "the war between the Greeks and the prehistoric people of Atlantis as the paradigmatic war between two orders of being: one perfect and the other degraded."[84]

It should be no surprise which attributes Dugin attaches to Eurasia and which are identified with the West. "Proclus said that the Greeks were connected to the earth and the Atlanteans to the sea."[85] Dugin somewhat mischievously claimed that Proclus was an ancient geopolitician.[86]

Dugin's Eurasia channels the mythical Northern Continent of Hyperborea.[87] Hyperborea fought against Atlantis in an ancient war that Dugin applied to the present day. In later mythology, the Greeks also fought Atlantis. The Greek-Atlantis war is strikingly similar to the Hyperborean-Atlantis conflict. "The Greeks were alongside the Olympian gods and the people of Atlantis alongside Titans," Dugin wrote.[88] "The maritime geopolitics of the Titans against the telluric geopolitics of the Gods," is how Dugin put it.[89]

Dugin projects the strife between Greece and Atlantis and Hyperborea and Atlantis into the present—Hyperborea/Greece representing Eurasia and Atlantis representing the West.[90]

Dugin continually contrasts the Western secular approach to geopolitical questions with his metaphysical beliefs. "Geopoliticians," Dugin stated for example, "stared at the fact of a fundamental difference between 'insular' and 'continental' powers, between 'western,' 'progressive' civilization and 'eastern,' 'despotic' and 'archaic' cultural forms," and missed a critical element.[91] Because, for Western geopoliticians, "the question about Spirit in its metaphysical and sacred comprehension never arose in modern science," they left it aside, wrote Dugin.[92] Western geopoliticians prefer "to evaluate the situation in different, more modern terms, rather than through the concepts of 'sacred' and 'profane,' 'traditional' and 'antitraditional.'"[93]

Dugin has written that he understands the Western affinity towards universalism, but he rejects any claim that universalism is inevitable.[94] While his "Eurasianism absolutely rejects the universal triumph of Atlantism and Americanism," Dugin admits that there is a pattern in the development of "Western-Europe and America," that possesses "many attractive features that can be adopted and praised."[95] With this admission, Dugin expressed the Eurasian idea of multipolarity, where the Atlantic Zone will remain—although, as merely a cultural system with a right to exist.

Clover pointed out that when Dugin wrote *Foundations of Geopolitics,* "it didn't seem to matter," that an inspired Eurasian trajectory in Russian policy "seemed completely insane."[96] At that time, Clover reported, "Russia's GDP was smaller than that of the Netherlands, while the once formidable Red Army had just been defeated on the battlefield and forced into a humiliating peace by a ragtag group of Chechen insurgents."[97] The depth of Russia's decline at the time may be a matter of some debate. Nevertheless, Clover was right; it did not matter so much in 1997. In light of the Russian resurgence, however, Dugin's ideas matter now.

A Spiritual Shift of the North-South Axis

Hyperborea, however real or mythic, disappeared long ago. But, it "does not exist on a physical level," it does remain "a spiritual reality," on which the spiritual vision of those enlightened reflects Hyperborea's original and Traditional position.[98] Dugin's Sacred Geography narrative is attempting to expose spiritual Truth within a Traditionalist understanding: "North in Tradition is a meta-historical and meta-geographical reality,"[99] Moreover, with equal certainty and the same Traditional approach, he affirms the existence of "the 'hyperborean race'—a 'race' not in the biological, but in [a] pure spiritual, metaphysical sense."[100]

Evola wrote in his autobiography that "three levels of racism ought to be distinguished in order to reflect the three kinds of races: the first level of racism pertaining to the race of the body, the second to the race of the character, and the third to the race of the spirit."[101] Dugin informed us that "the continents and their populations in our epoch have gone extremely far from those archetypes, which corresponded to them in primordial times."[102]

> Between real continents and real races (the realities of modern geopolitics), on the one hand, and meta-continents and meta-races (the realities of traditional sacred geography), on the other hand, today there exist not just a simple discrepancy, but almost an inverse correspondence.[103]

A metaphysical shift has occurred, and the Traditional views formerly held concerning the North and its Nordic Race have been transposed into the Sacred Geography of the East. Not only that, but the cosmic War of the Continents has also now become an east-west vice a north-south engagement. Herein lies Dugin's critical geopolitical and metaphysical concerns for today—the subsuming of the Sacred Geography of East and West into the current geopolitical juxtapositions of a multipolar and anti-modern East and a unipolar and a materially focused West.

Notes

1. Paul Coyer, "The Patriarch, The Pope, Ukraine, and the Disintegration Of The Russian World," *Forbes*, March 20, 2016, forbes.com/sites/paulcoyer/2016/03/20/the-patriarch-the-pope-ukraine-and-the-disintegration-of-the-russian-world/. Paul Coyer, Research Professor, The Institute of World Politics in Washington, D.C.

2. Coyer, "Patriarch Pope Ukraine."

3. Herein, these two terms are used interchangeably.

4. Cf. Dugin, "From Sacred Geography." This article, in its entirety, provides a window into Dugin's thinking and reveals clear examples of his metaphysical and esoteric mindset.

5. Cf. Rossman, "Anti-Semitism in Eurasian Historiography."

6. Ibid., 164. Here Rossman is quoting Dugin; Cf. Rossman's note: 1994b, i.e., "Apologiia natsionalisma." In Konservativnaiia revolutsiia. 142.

7. Dugin, "From Sacred Geometry," under, From Continents to Meta-Continents.

8. S.R. Burge, "Angels, Ritual and Sacred Space in Islam," *Comparative Islamic Studies* 5, no. 2 (2009): 221. Stephen R. Burge, Senior Research Associate, Institute of Islamic Studies.

9. Cf. Mircea Eliade, *The Sacred and the Profane: The Nature of Religion* (New York: Harcourt, Brace and World, 1959) and Eliade, *The Myth of the Eternal Return, or, Cosmos and History* (Princeton: Princeton University Press, 1954). Mircea Eliade, 1907-1986.

10. Geoffrey Simmins, *Sacred Spaces and Sacred Places* (Saarbrücken: VDM Verlag, 2009). A copy of this article may be accessed at dspace.ucalgary.ca/bitstream/1880/46834/1/Sacred%20Spaces.pdf. Also: scribd.com/document/135325460/Sacred-Spaces-pdf. Geoffrey Simmins, former Associate Dean, Research and Planning, University of Calgary's Faculty of Arts.

11. Simmins, *Sacred Spaces and Sacred Places*, 15ff.

12. Hui-Chih Yu, "A Cross-Cultural Analysis of Symbolic Meanings of Color," *Chang Gung Journal of Humanities and Social Sciences* 7, no. 1 (April 2014): 49-74

13. Bill Kirkpatrick, "Play, Power, and Policy: Putting John Fiske Back into Media Policy Studies," Fiske Matters: A Conference on John Fiske's Continuing Legacy for Cultural Studies. University of Wisconsin—Madison, June 11, 2010, billkirkpatrick.net/scholarship/fiske/. Emphasis added. Bill Kirkpatrick, Professor, University of Winnipeg.

14. Kirkpatrick, "Play, Power, and Policy."

15. Ibid.

16. Dugin, "From Sacred Geography," under, Symbolism of landscape. Brackets added.

17. Ibid., under, East and West in Modern Geopolitics.

18. Ibid. Brackets added.

19. Ibid. Dugin describes several of these axes in this article.

20. Ibid.

21. Ibid.

22. Philip Sheldrake, *Spaces for the Sacred: Place, Memory, and Identity* (Baltimore: Johns Hopkins University Press, 2001), 5. Cf. Eliade, *Images and Symbols: Studies in Religious Symbolism*, trans. Philip Mairet (Princeton, NJ: Princeton University Press, 1991), 40ff. Philip Sheldrake, Theologian, Cambridge, Georgetown, and other universities.

23. Sheldrake, *Spaces for the Sacred*, 1.

24. Dugin, "From Sacred Geography," under, East and West in Sacred Geography.

25. Rossman, "Anti-Semitism in Eurasian Historiography," 174. Rossman cites Dugin, "Ot sakralnoi geografii k geopolitike." *Elementi* 4, 42-43. Rossman suggests that for "the Atlantic origins of Jewish tradition," Cf. Guénon, "Mesto atlanticheskoi traditsii v Manvantare," *Milii Angel* 1, 16-17.

26. Ibid. Here Rossman is quoting Dugin. Dugin bestows the mantle of Hyperborea on the East.

27. Dugin, "From Sacred Geography," under, The People of the South.

28. Ibid.

29. Dugin, "From Sacred Geography," under, The People of the North.

30. John 17: 14-15, NASB.

31. Dugin, "From Sacred Geography," under, The People of the South.

32. Ibid.

33. Ibid.

34. Ibid.

35. Cf. José Ortega y Gasset, *The Revolt of the Masses* (New York: W.W. Norton, 1932); Originally published as, *Le Rebelión de las Masas*, 1930. José Ortega y Gasset, 1883-1955.

36. Ortega, *Revolt of the Masses*, 102.

37. Ibid.

38. Ibid.

39. Ibid.

40. Dugin, "From Sacred Geography," under, The People of the North.

41. Ibid. Cf. Ortega, *Revolt of the Masses*, 58ff. Consider Ortega's elaboration on the "mass man:" "the free expansion of his vital desires, and therefore, of his personality; and his radical ingratitude towards all that has made possible his ease of his existence."

42. Ibid.

43. Ibid., under, Sacred North and Sacred South.

44. Ibid., under, The People of the North. Soul is capitalized in the original.

45. Ibid., under, Sacred North and Sacred South.

46. Ibid. Brackets added.

47. Ibid. Brackets added.

48. Ibid., under, The People of the North.

49. Ibid.

50. Ibid.

51. Ibid.

52. Ibid., under, From Continents to Meta-Continents.

53. Ibid.

54. Ibid., under, The People of the North.

55. Ibid.

56. Ecclesiastes 1:9-10, NASB.

57. Dugin, "From Sacred Geography," under, Sacred North and Sacred South.

58. Ibid.

57. Ibid., under, From Continents to Meta-Continents.

58. Ibid., under, From Continents to Meta-Continents. Dugin makes this point with certainty—Traditionalism is an expression of ultimate Truth. Cf. numerous references herein.

59. Ibid., under, Sacred North and Sacred South. This theme is consistent throughout the article.

60. Ibid. This theme is also consistent throughout the article.

61. Ibid.

62. Ibid., under, From Continents to Meta-Continents.

63. Ibid.

64. Ibid.

65. Ibid., under, Land and Sea.

66. Ibid.

67. Dugin's use of terms *Atlantis*, *Atlantic*, and various associated and translation altered spellings, usually refer to the same subject: the sea-power orientation of America and most, if not all, of the Anglosphere. Cf. Hannan, *Inventing Freedom.*

68. Dugin, "From Sacred Geography," under, Land and Sea.

69. Ibid.

70. Ibid. Dugin writes that the example of Japan being Tellurocratic "is explained by the stronger 'attractive' effect of Eurasia."

71. Ibid., under, Symbolism of landscape.

72. Ibid.

73. Ibid.

74. Ibid.

75. Ibid.

76. Cf. "Sermon on the Mount," Oxford Biblical Studies Online, accessed February 28, 2018, oxfordbiblicalstudies.com/article/opr/t94/e1725.

77. Dugin, "From Sacred Geography," under, Symbolism of landscape.

78. Ibid.

79. Ibid.

80. Ibid.

81. Ibid.

82. Ibid.

83. Ibid.

84. Dugin, "The Figure of the Radical Subject," under, Part 1, Traditionalism and Sociology—The Modern and the Eternal.

85. Ibid.

86. Ibid.

87. I use "Channels" here considering the OED definition of the verb associated with a medium and spirit.

88. Dugin, "The Figure of the Radical Subject," under, Part 1, Traditionalism and Sociology—The Modern and the Eternal. Cf. ordoabchao.ca/volume-five/sacred-geopolitics?rq=sacred%20 for a viewpoint differing somewhat from Dugin's linkage of Hyperborea with Atlantis.

89. Ibid.

90. Ibid.

91. Dugin, "From Sacred Geography," under, East and West in modern geopolitics.

92. Ibid.

93. Ibid.

94. Dugin, *Fourth Theory*, 136.

95. Dugin, *Eurasian Mission: An Introduction to Neo-Eurasianism* (Leipzig: Renovamen Verlag, 2016), 44.

96. Clover, "In Moscow, a New Eurasianism," *Journal of International Security Affairs* Fall/Winter, no. 27 (2014). Cf. securityaffairs.org/sites/default/files/issues/fall_winter2014.pdf. Cf. the

Clover posted copy, "in Moscow, a New Eurasianism, StopFake.org. February 10, 2015, stopfake.org/en/in-moscow-a-new-eurasianism/. Clover has examined a multi-decade experience of Eurasianist study. Cf. *Black Wind, White Snow* and "Dreams of the Eurasian Heartland: The Reemergence of Geopolitics." Both deal directly with trends of the Russian geopolitical trajectory.

97. Clover, "A New Eurasianism."

98. Dugin, "From Sacred Geography," under, From Continents to Meta-Continents.

99. Ibid. Dugin makes this point with certainty – Traditionalism is an expression of ultimate Truth.

100. Ibid. Brackets added.

101. Evola, *The Path of Cinnabar: An Intellectual Autobiography*, trans. Sergio Knipe, ed. John B. Morgan (London: Integral Tradition Pub., 2009), 169. Here "racism" is intended as distinguishable characteristics rather than as a negative and pejorative characterization of a person or group.

102. Dugin, "From Sacred Geography," under, From Continents to Meta-Continents.

103. Ibid.

Chapter Four: Reviving Great Power Status

Concerning Russian Purposes and Intent

The Expert Commission on Norwegian Security and Defence Policy clearly expressed Russian intentions pointing out that Russia, "under President Vladimir Putin is an authoritarian and anti-Western state with significant great power ambitions."[1]

Recovering Great Power Status

It is interesting to note that a recent Carnegie report concerning Russia in the High North was published under the heading of *The Return of Global Russia.*[2] According to Laruelle, Russia's High North strategy "is based on three major objectives."[3]

1. First: considering its place on the world stage, Russia sees the High North "as a place to reassert its prestige and status as a great power."[4]

2. Second: considering security, "Russia wants to reassert its territorial sovereignty along the borders of the Arctic Zone of the Russian Federation (AZRF), established in 2013." This zone includes all the territories of Russia's Far North close to the Arctic Ocean or connected to it for economic reasons.[5]

3. Third: considering its domestic situation, "Russia's ambition is to consolidate the spatial unity of the country by reviving the economic development of the Far North."[6] "Moscow is seeking to improve the connection of its vast Siberian territory to the European and Far Eastern parts of the country."[7]

Tayloe would agree with Laruelle's first premise when writing that, "in the Arctic, Russia's new nationalist leaders have reached for great power status."[8] "The stated aim of Putin's regime is to re-establish Russia as a Eurasian great power" in this Norwegian view, while noting that Russia's ambitions "will have strong impact far beyond that region."[9]

Pavel Devyatkin, writing for the Center for Circumpolar Security Studies of the Arctic Institute, remarked that "the contextual importance of Russia's historical great power status is a common theme among critics of Russian actions in the Arctic."[10] Devyatkin notes that Ekaterina Piskunova, of the Université de Montréal, recognized this theme as "a coherent part of Russia's foreign policy, which is primarily concerned with regaining Russia's great power status."[11] "According to such scholars, restoring Russia's great power status is the principal objective of Russian foreign policy and the Arctic, as a region for Russian dominance, is no exception" Devyatkin claims.[12]

Dugin not only proposes Eurasian regional dominance in a multipolar world, Dugin, Devyatkin stated, openly advocates for an imperialist policy in the Arctic.[13] "According to Dugin," wrote Devyatkin, "the purpose of Russia's being is the expansion of space and the Arctic is rightful Russian territory."[14] The Arctic is therefore perceived to be part of Russia's Manifest Destiny.

Devyatkin wrote that Pavel Baev and Sergei Medvedev view Moscow's Arctic flexing as nationalistic rather than economically motivated.[15] "Baev criticizes Russia's conquest of the Arctic as "realpolitik with a Stalinist flavor," while "Medvedev argues that Russia's actions in the Arctic are solely based on "boosting patriotism at home while keeping up great power appearances abroad."[16] In either of these assessments, "rather than seeking collaboration with Arctic states, Russia's actions are based on hard security" and both contain "the growing prospect for military engagement."[17]

Avoiding singular security motivations, Laruelle more realistically ascribes multipurpose motives to Russia's objectives in the High North to secure transport routes that accompany this new frontier and to prepare for potential threats to its sovereignty from a place of geo-strategic advantage.[18] Tayloe, remarking on Russia's insecurity observes that, in fact, "potential threats seem to loom large from every direction."[19] Indeed, geopolitical author Robert Kaplan wrote that "insecurity is the quintessential Russian national emotion."[20] Paul Dibb, the former Professor of Strategic and Defense Studies at The Australian National University, elaborated:

Russia's vast geography left it open to waves of invasion, from the Mongols in the 12th century to the Nazis in the 20th. Russia's perduring vulnerability—it has no obvious or clear-cut topographical borders save for the Arctic and Pacific Oceans—accounts for the deep-seated militarization of its society and its endless search for security through the creation of a land-based empire.[21]

Echoing its anti-Containment Policy desires, Tayloe believes that "Russia has rationally sought strategic depth to mitigate its vulnerable geographic position."[22] Tayloe opines that Russia's "fear of collapse is not a paranoid abstraction," rather, "based on the experiences of 1917 and 1991," it is "a permeating reality," a fear based in history.[23] Tayloe offers that broadly, "Russian political and military elites have seized on the concept of strategic depth to prevent such an outcome."[24] Specifically, for this discussion, "Russian action in the Arctic thus must be understood in the context of the wider pursuit of strategic depth—a rational response to structural realities that have been present for centuries."[25] Tayloe correctly observed that the Containment Policy that "guided the West for decades" concentrated on building "'three walls' to the west, south, and east" around Russia "while geography and climate closed Russia off to the north."[26] Climate appears less able to provide the northern wall.

The basic conclusions of Mahanian and Mackinderian geopolitical theories have not changed but climate and technology have altered the dynamic. Heretofore, the trope intoning that rule of the Eurasian heartland is tantamount to rule of the world held sway. The Mackinderian theory presents a two-edged sword, however. Opponents of the possessor of the Eurasian heartland can deny world rule to the occupant if it can be confined within the very area that bestows it with such awesome power. Therefore, Mahan's ocean rule theory may prove to be a major driver of Russia's Arctic motivations and advancements.

The West (read NATO in current circumstances) has, for decades, been guided by the George F. Kennan's policy that contained the Soviet genie largely within its own heartland lamp.

Russia likely feels that dynamic expansion in the High North offers an escape from the constant chafe of Containment Policy. As northward expansion progresses, so some explanations go, Russia will no longer be susceptible to geographic isolation or encirclement.[28] Thus, Russia may hope for future success through Mahan's theory in addition to Mackinder's—with the Arctic Ocean opening the door to regional dominance and perhaps more.

Polar Projections Influence Air Power

Perhaps Russian hopes in the High North are pinned to neither Mahanian nor Mackinderian theories—at least not altogether. In a secular rendition of the historical cartographic depiction of Jerusalem as the center of the world, geographer George T. Renner placed the Arctic at the center of the world map.[29]

Adapted by Mud Pie Graphics from:
d1ftgt94wd5jml.cloudfront.net/2010/proj_orthographic.png

In Renner's mapping scheme, the first circle outside the pole is the Arctic Circle; a second, and larger, is the Tropic of Cancer; even further out, the Equator forms an even larger circle; outside

151

this is the circle formed by the Tropic of Capricorn; lastly—the farthest circle, the edge of Renner's map, is the Antarctic Circle surrounding the South Pole. Renner explained that his projection "is not hemispheric, but monospheric.[30] For Renner, the Arctic Ocean is the "World Mediterranean."[31]

> Renner stated that Eurasia (i.e., Europe and Asia) is indicated as a giant semicircle curved around the Arctic Mediterranean on any Arctic-centered map, noting Greenland and Iceland, which have two bulges with North America, almost complete the circle. Furthermore, like other geopoliticians, he also claimed that the center of gravity of the world lies in large areas of Russia, Siberia, Turkestan, and Western China. He asserted that these lands constituted an Earth center, or Heartland, that could barely be approached from land and inaccessible by ship, but was at a central position in an air-focused world. He noted that whoever holds this region would also take a dominant position in world affairs in the future.[32]

Renner suggested that in a fully developed *Air Age*, trade from to and from Eurasia and America, "would most likely pass through Greenland, the Franklin Archipelago, and the Arctic Sea."[33] Renner predicted that future wars are "likely to be waged for possession of the Arctic Mediterranean," an area on his map largely coinciding with the Arctic.[34] Selim Kurt notes that Giulio Douhet, contemporary of the 1920s air warfare advocates Walther Wever, Billy Mitchell and Hugh Trenchard, used the example that contact with the enemy employing the closest and most direct access is one of air power's most potent attributes.[35] Spykman, highlighted the proximity of North America and Eurasia.[36]

Renner's projection demonstrates the geographical advantage of polar routed flight paths, applicable commercially and most certainly militarily. Spykman presciently stated that the Arctic, especially a melting Arctic, "would give new and vital meaning to naval power and especially air power in the coming decades."[37]

Alexander Seversky also looked into the future and suggested it would be an "Air Age."[38] Seversky believed that Americans tend to visualize of Asia lying to the west and Europe to the east.[39] Kurt suggested that Seversky believed that, for purposes of air power, it is better to visualize the world from a Polar perspective.[40] Defense and security planning, relying on "old geographical perceptions," would have to be recast using an Arctic projection Seversky believed, or become "obsolete."[41]

The High North Forward

Dividing categories of contemporary Russian geopolitics into three camps, Sergey Sukhankin, Troy Bouffard and Whitney Lackenbauer remarked that in one of the camps, the Nationalist School participants insist "on Russia's need to increase Russia's military buildup in the Arctic."[42] Sukhankin, Bouffard, and Lackenbauer claim the Nationalist School is not sufficiently studied in the West.[43] "Consequently," these authors stated that the Nationalist School advocates' "role and influence on the Kremlin is misunderstood."[44] The Nationalist School is largely comprised of "authors coming from the ultra-conservative nationalistic Izborsk Club."[45]

> The Izborsky Club argues that the two major catastrophes of twentieth-century Russia—the fall of tsarism in 1917 and the collapse of the Soviet Union in 1991—resulted from the Russian state refusing to recognize a state ideology. According to the Club, the current regime does not have a specific ideology, and it has been unable to turn ideological fragments into a logical whole. The mission of the Club is thus to reopen the "cultural front" and to be "a laboratory where we will elaborate an ideology, an institute to engage in creating a forward-looking theory, a construction site to make an ideological weapon that we will send into combat without delay."[46]

Nationalist School participants insist "on Russia's need to increase Russia's military buildup in the Arctic."[47] Many of this school underscore the sacred nature of the Arctic Region as well as its strategic value. This metaphysical emphasis on geography is little studied in the West but "Alexander Dugin, Alexander Mazharov (deputy governor of the Yamal-Nenets Autonomous Region), Vyacheslav Shtyrov (former Head of the Sakha Republic), and devoted Stalinist Alexander Prokhanov are prominent members of this school, which envisages the Arctic region as 'the northernmost part of the Russian World.'"[48]

Tayloe posits that "the Arctic is currently the setting for a high stakes power play between the liberal, Western order and a revisionist Russia."[49] I believe that there may be no place left on earth, save the polar regions, that could play host to a redo of Great Game geopolitics.

Paul Arthur Berkman and Oran R. Young have suggested that "the Arctic could slide into a new era featuring jurisdictional conflicts, increasingly severe clashes over the extraction of natural resources, and the emergence of a new "great game" among the global powers."[50] The Neo-Eurasian characteristic of expansion and desire for great power status will continue to prove to be a significant source of competition and potential conflict.

Notes

1. The Expert Commission on Norwegian Security and Defence Policy, *United Effort*, Norwegian Ministry of Defence, 2015, 16. This report may be accessed from regjeringen.no/globalassets/departementene/fd/dokumenter/unified-effort.pdf.

2. Rumer, Richard Sokolsky, and Paul Stronski, *Russia in the Arctic—A Critical Examination*, Carnegie Endowment for International Peace, March, 2021.

3. Laruelle, "Russia's Arctic Policy: A Power Strategy and Its Limits," Russie.Nei.Visions, No. 117, Ifri, March 2019, 5.

4. Laruelle, "Russia's Arctic Policy," 5.

5. Ibid. Here Laruelle cites: I. Katorin, "Establishing the Arctic Zone of the Russian Federation as a Factor of the Regional Development:

Raising Questions (The Case of the Arkhangelsk Region)," Arctic and North, vol. 31, 2018, 28-40, arcticandnorth.ru.

6. Ibid., 6.

7. Ibid., 5-6.

8. Tayloe, "Projecting Power in the Arctic," 6.

9. The Expert Commission on Norwegian Security and Defence Policy, *United Effort*, 16.

10. Pavel Devyatkin, "Russia's Arctic Strategy: Aimed at Conflict or Cooperation? (Part I)," under, Realism, Russia and the Arctic, The Arctic Institute, February 6, 2012, thearcticinstitute.org/russias-arctic-strategy-aimed-conflict-cooperation-part-one/. Pavel Devyatkin, Senior Associate, The Arctic Institute.

11. Devyatkin, "Russia's Arctic Strategy," under, Realism, Russia and the Arctic. Cf. Piskunova E (2010) Russia in the Arctic: What's lurking behind the flag?, *International Journal*, 65, (4): 851-864.

12. Ibid.

13. Ibid.

14. Ibid. Cf. Devyatkin's footnote 15: Dugin A (1991) Misterii Evrazii, Moscow: Arctogaia: chapters 1 and 2.

15. Ibid.

16. Ibid., Cf. Devyatkin's notes 18: Trenin D and PK Baev (2010) The Arctic: A View from Russia, Washington, DC: Carnegie Endowment for International Peace; and 19: Medvedev S (2016) The Kremlin's Arctic Plans: More Gutted Than Grand, PONARS Eurasia Policy Memo, 430.

17. Ibid.

18. Laruelle, "Russia's Arctic Policy," 5-6.

19. Tayloe, "Projecting Power in the Arctic," 4.

20. Robert Kaplan, *The Revenge of Geography*, (New York: Random House, 2012), 159. Quoted in Tayloe, "Projecting Power in the Arctic," 4. Robert Kaplan, geopolitical author and commentator.

21. Tayloe, "Projecting Power in the Arctic," 5. Here, Tayloe cites Paul Dibb: (Dibb, 2006).

22. Ibid.

23. Ibid.

24. Ibid.

25. Ibid.

26. Ibid. Cf. 5 and 10.

27. Antrim, "The Next Geographical Pivot," 15-16. Quoted in Tayloe, "Projecting Power in the Arctic," 5.

28. Ibid.

29. Selim Kurt, "Importance of the Arctic in the Framework of Air Power Theory," *International Journal of Politics and Security*, Vol. 3, No. 1, 2021, 62-63. Cf. Kurt's footnote 33: George T. Renner, Human Geography in the Air Age (New York: The Macmillan Company, 1942), 21. Cf. archive.org/details/humangeographyin00rennrich/page/212/mode/2up. Selim Kurt, Professor, Giresun University.

30. Kurt, Importance of the Arctic in Air Power Theory, 63.

31. Ibid., 63.

32. Ibid., 64.

33. Ibid., 65. Cf. Kurt's footnote 43: Renner, Human Geography in the Air Age, 206-207.

34. Ibid. Cf. Kurt's footnote 43.

35. Ibid., Cf. Kurt's footnote 44: Douhet, The Command of The Air, 7-10.

36. Ibid., 65-66.

37. Ibid., Cf. Kurt's footnote 45: Kaplan, The Revenge of Geography, 16-17; Lambeth, "Air power, Space Power and Geography," 101.

38. Ibid., 66.

39. Ibid.

40. Ibid.

41. Ibid., Cf. Alexander P. de Seversky, Air Power: Key to Survival (New York: Simon and Schuster, 1950), 307. Alexander P. de Seversky, 1894-1974.

42. All quotes in this bullet appear in: Sergey Sukhankin, Troy Bouffard, and P. Whitney Lackenbauer, "Strategy, Competition, and

Legitimization: Development of the Arctic Zone of the Russian Federation," *Arctic Yearbook 2021*, arcticyearbook.com/images/yearbook/2021/Scholarly-Papers/12_AY2021_Sukhankin.pdf, 3.

43. Ibid., all quotes in this bullet from Sukhankin, Bouffard, and Lackenbauer, 3.

44. Ibid.

45. Ibid. Elsewhere found rendered *Izborsky Club*.

46. Laruelle, "The Izborsky Club, or the New Conservative Avant-Garde in Russia," The Russian Review 75 (October 2016): 626–44. 626. Laruelle cites, Izborskii klub: Russkie strategii, 2013, no. 10:32, and no. 2:4.

47. All quotes in this bullet from Sukhankin, Bouffard, and Lackenbauer, 3.

48. Ibid.

49. Tayloe, "Projecting Power In The Arctic," 1, from Tayloe's Abstract.

50. Paul Arthur Berkman and Oran R. Young, "Governance and Environmental Change in the Arctic Ocean," Science, 324, (5925), April 17, 2009, science.org/doi/abs/10.1126/science.1173200, 339.

Part IV

Chapter One: Political Theology

Not an Oxymoron

According to Saul Newman, *political theology*, as a definitive term, originated with the Russian anarchist Mikhail Bakunin.[1] Newman claims that Bakunin coined it "in a polemical essay from 1871 titled 'La théologie politique de Mazzini et l'Internationale.'"[2] In his essay, Bakunin reproached "the great Italian politician and republican Guiseppe Mazzini for illegitimately mixing religion and politics."[3] There is today a large and significant segment of Western political opinion that rather emphatically insists that *any* mixing of religion and politics is illegitimate. None-the-less, because Dugin is at any given time a political and theological figure of varying degrees, reception of his work should always be considered from both political and theological perspectives.

This dual reception approach is a much more comfortable process in Eastern rather than Western contexts. Applying Clooney's and Richard Hanson's thinking presents a practical understanding of Dugin's more Eastern view of this approach. Their understanding is germane to Dugin because "the full meaning of a theology, [in dialogical contexts], is no longer contained entirely within its own religious tradition"—it is the "'back and forth dynamic' of interreligious dialogue," described by Hanson, that is largely absent in Western geopolitical circles.[4]

Newman observed that "political theology, an enigmatic term, generally refers to the interpenetration of religion and politics."[5] "More precisely, it refers to the way in which political concepts, discourses and institutions—particularly sovereignty—are influenced, shaped and underpinned by religious categories of thought."[6] Dugin's particular geopolitical theology represents his expression derived from the broader field of political theology.[7] The extent and depth of his ideas in this area are abundantly evident as he declares that the state's very meaning is contained in its spiritual mission.[8]

Newman pointedly suggested that "Just as God transcends the world and nature, the state transcends and stands above society; the same principle of absolute sovereignty is at work in both."[9] "Religion and politics have always been intertwined," Newman wrote, elaborating that "the entire history of the Christian West, in its shifting relationship between religious and political power, between church and state, might be said to revolve around the politico-theological problem."[10]

Dugin's Use of Theological Language

Derived from Greek through Middle-English, theology is, quite literally, talking about God or the conclusions derived from such talk. Originally a word used in describing specialized biblical and ecclesial subjects among the academic clergy in a Christian context, theological terminology is now applied across religions. Hence a current definition implying "the study of religion and beliefs."[11]

Dugin's purpose in Fourth Political Theory is not to expound on theology, *per se*, but to build a geographic-centric political theology. In fact, Dugin develops Fourth Political Theory, in its entire array of conversations, using imprecise definitional applications concerning theology. Although, however imprecise his definition, Dugin's metaphysical references are ever-present and discernible, even if not always specifically religious or theological. While I consider theology as the contemplation, study, and discussion of God and Creation, and humankind's relationship to both, I feel Dugin may avail himself of less precise parameters. Dugin does not employ theology with any strict academic or ecclesial preciseness, but his purpose for implying its presence in his words and writings is germane.

Karl Barth wrote in a letter, "in the church of Jesus Christ there can and should be no non-theologians."[12] However, lack of a sufficient degree of academic rigor, a too broad multi-religious ecumenism, and infusion of mystical, gnostic, and even occultic characteristics in his geopolitical theology suggest that Dugin should not be approached through Fourth Political Theory as a strictly Christian theologian.[13] Still, it is evident that Dugin builds the geopolitical and theologically related elements of his theory in theologically derived conversation. Dugin undertakes to use theology with a more general understanding motivated by his desire to include it in his geopolitical scheme.

I address Fourth Political Theory and its included derivatives, Neo-Traditionalism and Neo-Eurasianism, as a form of God-talk. Dugin's political strands contain strong theologically related components. I presuppose that no proper examination of Dugin can succeed absent the assumption that geopolitical God-talk— that is, his political theology fused with geography—matters to Dugin. Beginning his discussion of Michael Fishbane's *Sacred Attunement: A Jewish Theology*, David Novak wrote that "the word *theology* means literally *God-talk*."[14] Commenting on Fishbane's approach, Novak noted that, for Fishbane,

> the movement toward theology begins from a nontheological starting point...This natural preparation for theology could be metaphysical, ethical, or aesthetic. That one can be led into theology metaphysically, owing to one's seeing the multiplicity of the natural phenomenal world, seems to presuppose a higher singularity lying beyond its horizon. (This is the way of medieval Jewish theologians from Saadia to Maimonides to Gersonides.)[15]

Dugin's approach in Fourth Political Theory, his God-talk, follows a path of metaphysical preparation. It is adamant in its insistence on interpreting "the multiplicity of the natural phenomenal world," especially evident in his view of Sacred Geography with "a higher singularity lying beyond its horizon."[16]

Dominican Bernard Bourdin, a political theologian himself, suggested that the influence of two political philosophers, Schmitt and Hans Blumenberg, were instrumental in twentieth century development of political theology.[17] Dugin envokes Schmitt as he establishes the basis of his Fourth Political Theory, and Blumenberg is remarkable for his contrasting views to those of Schmitt, thus, providing a foil to Dugin as well. I maintain that an essential element in understanding Dugin's geopolitical theology is summed up in Schmitt's statement:

160

All significant concepts of the modern theory of the state are secularized theological concepts not only because of their historical development—in which they were transferred from theology to the theory of the state, whereby, for example, the omnipotent God became the omnipotent lawgiver—but also because of their systematic structure, the recognition of which is necessary for a sociological consideration of these concepts.[18]

I accept Schmitt's conclusion and I believe it captures one of Dugin's underlying worldviews. I also presuppose that Schmitt's observation that "any decision about whether something is *unpolitical* is always a *political* decision, irrespective of who decides and what reasons are advanced," holds, by extension, that deciding whether something is *theological* or *non-theological* is, in fact, a theological decision.[19] I believe that Dugin embraces these same two conclusions. I contend that this understanding is critical to grasping the bedrock assumption that forges the link of Dugin's politics and its theological ingredients. As essential as this understanding is, it is not my intent to prove or disprove Dugin's assumptions; I am attempting to present his geopolitical theology systematically and to highlight the results of how his metaphysical and political visions may be becoming engrained and expressed in Russian political policy.

Viewing Dugin's theological inclusions as a form of Schmittian political theology seems the best course. I agree with Gavin Rae when applying my thoughts on Dugin's theology, in its geopolitical context, as Rae does in applying his thoughts to Schmitt:

The basic point guiding my argument is that Schmitt's thinking is premised on a particular theological sentiment that not only shapes the responses he gives to a number of the issues he engages with but also actually plays a fundamental role in the solutions he devises to them.[20]

161

Rae suggested "that we need a more nuanced understanding of what the 'theology' of political theology entails that does not reduce it to 'faith in (a) religion,' but which recognizes a more fundamental sense of political theology rooted in epistemic faith alone."[21] Rae's conclusion has direct applicability to Dugin's use of theology in his particular political ideology. Rae decided that "we need, therefore, to distinguish between two forms of theology: a religious form of theology, rooted in faith in divine revelation, and an epistemological form of theology, rooted in recognition of the limits of human reason."[22]

Dugin's geopolitical theology, like "Schmitt's political theology," adopting Rae's thinking, "is not premised on the truth of a religion, but on the narrower epistemological principle that faith or belief provides access to the truth."[23] The theological elements in Dugin's work are discernable in various manifestations. They may take the form of metaphysically infused political discussion, as an integral element of geopolitical projections (e.g., in his Neo-Eurasian ideas of Sacred Geography), or as elements of his engagement in theologically related areas such as eschatology and apocalypticism.

Criticality of Political Theology to Governance

My third presupposition is intimately connected and subordinate to my first and second. Dugin, echoing Schmitt, believes that proper governance involves an integrated political theology. Dugin uses "governance" in what his editor, John B. Morgan, styled as the "French" sense of "the art of governing."[24] *"Geopolitics is the science of how to rule,"* wrote Dugin.[25]

Theological and religious discussion matters to Dugin in the premise that political theology not only offers avenues of common-core dialogue with other nations, regions, and groups, but allows for acceptance and accommodation of the critical dimensions of the human spirit, society, and culture. Dugin emphasizes that in sizable portions of the world—certainly in Russia—religious strands are woven throughout politics and social life. Conversely, he stresses that the West is increasingly secular and prideful of Humanism derived from the Enlightenment. Dugin argues that adopting secularism ultimately

162

weakens the West by placing it in a position of being unable (or at least unwilling) to engage in constructive communication with a significant part of the world, especially Russia, in the present case.[26]

Though it may be able to stifle, secularism appears unable to succeed in removing theological discussion or some form of religious dialogue, from the political forum. The existence of former official Soviet apparatus supports the argument that, even in an avowedly secular government, a goal of abstaining from religious dialog is not practically achievable.[27] Even the self-proclaimed atheistic government of the former Soviet Union was unable to exclude religious engagement from its governance.[28]

A long-time debate continues in Western academic circles over the place of theology as subject matter within narrowly defined curricula.[29] While the actual merits of the discussion are not in question for my purposes, acknowledgment of the perception of exclusion, especially for the formally prominent inclusion of Judeo-Christian curricular material, is important. Dugin advocates for a broad religious presence in the public forum. His condemnation of Western secularism reflects a perception that the West is purposefully engaged in suppressing serious religious engagement, especially in its public expression.[30]

Commenting on the current perception of religious exclusion in the United States, R.C. Sproul wrote that there was a time when theology was known as "'Queen of the Sciences,' and all other disciplines saw her as their matron and themselves as her handmaidens."[31] James R. Stoner wrote that this time has passed, and theology has almost completely fallen away from the mainstream curricula of Western colleges today.[32] Stoner asked, "not whether theology ought to be restored as the queen of the sciences, but whether she belongs among them at all?"[33] He made the point that "holding theology not to be a form of knowledge creates the entire way religion is approached in our culture."[34] "When philosophers, following John Rawls, speak of 'public reason' as the test of what arguments and what positions are valid in public," Stoner said,

> they mean to subject public discourse to the censorship of the secular professoriate. They

163

know, I think, that they will never actually suppress the voice of faith in everyday politics, but they mean to exclude it from the higher reaches of the law, from journalism and the media, from professional and corporate networks, and the like.[35]

Theological Development of the State: Schmitt and Blumenberg

In 1922 Schmitt published his influential concepts of political theology, in which he articulated his theory of the state and its sovereignty.[36] Schmitt argued that the state, either installed through divine sovereignty or derived from it, can legitimately exercise the power of exception—to rule as seen fit during times of emergency or crisis. Having experienced the First World War, Schmitt attempted to influence the constitutional construction of the Weimar Republic in ways that would enhance its ability to establish and maintain order and respond to various disruptions with authority and effectiveness.[37] Schmitt was concerned that the concept of sovereignty had become corrupted in the nineteenth century movement toward secular democratic government.

Arthur Versluis wrote that, for Schmitt, "Hobbes's Leviathan arguably signals an intellectual point of origin for the modern secular state."[38] "Schmitt accepted the Hobbesian emphasis on the authority of the sovereign," according to Versluis.[39] Schmitt thought that the Sovereign of the Cosmos, "in the deistic view of the world," though conceived as residing outside it, "had remained the engineer of the great machine."[40] Newman stated that:

Schmitt saw the sovereign as analogous with God as the supreme lawgiver, and the state of exception as akin to the miracle in theology. The sovereign is the redeemer and saviour of the people in a time of nihilism and political neutralisation, which is why at the same time it demands absolute obedience and sacrifice.[41]

Schmitt explained the world instituted by a sovereign power, with the sovereign being analogous to a machine's engineer.[42] In Schmitt's combined political and theological outlook, the Sovereign of the Universe, as its creator, is the ultimate engineer, with earthly monarchs being subordinate operators of the machine-of-state.[43] Schmitt believed the Sovereign was being pushed aside by political movements that abandoned "theistic and transcendental conceptions."[44] An out of control machine-of-state was a chaotic afront to Schmitt, as it is to Dugin. "The machine now runs by itself," was Schmitt's observation, and absent the Sovereign Engineer a state is a self-driving machine running amuck.[45]

Schmitt saw the monarchical consistency of European states changing. He wrote that "the development of the nineteenth-century theory of the state displays two characteristic moments."[46] These moments were first, "the elimination of all theistic and transcendental conceptions," and second, "the formation of a new concept of legitimacy."[47] Thierry Gontier wrote that Blumenberg critiqued Schmitt's expression that "all significant concepts of modernity are secularized theological concepts," and labeled Schmitt's belief, "secularization theorem."[48] Gontier claimed that "it was Carl Schmitt who gave Blumenberg the model for the articulation of the secularization 'theorem.'"[49] Blumenberg stated that "the proposition that 'all the significant concepts of the modern doctrine of the state are secularized theological concepts' was first laid down by Carl Schmitt in 1922."[50]

Blumenberg went on to say of Schmitt's doctrine of the modern state, "both in the factual assertion that it contains and also in the deductions that it inaugurates, it is the strongest version of the secularization theorem."[51] Gontier wrote that Schmitt employed this theorem in contrast to "rationalistic and liberal modernity," and elaborated:

> The claims to autonomy advanced by this modernity are no more than illusory; the modernity of the Enlightenment is unable to liberate itself from the theological. It is, moreover, impossible for us ever to escape from the theological. The only real choice is that

between an orthodox, coherent political theology capable of accepting itself as such and a heterodox, contradictory, and latent political theology.[52]

Rae's analysis noted that Schmitt explained Western government in modernity originating from a transformation of God's sovereignty, with its attributes of monotheistic authority, transferred nearly one-for-one to the temporal sovereignty of the state.[53] Blumenberg rejected Secularization Theorem as mistaken. Western society did become modern, and Blumenberg recognized that it also became increasingly secular. However, Western society did not become more secular because of "the substitution of the absolute power of Man for that of God," according to Blumenberg.[54] "Modernity cannot be reduced to a process of secularization by which theological concepts are transformed into political ones," is the way Bourdin reduced Blumenberg's argument.[55]

Gontier, critiquing Schmitt's theory that ideas expressed in modernity are no more than secularized theological concepts, tentatively agreed that if Schmitt was correct, modernity arrived through a process of secularization.[56] On the other hand, Gontier thought that Blumenberg was not suggesting that politics are entirely devoid of theology.[57] "Modernity," as Gontier interprets Blumenberg, "expropriates theological notions, transferring them outside of their authentic semantic context and into another context in which they are trivialized and their meaning dissolved."[58]

In his comparison of the contrasting views of Schmitt and Blumenberg, Richard Faber offered that, in modernity, Schmitt viewed government as a transfer of God's sovereign authority to the state.[59] Faber concluded that Blumenberg, on the other hand, applied a polytheistic explanation in contrast to Schmitt's monotheistic characterization.[60] Faber explained the use of polytheistic terminology with the claim that polytheism is a metaphor for the more pluralist sovereignty of the modern state.[61]

Robert Wyllie explained Faber's interpretation this way:

Blumenberg, whose later work explores how metaphor orients thought, proposes a "polytheistic" alternative to "monotheistic" political theology. Polytheism is an early modern metaphor for plural sovereignty, underlying the checks and balances of liberalism.[62]

Though doubting Blumenberg's polytheistic influence on Dugin, his stance concerning theological characteristics of the state seems evident. Dugin certainly echoes Schmitt when claiming that proper understanding of political ideologies involves realizing that they are all renditions of theological modeling.[63] Schmitt claimed that liberal influences of the Enlightenment and the French Revolution eliminated "all theistic and transcendental conceptions," and replaced them with humanistic concepts of legitimacy.[64]

At a time when most European and Asian nations had transitioned or were moving away from monarchical political structures, with their various claims of divine association, Schmitt was critiqued as archaic.[65] If that charge was leveled then, how much more archaic must Dugin's adaption of Schmitt be seen by some critics today?

Eric Voegelin, interestingly, considering Dugin's penchant for gnosticism, claimed that, at its core, modernity is gnostic.[66] Voegelin's gnostic characterization can be paired to Versluis' observation that Blumenberg, in his *The Legitimacy of the Modern Age*, opened by asserting that modernity is properly identified with gnosticism.[67] Support of a contention that Dugin accepts some of Blumenberg's ideas might be found in Versluis' lack of surprise that Blumenberg began by referring to Voegelin's claim that the modern age "would be better entitled the Gnostic age."[68]

Voegelin, characterizing as a gnostic endeavor the move away from transcendent Christian monotheistic inspired society, including its governmental aspects, wrote that "a line of gradual transformation connects medieval with contemporary gnosticism."[69] Voegelin then speculated whether the present social environment should be classified as "Christian," owing to its outgrowth from medieval Christian heresies.[70] His conclusion was, "the best course will be to drop such questions and to recognize the essence of modernity as the growth of gnosticism."[71]

Schmitt recognized this perspective, championing his brand of political theology as an effort to break the gnostic line of gradual transformation and re-introduce recognizable monotheism back into the prevailing Western political discourse. Whatever the amount of Blumenberg's influence, Dugin can be witnessed endorsing the belief that Schmitt's political theology has been viewed as an attempt to revive the Sovereign and retrieve government from its gnostic trends.[72]

Dugin's Political Theology

Because Dugin is at any given time a political and theological figure in varying degrees, reception of his work should always be considered from both political and theological perspectives. Clooney, a scholar well versed in the concept of the reader becoming a receptive *homo lector*—a person who learns by conscious active and even passionate study—presents a practical understanding of this dual-reception in Dugin's case.[73] As previously noted, Clooney and Hanson advocate an interreligious aspect applicable to Dugin.[74] In the West, genuine "'back and forth dynamic' of interreligious dialogue," is often replaced by partisan agendas that substitute token civil religious offerings attempting to satisfy the real theological aspects of politics.[75]

Fourth Political Theory presupposes the collapse of the previous three political theories, and allows theology, all but excluded in Western Liberalism, to return and fill the vacuum. However, according to Peter J. Leithart, "the theology that returns isn't necessary [sic] the theology of Christian orthodoxy."[76] Despite Dugin's claims to a form of Russian Orthodoxy, the sources of his geopolitical theology include more ecumenical sources, including some from outside of Christianity. Dugin considers a wide range of theological and metaphysical aspects in tandem with his geopolitics.

It was his writing on geopolitics that first gained Dugin Western recognition, less visible to the Western eye was the metaphysical and theological substratum running below the entirety of Dugin's work. Epstein wrote of metaphysical and political relations within the context of Russian Nationalism in his 1994 study of conservatism and tradition.[77] In his study Epstein also provided an early introduction to Dugin and his political theology.[78] Capturing the essence of the Traditionalism adopted by Dugin, Epstein wrote:

> Radical traditionalism is the most extreme variety of Rightist Russian philosophy, challenging both liberalism and moderate, humanistic conservatism and attempting to make the twenty-first century the epoch of another worldwide revolution, spiritually opposed to the democratic and communist revolutions of recent history.[79]

Epstein's examination is pertinent, and, given the date of his research, groundbreaking. Epstein conducted his study into Russian conservatism and Traditionalism in the early years of the 1990s, thus providing valuable viewpoints from the time Dugin enjoyed scant recognition in the West. Searching for common ground available at the time of his Dugin research, Epstein selected Russian conservatism as a place to fix Dugin's geopolitical position. In his comparison of Dugin's Russian conservatism to that of Alexander Solzhenitsyn, Epstein made this observation:

> Traditionalists [of Dugin's geopolitical bend] distinguish themselves from more moderate conservatives, like Solzhenitsyn, since they do not want to restore the pre-revolutionary past, but rather to implement a new, Rightist revolution. Also in contradistinction with Solzhenitsyn, their political strategy is not isolationist, but presupposes the consolidation of Rightist movements all over the world.[80]

Recognizing the Symphonia bordering on *Papocaesarism* inherent in Dugin's Neo-Traditionalism, Epstein succinctly noted that "the connection between metaphysics and politics is dictated by the very essence of total traditionalism, which denies the liberal

169

principle of the separation of powers and specialization of knowledge."[81] Properly engaging with Fourth Political Theory requires a presumption that the geopolitical and the theological are inseparable. Separation of the two, more accurately the near-total absence of the latter, is a dominant presuppositional refrain one finds repeated in contemporary Western Liberal conversation.

Gordon R. Middleton frankly stated that the "Eurasia view is in stark contrast with the militant atheism of the Left and with the Right's reliance upon formal, organized religious entities for religious practice (which in the American version is done in complete separation from the political realm)."[82] He went on to note that "Dugin is emphatic that the primary means to achieve Eurasianism's goals are through spiritual, even theological, revival."[83]

Bonald and Lamennais recognized that traditional societal norms place humans in communal relationships that are similar and symbiotic in function. Modern aspects of society involve many individualistic selections made within a system requiring a high degree of what Émile Durkheim would address as *Division of Labor*.[84] Dugin favors communal relationships, with their symbiotic nature, when placed against the individualist characteristics of societies exhibiting a high degree of Division of Labor. Dugin's opposition to Western emphasis on individualism is a consistent marker of his Neo-Traditional stance. Another is his reliance on metaphysics rather than reason.

Edmund Burke's position on tradition challenges reason as an ultimate determinant in political discourse, and his view of the inherent inequality of rank and authority bear some noticeable traits later echoed in Dugin.[85] A trail can also be discerned from Thomas Hobbes and John Locke to Dugin, though the path from Plato through Burke to Dugin seems to be several degrees more natural. Burke is widely regarded as a founding spokesman of Western political conservatism.[86] Ian Harris stated:

> Burke's mind, by the time he left Trinity [Trinity College Dublin], had two facets: one was an orientation towards religion, improvement and politics, the other a philosophical method. The

170

latter derived from his university education, the former from reflection on the Irish situation.[87]

While perhaps not attended well enough in the current context of geopolitical affairs, Burke's thoughts on the French Revolution, British eighteenth century treatment of both the American Colonies and the Irish Catholics, combined with his diverse corpus of writing, deserves serious attention. "Burke is perhaps the least studied of political classics, but he is certainly amongst the small number with whom anyone who aspires to have an adequate political education must engage," in Harris' opinion.[88]

Speaking in political and philosophical terms that support ideas embedded within Fourth Political Theory, Burke viewed political elements possessing long-term attributes supporting societal legitimacy.[89] These attributes include traditions embedded within family, community, and common religion that provide societal cohesiveness.[90] Burke opposed over-reliance on reason, thinking that doing so undermines tradition; he classified much rational thought as a form of despotism.[91] Given these positions, Burke's thinking and Fourth Political Theory display several common themes. Burke's views concerning the utility of certain prejudices may likely be favorable to a Duginesque interpretation as well. Prejudice learned through social tradition may reflect protective and instructive elements to society that are positive and useful, according to Burke.[92]

Dugin classifies Burke as a "liberal conservative," and notes Burke's pushback to Enlightenment ideals after the French Revolution.[93] Liberal conservatives, according to Dugin, "are distinguished by the following qualitative structural characteristics: Agreement with the general trends of modernity, but disagreement with its more avant-garde manifestations, which seem excessively dangerous and unhealthy."[94] Burke viewed authority, rank, and the inequality inherently embedded in them as positives for society when they were deserved and applied using legitimate processes. Dugin's respect for traditional aspects of authority and his accommodational stance on hierarchical, perhaps even monarchical, aspects in government tend to mesh well with some aspects of Burkean political philosophy.

171

The Metaphysics of Debris

While Dugin's Neo-Traditionalism serves as the vehicle for much of his political theology, his geopolitics are largely expressed in his Neo-Eurasianism. Dugin arrived at the current station on his Neo-Traditional/Neo-Eurasian journey, in part, by building with material derived from previous construction attempts—both his and others. This pattern, developing modifications and adaptations of earlier Traditionalist and Eurasianist efforts, is Dugin's purposeful application of what he characterizes as the *Metaphysics of Debris*.[95]

Dugin described his formulation of Fourth Political Theory as a process that extended across years. As his project matured, Dugin eventually rejected the idea that neither communism nor fascism could be used to form a synthesis that eliminated the abhorrent manifestations of Soviet praxis and the unspeakable aberrance of Germany's National Socialist deviance. By way of explanation, Dugin stated that he rejected attempting any modification of Communism (as the Second Theory) or Fascism (as the Third Theory) beginning in 2008.[96] Since then, Dugin wrote, he concentrates "exclusively on the elaboration of [a] fully independent Fourth Political Theory."[97]

This independence involves some leeway to employ a kind of salvage operation of the second and third theories. Engaging Alexander Sekatsky's ideas on the Metaphysics of Debris, Dugin gleaned the marginal, discarded, and peripheral remains of communism and fascism, for useful Fourth Political Theory construction material.[98] Within the detritus of the second and third theories can be found items that "may, unexpectedly, turn out to be extremely valuable and saturated with meaning and intuition."[99] It is the marginal elements in communism and fascism, not their complete ideologies, that are worthy of consideration in Dugin's mind.[100]

Dugin rightfully rejects anything close to total trust in either the second or third of the political theories but does advocate examining the marginal elements remaining on the periphery of these two theories for useful salvage.[101] According to Dugin, his Fourth Political Theory may not be viewed as merely an extension of the second and third theories. Dugin stated that neither is acceptable as "starting points for resisting liberalism."[102]

Traditionalism, with its claims of possessing eternal Truth, is immensely attractive to Dugin. He identifies the presence of Traditionalist underpinnings supporting both Communism and Fascism while acknowledging that neither may have consciously realized their Traditional linkages.[103] Dugin's recognition of the Traditionalist threads in the second and third theories may at least partially explain why he mined them for salvageable material. He affirms that neither theory possesses correct orthodoxy but does not wholly disregard either as entirely worthless.

Dugin directly alluded to the concept of the rejected stone becoming the cornerstone as he contemplates his salvage operation.[104] "The second and third theories must be reconsidered," He wrote, "selecting in them what must be discarded and that which has value in itself."[105] In contrast, discernible Traditionalist threads in Liberalism (as the First Theory) are either non-existent or so obscure that Dugin deemed mining it an unproductive undertaking.[106]

Dugin suggests that the positives of communism include anti-capitalist, anti-liberal, anti-cosmopolitan, and anti-individualist elements.[107] But, allowing that even communism was stained by materialism and cosmopolitanism, Dugin insists that merely recycling communism will not do; these taints plus the considerable stumbling block of atheism eliminate communism from contention for resurrection.[108] As for fascism, Dugin rejects it as well—condemning it at the same time he does Western Liberalism, saying:

> As for the theories of the Third Way—which were dear, up to a certain point, to some traditionalists such as Julius Evola—there were many unacceptable elements, foremost among these being racism, xenophobia and chauvinism. These were not only moral failures, but also theoretically and anthropologically inconsistent attitudes. Differences between ethnicities do not equate to superiority or inferiority. The differences should be accepted and affirmed

without any racist sentiments of consideration. When one society tries to judge another, it applies its own criteria, and so commits intellectual violence. This ethnocentric attitude is precisely the crime of globalisation and Westernisation, as well as American imperialism.[109]

Dugin also mined Traditionalism in keeping with the Metaphysics of Debris. In doing so, he derived elements of his Neo-Traditionalism from various pieces of Integral Traditionalism he retrieved. "A tradition can give birth to a product at one stage of its existence which it could not produce at an earlier time," wrote Edward Shils.[110] Using this line of thinking, Dugin mines Integral Traditionalism for material that he then uses in his current construction project. Mining Traditional material places Dugin in a position described by the celebrated and influential sociologist, Talcott Parsons.[111] "While traditions work forward in time," Parsons explained, constructing an "inspirational tradition is a temporal movement in the reverse direction."[112]

As stated, Dugin does not view Fourth Political Theory as merely an extension of the failed second and third political theories of modernity. Dugin makes his case that neither can be the vehicle on which to construct or resurrect a Russia that can champion a multipolar world. However, he does not hesitate to explore leftover pieces of previous worldviews, ideologies, or geopolitical theories for reusable material. Even so, some are not so sure that Fourth Political Theory does not mean to produce "a copy of a totalitarian state from Europe's dark past, dressed in 21st century clothing."[113]

Notes

1. Saul Newman, *Political Theology: a Critical Introduction* (Cambridge, UK: Polity, 2019), 21. Saul Newman, Professor of Political Theory, Goldsmiths University of London.

2. Newman, *Political Theology*, 21.

3. Ibid.

4. Clooney, *Hindu God, Christian God: How Reason Helps Break Down the Boundaries Between Religions,* Oxford: Oxford University Press, 2001, 10, cited in, Richard Hanson, "A Dialogical Theism: Francis X. Clooney's Comparative Theology as a Resource for Interreligious Models of Ultimate Reality," *Journal of Inter-Religious Studies* 10, no. 10 (September 15, 2012): 66. Here Hanson is quoting Clooney. Cf. Hanson's footnote 12. Brackets in Hanson's original. Cf. Clooney, *Comparative Theology*. Richard Hanson, Senior Lecturer, University of Wisconsin.

5. Newman, *Political Theology*, 4.

6. Ibid., 5.

7. I do not argue for, or accept, Dugin as a theologian in either the academic or ecclesial sense. I do accept that he is a political theologian in the definitional sense explained, and that he pervasively embeds theologically related material and language, metaphysical references, and spiritual subject matter throughout his Fourth Political Theory.

8. Dugin, "Against Universalism."

9. Newman, *Political Theology*, 5.

10. Ibid., 5.

11. OED. Cf. e.g., Charles C. Ryrie, *Basic Theology* (Wheaton, IL: Victor Books, 1986), 13 and Charles Hodge, *Systematic Theology*, vol. 1 (Grand Rapids, MI: Eerdmans, 1952), 19f.

12. *Karl Barth's Letters 1961–1968*, Edited by J. Fangmeier and H. Stoevesandt. Translated and Edited by G. W. Bromiley (Edinburgh, T. and T. Clark, and Grand Rapids: Eerdmans, 1981), 284. Karl Barth, 1886-1968.

13. I confine this statement to considerations of his Fourth Political Theory and his ideas concerning Traditionalism and Eurasianism. As this is not a study of Dugin as a strict theologian (either Christian or otherwise), I confine him within the definition of political theology as explained.

14. David Novak, "Sacred Attunement: A Jewish Theology," *First Things*, (February 2009): 4, firstthings.com/article/2009/02/004-god-talk. Italics in original. Cf. Michael A. Fishbane, *Sacred Attunement: a Jewish Theology* (Chicago: University of Chicago Press, 2008). David Novak, Professor, Shiff Chair of Jewish Studies, University of Tornto. Michael A. Fishbane, Emeritus Professor of Jewish Studies, Divinity School, University of Chicago.

15. Novak, "Sacred Attunement," 4.

16. Ibid. Fourth Political Theory evidences a variety of God-talk as articulated by Fishbane, Novak, John Macquarrie and others, rather than theology originating from within strict academic or specific religious strictures. Cf. John Macquarrie, *God-Talk: An Examination of the Language and Logic of Theology* (London: SCM Press, 1978). Cf. Timothy Bradshaw, "John Macquarrie," in *The SPCK Handbook of Anglican Theologians*, ed. Alister E. McGrath (London: SPCK, 1998), 168. Timothy Bradshaw, Tutorial Fellow at Regent's Park College, Oxford.

17. Bernard Bourdin, The Theological-Political Origins of the Modern State: The Controversy Between James I of England and Cardinal Bellarmine, trans. Susan Pickford (Washington, DC: Catholic University of America Press, 2011), 1ff. Bernard Bourdin, Professor of Theology and the History of Religions, University of Lorraine. Hans Blumenberg, 1920-1996.

18. Schmitt, "Political Theology," 36. Originally published as *Politische Theologie: Vier Kapitel zur Lehre uon der Souveriinitat,* 1922, and in a revised edition 1934 by Duncker & Humblot, Berlin. Thomas McCarthy, Professor Emeritus of Philosophy, Northwestern University.

19. Ibid., 2. Italics in the original quotation, italics in the remainder of the sentence added.

20. Gavin Rae, "The Theology of Carl Schmitt's Political Theology," *Political Theology* 17, no. 6 (July 2015): 555. Gavin Rae, Research Fellow, Universidad Carlos III de Madrid. References and conclusions regarding Dugin's theological and related expressions throughout this study are too numerous to list.

21. Rae, "The Theology of Carl Schmitt's Political Theology," 557.

22. Ibid., 570.

23. Ibid., 571.

24. Cf. Morgan, in Dugin, *Fourth Theory*, footnotes 19 and 25.

25. Dugin, *Foundations*, 25. Malić notes that the emphasis was placed by Dugin in the original.

26. Dugin's critique of Western Secularism, Humanism, and embrace of Enlightenment ideas will be evident throughout.

27. The Fifth Directorate of the Soviet Government was responsible, as part of its charter, for the oversight of religious groups. That Fifth

Directorate existed is *prima facia* evidence of the claim made above. Cf. Coyer, "(Un)Holy Alliance: Vladimir Putin, The Russian Orthodox Church And Russian Exceptionalism," *Forbes*, May 21, 2015, forbes.com/sites/paulcoyer/2015/05/21/unholy-alliance-vladimir-putin-and-the-russian-orthodox-church/#497ea41427d5. Cf. e.g., loc.gov/exhibits/archives/anti.html; and, theguardian.com/commentisfree/belief/2017/oct/26/why-the-soviet-attempt-to-stamp-out-religion-failed.

28. Coyer, "(Un)Holy Alliance." A similar conclusion can be reached with respect to the current situation in China where the atheistic claims of the government do not preclude at least some religious dialogue (e.g., 2018 formal negotiations with the Roman Catholic Church regarding the selection process for bishops).

29. For just two of many, Cf. e.g., John G. Stackhouse, "Putting God in God's Place: Does Theology Belong in the University?," *Studies in Religion/Sciences Religieuses* 45, no. 3 (2016): 377-396; and, Tara Isabelle Burton, "The End of Theology," *The Chronicle of Higher Education*, January 24, 2016, chronicle.com/article/In-Defense-of-Theology/234986. John G. Stackhouse, Jr., Samuel J. Mikolaski Professor of Religious Studies, Crandall University. Tara Isabelle Burton, Theological Scholar, Columnist, and Writer.

30. Cf. e.g., Dugin, "Russians Must Save Europe from the Liberal Elites," Interview by *Il Foglio,* Geopolitica.ru., April 25, 2017, geopolitica.ru/en/article/russians-must-save-europe-liberal-elite. Geopolitica.ru. gives ilfoglio.it/ as its source for this question-and-answer article with Dugin.

31. R.C. Sproul, *Foundations: An Overview of Systematic Theology* (Stanford, FL: Ligonier Ministries, 1999), 2. Cf. Sproul, *Everyone's a Theologian: an Introduction to Systematic Theology* (Orlando, FL: Reformation Trust, 2014), 4 for a similar statement. "Thomas Aquinas called theology the 'queen of sciences,' using science in its medieval sense of a pursuit of knowledge or a knowledge-base." Kate Mertes, katemertes.com/theologyandreligionindexing.pdf. R.C. Sproul, 1939-2017. Kate Mertes, Indexer, Academic Texts (History, Art History, Law, and Humanities).

32. James R. Stoner, Jr., Stanley Hauerwas, Paul J. Griffiths, and David B. Hart, "Theology as Knowledge: A Symposium," *First Things*, May (2006): 21, firstthings.com/article/2006/05/theology-as-knowledge. James R. Stoner, Chair, Eric Voegelin Institute in the Department of Political Science, Louisiana State University. Stanley Hauerwas, Longtime Professor, Duke Divinity School, Duke University. Paul J.

Griffiths, Formally, Warren Professor of Catholic Thought, Duke Divinity School, Duke University. David B. Hart, Theologian.

33. Stoner, "Theology as Knowledge," 21.

34. Ibid., 22.

35. Ibid., 21. Cf. John Rawls, *Political Liberalism* (New York: Columbia Univ. Press, 1996). "From the Enlightenment onward, theology, far from being simply demoted to a handmaiden, became an outcast, a crazy aunt hidden in the basement of academia," was Sproul's droll comment on this situation. Sproul, *Foundations,* 2. John Rawls, 1921-2002.

36. Schmitt, "Political Theology," 5-66.

37. Arthur Versluis, "Carl Schmitt, Modernity, and the Secret Roads Inward," *Telos*, no. 148 (Fall 2009): Arthur Versluis, Chair of Religious Studies at Michigan State University. The First World War, World War I, also referred to as WWI.

38. Versluis, "Schmitt Secret Roads Inward," 31. Thomas Hobbes, 1588-1679.

39. Ibid.

40. Schmitt, "Political Theology," 48.

41. Newman, *Political Theology*, 2.

42. Schmitt, "Political Theology," 48.

43. I infer this from Newman, *Political Theology*, 2ff and Schmitt, "Political Theology," 48ff.

44. Schmitt, "Political Theology," 51.

45. Ibid., 48.

46. Ibid., 51.

47. Ibid.

48. Thierry Gontier, "Hans Blumenberg: The Legitimacy of the Modern Age," Voegelinview, November 12, 2011, under, The Secularization Theorem, voegelinview.com/modernity-and-secularization-pt-1/. "All significant concepts of the modern theory of the state are secularized theological concepts," can be found in Schmitt, "Political Theology," 36. It is unfortunate that *Secularization Theory*, the name given to ever-increasing secularization, which Schmitt opposed, is strikingly similar to *Secularization Theorem*, which Blumenberg used to describe

Schmitt's statement regarding secular concepts of modernity being theological in origin. Thierry Gontier, Professor of Political and Moral Philosophy, Université de Lyon.

49. Gontier, "Blumenberg Legitimacy," under, Modernity as Secularized Theology.

50. Hans Blumenberg, *The Legitimacy of the Modern Age*, trans. Robert M. Wallace (Cambridge, MA: MIT Press, 1983), 92.

51. Blumenberg, *Legitimacy of the Modern Age*, 92.

52. Gontier, "Blumenberg Legitimacy," under, Schmitt's Substitution of the State for Religion.

53. Rae, "Theology of Schmitt's Political Theology," 558.

54. Gontier, "Blumenberg Legitimacy," under, Blumenberg's Critique of Schmitt.

55. Bourdin, *Theological-Political Origins of the Modern State*, 4.

56. Gontier, "Blumenberg Legitimacy," under, Modernity as Secularized Theology.

57. Ibid., under, Deprecating All Modernity as "Secularization."

58. Ibid.

59. Richard Faber, "The Rejection of Political Theology: A Critique of Hans Blumenberg," *Telos* 1987, no. 72 (Summer 1987): 180. Cf. Teloscope, July 30, 2003, telospress.com/against-schmitts-political-theology-prometheus-or-pandora-hans-blumenberg-and-walter-benjamin-as-political-theologians/ for a transcript of this article. Richard Faber, Professor of Sociology, Free University of Berlin.

60. Faber, "A Critique of Hans Blumenberg," 180.

61. Ibid., 182.

62. Robert Wyllie, "Against Schmitt's Political Theology, Prometheus or Pandora? Hans Blumenberg and Walter Benjamin as Political Theologians," Teloscope, July 30, 2013, telospress.com/against-schmitts-political-theology-prometheus-or-pandora-hans-blumenberg-and-walter-benjamin-as-political-theologians/. This article is an examination of Faber's "Critique of Hans Blumenberg." Robert Wyllie, PhD candidate, Norte Dame, at the time of this writing.

63. Dugin, *Fourth Theory*, 174-5.

64. Schmitt, "Political Theology," 51.

65. Cf. e.g., Alain Pottage, "Conflicts of Laws," in *Territorial Conflicts in World Society: Modern Systems Theory, International Relations and Conflict Studies*, ed. Stephen Stetter (Routledge: New York, 2007),138-39. Alain Pottage, Professor of Law, London School of Economics and Political Science.

66. Cf. Eric Voegelin, *The New Science of Politics* (Chicago: University of Chicago Press, 1987). Eric Voegelin, 1901-1985.

67. Versluis, "Schmitt Secret Roads Inward," 34.

68. Ibid.

69. Voegelin, *New Science of Politics*, 126.

70. Ibid.

71. Ibid.

72. Cf. Geoffrey Sigalet, "Eric Voegelin: Political Theology in a New Key," Voegelinview, April 28, 2014, voegelinview.com/political-theology-new-key. Geoffrey Sigalet, Constitutional Law Postdoctoral Fellow, Stanford University.

73. Cf. Part IV Chapter One, especially note 4.

74. Hanson, "Dialogical Theism," 66.

75. Ibid.

76. Peter J. Leithart, "Fourth Political Theory," First Things, June 17, 2014, firstthings.com/blogs/leithart/2014/06/fourth-political-theory. Peter J. Leithart, President of Theopolis Institute, Senior Fellow of Theology, New Saint Andrews College.

77. Epstein, *Conservatism and Traditionalism*.

78. Ibid., 10ff.

79. Ibid., second page of Epstein's "Abstract."

80. Ibid., in Epstein's "Abstract," attached as a forward. Brackets added. Alexander Solzhenitsyn, 1918-2008.

81. Ibid., 18.

82. Gordon R. Middleton, "Religion in Russian Geo-Political Strategy," *Providence*, no. 9 (2017): 67. Parentheses in original. Gordon R. Middleton, Instructor, Director, Strategic Intelligence Program, Patrick Henry College.

83. Middleton, "Religion in Russian Strategy," 67.

84. Cf. Émile Durkheim, *The Division of Labour in Society*, Trans. by George Simpson. New York: Free Press. 1893. Durkheim built on previous ideas as far back as Plato; more recently, on the thoughts of Adam Smith. Cf. Smith's *An Inquiry into the Nature and Causes of the Wealth of Nations* in any one of its many editions. Émile Durkheim, 1858-1917. Adam Smith, ca. 1723-1790.

85. Jeff Weintraub's notes deal with Burke's widely recognized work, *Reflections on the Revolution in France*. Armitage provides insight into Burke's *Reason of State* perspectives. Armitage allows for contrasts and comparisons between Burke and Dugin to be drawn which are useful when considering Dugin's justifications for State power. Cf. Jeff Weintraub, *Handout #7: Reading Edmund Burke: Edmund Burke—Community, Authority, Tradition, and Conservatism*, 2012, Lecture Notes for PPE 475-302, University of Pennsylvania, handout "Making Sense of Modernity" covers Burke's impact on modernity—especially his impact on political philosophy; academia.edu/3884831/Edmund_Burke_Community_authority_tradition_and_conservatism, and David Armitage, "Edmund Burke and Reason of State," *Journal of the History of Ideas* 61, no. 4 (2000): 617-34. Cf. Edmund Burke, *Reflections on the Revolution in France: And Other Writings*, ed. Jesse Norman (London: Alfred A. Knopf, 2015). Edmund Burke, 1729-1797. David Armitage, Chairholder, Professor of History, Harvard University.

86. Cf. e.g., Weintraub, "Reading Edmund Burke."

87. Ian Harris, "Edmund Burke," *The Stanford Encyclopedia of Philosophy,* ed. Edward N. Zalta, Spring 2012, plato.stanford.edu/archives/spr2012/entries/burke/. Ian Harris, Lecturer, University of Leicester.

88. Harris, "Edmund Burke."

89. Weintraub, "Reading Edmund Burke."

90. Ibid.

91. Ibid.

92. Dugin, *Fourth Theory*, 91.

93. Ibid., 91-92.

94. Ibid., 91.

95. Ibid., 22-24

96. Dugin, "The Long Path." Cf. Dugin, *Fourth Theory*, 15ff.

97. Ibid., as part of his response to the first question which asked him to elaborate on his intellectual path. Brackets added.

98. Dugin, *Fourth Theory*, 22-24. Here Dugin discusses the three theories (Liberalism, Communism and Fascism) and mentions the "Metaphysics of Debris" while pointing out the utility of using "marginalia" and "marginal elements." Sekatsky is often rendered *Sekatski* in English. Alexander Sekatsky, Publicist, Philosopher, Academic, St. Petersburg State University..

99. Ibid., 24.

100. Ibid.

101. Ibid.

102. Ibid., 23.

103. Ibid., 24.

104. Ibid., 22 and Dugin's footnote 12. Cf. Mark 12:10, NASB: "Have you not even read this Scripture: The stone which the builders rejected, This became the Chief Corner Stone."

105. Ibid.

106. Dugin believes that Fourth Political Theory looks at everything preceding modernity for inspiration, thus he mostly excluded modernity from his mining operations. Cf. e.g., Dugin, *Fourth Theory*, 27.

107. Dugin, *Fourth Theory*, 195.

108. Ibid.

109. Ibid. As used here, the "Third Way" refers to Fascism.

110.. Edward Shils, "Tradition, Ecology, and Institution in the History of Sociology," *Daedalus*, 99, no. 4 (Fall 1970): 802. Cf. article may be accessed at: jstor.org/stable/20023974. Edward Shils, 1910-1995.

111. Talcott Parsons, 1902-1979.

112. Talcott Parsons, "The Informational Hierarchy of Control," *Critical Assessments*, Vol. 4. ed. Peter Hamilton, (London: Routledge, 1992), 151.

113. Rob Garver, "Putin Isn't Reviving the USSR, He's Creating a Fascist State," The Fiscal Times, May 26, 2015, thefiscaltimes.com/2015/05/26/Putin-Isn-t-Reviving-USSR-He-s-Creating-Fascist-State. Rob Garver, Correspondent, Fiscal Times.

Chapter Two: The Hermeneutics of Fourth Political Theory

Leaning on Brannan and Jeanrond

While other hermeneutical elements and themes are present in Dugin's work, three dominant categories falling under his overarching Hermeneutic of Political Theology—Traditionalism, Sacred Geography/Sacred Space, and Russia as the Third Rome— remain consistent, constant, and readily identifiable. Dugin's hermeneutical presuppositions drive Fourth Political Theory and all its associated accompaniments. Dugin's hermeneutics appear as refrains that are evident throughout his written works, spoken words, even in his choice of photographs and visual illustrations, and his allusions, and metaphors.[1]

To understand Dugin, first, understand his core hermeneutical assumptions. "Without this acceptance of the pre-suppositional hermeneutic," David Brannan assured, "the system will fail to convince."[2] Likewise, if Dugin's hermeneutical presuppositions are consistent within Fourth Political Theory, they will remain coherent—this is not to say universally evident, accepted, or correct, but coherent. "The central hermeneutic must be accepted," Brannan said—once acceptance is granted, all other suppositions fall into place below it.[3] Brannan's claims may be applied directly to Fourth Political Theory through his highlighting the centrality of hermeneutical presuppositions.

The detectable emphasis on the theological and metaphysical as an integral and essential component of Dugin's political thought is consistent with the Schmittian hermeneutic combining politics and theology. Dugin's classifications of themes and refrains suggest "hermeneutics as the methodology of interpretation," in keeping with the entry in the *Stanford Encyclopedia of Philosophy*.[4] Viewed from the academic perspective of hermeneutics as a refined subject area, Jean Grondin suggested confining hermeneutics to the "*theory* of interpretation."[5] "By 'hermeneutics' we mean the theory of interpretation," agreed Werner G. Jeanrond while lecturing in theology at Trinity College Dublin.[6]

Jeanrond provided the insight that "an ideology may be understood as a rigid attitude over against any object of understanding."[7] Going further, Jeanrond advocated a more holistic outlook with his claim that "the interpretation of the overall sense of our universe depends on the interpretation of the many textual or artistic approaches to reality, including the approach to the interpreter's own self."[8] I believe Jeanrond's expansion of his basic definition is critical to understanding Dugin's hermeneutical approach. For, in addition to extracting elements of Traditionalism and Eurasianism, including geographical, political, and theological ideas, to build his theory, Dugin is also "concerned with problems that arise when dealing with meaningful human actions and the products of such actions."[9] Dugin's hermeneutical usage agrees with the definitional expansions of Jeanrond and Chrysostomos Mantzavinos.

Dugin's hermeneutical categories may be arranged under his geopolitical theology as:

- **Political Theology**
- **Traditionalism**
  - Expressed as a Neo-Traditionalism
  - Anti-modernism/Anti-Westernism
- **Sacred Geography/Sacred Space**
  - Messianic Russia
  - Manifest Destiny
- **Russia as the Third Rome**
  - Revealing Antichrist
  - Russia as Katechon—the Restrainer that holds back Antichrist

A hermeneutical hierarchy in the structural framework of Fourth Political Theory is evident from the themes or refrains repeated throughout Dugin's written and spoken works. Dugin situates his Fourth Political Theory under the aegis of the *Hermeneutic of Geopolitical Theology*. Moreover, he expresses the theological aspects of his geopolitics from his Neo-Traditionalist viewpoint. Therefore, his *Hermeneutic of Traditionalism* is considered under his Geopolitical Theology.

Dugin's other hermeneutical subordinates are the *Hermeneutic of Sacred Geography/Sacred Space*, and his hermeneutics proclaiming *Messianic Russia* and *Russian Manifest Destiny*, accepting *Russia as the Third Rome* with its subsequent attempts of *Revealing Antichrist* and viewing *Russia as Katechon*—the Restrainer that holds back Antichrist.

Of the four major hermeneutical categories distinguishable under the over-arching Hermeneutic of Geopolitical Theology, the first three fall rather neatly underneath. The fourth, Russia as the Third Rome, is not quite as comfortable a placement as the three above it. This hermeneutical category contains both Traditional and sacred geographical elements. Russia is being distinctively Traditional when seeing itself as the successor of revealed Truth entrusted to Rome, then to Constantinople, when it assumed the sacred mantle for itself, and finally to Russia with the fall of Christian Byzantium. Russia, as the Third Rome, is also distinguished because of its sacred location. Third Rome advocates, like Dugin, ascribe Russia with remarkable sacred geographical characteristics.

Hermeneutic of Political Theology

A critical sub-set ingredient of Dugin's geopolitical theology is, of course, political theology. Dugin consistently expresses the Schmittian idea wherein politics contain a discernable theological component. There is a significant, distinguishable, and purposeful theme of intertwined or embedded political intent in Dugin's theologically connected presentation—and vice versa.

There is an active theological aspect, albeit decidedly esoteric, in Dugin's Fourth Political Theory. Dugin applies his spiritual outlook not only to his view of history but his view of the present and future as well. Dugin maintains the same position as that stated in Max Weber's observation and Schmitt's paraphrase: "it is possible to confront irrefutably a radical materialist philosophy of history with a similarly radical spiritualist philosophy of history."[10] In his Fourth Political Theory, Dugin demonstrates his belief in just such a claim. Dugin accepts Secularization Theorem and tends toward monotheistic rather than Blumenberg's polytheistic explanations. In Dugin's opinion,

185

"in order to understand politics, one must regard it as a religious phenomenon."[11] Schmitt, according to Dugin, wrote, "all political ideologies and systems are integral theological models with religions, dogmas, institutions, and rites of their own."[12]

I view Dugin's Hermeneutic of Political Theology following two pathways. The first "presupposes the existence of the political *telos*," its purpose or goal, "which can be constructed by man, like Hobbes' Leviathan."[13] The second recognizes political theology as being "of non-human construction, such as the [Roman] Catholic model of *imperium*, which was close to Schmitt's heart."[14] Dugin incorporates the first and espouses the second in his adoption of Hobbes and Schmitt. Dugin engages in the construction of Fourth Political Theory, believing, as he does so, in a theologically created imperium—that is, building with the authority of the Divine Sovereign.

Dugin, like Schmitt, finds "the machine" that "now runs by itself" objectionable. Also, like Schmitt, Dugin doubts that the machine that runs without the power of a sovereign in firm control, especially in times of crisis, will not likely run for long, or will careen into a collision and be destroyed. Moreover, as does Schmitt, Dugin finds ample reasons that the State requires a strong central authority equipped to exercise the exceptional force of the state. Finally, Dugin, agreeing with Schmitt, firmly believes in authority that possesses transcendent attributes, writing that, "society should be created not from below but from above."[15]

While Dugin no doubt believes that the state has the responsibility of "assuring citizens of order and stability," he does not make this responsibility the *raison d'être* of the state, as did Schmitt.[16] "The meaning of the State is its spiritual mission," Dugin claimed in more of a proclamation than a statement.[17] Indeed, it is the state's spiritual mission, its intertwining of the temporal and the spiritual—the fusion of political and theological elements, that likely makes Dugin, and by extension his Neo-Eurasian vision, so difficult for the West to accept. Dugin agrees with Hobbes' vision of the State's duty to law and security:

Hobbes used biblical imagery of Leviathan in his description of a powerful state able to keep peace and provide its citizens with security across the spectrum from personal to national. Hobbes was fain to envision the population of Leviathan, the State, contracting away most or all power to a single authority be it a single person or a relatively small authoritative council able to enforce the law and relieve the security concerns of the masses.[18] Dugin shares much of this Hobbesian philosophy of the power of the state but adds to it—blends with it—significant elements of theologically related metaphysics.

Hermeneutic of Traditionalism

Fourth Political Theory speaks to historically consistent Russian values and aspirations as well as to theological Truth in the Traditionalist sense of perennial norms and revelations. The mystical and esoteric nature of Dugin's Neo-Traditionalism is apparent throughout his writing and speaking, but nowhere more so than in his statement regarding the rationalism of Enlightenment-spawned Liberalism. "Tradition is an antithesis to Cartesianism," is Dugin's declaration of his belief.[19] "Formal logic," Dugin went on to say, "was where the Morning Star began the subversion of our majestic, sacral world."[20] Within these statements, Dugin is expressing a worldview that permeates his thinking and influences the articulation of all of his metaphysically grounded geopolitical theory. Cartesianism represents the Western Liberal worldview of formal logic and rationality, and the Morning Star, Dugin's allusion to Satan, has adopted the Cartesian approach in his usurpation of God and His Creation.[21]

Dugin's geopolitical theology involves a decidedly dualist view. Dugin sees Traditionalism as the worthy opponent to progressive Western Liberalism that asserts secular and civil religion dominance, and where long-established religious institutions and mores are subject to internal as well as external deconstruction. Dugin warned that "inter-confessional wars and tensions work for the cause of the kingdom of the Antichrist who tries to divide all the traditional religions in order to impose its own pseudo-religion, the eschatological parody."[22] Political figures and academics in the West, where only civil religion is safe ground, are not used to such counter-Enlightenment pronouncements boldly spoken by one who wields such a degree of potential influence.

187

Dugin is nowhere willing to cede the contest between Traditionalism and modernity to secular or civil religion. He wrote:

> In the spirit of Peter Berger, we can open up the prospect of "desecularisation" (throughout history, religious organisations frequently act as political subjects) or, together with Carl Schmitt, we can rethink the influence of Tradition on a political decision.[23]

Understanding Dugin's identified Traditional hermeneutic also provides a more unobstructed view of his preference for Sufist Islamic expressions, and its accommodation to Traditionalist views, as opposed to those of Wahhabist or Salafist leanings. Dugin insisted that "atomism is the doctrine of the asharitas and of the aggressively anti-Sufi, anti-esoteric theologian, Ibn Taymiyyah, father of contemporary Wahhabism and Salafism."[24]

Dugin embraces the conservatism inherent in Traditionalism. He places his Hermeneutic of Traditionalism beneath the overarching hermeneutical tent of Geopolitical Theology. Under this hermeneutical heading, Dugin arranges his anti-modernism, often expressed as anti-Westernism. Dugin took the anti-modernism found in Guénon's school of Integral Traditionalism, modified it with active elements of Evola's political brand of Traditionalist thought, and, using both, produced a hyper-anti-Western hybrid.

Anti-Modernism/Anti-Westernism

Dugin's Traditionalism yields an anti-modernism that expresses itself as anti-Westernism. Even a casual reader of Dugin quickly picks up on his anti-Western bias that is partially based on his vehement condemnation of globalism's rampant materialism. The constitutive ideology of the West contains efforts to expand Western globalism and the secular notion that elevates the individual over the traditional community. Dugin classifies both globalism and individualism as tenets of Western Liberalism.[25]

Dugin sees America as the flag bearer of Western Liberalism—
the "ominous and alarming country on the other side of the
ocean."[26] In a telling selection from Moss's English translation of
Absoliutnaia Rodina, Dugin stated that America is a country
"without history."[27] "It is the result of a pure experiment of the
European rationalist utopians."[28] It is also,

> without tradition, without roots. An artificial,
> aggressive, imposed reality, completely devoid of
> spirit, concentrated only on the material world
> and technical effectiveness, cold, indifferent, an
> advertisement shining with neon light and
> senseless luxury; darkened by pathological
> poverty, genetic degradation and the rupture of all
> and every person and thing, nature and culture.[29]

Dugin continued with his condemnation of America saying
that with "its planetary dominion, the triumph of its way of life,
its civilizational model over all the peoples of the earth," America
sees "progress" and "civilizational norms" only in itself.[30] Moss
wrote that, in Dugin's opinion, America refuses the right to choose
values and culture to everyone else on the planet.[31]

Hermeneutic of Sacred Geography/Sacred Space

The interwoven threads of place, metaphysics, and politics,
comprise the tapestry of geopolitical theology. In Dugin's case,
place is much more than physical reality. "The origins of
geography are entangled with the origins of Western philosophy
in Greek thought," wrote Tim Cresswell, addressing the ancient
origins of contemplating terrain.[32] Concepts addressing the
physical world are indeed ancient, but there is another aspect
addressed by both Cresswell and Sheldrake, at least as old.
Capturing the essential of Dugin's conception of Sacred
Geography, Sheldrake wrote that "the human sense of place is a
critical theological and spiritual issue."[33]

John Inge agreed, concluding that the narrative of the Old
Testament "supports a relational view in which God, people and
place are all important."[34] Not stopping there, he wrote that the

189

New Testament also supports the notion of place being of vital significance in God's dealings with humanity.[35] So, the ancient contemplation of the physical and the theological—the material and the metaphysical—are at play. Adding a third ingredient, old, but not ancient, using the term, *Russian Nationalism*, Rossman introduced geopolitics to the mix. He, like Clover, was one who described Dugin's affinity for Sacred Geography as a combination of geopolitics and religious ingredients.[36] Dugin wrote, "Russian nationalism is inseparably linked with space," and Rossman discusses this critical aspect extensively.[37]

There is also a direct contradiction between things considered "positive" by the majority of people in the West and those adhering to a belief in Sacred Geography/Sacred Space.[38] According to Dugin, in Western geopolitics, "such concepts as 'progress,' 'liberalism,' 'human rights,'" for example, "are today positive terms for the majority of people."[39] For those subscribing to Fourth Political Theory and a Sacred Geography/Sacred Space paradigm, evaluation of things "positive" spring "from a completely opposite point of view."[40]

Dugin's continued use of metaphorical language exposes his belief that deep-felt spiritual connections are inextricably part of the human condition. Superficially, many Westerners think they are entirely divorced from their ancient ancestral antecedents. Yet, even common expressions such as a person being under a cloud or describing the natural world as *Mother Nature*, betrays the persistence of uncanny awe and spiritual associations with nature's myriad phenomena. According to Dugin, "even in our antisacred world, at an 'unconscious' level almost always archetypes of sacred geography are preserved in their integrity, and are awoken in the most relevant and critical moments of social cataclysms."[41]

Shils, says Lawrence Cahoone, related that human societies seeking ultimate references for solidarity usually turn to either the sacred or the "objective ties of blood and soil."[42] Dugin takes a position contrary to the "blood" aspect of Shils' "blood and soil" ties.[43] Specifically, Dugin related that, contrary to other peoples, "Russians distinguish themselves not by blood, ethnicity, phenotype or culture."[44] Unlike others, Russians identify more with space, an identification that Dugin characterizes as a "national intoxication."[45] In the Russian mindset, geographical connections may supersede racial or ethnic ties. Put directly, "Russians regard space as sacred," according to Dugin.[46] This interpretation of their land as Sacred Space may help explain Dugin's observation that "in many cases Russians prefer non-Slavic people affiliated with Russian space to other Slavs."[47]

Comprising both the *Geo* of Dugin's Geopolitics and an essential element of the theology in his geopolitical theology is Dugin's realization of the sacredness of particular locations and geological features. For Dugin, geography comprises much more than the physical characteristics of land and sea. Dugin believes in a material world imbued with an inseparable spiritual dimension. Dugin weaves spiritual yarn throughout the projection of his Eurasian ideas with his concept of Sacred Geography/Sacred Space.

The concept of Sacred Geography/Sacred Space is present in the West, but mainly at a *sub rosa* level of awareness. Individuals may identify in some vague way with the concept that a place may possess a holy nature. Awareness may arrive, for example, through an ethereal experience in a cathedral, in elements of nature, while visiting the graves of loved ones, or in the space where something monumental has occurred.

Contemplating sites such as Stonehenge and New Grange as more than cultural and historical artifacts may be a first step in grasping concepts of Sacred Geography/Sacred Space. Considering examples that illustrate that closely integrated natural and spiritual realizations of the world were long the rule, rather than the exception, aids reception of Sacred Geography. The ancient Druids, for example, recognized strong ties between themselves and the spiritual aspects of the physical world. Appreciating this spiritual emphasis allows for the elevation of Sacred Space over purely physical interpretations of artifacts and geography in keeping with Dugin's Sacred Geography hermeneutic.

Native American peoples display a deep involvement with Sacred Space, perhaps the most accessible indigenous example in America that can contribute to an understanding of where Dugin is grounded. Though not in an exact correlation, Simmins and Dugin made similar claims, recognizing the common tendency of spiritual peoples to ascribe sacred attributes to geographical features, celestial geometry, and the bonds of place.

Simmins wrote that among the "aboriginal groups on the Great Plains, there is a conception of geography divided into realms, each of which are connected with cycles of life, the seasons, and particular abstract human attributes."[48] Dugin's perceptions also involve mystical geographic connections. Simmins related that the "cardinal points (and their associated life-cycles and seasons) are also connected with four elements: earth, wind, water and fire."[49] Contrasting the cardinal point applications of Native Americans to Dugin's cardinal point attachments also provide fascinating points of comparison.

Using the American Plains Indians as an example, Simmins made the point that their metaphysics consider human beings to "consist of four distinct parts."[49] These parts are distributed into categories: emotional, mental, physical, and spiritual.[46] The four distinctions are associated with the four cardinal points and are additionally linked with corresponding colors. Simmins listed the linkages as cardinal points, and associated colors, objects, and activities: physical (north, white, pipe holder); spiritual (east, red, sweetgrass); emotional (south, yellow, sweat lodge); mental (west, black, sun-dance).[47] Cardinal point, color, and object/activity associations with various sacred connections are not uncommon to cultures that embrace Sacred Space.

The compass directions and the colors referred to in the Hebrew and Christian Bibles yield such examples as the physical orientation of the Temple and the symbolic linking of colors to the four apocalyptic riders in the Book of Revelation in the Christian New Testament. There can be no doubting that the colors are purposely assigned to the horses. The color of the fourth horse, for example, demonstrates such a close association with its purpose that it repeatedly appears in literature in the metaphorical sense.

> I looked, and behold, an ashen horse; and he who sat on it had the name Death; and Hades was following with him. Authority was given to them over a fourth of the earth, to kill with sword and with famine and with pestilence and by the wild beasts of the earth.[50]

Simmins' association was by no means exclusive to the Plains Indians. There are numerous examples of cardinal point associations. For example, the Tabernacle, the Temple of Solomon, the restored Temple, and the rebuilt Temple were oriented facing to the east, toward Eden, and were said to model Paradise.[51] John M. Lundquist's research has shown that common temple design in the ancient Levant, South-West Asia, and Africa was, "oriented toward the four world regions or cardinal directions, and to various celestial bodies such as the polar star."[52] Due to their individually surveyed positioning, ancient temples may have served as astronomical observatories "to assist the temple priests in regulating the ritual calendar."[53]

In the contemporary world, references to east and west are often intuitive—the East is Oriental, and the West is Occidental—East is Asia, and West is Europe, North America, and the rest of the Anglosphere. Overlaying Sacred Space is allegorically and metaphorically consistent applied to east and west. The fact that the earth rotates so that the sun appears to rise in the east and set in the west is consistent with the mystical idea that beginnings, such as birth, have eastern associations, and endings, such as death, have western ones.

Many Christian churches and burial grounds are oriented to the east-west cardinal points. In churchyards, the head of the deceased is frequently arranged to the west and the feet to the east. This orientation recognizes that when Jesus returns to reign as Messiah-King, it will be realized first from the east, "for just as the lightning comes from the east and flashes even to the west, so will the coming of the Son of Man be."[54] Thus, the face of the person buried will be toward the coming Messiah when rising in the Resurrection.

The dramatic rise of civilization in the Northern Hemisphere, the eastern rotation of the earth, and the declination of the earth's axis at approximately 23.5° off vertical makes it easier to imbue Sacred Space with east-west allusions than with ones of north and south. Because solar events are typically witnessed as east-west events, it appears more consistent with Northern and Western Hemispheric experience to overlay east-west physical geography with east-west Sacred Geography than to make a north-south overlay. The fact that the sun seemingly rises in the east and sets in the west allows for scores of varied birth and death allusions. The tilt of the earth and the orbital rotation around the sun combine to produce the seasons as we know them, and seasons, as well as compass directions, abound with associations to birth and death.

Cardinal point associations are not limited to east-west allusions. Even considering the tendency favoring east-west associations, development of civilization in the Northern Hemisphere, with its profusion of writing, exploration, and trade, produced many allusions specifically relevant to north-south observations of physical geography. Comparisons related to heat and cold, observations of celestial events viewed from the Northern Hemisphere, and Northern cultural narratives fraught with allusions and allegory reflecting the world perceived through Northern eyes abound. Additionally, Dugin's interpretation of "Northness" and the assumption of Eastern attributes by the North must be taken into account.[55]

Dualism is prevalent in Chinese cosmology where the two universal principles of life are perceived and illustrated as being both tightly pressed against one another while yet remaining separate. Often thought of as opposites or contrasts—different, but somehow complementary—the Yin and Yang are symbolized within a circle separated by contrasting dark and light colors.[56] The Dualism displayed in the Yin and Yang is strongly reminiscent of the Anfisbena discussed in detail by Dugin.[57]

Combining Sacred Geography with Neo-Eurasian geopolitics may be difficult for Western geopoliticians to deal with, but it is necessary to do so in parsing Dugin's ideas. Because humans exist in a temporal dimension, place is a reality of being. It is, Inge related, where "meeting and activity" occur "in the interaction between God and the world."[58] The backdrop of Sacred Geography is an ever-present reality with Dugin. Critical to correctly viewing Dugin in the development of his Eurasian concept is realizing his consistent reliance on a spiritual understanding of geography. This element of geography and space is absent, or nearly so, in the West's geopolitical perception. Highlighting his anti-Western bias, Dugin believes that there is a conflict between the priorities of modern Western geopolitics and "the paradigm of sacred geography."[59]

Messianic Russia/Eurasia and Manifest Destiny

The overtly metaphysical attributes that Dugin espouses in his concept of Sacred Geography must find residence in Eurasia as the inheritor of Russia's messianic mission. "A major part of the rationale given by Putin as to why he annexed Crimea in 2014 was due to its 'sacred' nature as the spiritual birthplace of the Russian nation," explained Paul Coyer.[60] Putin made it very clear that Crimea has "sacred meaning for Russia, like the Temple Mount for Jews and Muslims."[61] Putin added that Crimea is "spiritual soil" and "the spiritual source of the formation of the multifaceted but monolithic Russian nation" where Russia's forebears first realized themselves as a nation.[62] So saying, Putin acknowledged Sacred Geography as part of the Russian narrative.[63] Coyer explained that it is in Crimea where Vladimir, Prince of Kiev, received the "Baptism of the 'Rus," his baptism into the Eastern Church, and thus, where the official conversion of his subjects simultaneously occurred.[64]

Coyer was probably correct that the linkage between Vladimir's Kievan state "and the political entity that later became 'Muscovy' and then evolved into modern day Russia," is questionable.[65] It is instructive to realize that the connection that Putin draws is reflective of the often allusion-rich and symbolic nature of Dugin's hermeneutic concerning place, not necessarily of empirical facts.

Dugin's Hermeneutic of Sacred Geography/Sacred Space allows him to project his vision of Eurasia through the lenses of Manifest Destiny terms and understandings. Woven deeply into the Hermeneutic of Sacred Geography/Sacred Space are the hermeneutically derived imperatives of Messianic Russia, expressed in Manifest Destiny terms and understandings, and passed on and expanded as a messianic Eurasian mission. While Manifest Destiny is often spoken of with derision in the postmodern West, Dugin does not express the concept in negative terms.

195

Dugin's mind—and this applies to many Russian thinkers—is Eastern, in that it contemplates theological and metaphysical considerations as a matter of course, unlike the purposeful intent of many Western thinkers who tend to exclude anything theological or spiritual altogether. It is instructive to observe that Dugin applies a theologically inspired approach to American development in its philosophical heritage, the effects of the Enlightenment on it, and to its geographical growth expressed in Manifest Destiny.

> As a historical product of Western Europe during its evolution, the New World very early on realized its "messiah" destiny, where the liberal-democratic ideals of the Enlightenment were combined with the eschatological ideas of radical protestant sects. This was called the theory of Manifest Destiny, which became the new symbol of belief for generations of Americans. According to this theory, American civilization overtook all cultures and civilizations of the Old World and in its current universal form, it is obligatory for all nations of the planet.[66]

Manifest Destiny terminology was coined by John L. O'Sullivan in an 1845 editorial "to urge the annexation of Texas, California, Oregon, and other western territories" into the United States.[67]

> Rather than a specific policy, manifest destiny was a belief in the superiority of the so-called Anglo-Saxon race and that westward expansion was divinely inspired, wise, and inevitable. This expansion would bring civilization and economic development to areas that previously had lain outside of areas of U.S. influence.[68]

Manifest Destiny is strongly associated with the expansionism that endows a state or people with a sense of transcendent guidance or implies inspiration—even the

196

command—of divine or spiritual force. "Proponents commonly pointed to the alleged inherent virtue of U.S. institutions and people and a divinely ordained mission to spread democratic institutions with a goal of remaking the rest of the world in the image of the United States," in Marc Becker's opinion.[69] For opponents, in the 1800s as well as today, it implies an unjustified and colonial sense of a privilege to subjugate through intimidation or application of force, either economic or militaristic.[70]

In an interview by *Alternative Right*, Dugin was asked by Tremblay, "you oppose American Manifest Destiny, but how does Orthodox Messianism differ?"[71] Dugin, in part, replied, "Manifest Destiny exists, not in the singular but in the plural."[72] Dugin suggested that, rather than a single Manifest Destiny, there are "*Manifest Destinies*: American, European, Russian, Islamic, Chinese, and so on."[73] Russia, too, possesses a messianic mission. There is a difference, however. Where Dugin implies a messianic destiny to the United States, he does so mainly in a metaphorical sense—underscoring America's expansionist fervor. When he addresses the messianic mission of Russia, he insists on its divine appointment. "We are a divine nation," is the distillation of Dugin's belief.[74] The messianic destiny assignation of the U.S. is mostly a metaphorical device to explain its expansionist motives. In contrast, the messianic mission of Russia envisioned by Dugin is actual, divinely directed, and divinely imperative. It is the exclusiveness of an American Manifest Destiny that Dugin opposes, and the divinely directed messianic mission of Eurasia that he proclaims.

William Cavanaugh claimed that the idea of what constitutes a messianic nation has its roots in the doctrine of election; "the doctrine of election is based in the notion of God's choice of a particular people at a particular moment in history."[75] In Christian theology, more particularly in Reformed Christian doctrine, election is an eternal reality from before the Creation and is thus predestined.[76]

Coyer wrote that the Russian Orthodox Church "strongly backed Putin's annexation of Crimea and intervention in eastern Ukraine, framing the conflict in apocalyptic, theological terminology in perfect harmony with Russia's historic sense of messianic destiny."[77] Coyer stated that both the Crimean

197

annexation and the Ukrainian conflict are framed as "Holy War" by the Kremlin and the Russian Orthodox Church.[78] He explained that the Kremlin and the Russian Orthodox Church view the Crimean and larger Ukrainian conflict "as a civilizational struggle between 'Holy Orthodox Russia' (a concept hundreds of years old) and an overly-secularized, morally decadent West (a Russian perception of the West that also predates Putin and Alexander Dugin by centuries)."[79] It is noteworthy to recognize the characterization of this conflict as a "civilizational struggle" given Coyer's claim that it "continues to be the most important field of civilizational conflict from Moscow's point of view."[80]

Hermeneutic of Third Rome

Marshall Poe stated that "several Russian philosophers of the late nineteenth century developed the thesis that Russia was a 'messianic' nation."[81] Poe's work revealed that by the turn of the twentieth century, "the 'messianic' understanding of 'Third Rome' was a commonplace that could be found in any number of influential historical surveys."[82] With the fall of First Rome—the Western portion of the Roman Empire—Constantinople became the seat of Roman power—Second Rome. The Bishoprics of Rome and Constantinople were nominally equal, but Rome more and more assumed not just the title of Chair of Peter, but also increasingly claimed the primacy. Eventually, internal doctrinal fighting led to the division of the Church into separate Eastern and Western entities.

Dugin wrote that "After the schism that split the Churches into Western (Catholic) and Eastern (Orthodox) hemispheres, the New Rome, Byzantium, remained the one guardian of true Christianity while the Catholics fell into the void of apostasy."[83] Second Rome fell as well. The Ottomans occupied Greece, formerly under Byzantine protection, after the fall of Constantinople in 1453. "But in a northern kingdom, in snowy and wild lands populated by a strange, pensive, contemplative people immersed in the fury of their secret mission, everything remained the same," Dugin related, "as if that terrible event," the fall of Second Rome, "had not taken place."[84] According to Dugin, when

Moscow took over the mission as the stronghold of Eastern Christianity, the Third Rome came into being.[85]

> So did Rus become the one country where the teachings and norms of true Christianity remained extant. Thus, the eternal city moved to the North, to Moscow. Henceforth, Moscow took upon itself the baton of being the subject of history. Later, a Patriarchy was established in Rus, and the "symphony of powers" was fully affirmed. Moscow became a synonym for Orthodoxy in the post-Byzantine era.[86]

Rossman wrote that Dugin believes that in the Russian view, "Orthodoxy is neither 'a branch of Christianity' (as Protestantism) nor the universal Catholic Church."[87] What then is it in Dugin's view?

> After the fall of Constantinople, Orthodox Russia became "the last shelter of Christ's truth in a world of apostasy" and "the last unspoiled bulwark of faith and sacredness in a world of evil." The doctrine of "Moscow—the Third Rome" of the monk Philotheus, Dugin argues, presupposes that Russia is the Fourth Empire and the "Restraining Force," "the catechon" of the second Epistle of Paul to the Thessalonians.[88]

The Rossman excerpt above is loaded with elements of Dugin's geopolitical theology. Dugin's hermeneutical presupposition of Russia, by extension, Eurasia, as the Third Rome, embodying a restraining force, the Katechon identified by Paul, is foundational to Fourth Political Theory. Versluis recognized Third Rome represents the "the paramount importance of historicity."[89] But, is historical authenticity Dugin's goal? His citation of Mikhail Agursky's work, *The Third Rome: National Bolshevism in the USSR*, in *The Fourth Political Theory*, and subsequent conversation, suggests the concept of Third Rome is more to Dugin than just a piece of historical foundation.[90] Dugin does not use theological material as a tangential contact with politics. Dugin attempts to saturate Fourth Political Theory with theological intent—the intent to support his scheme of geopolitical theology.

Poe reported that "the writings of the Russian monk Filofei of Pskov in the early sixteenth century," gave Third Rome its first recorded appearance.[91] Poe explained, "Filofei, like other clerics of the era, was concerned that the Russian monarchy was not doing enough to stamp out heresies such as astrology."[92] Filofei, Poe related,

> wrote a letter to an official in which he argued that the Muscovite grand prince was obliged to protect the church because he was the ruler of the "Third Rome." If the Russian ruler failed in this duty, humanity could not be saved, because, according to "books of prophecy" that Filofei never identified, there would be no "Fourth Rome" before the last judgment.[93]

In the Executive Summary to his study on Third Rome, Poe wrote that the Old Believers found Third Rome concepts important enough to ensure that in claiming the mantle of being the designated keepers of Third Rome they could be distinguished as holding the True Faith:

> The "Old Believers," a major sectarian movement of the second half of the seventeenth century, did adopt "Third Rome." They believed that the Russian orthodox church had abandoned the "true" faith and the obligations of being the "Third Rome." The Old Believers separated themselves from Russian orthodoxy and claimed their community alone represented the "Third Rome."[94]

As Poe concluded from his research, the influence of opinions supporting the Third Rome concept—Third Rome" as evidence—was accepted by several Russian philosophers.[95]

The idea first became politically significant in connection with the "Panslav" movement in the last quarter of the nineteenth century. The Panslavs believed that it was Russia's duty to protect and unite all orthodox Slavs in a federation under Moscow's control. They saw "Third Rome" as evidence that Russia was historically and even divinely destined to fulfill this task.[96]

Poe realized that by following up on the nineteenth century support for the Third Rome and Messianic Russia in the 1950s and 1960s, Western commentators connected the origins of Soviet "expansionism" to "Russian messianism" and thence to continuing Third Rome allusions.[97] "More recently," Poe explained, "Russians have begun to explore 'Third Rome' as a way to comprehend what they believe is their national psychology."[98] Although Dugin would probably not explain it as "national psychology," more likely preferring a description with overtones of inheritance of Divine Presence, he is most certainly one of the Russians who promote the Third Rome concept, as Poe suggests.

In the face of Dugin's use of Third Rome allusions underlying Fourth Political Theory, it is disappointing that Dugin's claims were not addressed in Poe's 1997 work.[99] Poe concluded that there is no historical validity in the contention of the past advocates of Third Rome.[100] Hence, there can be no validity for advocates, and Dugin is undoubtedly one, supporting the reality of a Third Rome. Despite Poe's assertion, of more concern in evaluating Dugin is the recognition given to his Third Rome assumptions. Wood wrote that

Russia has always had a singular conceit of itself as a Third Rome, an expanding imperial power, and then as the center of world revolution. The West has over the centuries been the object of both fascination and resentment for Russia. Russia's borders have enlarged and contracted over the centuries. The proposition that other

201

Slavs, like the Ukrainians, are somehow really
Russian has a long history.[101]

Poe's academic argument against the historicity of Third
Rome notwithstanding, it is Wood's opinion of Russian self-
identity as Third Rome coupled with geography that more
accurately reflects the West's interpretation of Russia's Historic
National Interest. It is hard to overestimate the role of geography
as a driver behind Russia's foreign policy," wrote Gurganus and
Rumer, adding that "geography has shaped Russian identity and
its rulers' understanding of security throughout the entire
existence of the Russian state."[102]

Recent events demonstrate the fact that Third Rome is a
living concept despite any weakness in its true lineage. Curiously,
the meeting between Pope Francis and Patriarch Kirill reinforced
Third Rome's conceptual viability. In the nineteenth century,
Vladimir Soloviev developed a philosophical and theological
ecumenism that called for a reconciliation of the Orthodox and
Roman Churches and "a mystical syncretism between Orient and
West."[103] But, this meeting of the Pope and the Patriarch "had far
more import for geopolitics than it did for the reconciliation of two
long-alienated branches of Christianity," in Coyer's opinion.[104]

Coyer stated three Russian goals for Kirill's participation in
the meeting which I feel are especially pertinent. The first was
gaining Francis's approval, and thereby, the Vatican's moral
authority, for Moscow's role in Syria. Russia portrays itself as
being in Syria partially for the critical reason of protecting
Christian minorities subject to the violence and under threat by
Daesh.[105] Russia, it must be remembered, takes the mission of
safeguarding Christians throughout Southwest Asia as a critical
element of its Historic National Interests.

Although Russia indeed recognizes and promotes
its cultural and religious pluralism since the
tsarist times, it is equally undeniable the
importance played by the Orthodox faith
throughout the centuries in the creation and
definition of the Russian identity and the shaping
of the foreign policy, as shown by the

202

"*Autocracy, Orthodoxy and Nationality*" 19th century doctrine or by the will to defend pilgrims and Christian worshippers living in the Ottoman-ruled Holy Land.[106]

Secondly, Kirill wanted Russia to gain visibility for Russian as a "Christian nation."[107] The third goal is most appropriate for this study: "the blunting of Turkey's ability to frustrate Russia's goals in Syria. As Sergey Kholmogorov wrote, a major Russian motivation for the meeting was "Third Rome [Moscow], Meeting First Rome [the Papacy], to Neutralize Second Rome [Constantinople/Turkey]."[108] Kholmogorov indeed connected the dots linking Moscow with Third Rome, and Coyer quickly picked up on the fact that he did so.[109]

Schmitt wrote that "The history of the Middle Ages is the history of a struggle for, not against Rome."[110] It was a struggle that attempted to recreate the idealized power and governance of the Roman Empire. The empire that constituted First Rome had become Christian but had fallen. The subsequent formation of what later became known as the Holy Roman Empire is evidence showing that the wish to recover that which was lost was much more than romantic nostalgia.[111] Dugin's hermeneutical endeavors fit together interdependently. Dugin employs a hermeneutical approach that recognizes Russia/Eurasia as the Third Rome and, as such, as Catechon—the Restrainer that holds back Antichrist—but, who or what is the Antichrist?[112]

Identifying Antichrist

The Apostle Paul warned his fellow Christians not to become overly concerned even if they got a letter purportedly written by him, not even if a spirit should deliver information that "the day of the Lord has come."[113] The clear implication being that such a letter must be a forgery, and such a message, even from a spirit, must be from an evil one. The reason such news could not be real is that such a day cannot come "unless the apostasy comes first."[114] Before the "day of the Lord," the "man of lawlessness" will be revealed.[115] This "man of lawlessness" is spoken of as if he is Antichrist if not, then some forerunner, prototype, or protégé.[116]

Dugin is confusing, sometimes even contradictory, concerning the specifics he attributes to the manifestation of the Antichrist. To arrive at a clearer understanding of how he entertains multiple Antichrist candidates, it is useful to realize Dugin's Orthodox and schismatic Old Believer background.[117] According to Rossman, Old Believer adherents claim, "that the Antichrist has already come and often identified him with one of the Russian emperors."[118] As an Old Believer, it would follow that Dugin would likely adopt a similar conclusion.

The Jewish Messiah as Antichrist

Rossman has also suggested that:

> Judaism does not have the soteriological element common in all other religions; the Messiah of Judaists does not bring any "good news" and does not promise the "return" to the original state. It is not surprising then that the Jewish Messiah is identified in "eternal Christianity" and other traditional religions with the Antichrist.[119]

Given Dugin's Traditional embrace of the "eternal Christianity" referred to by Rossman, it could follow that Dugin accepts that the Jewish Messiah is Antichrist.[120] Dugin contends that Judaism and Christianity share common terms regarding concepts such as eschatology, messiahship, and demonology, though they sometimes differ greatly as to their meanings.[121] For example, "in the Judaic consciousness the Messiah is not a Divine Hero who comes down from Heaven to rectify the worn cosmos and to save the degraded human community, as it is for the Christians," according to Dugin.[122] Dugin wrote that the messiah described in Judaic sources "cannot be identified with the direct and triumphal revelation of the Transcendental."[123] "Judaists believe that both the saving and the saved are this-worldly," therefore, Dugin claims that Judaism lacks soteriology.[124] He concluded that this Jewish Messiah would not usher in anything new—no New Heaven and New Earth as in Christian doctrine. Dugin ultimately decided that the Jewish Messiah is not on the side of Light and Truth.[125] Dugin's conclusions support the possibility of his acceptance of the Jewish Messiah as Antichrist.

A Collective Antichrist

A third possibility could be imbuing the Antichrist with a collective nature. Dugin suggests a "Moshiah of the World Government"—Antichrist manifested as the New World Order.[126] In the early 1990s, as President George H. W. Bush began proclaiming the arrival of a New World Order, Dugin began to announce its inherent evil. "After the Gulf War," Dugin wrote, "almost all mass media outlets in Russia, as well as in the West, injected into the common speak the formula 'New World Order,' coined by George Bush, and then used by other politicians including Gorbachev and Yeltsin."[127] Dugin immediately applied theological implications to these New World Order announcements claiming that Orthodox Christianity and Islam "clearly identify 'new religiosity,' New World Order, and Moshiah with the most sinister player in the eschatological drama, the Antichrist (Dadjal in Arabic)."[128]

Dugin's repeated claims that America is Antichrist, or a close associate, conflict with the Old Believer doctrine of the already accomplished appearance of Antichrist. His claims also seem to contradict any projection of the Jewish Messiah as Antichrist. As with much of Dugin's esoteric rhetoric, it is difficult to know how much to accept literally.

> I strongly believe that Modernity is absolutely wrong and the Sacred Tradition is absolutely right. USA is the manifestation of all I hate— Modernity, westernization, unipolarity, racism, imperialism, technocracy, individualism, capitalism. It is in my eyes the society of Antichrist.[129]

Russia, the core of Eurasia, is the opponent of a New World Order morphed from the Western inheritance of the

205

Enlightenment. To proponents of Fourth Political Theory, The Enlightenment, and hence the New World Order, produced a false faith, the pseudo-religion of Liberal Western globalism. The extensions spawned in evil—modernity, postmodernity, and the New World Order—represent the Moshiah, the Antichrist, of this world. Dugin Believes that the "Moshiah of the World Government is not simply a 'cultural project, new 'social myth,' or 'grotesque utopia,' but is something much more serious, real, terrible."[130]

Katechon (the Restrainer)

Before the thirteenth century, Rome and its successor monarchies and empires proved to be merely temporal. They were, nonetheless, continually striving to attain, then maintain, the power of Christian Rome. "The decisive historical concept of this continuity," according to Schmitt, "was that of the restrainer: katechon."[131] This desire to maintain the power of Rome "meant the historical power to restrain the appearance of the Antichrist and, the end of the present eon."[132] The image and acceptance of the katechon were mythically powerful in the time of the Holy Roman Empire. So much so that Schmitt stated that the "empire of the Christian Middle Ages lasted only as long as the idea of the katechon was alive."[133]

> The katechon represents, for Schmitt, a "historical concept" of "potent historical power" that preserves the "tremendous historical monolith" of a Christian empire, and it does so by opposing the perceived activity of Satan in others. One can hardly avoid the paramount importance of historicity here.[134]

A problem encountered with Dugin's hermeneutic concerning the Katechon is the identity of Antichrist.[135] The idea of Moscow (hence Russia or even Dugin's Eurasia) as Third Rome involves if or how it acts as the Restrainer. Accepting the Byzantine emperors as the Katechon assumes they restrained Antichrist for a time.[136] However, in making this assumption,

Antichrist should be present in the world today because after the Byzantine empire fell in 1453, there would have been no Restrainer. Absent the Katechon, Antichrist should have appeared.[137] Why did this not happen? Moss suggests that, as the Old Believers profess, "according to the great mercy of God," a kind of 'Indian summer' of truly Orthodox statehood, the 'Third Rome' of Moscow, prolonged the 'thousand-year reign of Christ' into the modern period."[138]

Confusion over dates when attempting to reconcile the Old Believer Millennial model creates calculation contradictions. Does the Millennial Reign of Christ depend on determining whether the Antichrist was loosed on the world since either 1656 or 1666-67, or until Peter I effectively set aside the Patriarchy in the early 1700's and attempted to continue his subordination of the Church to State rule?[139] Whatever the exact date, it is evident that Dugin believes that Russia is the Katechon divinely charged to resist the Collective Antichrist in the present day.

Versluis commented that, while discussing Hobbes, Schmitt "revealingly" acknowledged Guénon's views of the Antichrist.[140] Schmitt recognized the power of the Katechon in "Guénon's observation that the collapse of medieval civilization into early modernity by the seventeenth century came about because of secret forces operating in the background."[141] Schmitt realized that "Guénon saw the early modern period as inaugurating the progressive decline that modernity represented for him, which would conclude in the appearance of the Antichrist and the end of the world," Versluis wrote.[142]

Newman's comment that "it is difficult to tell whether sovereignty serves as the katechon ('restrainer') or conductor of the coming disorder," serves to underscore Dugin's criticism of Western governments, as they seem to be, in Dugin's view, risking the unleashing of Antichrist.[143] "The apocalyptic and nihilistic condition that Schmitt warned us of seems to be coming about precisely through the breakup of the liberal global order and uncanny return of the dream of sovereignty," Newman added, if it is aiding the "conductor."[144] Moss interprets Dugin's understanding of Russian history as one in which the Eastern Roman Empire continued to be viable through the times of the Tsars. More than that, it did not end with the Russian Revolution in 1917. "In some mysterious way," the Eastern Roman Empire "continued to exist under Soviet power, and continued to serve God and the True Church by opposing the real Antichrist—American power."[145]

In the midst of the continuing confusion over assigning identity to Antichrist to whatever or whomever the identity is properly assigned, Rossman's observation that Dugin accepts that, "Russians are the eschatologically chosen people entrusted with the 'mystery of grace' and empowered to prevent the appearance of the Man of Sin," is key.[146] In a profound combination of geopolitics and theology, Dugin believes that Russia/Eurasia is the Third Rome. Bound up in his belief is that Third Rome is the Restrainer, the Katechon that holds back Antichrist in whatever form revealed.

Dugin emphatically identifies Russia both past, present, and future as the Katechon.[147] "The mystery of lawlessness is already at work," Paul wrote, "only he who now restrains *will do so* until he is taken out of the way."[148] "He who now restrains" is part of the mystery surrounding the Antichrist. The idea of Russia as Katechon can be seen as Dugin's way of placing Messianic Russia in the divine position of Third Rome blocking the expansion of Western globalism—thus, restraining Antichrist.

Assigning Identity

To attach theological labels to Russia and the West, Dugin must bestow them with religious identities. As described by Brannan, establishing this identity is accomplished through a dynamic hermeneutical process.[149] Dugin has done this. He applied a hermeneutical method during his construction of Fourth Political Theory and Neo-Eurasian projections. Jeanrond's definitional expansion allows identity to be incorporated where required in Dugin's hermeneutical categories.[150] This expansion of hermeneutical parameters enhances Dugin's ability to apply mystical, symbolical, and conspiratorial metaphysical identity assignments to various players within his hermeneutical construction.

Jeanrond's expanded definition of hermeneutics, which allows identity as a constituent of hermeneutical construction,

208

permits Dugin to be interpreted through his assignment of various identifications. Jeanrond's expanded definition, combined with Brannan's conclusions on identity, permit Dugin's hermeneutical paradigms to become more apparent. Brannan conducted extensive research on self-defined Christian Identity groups in America in his study that resonates in Dugin's self-identity and the identity he applies to the West. Brannan's investigation into one group led him to report that:

> Those from within the movement took *Identity* as a name for their belief system from the idea that they—the descendants of White Europeans—were the literal and true Israel of God. Jewish people were not seen as descendants of the Old Testament people of God. Rather, the true "identity" of Israel, was to be found in the British, other European and American Caucasian people.[151]

Brannan highlighted the driving Hermeneutic of Christian Identity by stating that "the understanding or presupposition of Israel being hidden within the British and their extension elsewhere then serves as the predominant hermeneutic for their later exegesis of scripture."[152] "If one is willing to accept this all-important presupposition," that the true "identity" of Israel is now found elsewhere, in Christian Identity, "then later assertions appear to follow a coherent system of thought."[153] Brannan proposed a dynamic process, one that involves hermeneutical presupposition and the following acceptance of its subsequent hermeneutical subsets.

"Due to personal or social reasons," Jeanrond wrote, "ideological interpreters defend their particular 'readings' at all cost and remain hostile to all calls for a change of attitude, perspective or world-view."[154] Dugin's assertions of self-identity as a Traditionalist and Eurasianist fall within the boundaries of Jeanrond's observation. Dugin's aggressive application of identity to others and to ideologies not his own may be construed as demonstrations of Jeanrond's view. Identifying Russia-led Eurasia as the Third Rome, the Restrainer, and the West as

Antichrist are consistent with Brannan's and Jeanrond's conclusions.

Notes

1. E.g., a visit to any number of websites will support this last point by yielding photographs, book cover illustrations, and other graphics.

2. David Brannan's examination of Assigning Identity is useful in considering Dugin's hermeneutical approach in the designation of his specific identity labels. Cf. David Brannan, "Violence, Terrorism and the Role of Theology: Repentant and Rebellious Christian Identity," PhD diss., (University of St Andrews, 2007), 146. When explaining motivations and rationale behind identity, Brannan several times remarked to me, "it's all in the hermeneutics." By this, he meant that realizing how a text or idea is interpreted provides the real key to understanding the direction the interpreter will take it. My position maintains that Brannan's assertion holds true regarding Dugin. David Brannan, Professor at the Center for Homeland Defense and Security of the U.S. Naval Postgraduate School.

3. Brannan, "Rebellious Christian Identity," 150.

4. C. Mantzavinos, "Hermeneutics," *Stanford Encyclopedia of Philosophy,* ed. Edward N. Zalta, June 22, 2016, plato.stanford.edu/entries/hermeneutics/. Chrysostomos Mantzavinos, Professor of Philosophy, University of Athens.

5. Jean Grondin, *Introduction to Philosophical Hermeneutics* (New Haven, CT: Yale University Press, 1994), 18. Italics in original. Jean Grondin, Professor and Philosopher, specializing in Kant, Gadamer, and Heidegger. Cf. An applicable definition, when considering Dugin's approach to hermeneutics, is found in Alister McGrath, *Christian Theology* (Oxford: Blackwell Publishing, 2007), 490: "the principles underlying the interpretation, or exegesis, of a text, particularly of Scripture, and particularly in relation to its present-day application." The "present-day application" portion of this definition seems especially relevant to Dugin. Alister McGrath, Northern Ireland theologian.

6. Werner G. Jeanrond, *Theological Hermeneutics: Development and Significance* (New York: Crossroad, 1991), 1. Werner Jeanrond, Professor of Systematic Theology, University of Oslo.

7. Jeanrond, *Theological Hermeneutics*, 6.

8. Ibid., 5.

9. Cf. Mantzavinos, "Hermeneutics."

10. Schmitt, "Political Theology," 42. Here Schmitt evokes Max Weber in making his point that there is a counterargument to the purely rational approach of liberalism in issues of governance. Max Weber, 1864-1920.

11. Dugin, *Fourth Theory*, 175.

12. Ibid., 74-75.

13. Ibid., 75. The Editor's footnote 6 claims that *telos* is defined here meaning "purpose" or "goal" as in Classical Greek. Italics in original.

14. Ibid., 175. Italics in original. Brackets added.

15. Dugin, "Against Universalism."

16. George Schwab, "Introduction," in Schmitt, *Political Theology*, trans. George Schwab (Cambridge, Massachusetts: MIT Press, 1985), xix. George D. Schwab, Latvian born political scientist, co-founder of the National Committee on American Foreign Policy.

17. Dugin, "Against Universalism."

18. Cf. John Cody Mosbey, "Putin, Dugin, and the Coming Wild Ride on Leviathan," Modern Diplomacy, March 11, 2016, moderndiplomacy.eu/index.php?option=com_k2&view=item&id=1275 :putin-dugin-and-the-coming-wild-ride-on-leviathan&Itemid=480.

19. Dugin, "Cure You With Poison," under, Serpents against Serpents.

20. Ibid.

21. Cf. Isaiah 14:12-15, NASB. "How you have fallen from heaven, O star of the morning, son of the dawn!" (Verse 12). Although there is debate about the term *morning star* being applied to both Satan and Jesus in Scripture, it is clear here that Dugin's interpretation in his reference is to Satan. *Morning star* in Isaiah 14 is rendered *Lucifer* in the King James Bible. It is clear in the totality of the verse that it is not referring to Jesus, but to a created being (thus, "son of the dawn"). The desire of this being (the morning star, the son of the dawn) to be like God is more than adequate to assure that the subject is not Jesus the Messiah; verses 13-15 are clearly not referencing Christ.

22. Dugin, *Fourth Theory*, 196.

23. Ibid., 39-40. Cf. Dugin's footnote 25: Peter L. Berger, ed., *The Desecularization of the World: Resurgent Religion and World Politics*

(Grand Rapids, MI: Eerdmans, 1999). Cf. Schmitt, *Dictatorship* (Oxford: Blackwell, 2010), footnote 26. Peter Berger, 1929-2017, Founder, Institute on Culture, Religion, and World Affairs, Boston University, Sociologist of Religion.

24. Dugin, "The Figure of the Radical Subject," under, Part 1, Traditionalism and Sociology—The Modern and the Eternal. Cf. Part I, Chapter Two, Dugin's Self-placement as a Vertical Placement, for Dugin's condemnation of Atomism. Ibn Taymiyyah, Taqi al-Din Ahmad, 1263-1328.

25. Cf. e.g., Dugin, *Fourth Theory*, 88.

26. Moss, "Meaning of Russian History," under, Dugin's Eschatological Ecclesiology. Here Moss is quoting Dugin. Cf. Dugin, *Absoliutnaia Rodina* (Moscow: Arktogeia-Tsentr, 1999), 657. *Absoliutnaia Rodina*, [*Absolute Motherland*] is a compilation, edited, and somewhat expanded reprint of three previous Dugin works: *Ways of the Absolute*; *Metaphysics of the Gospel: Orthodox Esotericism*; and *Mysteries of Eurasia*.

27. Ibid.

28. Ibid.

29. Ibid.

30. Ibid. Cf. Dugin, *Absoliutnaia Rodina,* 658.

31. Ibid.

32. Tim Cresswell, *Place: an Introduction*, 2nd ed. (Chichester: John Wiley and Sons, 2015), 25. Tim Cresswell, Ogilvie Professor of Human Geography, University of Edinburgh.

33. Sheldrake, *Spaces for the Sacred*, 1.

34. John Inge, *A Christian Theology of Place* (Burlington, VT: Ashgate Publishing, 2017), 58. John Geoffrey Inge, Bishop of Worcester, Church of England, Member, House of Lords.

35. Inge, *A Christian Theology of Place*, 58.

36. Rossman, "Anti-Semitism in Eurasian Historiography," 164.

37. Ibid. Throughout this section, Rossman examines aspects of Russian Nationalism. Here Rossman quoted Dugin from "Apologiia natsionalisma," *Konservativnaiia revolutsiia*. Cf. Rossman's note 1994b: 142, 163-64. Rossman lists the components of Dugin's Russian Nationalism as: Religious and Messianic, Geopolitical, Imperial, and

Communal. In Rossman's interpretation of Dugin, the geopolitical aspects of Dugin's theological associations combine these four main features to produce a unique conception of Russian Nationalism.

38. Dugin, "From Sacred Geography to Geopolitics," *The Fourth Political Theory*, under, East and West in Modern Geopolitics, accessed June 12, 2017, 4pt.su/en/content/sacred-geography-geopolitics. A note on the manuscript states that this text appeared under the title "Ot sakral'noy geografii k geopolitike" in *Elementy*, 4, and as Chapter 7 of *Misterii Evrazii*, Moscow: 1996, Cf. evrazia.org/modules.php?name=News&sid=416. Note: There is potential for confusion in this (and similar footnotes) because of the obvious similarity of the title of Dugin's book (*The Fourth Political Theory*) and the Website (*The Fourth Political Theory* – 4pt.su).

39. Dugin, "From Sacred Geography," under, East and West in Modern Geopolitics.

40. Ibid.

41. Ibid.

42. Lawrence Cahoone, "Lecture Notes," in *The Modern Political Tradition: Hobbes to Habermas* (Chantilly, VA: Great Courses, 2014), 247. Lawrence Cahoone, Professor of Philosophy, College of the Holy Cross.

43. Cf. Rossman, "Anti-Semitism in Eurasian Historiography," 164.

44. Ibid. Here Rossman is quoting Dugin from "Apologiia natsionalisma," *Konservativnaiia revolutsiia*, 142.

45. Ibid.

46. Ibid.

47. Ibid.

48. Simmins, *Sacred Spaces and Sacred Places*, 15.

49. Ibid.

50. Revelation 6:8, NASB. Some translations famously render the translation "behold a Pale Horse." For other symbolic color examples, Cf. Micah 3:6, Job 30:6, Judges 8:26, Daniel 5:7, Mark 15:17, Isaiah 1:15, among others.

51. Gregory K. Beale, "Eden, the Temple, and the Church's Mission in the New Creation," *Journal of the Evangelical Theological Society* 48, no. 1 (March 2005): 7. "The earthly temple is also seen as a copy or

counterpart of a heavenly model." Cf. John M. Lundquist, "The Common Temple Ideology of the Ancient Near East," in *The Temple in Antiquity: Ancient Records and Modern Perspectives*, ed. Truman G. Madsen (Provo, UT: Religious Studies Center, Brigham Young University, 1984), 53-76. Cf. Exodus 25: 8-9 and Hebrews 8: 5. Gregory K. Beale, J. Gresham Machen, Chair of New Testament, Westminster Theological Seminary, Glenside, PA. John M. Lundquist, Chief Librarian of the Asian and Middle Eastern Division, New York Public Library.

52. Lundquist, "What Is a Temple? A Preliminary Typology," essay, in *Temples of the Ancient World*, ed. Donald W. Parry (Salt Lake City: Deseret Book Company, 1994), 92. Cf. Lundquist, "Common Temple Ideology."

53. Lundquist, "What is a Temple?" 92. Some ancient temples, like Solomon's Temple and the later rebuilt Jewish Temples, shared this modeling aspect.

54. Matthew 24:27, NASB.

55. Dugin espouses Northern superiority, "the sacred North, the archetype of North," half immersed in history derived from the natural landscape, and half immersed in Nordism—the concept of being Northern. Cf. e.g., Dugin, "From Sacred Geography," under the headings Sacred North and Sacred South and The People of the North.

56. Hui-Chih Yu, "Symbolic Meanings of Color," 55. Footnote 5 credits Hartley Burr Alexander, *The World's Rim: Great Mysteries of the North American Indians*, (Lincoln: University of Nebraska Press, 1953), 13. Footnote 6 cites Charles Alfred Speed Williams, *Chinese Symbolism and Art Motifs*, (Tokyo: Tuttle, 1999), 458. "Yang signifies heaven, sun, light, vigor and male. It is symbolized by the Dragon and is associated with azure color. Similarly, Yin stands for earth, moon, darkness, female. It is symbolized by the Tiger and is associated with orange color." Hartley Burr Alexander, 1873-1939. Charles Alfred Speed Williams, 1884-unk.

57. Cf. Part 1, Chapter Three under, Examples of Dugin's Metaphysical Esoteric Mindset for a more detailed treatment of the Anfisbena.

58. Inge, *A Christian Theology of Place*, 58.

59. Dugin, "From Sacred Geography," under, East and West in Modern Geopolitics.

60. Coyer, "Patriarch Pope Ukraine."

61. Ibid. Putin made this and other references to the sacred nature of Ukraine in his annual "state of the nation" speech at the Grand Kremlin Palace December 4, 2014. Cf. en.kremlin.ru/events/president/news/47173.

62. Ibid.

63. Cf. Sheldrake, *Spaces for the Sacred*, 1. "The concept of space refers not simply to geographical location but to a dialectical relationship between environment and human narrative."

64. Coyer, "Patriarch Pope Ukraine." Here Coyer went on to say, "What is not mentioned by either the Kremlin or the ROC is that Vladimir converted not for reasons of piety, but in order to marry the Byzantine Emperor's sister and to tie himself geopolitically to the Byzantine Empire, which significantly boosted his domestic political prestige and also gave him a valuable foreign alliance."

65. Ibid. Coyer referred to Harvard historian Edward Keenan, 1935-2015, who taught that "the medieval state of Muscovy did not exhibit any consciousness of being a continuation of the Kievan state—that historical narrative was a later creation." Cf. Marshall Poe, *Moscow, The Third Rome*, report (Washington: National Council for Soviet and East European Research, 1997), for additional treatment of this opinion. Marshall Tillbrook Poe, American Historian, Writer, and Russian Scholar.

66. Dugin, "The Eurasian Idea," under, The New World as Messiah.

67. Marc Becker, "Manifest Destiny," *Encyclopedia of U.S. Military Interventions in Latin America*, ed. Alan McPherson, vol. 2 (Santa Barbara, CA: ABC-CLIO, 2013), 368. Cf. John O'Sullivan, "Annexation," *The United States Magazine and Democratic Review* 17, no. 1 (July/August 1845): 5-10, pdcrodas.webs.ull.es/anglo/OsullivanAnnexation.pdf. Marc Becker, Professor specializing in Latin American Studies at Truman State University. John L. O'Sullivan, 1813-1895.

68. Becker, "Manifest Destiny," 367-68.

69. Ibid., 368.

70. Ibid.

71. Dugin, "Against Universalism."

72. Ibid.

73. Ibid. Emphasis in original.

74. Dugin, "Dostoyevsky and the Metaphysics of St. Petersburg," under The Capital, Eurocontinentalism Journal, September 13, 2013, archive.md/5KtwU. Cf. archive.is/eurocontinentalism.wordpress.com.

75. William Cavanaugh, "Messianic Nation: A Christian Theological Critique of American Exceptionalism," *University of St. Thomas Law Journal* 3, no. 2 (Fall 2005): 262. Although written about messianic nation arguments concerning America, this article is useful for understanding other messianic nation concepts as well. William T. Cavanaugh, Director of the Center for World Catholicism and Intercultural Theology and professor of Catholic Studies, DePaul University.

76. Cf. e.g., Wallace M. Alston and Michael Welker, eds., *Reformed Theology* (Grand Rapids, MI: Eerdmans, 2007).

77. Coyer, "Patriarch Pope Ukraine."

78. Ibid.

79. Ibid. Parentheses in original.

80. Ibid. Cf. e.g., Part Two, Chapter 2 for comments on civilizational conflict from Dugin's and Huntington's perspective.

81. Poe, *Moscow Third Rome*, i.

82. Ibid., ii.

83. Dugin, "Moscow as an Idea," The Fourth Political Theory, April 9, 2018, 4pt.su/en/content/moscow-idea. Cf. beneath the translator's notes is this notation: Chapter 1 of Part II of Book 2 of Osnovy geopolitiki [Foundations of Geopolitics] (Moscow: Arktogeya, 2000). Parentheses in original.

84. Dugin, "Moscow as an Idea."

85. Ibid.

86. Ibid.

87. Rossman, "Anti-Semitism in Eurasian Historiography," 164. Parentheses in original. Cf. Rossman's footnote 36. Here Rossman noted, "Dugin refers to the theory of the Old Believers, schismatics who split from the Orthodox Church in the late seventeenth century. They believe that the Antichrist has already come and often identified him with one of the Russian emperors."

88. Ibid.

89. Versluis, "Schmitt Secret Roads Inward," 31.

90. Cf. Mikhail Agursky, *The Third Rome: National Bolshevism in the USSR* (London: Westview Press, 1987). Mikhail Agursky, 1933-1991, pen name of Melik Agursky, Historian of National Bolshevism.

91. Poe, *Moscow Third Rome*, i.

92. Ibid.

93. Ibid.

94. Ibid.

95. Ibid.

96. Ibid., ii.

97. Ibid.

98. Ibid., i.

99. This is puzzling because Epstein had covered Dugin quite extensively in his work published some three years earlier as part of the same overall National Council for Soviet and East European Research project. It seems that Epstein's work should have been familiar to Poe.

100. While there may be merit in continuing the debate over the validity of the Third Rome claims, this is not that forum.

101. Wood, "Cold War II?"

102. Gurganus and Rumer, "Russia's Global Ambitions in Perspective."

103. Laruelle, "Orient in Russian Thought," 21. Vladimir Soloviev, 1853-1900.

104. Coyer, "Patriarch Pope Ukraine."

105. Ibid. Daesh is an Arabic acronym referring to the same group known as IS (the Islamic State), Isis or ISIS (the Islamic State of Iraq and Syria), and Isil or ISIL (the Islamic State of Iraq and the Levant). Cf. e.g., the BBC reported that "Daesh is essentially an Arabic acronym formed from the initial letters of the group's previous name in Arabic— 'al-Dawla al-Islamiya fil Iraq wa al-Sham.' Although it does not mean anything as a word in Arabic, it sounds unpleasant and the group's supporters object to its use." Cf. bbc.com/news/world-middle-east-27994277.

106. Emanuel Pietrobon, "Russias Return as Defender of Christianity," Inside Over, November 6, 2019, insideover.com/religion/russias-return-as-defender-of-christianity.html. Cf. Leonid Issaev & Serafim Yuriev,

"The Christian Dimension of Russia's Middle East Policy," The Sharq Forum, March 2017, hse.ru/mirror/pubs/share/217045866: "From the Russian Church's perspective, any kind of aid to suffering Christians wherever they are in the world is undoubtedly a positive thing, fully reflecting the historic mission of Russia as a katechon state – the strongest Orthodox power and the successor to the Byzantine Empire in the role of protector of Orthodox Christians throughout the world." (Katechon – τὸ κατέχον, `that what withholds`, or ὁ κατέχων, `the one who withholds`). Katechon is often encountered spelled as Catechon). Katechon/Catechon is addressed in other chapters herein as well. Cf. *Brittianica*: "Orthodoxy, Autocracy, and Nationality, Russian Pravoslaviye, Samoderzhaviye, I Narodnost, in Russian history, slogan created in 1832 by Count Sergey S. Uvarov, minister of education 1833–49, that came to represent the official ideology of the imperial government of Nicholas I (reigned 1825–55) and remained the guiding principle behind government policy during later periods of imperial rule." Emanuel Pietrobon, University of Turin educated scholar of geopolitics, religion, and Russian conflict issues. Leonid Issaev, Senior Lecturer, Department for Political Science, Russian National Research University Higher School of Economics. Serafim Yuriev, Deputy Head of the Faculty of Social Sciences, Higher School of Economics, Russian National Research University.

107. Coyer, "Patriarch Pope Ukraine."

108. Ibid. Brackets in original.

109. Coyer claims that Sergey Kholmogorov is a former Russian politician with strong ties to the Kremlin.

110. Schmitt, "The Nomos of the Earth," in *International Law of the Jus Publicum Europaeum*, trans. G. L. Ulmen (New York: Telos, 2006), 59.

111. It is interesting to note that before the middle of the twelfth century to as far back as at least 1034 it was referred to simply as *the Roman Empire* vice the *Holy* Roman Empire. Cf. e.g., Geoffrey Baraclough, "Holy Roman Empire (Historical Empire, Europe)," *Encyclopædia Britannica*, updated, July 25, 2018, britannica.com/place/Holy-Roman-Empire. Perhaps, by adopting the moniker, it was thought that the lost power of the actual First Rome could be restored. Geoffrey Baraclough, 1908-1984.

112. Dugin, "Ideology of the World Government," The Fourth Political Theory, September 28, 2012, 4pt.su/en/content/ideology-world-government. This article apparently appeared as, Dugin, "Ideology of

218

the World Government," trans. Victor Olevich, Arctogaia, December 20, 1998, arctogaia.com/public/eng-ed2.htm. A search for this site failed to locate this article.

113. 2 Thessalonians 2: 2, NASB.

114. Ibid., 2: 3, NASB.

115. Ibid. "Let no one in any way deceive you, for *it will not come* unless the apostasy comes first, and the man of lawlessness is revealed, the son of destruction."

116. Ibid., 2: 9, NASB, "that is, the one whose coming is in accord with the activity of Satan, with all power and signs and false wonders."

117. Cf. other references to Dugin's identification as an Old Believer/Old Ritualist herein. Throughout, mentions of Old Ritualist and Old Believer are used interchangeably. Old Ritualists/Old Believers are Orthodox schismatics who split from mainstream Orthodoxy in 1666. Patriarch Nicon introduced the New Rite ca. 1666-67 resulting in placing the Old Ritualists/Old Believers under Anathema. Anathema was officially rescinded in 1971, but a lack full restoration remains evident.

118. Rossman, "Anti-Semitism in Eurasian Historiography," 164. Cf. Rossman's footnote 36.

119. Ibid., 174.

120. Ibid. Cf. other references referring to *authentic, original*, and *eternal* Christianity and the association of these terms with Old Believer/Old Ritual Orthodoxy.

121. Ibid.

122. Ibid. Cf. note 1994e: 257–58. Here Rossman cites and credits Dugin, "Golem I evreiskaiia metafizika," *Konservativnaiia revolutsiia*, 257-58.

123. Ibid. Rossman credits Dugin as above.

124. Ibid. Again, crediting Dugin as above.

125. Ibid.

126. Dugin, "Ideology of World Government." What Dugin renders here as Moshiah is also encountered as *Moshiach* or *Mashiah*—the Messiah—in Jewish messianic interpretations. Cf. e.g., Hodge, *Systematic Theology*, vol. 3, 813-14 for discussion of the Antichrist as not necessarily being an individual, perhaps instead being a power.

127. Ibid. While Dugin and others apply various theological interpretations to Bush's New World Order proclamations, there is scant evidence from Bush's several speeches on the subject that he attached any religious emphasis to the concept. For Bush, the New World Order references appear to be political and promote the advancement of the attributes of Western Liberal Democracy absent any overt religious agenda. Mikhail Gorbachev, 1931-2022.

128. Ibid. Here messianic mention is more in the vein of traditional Judaism (still anticipating the coming) than the Orthodox Christian belief in Messiah Jesus as an already accomplished temporal and spiritual fact. Parentheses in original.

129. Dugin, "Maoism Is Too Modern for Me," under, Five Questions for Alexander Dugin, The Fourth Political Theory, March 26, 2015, 4pt.su/en/content/maoism-too-modern-me. E.g., Dugin alternately applies Antichrist to America, the New World Order, the Roman Catholic Church, the Jewish Missiah, and Western Culture in general. This was part of Dugin's response to the first question.

130. Dugin, "Ideology of World Government."

131. Schmitt, "Nomos of the Earth," 59.

132. Ibid.

133. Ibid., 60.

134. Versluis, "Schmitt Secret Roads Inward," 31.

135. The issue is one of just who or what is being restrained? Is an individual being restrained or is the Antichrist a collective subject?

136. 2 Thessalonians 2: 6, NASB, "And you know what restrains him now, so that in his time he will be revealed."

137. Moss, "Meaning of Russian History," under, Dugin's Eschatological Ecclesiology.

138. Ibid. Dugin then would have the roughly 1000-year Byzantine Period from the Edict of Milan (312) to the fall of Constantinople in 1453 equate to the "thousand-year reign of Christ" in Revelation 20.

139. Ibid. Moss notes that in 1656, Patriarch Nicon introduced the New Rite. The Council of 1666-67, placed the Old Rite under Anathema. Peter the Great, set aside the Patriarchate ca. 1721, culminating years of his resistance to allowing a Patriarch to be named.

140. Versluis, "Schmitt Secret Roads Inward," 31.

141. Ibid.

142. Ibid. Schmitt referred to Guénon, *La Crise du monde moderne*, Paris, Bossard, 1927. Note the similarity with Dugin's Collective Antichrist ideas.

143. Newman, *Political Theology*, 3-4.

144. Ibid., 4.

145. Moss, "Meaning of Russian History," under, Dugin's Eschatological Ecclesiology.

146. Rossman, "Anti-Semitism in Eurasian Historiography," 164. The "mystery of grace" connotation may apply in this instance to the granting an understanding about the Messiah given to specific prophetic voices throughout the ages and/or to a blessing upon Russia of the ability to make such understanding known. For an example of the "mystery of grace" discussion, Cf. George Vandervelde, "The Grammar of Grace: Karl Rahner as a Watershed in Contemporary Theology," *Theological Studies* 49, no. 3 (September 1, 1988): 445-59. George Vandervelde, 1939-2007.

147. References throughout support this contention.

148. 2 Thessalonians 2: 7, NASB. Italics in original in the quoted edition.

149. Brannan, "Rebellious Christian Identity," 14. Cf. footnote 2 above.

150. Cf. Jeanrond, *Theological Hermeneutics*, 6. I believe Jeanrond's expansion combined with Brannan's conclusions regarding acceptance of a hermeneutical position is useful when considering Dugin's assumptions.

151. Brannan, "Rebellious Christian Identity," 14.

152. Ibid., 146.

153. Ibid.

154. Jeanrond, *Theological Hermeneutics*, 6.

221

Chapter Three: Dugin's Eschatology

Acute Awareness of the End Times

Eschatological thinking figures prominently in Dugin's theological projections of Fourth Political Theory. As an example, Dugin interpreted the fall of communism as an eschatological event. Evident in his remark that "the victory of liberalism over communism was the proof in my eyes of its eschatological nature," is Dugin's belief in the overt theological presence in the conflict of the three political theories preceding the introduction of his fourth one.[1] Dugin has no wish to remain fixed within the reign of Antichrist; a reign either already present or coming after the chains of the Restrainer are removed. For Dugin, it seems that there are only two possible alternatives—endure the abominations of Antichrist or hasten its/his exit. "As follows from the very logic of apocalyptic drama," Dugin stated, "in the course of the last struggle, the clash will occur not between the Sacred and the profane, nor between Religion and atheism, but between Religion and pseudo-religion."[2]

Dugin is quick to demonstrate his default setting to metaphysics where *mondialism*, a broad term encompassing the concept of a unipolar world, is concerned. A kingdom here on earth ruled over by the Jewish Messiah, awesome and powerful as it may be, is absent the presence of the Divine Hero Messiah. For Dugin, the reign of a collective Antichrist is no less a calamity than the rule of an individual one. Dugin has no desire for a secularized Jewish Messiah, nor has he any appetite for the triumph of Fukuyama's End of History. No matter that Liberalism has succumbed to post-liberalism, the environment is still conducive to globalism and Western hegemony.

Hastening the Apocalypse

As Dugin opposes Fukuyama's 1990s vision of the End of History, he also opposes Kabbalistic Eschatology that would terminate history with the kingship of the Jewish Moshiah. However, it is a mistake to think that Dugin is entirely opposed to the End of History in reality. On his terms, "Dugin has expressed that Russia's messianic role—a role that may involve hastening the end of the age coinciding with the defeat of Antichrist—is also Russia's eschatological purpose."[3] "The End Times and the eschatological meaning of politics will not realize themselves on their own," Dugin wrote in *The Fourth Political Theory*.[4] With this and similar statements, Dugin suggests the possibility of hastening the Apocalypse. "If the Fourth Political Practice is not able to realise the end of times, then it would be invalid," Dugin says, perhaps implying that the arrival of the end-times may benefit by the application of his theory.[5] Dugin answers the question of why the Traditionalists should desire to be in *Gottesnacht* by stating that it is to help bring about the end of the modern world.[6]

Concerning Dugin's Apocalyptic Eschatology

Much apocalyptic literature is theologically dualistic in nature. Dugin's eschatology tends to dualistic expressions as well. When Mervyn F. Bendle compared Dugin's various eschatological apocalyptic expressions, he concluded:

> Dugin's view is dualistic, depicting the world as a battleground within which the forces of good and evil, light and darkness, spirit and matter, contend for the fate of the planet. In Dugin's version of apocalypticism, it is the "Atlanticist New World Order" based on liberalism, modernity, and materialism, that represents the forces of evil, while the peoples of Eurasia with their stronger spirituality constitute (or will soon constitute) the "New Eurasian Order" and form the vanguard for the forces for good.[7]

According to Moss, Dugin employs a three-phase chronology of Church history.[8] The first Moss labels the "Pre-Constantinian Phase," noting that it lasted until the Edict of Milan in 312.[9] The second is the "Byzantine Phase," from 312 until the Fall of Constantinople in 1453.[10] Moss highlighted that this phase corresponds to the thousand-year reign of Christ of Revelation

20.[11] The third is the "Post-Byzantine Phase," in which we find ourselves today—the reign of Antichrist.[12]

Two other views indicate interpretations of Dugin's eschatology. First, Rossman said that for Dugin, "mondialism, especially the mondialistic concept of the 'end of history,' is only a secularized version of Jewish 'kabbalistic eschatology,' which lacks a soteriological dimension."[13] The second example comes from *The Fourth Political Theory* itself, and suggests that Dugin appreciates Agursky's ideas, especially his "review of the Soviet period as a special, 'eschatological' version of the traditional society."[14] Whatever he specifically had in mind regarding Agursky's eschatological reference, Dugin's interest in the relevance of various eschatological references and approaches reveals either a less than fully developed theology in this area, or an as yet immature Western interpretation of it.

"One approach to the enigma of Dugin," said Moss, "is through a discussion of his little-known 'eschatological ecclesiology,' and his understanding of the role of the Orthodox Church and Russia in the last times."[15] If correct, the entirety of Dugin's chronology of Church history, viewed from Moss' perspective, firmly positions the current world circumstance in the post-Byzantine period of the reign of Antichrist.

Comparing Some Secular Apocalyptic Manifestations

Aiding and abetting Armageddon is not a Dugin exclusive. Commentators have considered Dugin's views and the views of others regarding attempts to provide catalytic action triggering the apocalyptic end of the present age on earth.[16] A brief examination of examples reflecting some similarities with Dugin's position offer perspective.

The violent religiously radical group, Aum Shinrikyō, attacked the Tokyo Subway System in March 1995 with the Apocalypse in mind. In addition to the innovative use of sarin gas, a non-explosive weapon of mass destruction, as the fatal medium, Aum Shinrikyō combined Tibetan Buddhism and the New Testament book of Revelation into the metaphysical basis for their attempt to accelerate the End of Days. Matthias Riedl, wrote that the ideology of Aum Shinrikyō was "based on the teaching of their guru Shōkō Asahara."[17] Asahara, in turn, drew on Tibetan Buddhism and other Eastern spiritual sources.[18] Claiming divine intervention, Asahara said, "My guru, the god Shiva, suddenly said to me: 'Now is the time to decode the Book of Revelation, receive its message, and start Aum's salvation work,'" psychiatrist Robert Lifton reported.[19]

There are also similarities between the aims of Aum Shinrikyō and Dugin's proclaimed mission to hasten the Apocalypse. From Lifton's viewpoint, "the gas attack was meant as a 'self-assigned project of making Armageddon happen.'"[20] Similar too is the esoteric characteristic of Shōkō Asahara to selectively draw from multiple religious traditions.

It is tempting to lump the apocalyptic efforts of Dugin and Asahara with other advocates of radical change, but care demands that the element of spiritual inspiration claimed by Dugin and Asahara be a defining factor. The degree of metaphysical motivation involved alone is a reason to distinguish between theologically inspired kinetics and that fueled by secular anarchism or Luddite leanings.[21] Riedl, in his paper on Apocalyptic Politics, drew on source material as varied as the Federal Bureau of Investigation's, *Project Megiddo,* and Voegelin's essay, *The Political Religions.*[22] Despite similarities, when considering the Oklahoma City Murrah Federal Building bombing, Riedl found that Timothy McVeigh relied on secular apocalyptic texts rather than sacred sources:

> McVeigh—like other far-right terrorists—was inspired by the racist novel The Turner Diaries, published pseudonymously in 1978 by the far-right leader William L. Pierce. McVeigh had followed in detail the description of a car bomb attack on a federal building that he found in the book.[23]

Riedl also stated a basis for a valid apocalyptic comparison. *"The Turner Diaries* are more than just a terrorist manual in the disguise of a novel," Riedl concluded, "they are also an apocalypse."[24] *The Turner Diaries* "emulate the narrative of ancient apocalypses," Riedl wrote, "when the hero is granted inspection of a secret book and in an ecstatic vision gains insight into the whole course of human history."[25]

Riedl's association of *The Turner Diaries* with apocalyptic literature notwithstanding, McVeigh left no substantive writings to indicate he subscribed to the eschatological leanings of *The Turner Diaries*. While he attempted to ascribe a political motive to his actions, there is little to no evidence that he associated his extreme violence with any form of apocalyptic vision. Likewise, Theodore Kaczynski did not write or promote any significant eschatological message in his attempts to thwart a technological society that he viewed as decidedly opposed to his concepts of Natural Law. Kaczynski, the so-called Unabomber, is anti-modern—especially anti-technological—but cannot be classified as metaphysical.[26]

Anders Breivik, still imprisoned in Norway for the deaths of scores of mostly young people, comes closest of the three (McVeigh, Kaczynski, and himself) to imbuing his cause with religious elements and promoting a form of spiritual conflict through a bizarre form of retro-Templar "knighthood." Nevertheless, Breivik's writings exhibit a dearth of definable eschatological elements.[27] So, while he may have displayed tinges of gnostic trappings associated with an apocalyptic genre, Breivik too, fell well short of a credible Dugin-like comparison.

Anti-modern praxis does not require a definitive apocalyptic framework, so there is more than just anti-modernism at work in Dugin's eschatology. Dugin's Neo-Traditionalism begins on a religious foundation and concludes with eschatological certitude; it is, therefore, more than just the revenge, anti-modernism, or xenophobia witnessed in McVeigh, Kaczynski, and Breivik—despite whatever degree of Luddism they possess in common.

Notes

1. Dugin, "The Long Path," as part of his response to the first question.

2. Dugin, "Ideology of World Government."

3. Mosbey, "Wild Ride on Leviathan."

4. Dugin, *Fourth Theory*, 183.

5. Ibid.

6. Dugin, "The Figure of the Radical Subject," under, Part 2, The Figure of the Radical Subject and the Traditionalist without Tradition.

7. Mervyn F. Bendle, "Putin's Rasputin," Quadrant On-Line, September 3, 2014, quadrant.org.au/magazine/2014/09/putins-rasputin/. Mervyn F. Bendle, Senior Lecturer, James Cook University.

8. Moss, "Meaning of Russian History," under, Dugin's Eschatological Ecclesiology. Moss credits Dugin, *Absoliutnaia Rodina*, for his understanding of these three epochs.

9. Ibid. The Edict of Milan was a "proclamation that permanently established religious toleration for Christianity within the Roman Empire. It was the outcome of a political agreement concluded in Mediolanum (modern Milan) between the Roman emperors Constantine I and Licinius in February 313. The proclamation, made for the East by Licinius in June 313, granted all persons freedom to worship whatever deity they pleased, assured Christians of legal rights (including the right to organize churches), and directed the prompt return to Christians of confiscated property." Cf. *Encyclopædia Britannica*, s.v. "Edict of Milan (Roman History)," updated August 8, 2019, britannica.com/topic/Edict-of-Milan.

10.   Ibid.

11.   Ibid. Revelation 20: 1-3, NASB. "Then I saw an angel coming down from heaven, holding the key of the abyss and a great chain in his hand. 2 And he laid hold of the dragon, the serpent of old, who is the devil and Satan, and bound him for a thousand years; 3 and he threw him into the abyss, and shut *it* and sealed *it* over him, so that he would not deceive the nations any longer, until the thousand years were completed; after these things he must be released for a short time."

12.   Ibid.

13.   Rossman, "Anti-Semitism in Eurasian Historiography," 175.

14.   Dugin, *Fourth Theory*, 21. Cf. Morgan's editorial footnote 9. Cf. Agursky, *Third Rome.*

15.   Moss, "Meaning of Russian History." This quote is from the introduction portion of the post. Whereas Shekhovtsov and Umland have focused an argument criticizing the authenticity of Dugin's Traditionalism, Moss, writing from an Orthodox perspective, criticizes the authenticity of his adherence to Orthodox Church doctrine.

16.   Cf. e.g., Matthias Riedl, "Apocalyptic Politics—On the Permanence and Transformations of a Symbolic Complex." Paper Delivered to The Franklin Humanities Institute—Politics and Religion: A Humanities

Futures Cross-Departmental Seminar, Duke University, Durham, NC, December 3, 2014, 5. Riedl explains that "Apocalypsis means a revelatory unveiling of a historical structure of decline, which will culminate in the battle between good and evil at the end of times and Judgment Day. Then will follow the destruction of this world and the dawn of a new world, into which the true believers will be transferred and where they will establish a truly theocratic society, the Heavenly Jerusalem." Matthias Riedl, Chair of Comparative Religious Studies, Central European University.

17. Riedl, "Apocalyptic Politics," 3.

18. Ibid. Cf. Christopher H. Partridge, *New Religions: A Guide: New Religious Movements, Sects, and Alternative Spiritualities* (New York: Oxford University Press, 2004). Christopher H. Partridge, Professor, Lancaster University, also Co-Director of the Centre for the Study of Religion and Popular Culture.

19. Ibid. Riedl cites Robert J. Lifton, *Destroying the World to Save It: AumShinrikyō, Apocalyptic Violence, and the New Global Terrorism* (New York: Metropolitan, 1999), 47; Cf. Riedl's note: Lifton 1999, 47. Robert J. Lifton, Psychiatrist, Writer, and Researcher known for his studies of the psychological causes and effects of wars and political violence.

20. Ibid. Cf., Lifton, *Destroying the World to Save It*, 4, note: Lifton 1999, 4; Cf. *Proceedings* of *Politics and Religion: A Humanities Futures Cross-Departmental Seminar*, The Franklin Humanities Institute, Duke University, Durham, NC, under, Modern Terror as Apocalyptic Violence, accessed February 9, 2015, humanitiesfutures.org/papers/apocalyptic-politics-on-the-permanence-and-transformations-of-a-symbolic-complex/.

21. OED: "A person opposed to new technology or ways of working." Historically: "A member of any of the bands of English workers who destroyed machinery, especially in cotton and woolen mills, that they believed was threatening their jobs (1811–16)."

22. Riedl, "Apocalyptic Politics," 2. Cf. U.S. Government, Federal Bureau of Investigation, *Project Megiddo* (Washington, DC: FBI, 1999), permanentaccess.gpo.gov/lps3578/fbi.gov/library/megiddo/megiddo.pdf. Also available from other sites, e.g., constitution.org/y2k/megiddo.pdf. Cf. Voegelin, "The Political Religions," in *Modernity Without Restraint*, *The Collected Works of Eric Voegelin* (Columbia: University of Missouri Press, 2000), 19-73.

23. Ibid. Cf. William L. Pierce, *The Turner Diaries* (Hillsboro, WV: National Vanguard Books, 1999). Pierce used the pseudonym, Andrew McDonald. William L. Pierce, 1933-2002. Timothy McVeigh, 1968-executed in 2001.

24. Ibid. Italics added.

25. Ibid.

26. Cf. Howard Kurtz, "Unabomber Manuscript Is Published Public Safety Reasons Cited in Joint Decision by Post, N.Y. Times," *Washington Post* (Washington, DC), September 19, 1995, A01. Howard Kurtz, American Journalist.

27. Published under the pseudonym of Andrew Berwick on July 22, 2011, this Manifesto is over 1500 pages in length. Cf. Anders Breivik, "Anders Behring Breivik's Complete Manifesto '2083—A European Declaration of Independence,'" Public Intelligence, July 28, 2011, 2915, publicintelligence.net/anders-behring-breiviks-complete-manifesto-2083-a-european-declaration-of-independence/. Breivik had his name legally changed to Fjotolf Hansen in 2017.

Part V

Chapter One: Traditionalism

The Search for Eternal Truth

Traditionalism refers to the belief that there exists a body of Truth inherited from the past—Truth correctly handed-down from time-out-of-mind.[1] This Truth was present from before the Fall described in the Hebrew and Christian Scriptures. Traditionalism holds that this Truth is contained in a body of knowledge that exists unchanged and unaltered from the time of original divine revelations. The OED states that the historical definition of religious tradition is "the theory that all moral and religious truth comes from divine revelation passed on by tradition, human reason being incapable of attaining it." Despite being somewhat circular, this definition is adequate for a broad understanding. I turn to well-recognized writers within the fields of Traditionalism and fundamentalism for elucidation.

I have encountered several attempts to define Traditionalism but do not offer any one of them as being precise. I prefer to allow for some definitional slack to be present as various contributors suggest their views and understandings of tradition and Tradition. While current scholarship attaches the term *Integral* Traditionalism or *Classic* Traditionalism with Guénon's work, I found no evidence that he favored either descriptor. More consequential here is Dugin's explanation of Traditionalism. He expresses a Traditionalism that contains politically active elements not found in Integral (Classical) Traditionalism. Though acknowledging Dugin's Traditionalist beliefs and their application to his geopolitical theology, it is not my purpose to advocate a specific disciple of Traditionalism.

I first traced Traditionalism's historicity through its association with Perennialism. I then explored Dugin's adaptations of Integral Traditionalism. However, I do not dwell on Dugin's interpretation of Traditionalism for anything more than its utility as a foundational element in his geopolitical theology. I briefly examine fundamentalism because I view Dugin as a fundamentalist in its expanded definition, because of its kinship to Traditionalism, and because of the potential toxicity in the West associated with the fundamentalist label.[2]

I recognize the claims that Traditionalism is an understanding and acknowledgement of eternal Truth expressed as both a worldview and a lifestyle. I view Traditionalism mainly from the perspective of the Integral Traditionalism ascribed to Guénon and adherents to the twentieth century and twenty-first century expressions of his beliefs and practices. Because Dugin claims to be a Traditionalist, proclaims his heritage to be derived through Guénon and Evola, and emphatically states that Traditionalism is a critical element of Fourth Political Theory, it is necessary to expound on just what he is claiming for himself and his theory.[3]

Perennialism

Traditionalism is closely related to Perennialism. Traditionalist claims are practically identical with those of Perennialism, so close that treating them as such will serve my purposes here. A current explanation of Traditionalism and Perennialism notes that both "are nearly synonymous and are, most often, interchangeable."[4] However, Traditionalism, rather than Perennialism, seems to have become the more common identifier, although either term is encountered in literature and other media. Descriptive language regarding Traditionalism is remarkably like that applied to Perennialism. Traditionalism incorporates the Perennialist assumption that revelation of unchanging Truth has transcendental origins and that certain of the Ancients were aware of the pure form and worthiness of passage via tradition (apostolic-like linkages) from initial reception to succeeding generations.

Reference works tend to apply similar definitions of Traditionalism and Perennialism.[5] Apparent are the visible overlapping definitions of terms—essential elements appear blurred from the outset. A Traditionalist website states, for example:

> All of the major twentieth [century] writers in this
> area wrote of Tradition. By this they meant the
> entirety of the intellectual, religious, cultural, and

artistic aspects that tie a people to a Revelation or to a sacred origin. Thus, such an entity as this *Tradition* is itself considered sacred. All things centered on this Tradition, such as a civilization, its arts or crafts, doctrines, etc., all can be referred to as "traditional."[6]

And:

"Traditional" is not used by these writers [Traditionalists] just to designate cultural artifacts passed along from one generation to another by sheer habit. Instead, it is used to indicate, for example, those civilizations whose ideas, practices, creations, and so on are still guided and formed by the attraction to and the principles of the domain of the Spirit. People who study Tradition are called "traditionalists," and all such traditionalists accept the premises of the Perennial Philosophy.[7]

In the Western Liberal environment, Traditional strands or threads are sometimes difficult to discern because both the lenses used to bring them into focus and the labels applied to them are products of historicism—an assumption that the Renaissance and Reformation eclipsed the esotericism of the Middle Ages. Will-Erich Peuckert, in Wouter J. Hanegraaff's view, denied this assumption, positing that esoterism adapted and survived.[8] Historians, Hanegraaff observed,

looked at the early modern period either from the perspective of "Reformation versus Counter-Reformation," or from that of the Renaissance as a rebirth of antiquity. Both perspectives, Peuckert observes, are essentially "catastrophe theories:" they describe how the old breaks down and vanishes at the arrival of the new. As a result of this narrow focus, historians overlooked the many ways in which pre-modern thinking *continued* right into the early modern world and took on new creative shapes.[9]

Peuckert identified closely with Theophrastus von Hohenheim, best-known by his pseudonym, Paracelsus.[10] Paracelsus claimed that "two wisdoms exist in this world, one that is eternal and one that is mortal; the eternal one springs from the light of the Holy Spirit, the other one from the Light of Nature."[11] "What it comes down to," in Peuckert's judgment, is that "Paracelsus develops a new understanding of magic grounded in the double light of Nature and Grace."[12] What Peuckert told us is that Traditionalism is still with us; it has not been eclipsed, has not vanished, and remains just beyond the vision of myopic modernism. Modernism, looking through the lens of Nature only, sees what is mortal and does not see Traditionalism that is only visible in light that is eternal.

Unlike the Christian Fundamentalist movement, with its discernible chronological beginnings, Perennialism and its later-defined near-twin, Traditionalism, has its origins in a much more distant and less-discernible past. Still not well developed, the historical background of Traditionalism is sketchy in mainstream academic literature before Guénon, and the other Integral School Traditionalists, made the subject better known.[13] Often searches under the Perennialist identifier have to be relied on to demonstrate historical linkages. Although Perennialist evidence also lacks a consistent written historical trail, it provides a more discernible look into the distant past when compared to available sources found under the Traditionalist heading.

Realizing that Perennial sources often rely on material that is esoteric and sometimes occultic, making empirical determinations difficult, Vojtěch Hladký's consideration of Plethon provided a Zoroastrian perspective.[14] Through Plethon, Hladký linked Perennialism back in antiquity to Zoroaster (Zarathustra), suggesting an ancient pedigree. Also noteworthy is Hanegraaff's study of the life and influence of Peuckert.[15] Hladký and Hanegraaff help establish the link, admittedly often slender and usually esoteric, between twentieth century Traditionalism and its antecedents.

Aldous Huxley traced Perennialism stretching back through Gottfried Wilhelm Leibniz to the sixteenth century writings of Augustinius Steuchius and beyond.[16] Along with Huxley, Randolph Dible, Renaud Fabbri, and other scholars have provided evidence of Perennial thought in deep antiquity.[17] However, there is a vast and perhaps unbridgeable gap in Perennial literature from the Late Middle Ages until the more mainstream writing on the subject was taken up by the Traditionalists and Huxley.[18] The gap remains mostly unfilled unless one relies on overtly gnostic, esoteric, and occultic literature—a remedy outside the scope of my present intentions.

The thoughts and works of Guénon and Evola are prominently featured in writing emanating from within Traditionalism, and they are subjects of continuing scholarship from external sources as well. I must recognize both here primarily due to the frequency of their mention within *The Fourth Political Theory* and other of Dugin's works. Guénon, the preeminent Integral or Classical Traditionalist, and Evola, the Italian Traditionalist with his pronounced political focus, are often credited with having exerted a significant influence on Dugin.[19]

Along with Guénon, there are other significant Integral Traditionalists.[20] However, when considering Dugin, noteworthy proponents such as Ananda K. Coomaraswamy, Ali Lakhani, Seyyed Hossein Nasr, and others are considered secondarily to Guénon and Evola when concentrating on Fourth Political Theory.[21] Frithjof Schuon, for example, is notable for creating the Maryamiyya along with Titus Burckhardt.[22] The Maryamiyya, a Sufi order, became a principal Traditionalist religious locus. Schuon followed Guénon's Traditionalism—even into Sufism— and became a well-known Traditionalist proponent although he and Guénon eventually fell out.[23] Schuon receives less attention here because most of his concentration is centered within Sufism and Buddhism; therefore, he is of less direct significance to Dugin's Neo-Traditionalism with its defining active component.[24]

Mark Sedgwick continues to conduct significant contemporary exploration into Traditionalism. He covered both a broad overview and a good deal of in-depth study in his *Against the Modern World*, the title of which purposefully recalls Evola's *Revolt Against the Modern World* and Guénon's *Crisis of the*

Modern World.[25] Sedgwick's book is the source of much renewed interest in Traditionalism. For many in the West, it was their first introduction to Guénon, Evola, and Dugin. Additionally, *Against the Modern World*, is germane because it emphasizes the conflict between Traditionalism and Western Liberalism that Dugin so often highlights in his work.

There is a body of Perennialist/Traditionalist work in Theosophy as well as an ample selection of esoteric and occultic subject matter originating in the nineteenth century. The primary nineteenth century proponents of Theosophy were Helena Petrovna Blavatsky and Colonel Henry Olcott.[26] Aleister Crowley left an enormous volume of work that is the subject of attention from within the Academy proper and in the literature of the occult.[27] Mysticism and esotericism, are also evident in the avant-garde art, music, and writing of those nineteenth century times. Active remnants in these media are discernable today.

Although outside the boundaries of this study, comprehensive research focused on Traditionalism *per se* should include inquiry into kindred strands of Traditionalism, including Theosophy, Kabbalism, and the occult adaptations of Crowley and others. Sedgwick has given just such attention to these subject areas.[28] Various threads connecting Dugin's esoteric and mystic inclinations to the much broader and deeper regions of the occult and other metaphysical manifestations do appear herein, but his Traditionalist proclivities are noted without my becoming side-tracked into fascinating but distracting corollary inquiries.

Timeless *Tradition* and Temporal *tradition*

Jaroslav Pelikan contributed valuable conversation on traditionalism.[29] Pelikan demonstrated aspects of more conventional traditionalism in his Jefferson Lectures and his subsequent book, *The Vindication of Tradition*.[30] Pelikan's comments on the themes of tradition in the music and lyrics of *Fiddler on the Roof* are anything but shallow; they are very much on-point.[31] Religious milieus often inspire varied artistic genres. *Fiddler on the Roof* expounds traditional themes, but in some creative media Integral Traditionalism is also recognizable. The poetry of T.S. Eliot and the writing of Eco offer two well-known examples of the latter.[32] Sedgwick addressed Traditionalism in the fine arts in his article, "Traditionalism and art—and perhaps more than art."[33] Eco's writing frequently explores Traditionalist themes and conspirology.[34] For more on the subject of Traditionalism's reach beyond the strict confines of its spiritual borders, Eliot's essay, "Tradition and the Individual Talent," is instructive.[35]

The Traditionalist movement, according to Sedgwick, views Tradition, "as belief and practice transmitted from time immemorial—or rather belief and practice that *should* have been transmitted but was lost to the West during the last half of the second millennium A.D."[36] Tradition *is* tradition, but it is also more than tradition. Tradition contains the preserved essential Truth and knowledge of the ages. Therefore, Traditionalism, as viewed by Integral Traditionalists, is not merely the tradition of customs, practices, or general history preserved from generation to generation.

Transmission and the content transmitted are critical to Traditionalists. Guénon's consideration of Traditionalism permeates the main body of his published work, but concise treatment is contained in his article, "What is meant by Tradition?"[37] Guénon defined Traditionalism by first addressing tradition. "Etymologically," he wrote, "tradition simply means 'that which is transmitted' in some way or other," an opinion endorsed by both Sedgwick and contemporary Traditionalist, James Cutsinger.[38] Agreeing, Fabbri stated, "tradition implies the idea of a transmission (*tradere*)."[39] Guénon, Sedgwick, Cutsinger, and Fabbri all agreed that Traditionalism is more expansive in its concept than the mere act of transmission. Ordinary transmissions, however accurate, may or may not convey truth, or more pointedly, in this case, Truth. Cutsinger added that things merely customary or nostalgic cannot be the criterion for Traditionalism.

> The passing along of a thing received also accounts for mere custom and habit. This, of course, is the concern of the critic: that the conservative is simply nostalgic for the way things were done in the past, irrespective of their truth or adequacy. One would perhaps be justified

in replying to this observation by pointing out that the very length of a given usage almost certainly implies a correspondingly deep human need. But this is not my response here. I prefer to admit instead that a greater precision is called for than is afforded by etymology.[40]

All tradition involves knowledge or practices acquired from the past, yet much passed down material does not qualify as Integral Traditionalism. As Cutsinger explained, tradition "is the action or result of handing down or transmitting."[41] Careful not to allow everything handed-down to be counted as Traditional, Cutsinger hastened to add that, "at the same time it is important to clarify that not everything handed-down is traditional in the sense at stake here."[42]

Although Traditionalism (as identified with the uppercase T) is not contained within tradition (as identified with the lowercase t), it is not correct to say that tradition is absent in Traditionalism. Guénon reminded us that certain traditional elements are foundational for Traditional construction. Regarding the presence of tradition in things Traditional, Guénon pointed out that within Tradition "it is necessary to include "secondary and derived elements" that are present and "important for the purpose of forming a complete picture."[43]

Cutsinger used Scripture to provide clarity concerning Traditional and traditional.

The Thessalonians were exhorted to stand fast and to hold the tradition they received from Saint Paul, but the Colossians were warned against the traditions of men. It appears that not every giving and receiving is good for us. The fact of a transmission itself, let alone its duration or the number of its successive receptions, is not the point. Any particular custom may be older than any particular tradition.[44]

Cutsinger stressed the difficulty of the Traditionalist's task. "Not only must he [the Traditionalist] find fresh words for a

237

familiar topic so as to say something new about something old," Cutsinger concluded that "he must insist in this case that the old really is the new."[45] While tradition and custom are tied to a temporal process of handing down, Lakhani observed Coomaraswamy's missive that "Tradition has nothing to do with any 'ages,' whether 'dark,' 'primaeval,' or otherwise."[46] Coomaraswamy underscored the timeless characteristic of Tradition; the unchanging principle is one that implies that it has been, and is, and will be, unchanged and unchanging. Thus, Coomaraswamy separated Traditionalism from a strictly historical perspective.

Study involving Traditionalism encounters definitional overlaps between Traditionalism and traditionalism.[47] While traditionalism, with its adherence to custom and historical practice, is discernible within Traditionalism, the two concepts are not identical. Traditionalism claims unbroken links to eternal Truth and is often accessible only through gnostic pathways, while traditionalism is much more the recognition of associated practices closely akin to custom.[48]

Recognizing the uppercase T is essential as it emphasizes that the Truth of Tradition may be separated temporally from either truth or tradition in the lowercase. "Tradition," Coomaraswamy continued, "represents doctrines about first principles, which do not change."[49] As "first principles" are deemed eternal and unchanging, so must Tradition be eternal and unchanging.[50] Coomaraswamy's explanation was that Tradition is eternal and detectable as consistent Truth that is conveyed generationally in the temporal human realm—the unchanging Truth that passes from the past to present to future.[51] If there is one thing that definitively separates lowercase tradition from uppercase Tradition, it is the addition of Revelation. Traditionalism claims it possesses divinely revealed Truth. Notably, tradition does not attempt to make this claim.

The Added Ingredient of Revelation

Cutsinger, a practicing Orthodox Christian in addition to his being a Traditionalist scholar, provides clarity to two critical areas evident at this stage. First, Cutsinger provides definitional insight

238

into Traditionalism; his writing is clear and concise, as he explains Traditionalism from a current perspective. Second, he presents the foundational elements of Traditionalism in a readable style, but with a depth indicative of a subject matter expert.[52]

While custom and Tradition involve repetitive transmission, Tradition possesses the added ingredient of revealed Truth. In Cutsinger's words, the Traditionalist "must defend what is old, not as old but as true, as the temporal expression of something which is always springing fresh from eternity."[53] It is not that everything old is also true, rather that the Traditionalist defends and conveys what is both old *and* true—unchanging Truth handed-down from the most distant times.

The Truth Cutsinger is referring to above is derived from revelation. Cutsinger stated that Traditionalism should be "paired with revelation."[54] The essential ingredient differentiating Tradition from custom is its "contact with revelation and thus with God."[55] Fabbri suggested that "for Guénon and his followers, tradition does not have a human origin and may be considered as principles revealed from Heaven and binding man to his divine origin."[56] Lakhani provided a further explanation when comparing Tradition against things modern; Tradition, in contrast to modernity, designates those immutable principles, the *Sophia Perennis* or primordial wisdom, which are rooted in the Transcendent.[57]

The transcendent nature of Traditionalism became even more apparent with Cutsinger's definitional clarity:

> My own definition of tradition requires that it be paired with revelation. The former, we might say, is horizontal, while the latter is vertical. Where revelation is the projection of God into space, tradition is the extension of revelation through time...The distinction of space from time is too simplistic, of course. In entering space, God also enters time. And in their extension through time, the modes by which tradition carries the force of revelation—be they words, gestures, symbols, saints, shrines—take up a certain space. But however one pictures it, revelation and tradition

are to be seen, I suggest, as two parts of a single movement from God to man.[58]

Cutsinger reinforced Guénon's contention that "there is nothing and can be nothing truly traditional that does not contain some element of a super-human order."[59] Cutsinger also echoed Guénon's claim that the supernatural quality of Tradition "is the essential point, containing as it were the very definition of tradition and all that appertains to it."[60] Schuon agreed that Tradition emanates from a divine source.[61] Lakhani emphasized revelation in explaining the metahistorical nature of Traditionalism in contrast to a particular religious tradition that embraces it. Noting the eternal attribute of Revelation, Lakhani related that it "is not a historical event: it is based in the eternal present and is continuous."[62] Lakhani's clarification addressed the eternal nature that Divine Revelation brings to Traditionalism, thereby endowing it with an ingredient that transcends history. As will be apparent, Dugin, professing a Traditionalist position, does not hesitate to proclaim supernatural intervention in his Neo-Eurasian development.

The Battle Line between Traditionalism and Modernity

Time against eternity can be the motto of the ongoing conflict between modernity and tradition, Dugin claimed.[63] Pelikan Famously stated, "Tradition is the living faith of the dead, traditionalism is the dead faith of the living."[64] Provocative this may be, but Pelikan used the statement not so much to provoke as he did to cast doubt on the tendency to glorify a return to an atavistic state. One of the primary friction points between embracing Traditionalism and living in the present is the strife—often described as "revolt"—which Traditionalism promotes against modernity.[65]

Pelikan put his finger on the friction point between Traditionalism and modernity by stating that "reformers of every age, whether political or religious or literary, have protested against the tyranny of the dead, and in doing so have called for innovation and insight in place of tradition."[66] Thus, is the battle

240

line between the inherently progressive nature of modernity and the inherently conservative nature of Traditionalism drawn.

Notes

1. The use of uppercase Truth here is employed to contrast a divinely inspired and unchanging sacred characteristic of Traditionalism with the profane truth of factual statements, concepts, or beliefs.

2. The Traditionalist/Fundamentalist topic is expanded in Part V, Chapter Two. Cf. Rosalind Marsh, "The 'New Political Novel' by Right-Wing Writers in Post-Soviet Russia," *Forum Für Osteuropäische Ideen -und Zeitgeschichte* 14, no. 2 (2010), for her comments on the St. Petersburg Fundamentalists and relationships with the RNR. Dugin is mentioned in Marsh's article several times. Cf. doi.org/10.7788/frm.2010.14.2.159 for a copy of this article. Rosalind Marsh, Emeritus Professor of Russian Studies, University of Bath.

3. Cf. e.g., Dugin, *Fourth Theory*, 193ff. Julius Evola, 1898-1974.

4. "Are Perennialists and Traditionalists the Same or Different?," World Wisdom, under, A Definition of the Perennial Wisdom, accessed June 13, 2016, worldwisdom.com/public/slideshows/view.aspx?SlideShowID=41&SlideDetailID=376.

5. The OED states that Traditionalism is "the upholding or maintenance of tradition, especially so as to resist change." The OED does not address Perennialism as such, but definitions similar Traditionalism are common in other sources. Fundamentalism is defined in the OED as "a form of a religion, especially Islam or Protestant Christianity, that upholds belief in the strict, literal interpretation of scripture." Note that the OED here applies current usage. Historical development of the term is addressed here and elsewhere in the body of this study.

6. "Are Perennialists and Traditionalists the Same or Different?," under, "Definition of Perennial Wisdom." Brackets added. Italics in original.

7. Ibid. Brackets added.

8. Wouter Hanegraaff, "Will-Erich Peuckert and the Light of Nature," in *Esotericism, Religion, and Nature*, ed. Arthur Versluis, et al (East Lancing: North American Academic Press, 2009), 285. Will-Erich Peuckert, 1895-1969. Wouter Hanegraaff, Professor of History of Hermetic Philosophy, University of Amsterdam.

9. Hanegraaff, "Peuckert and the Light," 285. Here referring to Peuckert, *Pansophie,* IX. Italics in original.

10. Ibid. Here the quotations are assumed to be from Peuckert. Theophrastus von Hohenheim, ca. 1493-1541. As a physician, Paracelsus attempted to reform the medical practices, in the vein of Martin Luther. This effort earned Paracelsus censure and professional marginalization for much of his life. Cf. e.g., Sašo Dolenc, "Paracelsus - Martin Luther of Medicine,"Kvarkadabra, June 18, 2016, under, A new approach to healing, kvarkadabra.net. Sašo Dolenc, Writer and Philosopher of Science, Editor-in-Chief of the online science journal *Kvarkadabra.*

11. Ibid., 288.

12. Ibid., 291.

13. *Integral* is sometimes rendered *Classical* especially when distinguishing it from Neo-Traditionalism. Cf. Julius Evola, "René Guénon & Integral Traditionalism," Counter Currents Publishing, June 7, 2016, counter-currents.com/2016/06/rene-guenon-and-integral-traditionalism/. This article is translated from: Evola, *Ricognizioni: Uomini E Problemi* (Rome: Edizioni Mediterranee, 1974).

14. Cf. Vojtěch Hladký, "From Byzantium to Italy: 'Ancient Wisdom' in Plethon and Cusanus," ed. Paul Richard Blum, in *Georgios Gemistos Plethon: The Byzantine and the Latin Renaissance*, ed. Jozef Matula (Olomouc: Palacke University, 2014), 278ff. References and discussion of Zoroaster are found throughout this article. Plethon, 1355-1452, is also known as George Gemistos. Vojtěch Hladký, member of the faculty of Charles University, Prague.

15. Cf. Hanegraaff, "Peuckert and the Light." Cf. Hanegraaff, *Esotericism and the Academy: Rejected Knowledge in Western Culture* (Cambridge: Cambridge University Press, 2013).

16. Aldous Huxley, *The Perennial Philosophy* (London: Chatto & Windus), 1947, 1. Huxley claimed an unbroken chain of some 2500 years. Aldous Huxley, 1894-1963. Gottfried Wilhelm Leibniz, 1646-1716. Augustinius Steuchius, 1497-1548.

17. Cf. Randolph Dible, "The Philosophy of Mysticism: Perennialism and Constructivism," *Journal of Consciousness Exploration & Research* 1, no. 2 (March 2010): 173-83, W.T. S. Thackara, "The Perennial Philosophy," *Sunrise Magazine*, April/May 1984, and Renaud Fabbri, "Introduction to the Perennialist School," Religio Perennis, accessed June 13, 2017,

242

religioperennis.org/documents/Fabbri/Perennialism.pdf; and Cicero, *Tusculan Disputations* I. Randolph Dible, Lecturer, St. Joseph's College. Renaud Fabbri, formally Visiting Scholar at the Center for the Study of World Religions, Harvard Divinity School.

18. *Middle Ages* is an imprecise term referring to a period of time from (roughly) the fall of the Roman Empire in the West to the Fall of Constantinople in 1453. Cf. *Encyclopædia Britannica*, s.v. "Middle Ages (Historical Era)," updated July 4, 2019, britannica.com/search?query=Middle+Ages+. The *Britannica* states that the Middle Ages cover "the period in European history from the collapse of Roman civilization in the 5th century CE to the period of the Renaissance (variously interpreted as beginning in the 13th, 14th, or 15th century, depending on the region of Europe and on other factors)."

19. Dugin himself makes this connection.

20. E.g., Sedgwick identifies seven significant Traditionalists: Coomaraswamy, Dr, Ananda Kentish (1877–1947), British, then American, art historian; Guénon, René (1886–1951), French, then Egyptian, developed Traditionalism; Evola, Baron Julius (1896/8–1974), Italian, developed political Traditionalism; Eliade, Dr. Mircea (1907–86), Romanian, then American, scholar of religions; Schuon, Frithjof (1907–98), German, later French, then Swiss, finally resident in America, developed Sufi Traditionalism and established the Alawiyya (later the Maryamiyya) Sufi order; Nasr, Dr. Seyyed Hossein (1933–), Iranian, then American, introduced Islamic Traditionalism to Iran and other parts of the Islamic world; Dugin, Alexander (1962–), Russian. Developed Neo-Eurasianism. Cf. Sedgwick, *Against the Modern World,* xiii. Mark Sedgwick, Professor of Arab and Islamic Studies, Aarhus University.

21. Cf. e.g., Ananda K. Coomaraswamy, *The Essential Ananda K. Coomaraswamy*, ed. Rama P. Coomaraswamy (Lahore, Pakistan: Suhail Academy, 2011), M. Ali Lakhani, "Understanding 'Tradition,'" in *The Timeless Relevance of Traditional Wisdom* (Bloomington, IN: World Wisdom, 2010), 3-4, Ali Lakhani, Editorial, "Understanding Tradition," *Sacred Web* 9 (2002), sacredweb.com/online_articles/sw9_editorial.html, Seyyed Hossein Nasr, *Knowledge and the Sacred* (Albany, NY: State University of New York Press, 1989), and Guénon, *Essential Guénon*, 93-6. Ananda K. Coomaraswamy, 1877-1947. M. Ali Lakhani, QC, Canadian lawyer, also writer of metaphysics and Perennialism. Seyyed Hossein Nasr, Islamic Philosopher, Professor Emeritus of Islamic studies, George Washington University.

22. Maryamiyya was originally known as the Alawiyya. Schuon renamed it after experiencing a vision of the Virgin Mary. Cf. Sedgwick, *Against the Modern World*, chapter titled, The Maryamiyya. Cf. oxfordindex.oup.com/view/10.1093/0195152972.003.0008. Titus Burckhardt, 1908-1984. Frithjof Schuon, 1907-1998.

23. Ca. 1950.

24. Cf. Frithjof Schuon, *Understanding Islam* (London: Allen & Unwin, 1963) and Schuon, *In the Tracks of Buddhism* (London: Allen & Unwin, 1968).

25. Evola, *Revolt Against the Modern World*, trans. Guido Stucco (Rochester, VT: Inner Traditions International, 1995). René Guénon, *The Crisis of the Modern World*, trans. Marco Pallis, Arthur Osborne, and Richard C. Nicholson (Hillsdale, NY: Sophia Perennis, 2001).

26. Helena Petrovna Blavatsky, 1831-1891. Colonel Henry Olcott, 1832-1907. The two well-known works attributed to Blavatsky are, *Isis Unveiled: A Master-key to the Mysteries of Ancient and Modern Science and Theology* and *The Secret Doctrine: The Synthesis of Science, Religion and Philosophy*. Cf. Blavatskaja, *Isis Unveiled: A Master-Key to the Mysteries of Ancient and Modern Science and Theology* (New York: Bouton, 1893) for one of many reprints. Cf. Blavatsky, *The Secret Doctrine: The Synthesis of Science, Religion and Philosophy* (London: Theosophical Pub. House, 1893) for one of the various editions of this work. "Authorship of both books," wrote Sedgwick, "was attributed to ethereal sources, but both were in fact drafted by Blavatsky and then turned into publishable form by human 'ghost' writers—by Olcott in the case of *Isis Unveiled*, and in the case of *The Secret Doctrine*, by two English brothers who took over after Blavatsky's original choice of editor had refused the task in dismay on reading her disorganized first draft." Cf. Sedgwick *Against the Modern World*, 44 footnote 25, where he credits Bruce F. Campbell, *Ancient Wisdom Revived: A History of the Theosophical Movement* (Berkeley: University of California Press, 1980), 34, 40. I do not explore Theosophy it in any depth primarily due to Dugin not writing of it in any substantial way when compared to his emphasis on the Traditionalism of Guénon, other Integral Traditionalists, and Evola. The second reason is that Guénon criticized Theosophy thoroughly, the subject becoming the basis of books he published in 1921 and 1923. Sedgwick wrote that Guénon's criticisms amounted to "sophisticated demolitions of Theosophy, spiritualism, and occultism, proceeding from a familiarity with the occultist milieu that Guénon had acquired

between 1906 and 1912." Cf. Sedgwick, *Against the Modern World*, 24.

27. Aleister Crowley, 1875-1947. Cf. Hanegraaff's "Foreword" in *Aleister Crowley and Western Esotericism* is an example of the greater attention afforded Crowley and other nineteenth century proponents of popular mysticism, much of it the carnival variety then in vogue. Cf. Hanegraaff, "Forward," in *Aleister Crowley and Western Esotericism: An Anthology of Critical Studies*, ed. Henrik Bogdan and Martin Starr (Oxford: Oxford University Press, 2012), vii–x.

28. I avoided chasing after the amazingly prolific Joséphin Péladan, the poetry of Stanislas de Guaita, the music of Erik Satie, Symbolist expression in fine art, and the occultism and gnostic metaphysics of Martinism of the late eighteenth and nineteenth centuries. Cf. A Martinist, according to the OED, adheres to "a form of mystical pantheism developed by the French philosopher L. C. de Saint-Martin (1743–1803)."

29. Here I am referring to tradition as social and cultural custom rather than in the context of Traditionalism's revealed Truth claims. Jaroslav Pelikan, 1923-2006.

30. Jaroslav Pelikan, *The Vindication of Tradition* (New Haven: Yale University Press, 1984).

31. Lyrics may be accessed at allmusicals.com/f/fiddlerontheroof.htm.

32. As Sedgwick and Patrick Ringgenberg inform us, expressions of the visual arts are conspicuously absent in Traditionalism. Cf. Sedgwick, "Traditionalism and Art - and Perhaps More than Art," Traditionalists, June 18, 2010, traditionalistblog.blogspot.ie/2010/06/traditionalism-and-art-and-perhaps-more.html. Ringgenberg's 2010 dissertation, "Les Théories De L'artdans La Pensée Traditionnelle. René Guénon - Ananda K. Coomaraswamy - Frithjof Schuon - Titus Burckhardt," may be accessed at, academia.edu/38298407/Les_th%C3%A9ories_de_lart_dans_la_pens%C3%A9e_traditionnelle_Gu%C3%A9non_-_Coomaraswamy_-_Schuon_-_Burckhardt. Subsequently, this dissertation was published, Cf. Ringgenberg, *Les théories de l'art dans la pensée traditionnelle: Guénon, Coomaraswamy, Schuon, Burckhardt* (Paris: Editions L'Harmattan, 2011). This lack of visual expression may be due to the rejection of contemporary society so prevalent in Integral Traditionalism. Perhaps too, the degree of Islamic influence on the

Integral Traditionalists may have curtailed visual artistic expression. T.S. Eliot, 1888-1965.

33. Sedgwick, "Traditionalism and Art."

34. Cf. Part I, Chapter Three, footnote 17 for examples of Eco's writing that include Traditionalist and conspirology themes and references.

35. Thomas Stearns Eliot, "Tradition and the Individual Talent," in *The Sacred Wood* (New York: Alfred A. Knopf, 1921). Although Dugin reserves most of his comments on the arts to criticize the decadence of the West, it is evident that he admires Traditionalist expressions in poetry, for example in the works of Hölderlin and Arthur Rimbaud. Dugin mentions Hölderlin in connection with Heidegger, specifically Hölderlin's poem, "Bread and Wine." Cf. *Fourth Theory*, 29, and Heidegger, *Off the Beaten Path*, 200-41. Jean Nicolas Arthur Rimbaud, French poet whose poetry was filled with symbolism. It may be the symbolic nature of Rimbaud's poetry that first attracted Dugin. Jean Nicolas Arthur Rimbaud, 1854-1891.

36. Sedgwick, *Against the Modern World*, 21.

37. Guénon, *Essential Guénon*, 93-5.

38. Ibid., 93.

39. Fabbri, "Perennialist School," under, Modernity, tradition and Primordial Tradition.

40. James Cutsinger, "An Open Letter on Tradition," *Modern Age*, Spring, 36, no. 3 (1994): 295. This article may be accessed at unz.org/Pub/ModernAge-1994q2-00294?View=PDF. James Cutsinger, Professor Emeritus, University of South Carolina.

41. Cutsinger, "An Open Letter," 295.

42. Ibid.

43. Guénon, *Essential Guénon*, 93. Cf. worldwisdom.com/public/library/default.spx.

44. Cutsinger, "An Open Letter," 295.

45. Ibid., 294.

46. Lakhani, "Understanding 'Tradition,'" 52. Lakhani attributed this quote to Coomaraswamy with the notation "*Correspondence*, 1946." Ramin Jahanbegloo stated that Coomaraswamy wrote this explanation of Tradition "in a letter to Alfred O. Mendel." Cf. Ramin Jahanbegloo, "Ananda Coomaraswamy: A Metaphysical Critique of Modernity,"

Ramin Jahanbegloo, October 15, 2012, jahanbegloo.com. Ramin Jahanbegloo, Political Philosopher.

47. This holds true for the variants of both: Traditionalist/traditionalist, Traditional/traditional, etc.

48. Paradoxically, perhaps by circular definitions, it is accurate to state that Traditionalism contains traditionalism, but traditionalism does not contain Traditionalism.

49. Ibid. From Coomaraswamy, *Correspondence*, 1946.

50. Ibid.

51. Ibid.

52. Cf. Cutsinger, "An Open Letter."

53. Ibid., 300.

54. Ibid., 294-95.

55. Ibid., 295.

56. Fabbri, "Perennialist School," under, Modernity, tradition and Primordial Tradition.

57. Lakhani, "Understanding 'Tradition,'" 52-53. Here Lakhani offered his take on Nasr's conceptions of "modern" and "traditional." Lakhani noted that this article is adapted from an editorial that appeared in *Sacred* Web volume 9, July 2002. Cf. "Understanding 'Tradition,'" reposted from religioperennis.com, and dated July 17, 2005, elkorg-projects.blogspot.com/2005/07/ali-lakhani-understanding-tradition.html. Cf. traditionalhikma.com/wp-content/uploads/2015/02/Understanding-Tradition-by-M.-Ali-Lakhani.pdf.

58. Cutsinger, "An Open Letter," 294-95. Compare with Dugin's use of vertical/horizontal representations in Part I, Chapter Two, under, Dugin's Self-placement as a Vertical Platonist.

59. Guénon, *The Reign of Quantity and the Signs of the times*, trans. Walter James (Hillsdale, NY: Sophia Perennis, 2004), 253.

60. Guénon, *Reign of Quantity*, 211.

61. Deon Valodia, "Glossary of Terms Used by Frithjof Schuon," frithjof-schuon.com/Glossary%20Schuon%20Revised.pdf.

62. Lakhani, "Understanding 'Tradition,'" 53.

63. Dugin, "The Sovereignity [sic] of the Eternity vs the Imperialism of the Time," Геополитика.RU, May 26, 2017, geopolitica.ru/en/article/sovereignity-eternity-vs-imperialism-time. According to the article the contents are derived from "Alexander Dugin's speech at the conference, 'From the Atlantic to Pacific: for a common destiny of Eurasian peoples'" (May 26-27, Chişinău)."

64. Pelikan, *Vindication of Tradition*, 65.

65. Cf. e.g., Sedgwick, *Against the Modern World*, Guénon, *The Crisis of the Modern World*, trans. Marco Pallis, Arthur Osborne, and Richard C. Nicholson (Hillsdale, NY: Sophia Perennis, 2001), and Evola, *Revolt Against the Modern World*.

66. Pelikan, *Vindication of Tradition*, 65.

Chapter Two: The Fundamentalism/Traditionalism Relationship

Closer than Cousins

Fundamentalism, in its more strict and historical definition, shares essential common threads with Traditionalism. One of the most critical threads being an imperative to ensure proper transfer and reception of unaltered Truth. Indeed, knowing, discovering, or uncovering the exact body of revealed Truth, faithfully engaging its precepts, preserving it, and consequently passing it on intact, comprises the *raison d'être* of Traditionalism and Fundamentalism.

In its treatment of fundamentalism, the OED states, "fundamentalists reject a larger portion of secular society, maintain strong commitments to strict literalism, premillennial dispensationalism, and moral traditionalism." The terms *fundamentalist* and *Traditionalist* refer to similar things. However, definitional interpretations have sometimes been derived directly from practitioners of fundamentalism or Traditionalism. At other times, definitions have been profoundly influenced by twentieth and twenty-first century writers and thinkers who constructed definitions from outside the accepted definitional elements applied by those within either belief system.

In the literature, fundamentalism and Traditionalism share several common characteristics evident in the way both project their Truth claims. Christian Fundamentalism, as a self-identified biblical hermeneutic, has identifiable reactionary beginnings. Michael O. Emerson and David Hartman concluded that early twentieth century fundamentalism "was not so much a battle with the secular state as it was an intrareligious fight" between American Protestants.[1] The fundamentalist movement began when specific aspects of modernism that had pervaded Christian denominations were interpreted by the initial Christian fundamentalists as being non-biblical, heretical, and dangerous.[2]

The militant nature of fundamentalism received useful treatment from historian George Marsden and theologian Rolland McCune.[3] Perhaps the most instructive work to this end was that of Michael Barkun. Barkun's work is remarkable for its

249

clarification of violent tendencies present in current interpretations of fundamentalism vice the original nonviolent characteristics of the Christian fundamentalist movement.[4] Additionally, baseline research into fundamentalism includes Yvonne Luven's extensive *Scoping Study*.[5] Seminal research in the field by Martin E. Marty and the *Fundamentalism Project* is another very relevant, in-depth, and informative study.[6]

Karen Armstrong's, *The Battle for God*, and "Fundamentalism and Literature," by Ihab Hassan, are both concerned with fundamentalism, and expand its definition.[7] Both of these works examine elements of non-Christian-centric fundamentalisms, including Islamic and other manifestations, in scholarly and well-documented forums. *The Battle for God* provides foundational information but is dated in its presentation of specific fundamentalist groups. Hassan's presentation is especially impressive as it covers art and literary topics in their organic relationship with fundamentalism in a non-typical literary style reminiscent of the sophisticated writing of Eco. Hassan expanded fundamentalism's artistic and literary connections much as Pelikan and Eliot did for Traditionalism. Armstrong considered the evolution of violent groups claiming religious purity and orthodoxy, and acknowledged characteristic resemblances found among these fundamentalist groups.[8] The importance of family-like resemblance in the context of organized movements is underscored by the supporting literature of Huntington and others.[9]

Fundamentalism's Evolution

According to Emerson and Hartman, "the term fundamentalism was first used to describe a conservative strain of Protestantism that developed in the United States roughly from 1870 to 1925."[10] As a descriptor, fundamentalism was initially applied in the first quarter of the twentieth century.[11] However, fundamentalist threads linked to the movement that emerged are traceable to the Puritans and other dogmatic sects or groups.[12]

The Protestant fundamentalists were reacting in part to the residual effects of the Enlightenment. Liberalism in the form of more secular or popular religious interpretations spawned significant changes in Protestant hermeneutics, especially in the latter nineteenth and throughout the twentieth centuries. The reaction of some Protestants regarding their understanding of changing theological dogma away from traditional interpretations was, in its way, an expression of anti-modernism; it was their revolt against the modern world.

After a purely Christian attempt to return to the basic tenants of the Faith determined by the original definers, the second phase of fundamentalism's evolution involved the infusion of militancy into its definitional character. There can be little doubt that the inclusion of a militant aspect within fundamentalism has contributed to broadening its definition to include non-Protestant actors that express ideology with militancy, aggression, and violence. Fundamentalism's time confined within the definitional boundaries of foundational Christian beliefs in response to, and in opposition of, modernism was short-lived. The rapid evolution of Christian Fundamentalism quickly resulted in broader definitional descriptions that are now commonly held.

Following mostly unsuccessful forays into the public arena of the 1920s and 1930s, Christian Fundamentalism adopted a more separatist or isolationist posture. This posture was prevalent until moves, especially noticeable since the 1970s, toward a more open and visibly combative stance occurred. Whatever the original intentions of the founders of the Christian Fundamentalist movement, its evolution soon exhibited militant characteristics.

Fundamentalist Aspects of Dugin's Political Theology

The political theology of Schmitt, Bonald, Lamennais, Durkheim, and the political philosophy of Burke are important to placing Dugin firmly in a specific geopolitical position. However much the location of Dugin's position is determined by his political, theological, and philosophical influencers, accurate reception of Dugin requires understanding that he is conservative to the point of being fundamentalist. That is, his conservatism exhibits decidedly fundamentalist characteristics evident in both his Neo-Traditionalism and is Neo-Eurasianism.

Although perhaps an unintentional pun, "the influence of Traditionalism on Dugin seems to be fundamental: it constitutes

251

his main intellectual reference point and the basis of his political attitudes as well as his Eurasianism," wrote Laruelle.[13] Dugin is emphatic on this point as well.[14] Not only was Traditionalism's influence fundamental, but Dugin's Traditionalism is also, in itself, fundamentalist. "Dugin's Eurasianism embodies a triumphalist form of cultural fundamentalism (Traditionalism) which attempts to bridge ethnic divisions by a call to pre-historic glory and persisting common elements," observed Middleton.[15] With this remark, Middleton reinforced the link between Traditionalism and fundamentalism and connected both with Dugin.

Dugin's awareness and acceptance of Schmitt are noteworthy on multiple levels, not the least of which is how political theology emanating from conservative sources (both Dugin and Schmitt, for example) has gained attention in the West. Dugin's entry into the light of Western recognition coincides with Schmitt's. I previously introduced Dugin's initial reception, and Joseph W. Bendersky wrote of Schmitt's that "until the 1980s few in North America had even heard of Schmitt—and most of them worked under the then prevalent, though erroneous notion, that he was a Nazi thinker."[16]

Bendersky's mention of Nazi associations attached to Schmitt is pertinent because of similar proclivities frenquently attached to Dugin.[17] Indeed, Schmitt was academically shunned in the West for many years due to his willingness to work within the prevailing governmental system, whether it was the Weimar Republic or Hitler's National Socialist regime.[18] Schmitt is still labeled as an evangelist of National Socialism—John P. McCormick being one accuser.

Bendersky remarked on McCormick's fear of "Schmittian paths in America, Europe and the Third World."[19] McCormick identified these paths as "neo-Nazism, militia movements, 'Christian identity' ideologies, ethnic cleansing, racially motivated mass rape, violent attacks on emigrant workers and foreigners," as well as, "bombing of abortion clinics and state administrative buildings."[20] Bendersky countered that "Scholars in Europe, Japan, and America have long refuted the 1950s interpretations of Schmitt as someone who undermined the

Weimar Republic and saw his ideas come to fruition in the Third Reich."[21]

The McCormick and Bendersky dispute involving supposed "Schmittian paths" leads to considerations of extremist political theologies, and expressions of radical political theologies often include fundamentalist language. It is evident, given his characterization of Schmittian paths, that McCormick ascribes Schmitt's political theology with militant attributes. Discussing the intersection of militancy and fundamentalism, McCune stated that militancy "has been a defining characteristic of fundamentalism from the beginning."[22]

Militancy, most evident in its use of confrontational methods, became distinguishable within fundamentalism very early on. McCune made direct references that focus attention on this militant characteristic. These references include the observation by George Dollar that "the militant exposure of all non-Biblical expositions and affirmations and attitudes" became a part of the accepted definition of Christian Fundamentalism.[23] Marsden wrote that the attributes of an early Christian Fundamentalist included being a "believer in the fundamentals" who was "willing to take a militant stand against modernism."[24] This militant stand is evident in Fourth Political Theory.

McCune summed up the second stage of the evolutionary process of fundamentalism in contrast to its primary stage by noting that, "the most clearly observable distinctives [sic] of the movement are militancy and separatism."[25] Here similarities between Fourth Political Theory and early developing Christian Fundamentalist thought are evident in the multipolar aspirations of Dugin's Neo-Eurasianist efforts. Hoffer provided insight:

> Those who are awed by their surroundings do not think of change, no matter how miserable their condition. When our mode of life is so precarious as to make it patent that we cannot control the circumstances of our existence, we tend to stick to the proven and the familiar.[26]

"As for the hopeful," Hoffer wrote, "they all proceed recklessly with the present, wreck it if necessary, and create a new world."[27] The militancy of fundamentalism is rooted in its hope for change, not in hopelessness that things will never change. Hoffer's observation highlights Dugin's hopefulness and is reflected in the growing recognition of Rightist movements in Europe and elsewhere.[28]

Movements demanding strict orthodoxy and orthopraxis often reject elements of the contemporary society and culture where they find themselves.[29] The same goes for believers who find identity in a designated hermeneutical position or a specific exegesis. Adherents of movements that adopt identities purposely away from the center tend to collect at one of the poles of a given social continuum, not because they do not wish to occupy the center, but because they are pushed away by political and societal power. In response, fundamentalists of all stripes, including Dugin, push back against being marginalized. Their reaction to assignment at the social and political margins is often to adopt radical activism calling to mind Armstrong's observation that in their strife with modernity,

> Fundamentalists do not regard this battle as a conventional political struggle, but experience it as a cosmic war between the forces of good and evil. They fear annihilation, and try to fortify their beleaguered identity by means of a selective retrieval of certain doctrines and practices of the past.[30]

Marty pointed out the polemical nature of fundamentalist thinking and identified friction points along the fault lines of internal division and external separatism:

> fundamentalisms are Manichaean in the sense that they sharply differentiate between the realm of their god and their satan, between the elect people and the outsiders, between "us" and "them," allowing for no middle ground. Because of this characteristic, fundamentalisms may and often do resist some features of political life, including compromise. In fact, fundamentalists

tend to be more disdainful and wary of the moderates within their own religious complexes than they are of liberals or representatives of other faiths, who are unmistakably "other."[31]

Fourth Political Theory resonates with similar Manichean dualism in its claims of Messianic Russia and the evil otherness of the Western Antichrist.

Barkun thought that "What is usually referred to as 'fundamentalism' is in effect any claim to exclusive authenticity within a religious tradition."[32] Traditionalists make this claim with their insistence on their knowledge of unaltered Truth; Dugin makes it in stating his case for the authentic Christianity of the Old Believers. Barkun's opinion demonstrates just how far fundamentalist labeling has traveled along the trail of etymological evolution. It also underscores the family resemblance and fundamentalist nature of Traditionalist and Old Believer elements within Fourth Political Theory.

Notes

1. Michael O. Emerson and David Hartman, "The Rise of Religious Fundamentalism," *Annual Review of Sociology* 32, no. 1 (August 11, 2006): 132. Michael O. Emerson, provost of North Park University. David Hartman, researcher at the University of Notre Dame when this article was published. In this chapter especially, uppercase treatment of the term *Fundamentalism* is somewhat problematic. Very often in the literature, *fundamentalism* is not capitalized in accordance with no particular rule I have encountered. Therefore, acknowledging the internal inconsistency, there may appear to be little method in upper- and lower-case renditions of the term herein.

2. Cf. Karen Armstrong, *The Battle for God* (London: Harper Perennial, 2004), for an example of an attempt to trace the historical roots of Christian Fundamentalism far earlier than the 1800s. Karen Armstrong, Religious Scholar and Author.

3. Cf. George M. Marsden, *Reforming Fundamentalism* (Grand Rapids, MI: Eerdmans, 1987), and Rolland D. McCune, "The Self-Identity of Fundamentalism," *Detroit Baptist Seminary Journal*, Spring, 1, no. 1 (1996): 9-34. George M. Marsden, Professor Emeritus at Notre Dame and religious historian. Rolland D. McCune, Former Professor of

Systematic Theology and president of the Detroit Baptist Theological Seminary.

4. Michael Barkun, "Religious Violence and the Myth of Fundamentalism," *Totalitarian Movements and Political Religions* 4, no. 3 (2003): 55-70. Michael Barkun, Professor Emeritus of Political Science at the Maxwell School of Citizenship and Public Affairs, Syracuse University, recognized for his work in the field of religious violence.

5. Yvonne Luven, *Engaging Religious Fundamentalisms* (Dublin: Irish School of Ecumenics, Trinity College Dublin), 2008. This report is designated as a *Scoping Study* by the Irish School of Ecumenics. Yvonne Luven, scholar of comparative religion in Dublin.

6. Martin E. Marty, "Too Bad We're So Relevant: The Fundamentalism Project Projected," *Bulletin of the American Academy of Arts and Sciences* 49, no. 6 (March 1996). This report was presented to the American Academy of Arts and Sciences at conclusion of the well recognized 6-year Fundamentalism Project and may be accessed at illuminos.com/mem/selectPapers/contentsSelectList.html. Martin E. Marty, Fairfax M. Cone Distinguished Service Professor Emeritus of the History of Modern Christianity, University of Chicago.

7. Cf. Armstrong, *Battle for God* and Ihab Hassan, "Fundamentalism and Literature," *Georgia Review*, Spring, 62, no. 1 (2008): 16-29. Hassan's article may be accessed at jstor.org/stable/41402956. Ihab Hassan, 1925-2015. Fundamentalism's expanded definition, as employed by Armstrong and Hassan, includes religious associations outside of those included in the original twentieth century Christian application.

8. Armstrong, *Battle for God*, xii.

9. Cf. e.g., Huntington, *The Clash of Civilizations and the Remaking of World Order* (New York: Simon and Schuster, 1996), 96, T. E. Lawrence, *Seven Pillars of Wisdom* (Private Edition, 1926), (several public editions have been subsequently produced), and Hoffer, *The True Believer: Thoughts on the Nature of Mass Movements*, originally published by Harper & Row in 1951, Cf. Hoffer, *The True Believer: Thoughts on the Nature of Mass Movements* (New York: HarperPerennial, 2010). T.E. Lawrence 1888-1935.

10. Emerson and Hartman, "Rise of Religious Fundamentalism," 131.

11. *Online Etymological Dictionary*, s.v. "Fundamentalist," accessed February 23, 2018, etymonline.com/word/fundamentalist. Excerpts:

1920 in the religious sense (as is *fundamentalism*),
from *fundamental* + *-ist*. Coined in Amer.Eng. to name a movement
among Protestants c.1920-25 based on scriptural inerrancy, etc., and
associated with William Jennings Bryan, among others.
Fundamentalist is said (by George McCready Price) to have been first
used in print by Curtis Lee Laws (1868-1946), editor of "The
Watchman Examiner," a Baptist newspaper. The movement may have
roots in the Presbyterian General Assembly of 1910, which drew up a
list of five defining qualities of "true believers" which other
evangelicals published in a mass-circulation series of books called "The
Fundamentals." A World's Christian Fundamentals Association was
founded in 1918. The words reached widespread use in the wake of the
contentious Northern Baptist Convention of 1922 in Indianapolis. In
denominational use, *fundamentalist* was opposed to *modernist*.

12. David S. New, *Christian Fundamentalism in America: a Cultural History* (Jefferson, NC: McFarland, 2012), 4ff. David S. New, Canadian religious scholar.

13. Laruelle, *Russian Version of European Radical Right*, 10.

14. Cf. e.g., Dugin, *Fourth Theory*, 193-94.

15. Middleton, "Religion in Russian Strategy," 67-68.

16. Joseph W. Bendersky, "The Definite and the Dubious: Carl Schmitt's Influence on Conservative Political and Legal Theory in the US," *Telos* 122 (2002): 34. Joseph W. Bendersky, Schmitt scholar, Virginia Commonwealth University.

17. Cf. Part VI, Chapter Three for a discussion of Dugin's reception as a fascist.

18. The National Socialist German Workers' Party (NSDAP): *Nationalsozialistische Deutsche Arbeiterpartei*.

19. Bendersky, "Definite and Dubious," 35. Here Bendersky quotes McCormick. Cf. John P. McCormick, *Carl Schmitt's Critique of Liberalism: Against Politics as Technology* (Cambridge: Cambridge University Press, 1997), 305. John P. McCormick, Professor, Political Science, University of Chicago.

20. McCormick, *Schmitt's Critique of Liberalism*, 305. Cf. Bendersky, "Definite and Dubious," 35.

21. Bendersky, "Definite and the Dubious," 35.

22. McCune, "Self-Identity of Fundamentalism," 22.

23. George W. Dollar, *A History of Fundamentalism in America* (Greenville, SC: Bob Jones University Press, 1973), xv; quoted in McCune, "Self-Identity of Fundamentalism," 22. George Dollar, 1917-2006.

24. Marsden, *Reforming Fundamentalism*, 10; quoted in McCune, "Self-Identity of Fundamentalism," 23.

25. McCune, "Self-Identity of Fundamentalism," 10. Brackets added.

26. Hoffer, *The True Believer*, 10. For additional views on change, Cf. Hoffer, *The Ordeal of Change* (New York: Harper & Row, 1967).

27. Ibid.

28. It may be that the rise of Trump and his impact lends itself to fundamentalist interpretations and expressions.

29. E.g., Hasidic Jews and the Amish, to name two.

30. Armstrong, *Battle for God*, xii.

31. From Marty's presentation to the American Academy of Arts and Sciences at the conclusion of the Fundamentalism Project, Cf. illuminos.com/mem/selectPapers/contentsSelectList.html. Cf. Marty, "Too Bad We're So Relevant."

32. Barkun, "Violence and the Myth," 60.

Chapter Three: Dugin's Traditionalism

Dugin's Employment of Traditionalism as a Political Theology

Dugin's modified Traditionalism embodies his revolt against modernity and forms the basis for the anti-modernism found within Fourth Political Theory and the theological framework on which he overlays his Eurasianist geopolitical worldview. Dugin's understanding was expressed well by Voegelin: "All the early empires, Near Eastern as well as Far Eastern, understood themselves as representatives of a transcendent order, of the order of the cosmos; and some of them even understood this order as a 'truth.'"[1] Dugin would share Voegelin's understanding of temporal imperial power endowed with transcendent authority. He welcomes its fruition in a Eurasian reality.

Considering the conflicted viewpoints of Schmitt and Blumenberg, Pini Ifergan, a Blumenberg scholar, addressed political theology coinciding with Dugin's understanding. "The term *political theology* conceptualizes an attempt to rediscover and expose the theological dimension entwined within the fabric of politics," wrote Ifergan.[2] He was correct that the current practical understanding of Western governments, free from overt religious influence, is a youthful one considering the centuries of non-separation prior to the monumental eighteenth century social and political revolutions.[3]

Ifergan's conception of rediscovering theology entwined in the political fabric is especially applicable to Dugin. The theological dimensions of Traditionalism, Orthodox Christianity, gnosticism, and other esoteric and metaphysical elements Dugin weaves into the fabric of Fourth Political Theory are evident. Dugin does not hesitate to use Traditional ideas, with a culture-particular logic, in the vision of Eurasia that emerges from Fourth Political Theory. By stressing the interweaving threads of theology and politics within a composite fabric, Ifergan's understanding and Dugin's find common ground.

As Dugin overlays his Neo-Traditionalism with purposeful geopolitical elements, he moves it significantly away from the center to a point beyond the pale of Integral Traditionalism. With

259

this movement, Dugin mounts forays into apocalyptic territory with an active Traditionalism that Evola may have condoned, but Guénon never would.[4] Adding active political motives and eschatological purposes to his Neo-Traditionalism innovation marks the separation of Dugin from Guénon.

Dugin's geopolitical theology can be examined considering his treatment of it in the following areas:

- **Neo-Traditionalism**
- **Neo-Eurasianism**
- **Hermeneutics—the geopolitical and theological categories of Dugin's interpretations**
- **Assigned Identity—how Dugin views Eurasia in contrast to the West**
- **Conspirology—Dugin as Conspirologist**
- **Russian Orthodoxy—Dugin's expression of Orthodox Christianity in his Neo-Traditionalist terms**
- **Eschatology—Dugin's Apocalyptic view of Armageddon**

Development of Dugin's Neo-Traditionalism

Applying a Traditionalist label to Dugin and determining the depth of his acceptance of it allows for more accurate and usable insight into Fourth Political Theory. What this theory's message is, how Dugin envisions it, and why knowledge about it matters, must be considered given Dugin's claim that Fourth Political Theory is laid on Traditionalist foundations. What exactly is Dugin claiming to be, does he belong in a Traditionalist belief-system category, and what are the implications of the answers to these questions?

Traditionalism, while not a religion *per se*, involves religiously related discourse intensely interested in uncovering, recovering, and passing on Truth imparted to humankind through divine revelation but mostly lost to the major religions today. It is gnostic in its belief that correct ancient understandings have been passed down through the ages through sages and holy men.

260

Integral Traditionalism rejects the materialism of modernity in favor of a contemplative approach to understanding the cosmos through initiation into awareness of Truth.

Dugin credited Guénon, Evola, Burckhardt, Leopold Ziegler, and other Traditionalists for mounting a twentieth century defense of Traditionalism.[5] While not claiming to duplicate their Traditional views, Dugin emphasized that he shares "the vision" of Guénon and Evola,

> who considered Modernity and its ideological basis (individualism, liberal democracy, capitalism, consumerism, and so on) to be the cause of the future catastrophe of humanity and global domination of the Western lifestyle as the reason for the final degradation of the earth.[6]

Traditionalism constantly clashes with modernity. Dugin highlighted the contrast using the example of Traditionalism and sociology:

> The difference between traditionalism and sociology lies in the fact that sociology starts from modernity and judges Tradition from the point of view of modernity. Traditionalists do the opposite: they see modernity from the standpoint of Tradition. Modernity puts all reality in time, in history. Tradition considers things in light of eternity. So sociologists think pre-modernity diachronically as something past. Traditionalists regard modernity as an aspect of eternity.[7]

Dugin includes what amounts to Traditionalist redux as a foundational part of his Fourth Political Theory. As presented, it is a modified Traditionalism—a Neo-Traditionalism—genetically altered to display an active characteristic Guénon would have no doubt rejected.[8] Integral Traditionalists consider themselves to be something of an ideologically consistent community of a mostly static body of Traditional belief and practice across their various religious affiliations. In contrast, Dugin considers Traditionalism to be part of a present, potent, and active force with a political aspect; and he applies it accordingly. Hence, Dugin's version is appropriately labeled *Neo-Traditionalism*.[9]

Dugin applies elements of the Integral Traditionalism of Guénon and other Traditionalist interpreters with the much more politically active adaptations of Evola. Dugin's Neo-Traditionalism differs from Integral Traditionalism in two essential ways: it is active, and it is applied.[10] Dugin's applied Neo-Traditionalism is part of his geopolitical theology, not a specific self-fulfilling end in-and-of-itself. Where Integral Traditionalism aims at an inwardly directed spiritual perfection, Dugin's applied Neo-Traditionalism manifests itself as an active part of an overall opposition to Western Liberalism. Where Integral Traditionalism strives for a passive internal realization of Truth, Dugin's applied Neo-Traditionalism intends to project itself outwardly as part of a viable political theology alternative to Western political and cultural hegemony.

Dugin is entirely capable of holding forth on Integral Traditionalism. His discussions of the early twentieth century Traditionalists, historical figures, events, thoughts, and concepts derived from Traditionalist and Perennialist sources attest to his knowledge and understanding of the subject. Dugin pulls from a range of mystically oriented sources, and in doing so, displays the broad inclusionary traits characteristic of Traditionalists.

Dugin wrote that Guénon was "the most correct, the most intelligent and the most important person of the twentieth century."[11] Dugin claimed that, in his youth, he "was deeply inspired" by the Traditionalism of Guénon and Evola.[12] Dugin insisted, like Guénon and Evola before him, that his position is "on the side of sacred Tradition against the modern (and post-modern) world."[13]

Moreover, Dugin openly connects his Traditionalist philosophy with Russian Orthodox practice. He has "laid the basis for Traditionalist thought trying to apply the ideas of Guenon and Evola to the Russian Orthodox Christian tradition."[14] Western reception of Dugin and Fourth Political Theory must give considerable weight to his assertion that he stands "for spiritual and religious values against actual decadent materialist and perverted culture."[15] Recognition also must be afforded to Dugin's claim that his Traditionalism "rests central [sic] as the philosophic focus of all my later developments."[16]

To determine the depth of Dugin's Traditionalist credentials correctly, examples taken from along Dugin's path are useful. Dugin became a Traditionalist, at least by his reckoning, years before his Neo-Eurasianist impact was felt in Russia, and many years before it gained recognition in the West. Laruelle reported that Dugin was part of a group that created the "New University" founded in 1998.[17] This educational endeavor undertook to provide Traditionalist and occultist teachings.[18] In the 1980s, Dugin became acquainted with an active group of Traditionalists.[19]

> Depressed and alienated from the Soviet reality around him, he encountered by chance, through a neighbor of his parents, a secretive group of intellectuals who gave him the existential home he sought. The three most important members of this circle, who first came together in the 1960s, were all scholars steeped in the mystical traditions of Europe or the Orient: Yevgeny Golovin, a specialist in European mystical literature and poetry; Yuri Mamleyev, a Christian philosopher; and Geidar Jemal, a Muscovite of Azeri origin who specialized in the metaphysics of Islam.[20]

During this New University period, Dugin began translating works in English, French, and German. Through this work and his Traditionalist friends, he became familiar with the literary works of Guénon and Evola.[21] Shenfield remarked that at this time, "Dugin rapidly made himself a valued member of the Golovin circle."[22] Also, by Shenfield's account, "Dugin spent much of 1989 on visits to West European countries, where he strengthened his links with such European New Right (ENR) figures as the Frenchman Alain de Benoist, the Belgian Jean-François Thiriart, and the Italian Claudio Mutti."[23]

263

Dugin's Drift Toward Evola

Even as Dugin acknowledged the influence of both Guénon and Evola, there is no clear evidence that Dugin was ever a strict follower of the former.[24] If Dugin was initially a disciple of Guénon, he is no longer on the same path, Dugin's Neo-Traditionalism is much more that of Evola. Shekhovtsov and Umland found some redemptive value in Dugin's translation and publication of Traditionalist literature, and they acknowledged these activities as a genuine contribution to Integral Traditionalism.[25] But, they and some other Dugin critics, have never fully endorsed Dugin's Traditionalist claims. This situation is probably due, in part, to the difficulty encountered in reconciling the characteristically active Neo-Traditionalist praxis of Dugin, strongly influenced by Evola, with the more passive and contemplative Traditionalism of Guénon.

Dugin employs his Traditionalist beliefs within his active geopolitical agenda—something Guénon assuredly would not have done. Dugin is thus compelled to adopt a Neo-Traditionalism, instead of Guénon's version, to mesh with his active and somewhat complicated mix of theology, geopolitics, and assigned identity. The action-infused characteristic of Dugin's applied Neo-Traditionalism is more closely related to the militant aspects of fundamentalism than it is to the passive nature of its Integral forebearer. Dugin's Neo-Traditionalism allows him the flexibility to be overtly active—even militant, while at the same time, bringing the full weight of Traditionalism's anti-modernism down on the West, especially the United States.

Guénon is recognized in practically all discussions of Traditionalism. This one is no exception, but what are we to make of Dugin's statements concerning the supremacy of Guénon?

> What can you say about postguenonism (Traditionalism) in relation to the Russian situation? For us, the implementation of the programme of postguenonism is paramount, the only major state, national, social and cultural task. We only have one author that should be read is [sic] Rene Guenon.[26]

The conclusion can only be that Dugin initially grounds himself in Traditionalism but then adapts it to the activism of Fourth Political Theory. As I attempt to systematize Dugin's geopolitical theology, Integral Traditionalism becomes less the focus, and more the foil, for Dugin's Traditionalism is not a copy of Guénon's.[27] Within the parameters of Guénon's work, Integral Traditionalism is restricted to passive expressions allowing Dugin's more active innovations to be examined and considered in contrast. Dugin is engaged in direct action against Western Liberalism, and in daring to face it down, his fundamentalist expressions of Neo-Traditionalism become the objects of Western Liberalism's concentrated scorn.

As Dugin moved away from Integral Traditionalism, Evola began to overtake Guénon in the Neo-Traditional pantheon.

> Evola is a paradigmal figure of traditionalism, along with Guenon. The more time passes, the more impressive his shape. None of the Guenonists—Burkhardt [sic], Valsana, Schuon, not to mention the less important, could even relatively compare to Evola. Guenonists are becoming commonplace, have become conformists and Masons or fell into a weak-minded "new age," but Evola's case remains a monument of spirit in this dark age.[28]

Dugin stresses that, as a product of modernity, Western Liberal Democracy elevates the individual. All Traditionalists tend to emphasize communal or collective cohesiveness. Dugin cited the opinion of sociologist Louis Dumont in describing "two types of society—the holistic society and the individualistic society," concluding that "Modernity is essentially individualistic."[29] Dugin's Neo-Traditionalism "emphasizes the dualism that exists between two worlds: the world of tradition and the modern world."[30]

Epstein suggested that a long-reach look-back into the past is an inherent aspect of Dugin's Neo-Traditionalism:

Among the multiplicity of conservative movements that arose with the collapse of Soviet Marxism, one stands out as perhaps the most radical, both in political and metaphysical terms. Its radicalism is paradoxical because it calls for the resurrection of ancient esoterism as the antithesis of contemporary rational and democratic convention; hence the movement often identifies itself as "radical traditionalism," though it goes by a number of other names, such as "continentalism," "anti-mondialism," "the third way," "revolutionary conservatism," etc.[31]

Epstein pointedly connected Dugin with the "radical traditionalism," he mentioned. "The two preeminent spokespersons of this movement," Epstein claimed, "are Alexander Prokhanov and Alexander Dugin."[32] Epstein concluded that Dugin's conception of Traditionalism, his radical version, consists of four distinct levels of meaning. At its deepest level, Dugin places "a direct knowledge of the Divine accessible only to a spiritual elite."[33] Where the first level is esoteric, the second is exoteric. Epstein also recognized Dugin's strong affinity for Church and State syncretism at the second level.[34]

Dugin is anxious to distinguish the genuine traditionalist esoterism, which recognizes traditional religions and Church dogmas, from Satanic distortions of esoterism, which attack Christianity and Islam and attempt to destroy the dogmatic integrity of Tradition. That is why a second level of Tradition is exoterism, the sphere of sacred knowledge open to everyone, as long as they participate in the life of the Church. In this sense, traditionalism supports theocracy, [and] "presupposes the restoration of the central position of the Church in the State."[35]

Achievement at the third level involves the "spiritual stratification of society and the establishment of a hierarchy of

266

estates or castes."[36] Epstein indicated he believes Dugin is suggesting that a "truly sacred civilization" recognizes different types of people based on their "spiritual origins."[37] At the fourth level, sacred science and art regain their rightful places.[38] This level indicates a return to various teachings of alchemy and magic arts, and holds that science, as it is known and practiced in advanced societies today, is profane and material. Society at Dugin's fourth level moves away from modernity's view of science to a position far less empirical.

Peter Brooke, holding an Orthodox Christian perspective, pointedly asked, "What does Dugin mean by 'Tradition'?"[39] Rather than declare what Dugin is not when compared to the Integral Traditionalists, Brooke directly addressed the critical question. Brooke did not ask intending to challenge the orthodoxy of Integral Tradition; instead, he asked to get to the heart of how Dugin differs from the earlier twentieth century Traditionalists. Shekhovtsov and Umland asked as well. They argued persuasively against Dugin being a Traditionalist in the mold of Guénon.

Shekhovtsov and Umland associated Dugin much closer to Evola than to Guénon, and thus, established parameters of Dugin's Neo-Traditionalism. Although not precisely labeling Dugin's derivative of Integral Traditionalism as Neo-Traditional, Epstein was prescient in his understanding of how Dugin, in contrast to Solzhenitsyn, would employ it. Epstein noted the dynamic nature of Dugin's brand of Traditionalism, its revolutionary character, and its designs outside Russia proper. In practice, Dugin exhibits a practical Traditionalism rather than the profoundly spiritual one found in that of Guénon and the leading twentieth century adherents of the Integral School. Dugin's Neo-Traditionalism adopts characteristics identified with Integral Traditionalism, such as anti-modernism, but it is recognizably different in its employment of overt action in the political arena.

Traditionalism evaluates tradition and judges the purity of its initial revelation as well as its continuity through time. Herein lies the criticism that Traditionalism is self-validating. Mostly unidentified elements within Traditionalism itself determine what traditional elements constitute Truth. Although a valid criticism, self-validation is commonly employed, wide-spread, and not

267

exclusive to Traditionalism.[40] Muhammad Legenhausen offered an additional challenge to Traditionalist claims addressing apparent gaps in empirical evidence linking current Traditional awareness to the Ancients. "Traditionalism is a modern European reaction against modernism," Legenhausen wrote, noting its appearance "in a variety of religious movements: Jewish, Catholic, Protestant and Islamic."[41]

Legenhausen pointedly fixed Traditionalism as a reactionary actor. That is, Traditionalism is a response to the nineteenth century European shift toward the secular that continued to expand on the anti-religious ideas of the Enlightenment.[42] To Legenhausen's mind, Traditionalism's reactionary beginning evidenced a relatively recent construct leaving Traditionalism without any legitimate claims to its ancient pedigree. Legenhausen's bottom line criticism was that Traditionalism uses intuition as validation, not historical facts.[43]

Dugin cannot now be considered an Integral Traditionalist. Still, one cannot arrive at understanding and appreciating Dugin's Neo-Traditional stance without at least a brief requisite journey along the Integral Traditionalist paths of Guénon and his colleagues. Traditionalists trace their development using a preponderance of Eastern sources, and these sources are decidedly esoteric. The Western Academy has been reluctant, perhaps ill-equipped and ill-disposed, to afford esotericism a place in the rationally and empirically dominated arena of historical evidence. Legenhausen's anti-Traditional argument may be valid, but divorcing Traditionalism from any traceable esoteric connections to a Perennialist heritage risks being subject to the charge of excluding evidence for mostly Western cultural reasons.

Lakhani did not directly dispute Legenhausen. He did address the historicity of Traditionalism differently, emphasizing both the non-historical and the transcendental nature of Traditionalism through his interpretation of Traditionalism as a "metahistorical" revelation.[44]

> [Traditionalism's] only relation to the past resides
> in the linkage of a particular religious tradition to
> its original source, which is to say, the revelation
> that authenticates it, the foundational scripture

and its expressive forms of worship transmitted
through the protective medium of the particular
tradition. But this relation between a particular
tradition and its historical origins is in a sense
merely incidental. The relation between Tradition
as such and Revelation as such transcends
history.[45]

Granted, Traditionalism's kinship with Perennialism is
discernible in its gnostic interpretation of Truth. However,
acknowledging this kinship does not constitute empirical proof
that Traditionalism is the recipient of an unbroken chain of
uncorrupted divine revelation. To accept that a significant body of
perennial Truth has been passed untainted and intact from the
ancient Adepts via face-to-face and mouth-to-ear transmission to
the initiated Traditionalist adherents today is not adequately
supported by the available evidence. To argue that the evidence
exists, but that it is hidden, secret, and protected, requires
acceptance of self-validation as equal to empirical proof. For the
Academy to recognize Traditionalism as a revival of
Perennialism's precepts and principles is undoubtedly feasible; to
accept it as a set of provable facts passed down via a continuous
and inerrant initiatory process is not.

Legenhausen argued Traditionalism's historicity
legalistically. Lakhani expressed the position that Traditionalism
possesses transcendental elements that render its truth-claims
immune from the rigidity of legalism. Legenhausen denied
Traditionalism's claim to an unbroken chain-of-custody and
argued that this deficiency is fatal. Lakhani's implied retort was
that, even if empirical evidence does not support the chain,
Traditionalism's transcendent revelations overcome that
deficiency. This Enlightenment-permeated Western worldview
conflict with Eastern Esotericism is another in the continuing
battle of modernism versus Traditionalism.

Asking what Dugin means when invoking Tradition, Brooke
agreed with other Dugin scholars in that Dugin "has said that he
regards Guénon, together with Heidegger, as the most important
influence on his thought."[46] However, when Brooke compared
Dugin and Guénon, he questioned Dugin's Traditional orthodoxy.

"Contrary to the spirit of Guénon," Dugin, "is not at all concerned with whether or not these traditions are authentic," Brooke explained.[47] Brooke stated that Dugin appealed "to the huge body of twentieth century anthropological writings, notably Franz Boas and Levi-Strauss, to argue that, however mutually contradictory they may be, different cultures dismissed by the modern world as 'backward' have their own logic."[48] Brooke offered that "this individual and multipolar logic "is in its own terms perfectly valid" to the culture applying it to itself.[49]

Is Dugin a Heretical Traditionalist?

When ideologies, philosophies, and religions begin, a first phase development of orthodoxy and orthopraxis is recognized. In the second phase, orthodoxy matures. At this juncture, bureaucratic and institutional orthopraxis may begin to overshadow orthodoxy. In the third phase, orthodoxy and orthopraxis continue to develop, alternative or counterarguments arise, collide with their mature parent planets, and heresies spin-off as fragments. Finally, new orthodoxies may evolve from the fragments and become new orthodox planets themselves.

One utility of a belief system becoming orthodox is that it allows for heresy to exist. For, without orthodoxy, there can be no heresy. Heresy affords both followers and critics a choice by providing opportunities to evaluate alternatives and deviations from orthodox positions. Heresy develops in cyclic stages where departure from orthodoxy, given time, spawns heresy, which, given time, may generate an entirely new orthodoxy. Hence, the heretical Judaism of Jesus' followers became Christianity, and the heretical Christianity of Luther and the Reformers became Protestantism.

Traditionalism can likewise spin-off heresies. Integral Traditionalists consider Dugin's Neo-Traditionalism to be one. Dugin himself speaks of modernism as a Traditional heresy—perverted Tradition—with his recognition of Guénon's classification of modernity as a "great parody" of ancient Atlantis.[50] The body of religious, spiritual, and academic writing concerning Guénon, and his beliefs, increased as he gained followers. After Guénon, the work and ideas of other

270

Traditionalist School founders and their followers coalesced into Integral Traditionalism. Heresy then appeared as should have been expected. Thus, the twenty-first century's Neo-Traditionalist heresy is a product of the third and final evolutionary stages.

Evola and Dugin are the designated heretics, at least as characterized by Shekhovtsov and Umland. In their challenge to the legitimacy of Dugin's Traditionalism based on their interpretation of Integral Traditionalism's Guénonian orthodoxy, Shekhovtsov and Umland claimed that,

> Dugin's case raises a question also applicable to the assessment of Evola's and the ENR's interpretation of Integral Traditionalism: are Evola's theories and the ENR's ideology legitimate successors of Guénon's teaching? The answer, we believe, is that they are not, or that they are at best skewed reinterpretations of Integral Traditionalism.[51]

The orthodoxy ascribed to Guénon's articulation of Traditionalism is evident in Shekhovtsov and Umland as they proceeded to offer specific examples of Evola's and Dugin's heretical deviations:

> The universalist core of the deist worldview of classical Traditionalism is lost in the outlooks of Evola, the ENR, and the disciples of "neo-Eurasianism." Dugin plainly rejects the "transcendent unity of religions"—a central concept of Integral Traditionalism.[52]

"Neither Evola's worldview nor the doctrines of the ENR and Dugin constitute the unequivocal rejection of Modernity that Integral Traditionalism explicitly demands," wrote Shekhovtsov and Umland.[53] Despite the volume of his rhetoric, Dugin only partially rejects modernism, accepting perhaps the technological aspects of progress in much the same way the Soviet Union desired to possess technology that rivaled the West without adopting the liberalism that would usher in Liberal Democracy and Cultural Westernization.[54]

Brooke observed that in *The Fourth Political Theory,* Dugin does not seem to be overly concerned with the authenticity of Integral Traditionalism as it relates to Truth as a "single, universal, potentially knowable" reality.[55] Brooke's interpretation, questioning Dugin's Integral Traditionalist credentials, supports the charge of heretical Traditionalism. Brooke also stated that Dugin wishes to measure cultural logic "by the (again very un-Guénonian) values of sophistication, consistency and complexity."[56]

Shekhovtsov and Umland may have correctly identified heresy in the Traditionalism of Evola and Dugin. However, heterodoxy versus orthodoxy in the academic or theological sense will not be the overriding concern if Dugin's Fourth Political Theory becomes manifest in Russian geopolitics. Nevertheless, the activity involved in creating a Fourth Political Theory-inspired Eurasia would by itself confirm Dugin's heresy. "'Contemplation' versus action was one of the most fundamental antitheses for Guénon, who considered contemplation or cognition an expression of the 'traditional spirit,' and action itself an 'anti-traditional' one," according to Shekhovtsov and Umland.[57] So, by the orthodox precepts of Integral Traditionalism, the application of action, however dressed-up as Traditionalism, would relegate Fourth Political Theory into the realm of Traditional heresy.

Shekhovtsov and Umland admitted that "many of Dugin's works are an amalgamation of Traditionalist concepts, Evola's theories, geopolitical ideas, and the ideology of the German interwar 'Conservative Revolution.'"[58] It is noteworthy that Dugin claims Traditionalism, yet the ingredients and applications of the "amalgamation" contribute a great deal to the rightful exclusion of Evola and Dugin from the halls of orthodoxy. Fabbri speculated that Evola was infected with Friedrich Nietzsche's philosophy and racist ideas before he came under the influence of Guénon.[59] Nietzsche's influence led to Evola's deviation "from the core of Perennialist teaching on far too many points to be considered as part of Guénon's legacy."[60] Dugin's attraction to Evola may be symptomatic of Dugin's deviations as well.

272

Shekhovtsov and Umland conceded, "There is no doubt that Dugin has contributed to the development of Russian Traditionalism."[61] They stated that Dugin's contribution might be due to his industrious publishing rather than as a Traditional thinker or writer.[62] Ultimately, given the totality of his contributions and the extent of his adaptations of Guénon and Evola, I suggest that the conclusion must be that Dugin is a Traditionalist—but a heretical one.

Dugin's Infusion of Traditionalism into Neo-Eurasianism

Postmodern Neo-Eurasianism challenges Western Liberalism, its postmodern rival, and adds an infusion of Tradition. Neo-Traditionalism will not just generally oppose its presumed evil postmodern rival; it will directly challenge it. Dugin believes that the Traditionalism of his Neo-Eurasianism will prevail where more general traditionalism did not.

It is not overly difficult to connect the dots, as Dugin does, and arrive—as one is bound to do—firmly at the intersection of lowercase traditionalism and Eurasianism. Arrival at the intersection of uppercase Traditionalism and Eurasianism is not as obvious, but Dugin erased any doubt of his view of this confluence in his explanation. Neo-Eurasianism "implies a positive re-evaluation of the archaic, of the ancient," in Dugin's mind.[63]

Providing crossover between Traditional and Eurasian relationships, Dugin noted Eurasianism's closeness to "the traditionalism of Guénon, who also thought that 'contemporiety' was a 'western' notion."[64] Dugin also pointed out that it is not a coincidence that the first Russian author who referenced "Guénon's book *East and West*, was the Eurasianist N.N. Alekseev."[65]

The Eurasian legacy, "fervently refers to the past, to the world of Tradition."[66] Neo-Eurasianism involves the development of a cultural process with a new emphasis on the archaic—"the insertion of original cultural motives in the fabric of modern forms."[67] "Conservatism," in Dugin's words, "in its most general sense means *a positive attitude towards historical tradition.*"[68] "The priority in this area is given back to national motives, to the

273

sources of national creativity, to the continuation and revival of traditions," says Dugin.[69] The standard of Neo-Eurasian conservatism is also the standard of Russian conservatism. Dugin made this clear in his comparison that "contemplating contemporary Russian conservatism is basically contemplating Eurasianism, which is a synthesis of Russian political history on the basis of a unique geopolitical and civilisational methodology."[70] "Moreover," Dugin wrote, "conservatism is based on the premise that the people and the state have a certain historical mission."[71]

Dugin believes that Russia's historic mission lies in a messianic Manifest Destiny, which is an essential element of Russian national identity.[72] For a Traditional conservative, past, present, and future "are tied together in a single integral project striving toward a clear national goal."[73] Believing in the ultimate messianic triumph of Eurasianism, implying divine favor, and linking conservatism with Traditionalism through ageless correctness, Dugin stated, "after all, as Arthur Moeller van den Bruck once said, 'Conservatism has eternity on its side.'"[74]

Notes

1. Voegelin, *New Science of Politics*, 54.

2. Pini Ifergan, "Cutting to the Chase: Carl Schmitt and Hans Blumenberg on Political Theology and Secularization," *New German Critique*, 111th ser., 37, no. 3 (Fall 2010): 149. Italics in original. Pini Ifergan, Scholar at Bar-Ilan University.

3. Ifergan, "Cutting to the Chase," 149ff.

4. Guénon was opposed to having Traditionalism be associated with active political engagement. Cf. e.g., Guénon, *Crisis of the Modern World*, 33ff. In the chapter titled "Knowledge and Action" Guénon makes the case of the superiority of contemplation over action. Cf. page 37 in particular, where Guénon stated that "the Eastern doctrines are unanimous, as were the ancient doctrines of the West, in asserting that contemplation is superior to action, just as the unchanging is superior to change." The critique of Dugin made by Shekhovtsov and Umland also addresses Guénon's resistance to action.

5. Dugin, *Fourth Theory*, 88. Leopold Ziegler, 1881-1958.

6. Ibid., 193.

7. Dugin, "The Figure of the Radical Subject," under, Part 1, Traditionalism and Sociology—The Modern and the Eternal.

8. Cf. e.g., references throughout remarking on Guénon's objections to an active Traditionalism.

9. Dugin's characterization as a Neo-Traditionalist is attested to throughout this study. Cf. citations of Shekhovtsov, Umland, Laruelle, Epstein, et al.

10. Cf. Epstein, *Conservatism and Traditionalism*, 10-11 for Epstein's discussion of Radical Traditionalism.

11. Dugin, "Traditionalism as Language," under, Rene Guenon.

12. Dugin, "The Long Path," as part of his response to the first question.

13. Ibid.

14. Ibid.

15. Ibid.

16. Ibid. Brackets added.

17. Laruelle, *Russian Version of European Radical Right*, 1.

18. Ibid.

19. Shenfield, *Russian Fascism*, 192.

20. Ibid.

21. "Alexander Dugin," Geopolitica.ru.

22. Shenfield, *Russian Fascism*, 192.

23. Ibid.

24. Cf. e.g., Shekhovtsov and Umland, "Is Aleksandr Dugin a Traditionalist? 'Neo-Eurasianism' and Perennial Philosophy," *The Russian Review* 68, no. 4 (2009): 668, footnote 29. Here Guénon is being referenced from, Guénon, *Crisis of the Modern World*, 33-36.

25. Shekhovtsov and Umland, "Is Dugin a Traditionalist?," 672.

26. Dugin, "Traditionalism as Language," under, Traditionalism and Russia. Brackets added.

27. This is adequately supported by Sedgwick, Shekhovtsov, Umland, and others referenced throughout.

28. Dugin, "The Mission of Julius Evola," Open Revolt, October 27, 2011, under, Point 1, openrevolt.info/2011/10/27/the-mission-of-julius-evola/. Michel Valsan (Valsana), 1911-1974. Brackets added.

29. Dugin, "The Figure of the Radical Subject," under, Part 1, Traditionalism and Sociology—The Modern and the Eternal. Louis Dumont, 1911-1988. Cf. Louis Dumont, *Essays on Individualism: Modern Ideology in Anthropological Perspective*, trans. Joseph Erhardy, Paul Hockings, and Louis Dumont (Chicago: University of Chicago Press, 1992).

30. Ibid.

31. Epstein, *Conservatism and Traditionalism*, 10-11. I submit that Dugin's Neo-Traditionalism conforms to Epstein's idea of Radical Traditionalism.

32. Ibid., 11. Epstein notes that "Dugin associated himself with the extreme nationalist factions: *Pamiat'* and *Natsional'noe edinstvo,*" also noting that Dugin "was editor in chief of *Cherished Angel* and *Elements* and is the author of the books *Mysteries of Eurasia* (1991), *Hyperborean Theory* (1992), and *Conspirology* (1992)." Epstein said Prokhanov is a well-known Russian novelist and writer, and claimed that he "in Brezhnev's time, was celebrated as the bard of the Soviet invasion of Afghanistan and was mocked by the liberal press as the 'Nightingale of the General Staff.'" Lionid Brezhnev, 1906-1982.

33. Ibid., 12.

34. Ibid.

35. Ibid. Brackets added. Herein, Epstein quotes from a *Milyi Angel* editorial; Cf. Epstein's footnote 31: nashem zhurnale. Kak my ponimaem traditsiiu. [Editorial] *Milyi Angel. Ezotericheskoe reviu.* Moscow: Arktogeia, 1991, vol.1, 1. Brackets in Epstein's original reference.

36. Ibid., 12-13.

37. Ibid.

38. Ibid, 13.

39. Peter Brooke, "'Third Rome, Third International, Third Reich'—Alexander Dugin and the 'Fourth Political Theory,'" under, Against 'modernity,' *The Heidegger Review*, no. 1 (July 2014),

heideggerreview.org/table-of-contents-no-1/third-rome-third-international-third-reich-alexander-dugin-and-the-fourth-political-theory/. This article can also be accessed at: peterbrooke.org/politics-and-theology/dugin-index/. Although Brooke characterizes his article as a review of *The Fourth Political Theory*, it is more like an article and is comprehensive compared to standard literary reviews. Peter Brooke, Northern Ireland born artist and Dugin scholar.

40. E.g., Despite the often proclaimed Western proclivity for the scientific method, internal validation yet remains prevalent in institutional settings. U.S. Governmental agencies frequently make internal decisions on findings, then make requirements, enact codes and regulations, enforce compliance, and adjudicate violations in a closed system of self-validation.

41. Legenhausen, "Not a Traditionalist," 1.

42. Ibid., 2.

43. Ibid., 8-9. Here Legenhausen stated, "The Traditionalists, on the other hand, claim that through intellectual intuition they are able to discern the common essence. The method used is implausible. It is assumed at the outset that the religions have a common esoteric essence, and the texts are interpreted so as to accord with this principle. This is question begging."

44. Lakhani, "Understanding 'Tradition,'" 53. Legenhausen, in fact, took this tact when he examined "Balance and Truth Seeking." Cf. Legenhausen, "Not a Traditionalist," 20ff.

45. Ibid. Here Lakhani expounded on his interpretation of Nasr.

46. Brooke, "Third Rome, Third International, Third Reich," under, Against 'modernity.' Here, as a sub-heading, Brooke directly asks, "What does Dugin mean by 'Tradition'?" Evola is noteworthy here due to absence of his being mentioned. It would be wrong to make too much of this omission as Brooke is emphasizing the Dugin-Guénon relationship at this point in this article. Brooke, other Dugin commentators, and Dugin himself have all acknowledged Evola's influence.

47. Ibid.

48. Ibid.

49. Ibid.

50. Dugin, "The Figure of the Radical Subject," under, Part 1, Traditionalism and Sociology—The Modern and the Eternal.

51. Shekhovtsov and Umland, "Is Dugin a Traditionalist?," 666. Cf. their footnote 16. Here the authors refer to Dugin's *Filosofiia traditsionalizma* (Moscow, 2002), 42–3, 100–1, as evidence from Dugin's own work. To access an interview with Benoist, the key ENR proponent, Cf. Alain de Benoist, "The 'European New Right': Defining and Defending Europe's Heritage," Interview by Ian Warren, *Journal of Historical Review*, 1994, 28-37. A transcript of this interview is available online at, ihr.org/jhr/v14/v14n2p28_Warren.html. Ian Warren, pen name of Donald Warren, Professor at Oakland University. Donald Warren, 1935-1997.

52. Ibid. Cf. their footnote 59.

53. Ibid., 669.

54. Ibid. Cf. e.g., Legenhausen, "Not a Traditionalist," 21, for a similar argument.

55. Brooke, "Third Rome, Third International, Third Reich," under, Against 'modernity.'

56. Ibid.

57. Shekhovtsov and Umland, "Is Dugin a Traditionalist?," 668, footnote 29. Here Guénon is being referenced from, Guénon, *Crisis of the Modern World*, 33-36.

58. Ibid., 665.

59. Fabbri, "Perennialist School," under, Julius Evola and the Perennialist School. Friedrich Nietzsche, 1844-1900.

60. Ibid.

61. Shekhovtsov and Umland, "Is Dugin a Traditionalist?," 672.

62. Ibid. Shekhovtsov and Umland may be engaged in academic hair-splitting but so it is within the academy where orthodox and heretical arguments are involved.

63. Dugin, "Eurasia Above All," under, Priorities of the Eurasia movement.

64. Dugin, *Fourth Theory*, 99. I assumed that Dugin means Integral Traditionalism in this case. It is interesting to note that in at least one online version of *The Fourth Political Theory*, the passage is rendered, "eurasianists partly draw closer with Guénon's traditionalism who also considered that 'modernity' is a 'western' concept." Cf. scribd.com/document/233578477/The-Fourth-Political-Theory, 137.

65. Ibid. Cf. Guénon, *East and West*, trans. Martin Lings (Gent: Sophia Perennis, 2001) and Dugin, "Eurasianism above all," under, Priorities of the Eurasia movement. N.N. Alekseev, 1879-1964.

66. Dugin, "Eurasianism above all," under, Priorities of the Eurasia movement.

67. Ibid.

68. Dugin, *Putin vs Putin: Vladimir Putin Viewed from the Right* (Leipzig: Renovamen Verlag, 2016), 145. Italics in original.

69. Dugin, "Eurasia Above All," under, Priorities of the Eurasia movement.

70. Dugin, *Putin vs Putin*, 156. Cf. Dugin's footnote 24: "Kievan Rus' was a loose tribal confederation that had its capital in Kiev, and from which the modern-day states of Russia, Ukraine and Belarus are descended. It lasted from the tenth until the thirteenth centuries." Cf. Dugin, *Putin vs Putin: Vladimir Putin Viewed from the Right*, (London: Arktos, 2014); apparently Dugin's book was also published by Arktos in 2014. Cf. scribd.com/document/268017818/alexander-Dugin-Putin-vs-Putin-pdf.

71. Ibid., 146.

72. Cf. references to Russian Identity and Manifest Destiny.

73. Dugin, *Putin vs Putin*, 146.

74. Dugin, *Fourth Theory*, 66. Cf. Dugin's footnote 32, where Dugin cites Bruck, Cf. Arthur Moeller Van Den Bruck, *Germany's Third Empire* (London: Arktos Media, 2012). Moeller van den Bruck, 1876-1925.

Part VI

Chapter One: Reception

Giving and Taking

Reception is a process, as the label implies, of receiving, and receiving is a dependent response to transmission. Some scholars have characterized the method of transmitting and receiving as a linear construction progressing from the originator to the listener, reader, or viewer. Others have conceptualized more complex models, including feedback loops and other transmitter-receiver interactions. Considering various models is useful in achieving a better understanding of how reception occurs as the sender's intent and intensity, and the reaction or response of the receiving audience translates into observable action. Observable action is the activity best able to gauge the current traction of Fourth Political Theory.

John F.A. Sawyer, known for his research into biblical reception, told us that "reception in the analysis of literary texts," is not a new thing.[1] The ancient Greeks were deeply appreciative of the transmission and reception of spoken and written words. Transmission and reception have always been crucial to communication. Sawyer added that "although the terms are relatively new, the importance of reception in the analysis of literary texts was appreciated already in ancient Greece."[2]

The Greeks developed entire schools of thought dedicated to the transmission and reception of spoken and textual words. The Greeks admired those who were proficient with words and much admired those who were masters of rhetoric. Hoffer instructed that "the preliminary work of undermining existing institutions, of familiarizing the masses with the idea of change, and of creating a receptivity to a new faith, can be done only by men who are, first and foremost, talkers or writers and are recognized as such by all."[3]

The medium of the written word has exploded, as have correspondingly similar eruptions in other media, in the latter part of the twentieth century and the first part of the twenty-first. Adaptations of the various reception theories must likewise

280

expand. A wide range of transmission options, especially in the rapidly enlarging arena of social media, must be considered in attempts to understand the relationship between the intent of the original transmitter and the acceptance and response of the receiver. Sawyer recognized these phenomena by noting that reception is no longer limited to the study of literature:

> Businesses spend millions on consumer research to analyze the effect marketing strategies have on their customers. The success of films is measured by box office returns, and television programmes are judged by their share of the potential viewing public.[4]

Emphasizing the transmission and reception of rhetoric, Sawyer stressed that, "rhetoric, after all, is the art of persuasion and is very much concerned with the effect a text has on its readers."[5] Transmission is complex. "It refers to all those literary devices designed to get the reader or listener to respond to a text in various ways," According to Sawyer.[6] Plato's warning that "letting people read literature that might arouse in them emotions that are difficult to control," is apropos to Dugin—and Dugin well illustrates these lessons of Sawyer, Hoffer, and Plato.[7] There can be no argument that Dugin intends for his words to affect his audience, arouse emotions, and elicit responses.

Reaction is a function of reception. How the West reacts to Dugin, and his geopolitical and theological endeavors, is a function of how the West receives Dugin and perceives the content of his transmissions. Dugin should be considered in the context of his claims that Fourth Political Theory continues the historical consistency of revealed Truth through Traditionalism and supports the rejection of a unipolar world through the reality of Neo-Eurasianism.[8] Affirming or rejecting Dugin demonstrates reception in either case. So, in the bigger picture, it is the interpretive reception of Dugin's geopolitical theology rather than the accuracy of its transmission that will determine any subsequent response from the West.

If Russia's future national policies employ Dugin's proposals, its strategic decisions reflecting Duginesqe elements will influence the West's response to Russian actions regardless of whether Dugin is acknowledged or not. Western reception will determine Western response. While even the most informed and accurate interpretation of Dugin's reflected influence on Russian policy may not prevent potentially dangerous friction, a misinformed and inaccurate interpretation will likely ensure it.

The Reception Process

Like Hoffer, Sawyer explained that rhetoric is concerned with the effect of a text on its readers through the psychological impact of words.[9] Sawyer employed the term *Rezeptionsaesthetik*, noting its similarity to *Reader-Response Criticism*, in referencing the historical development of reception.[10]

The Konstanz School Approach

In Sawyer's words, "the term reception theory itself or *Rezeptionsaesthetik* goes back to the Sixties and to the Konstanz School of literary studies."[11] Going further, Sawyer identified *Rezeptionsaesthetik* as the "German equivalent of the preferred American term 'Reader-Response Criticism.'"[12] Sawyer suggested that the writer and reader may or may not share the interpretation of a transmission. For Western receivers, the notion "that the reception of a text is more important than the text itself," is paramount.[13] Sawyer's explanation of this perception was that,

> it is like the philosophers' old question: If a tree falls in the forest and no-one hears it, does it make a sound? A text without a reader has no meaning. It is the readers of a text that imbue meaning. In a sense, the reader creates at least as much textual meaning as does the author.[14]

Sylvia Plath was not willing to allow the writer even this much ownership. "Once a poem is made available to the public," she said, "the right of interpretation belongs to the reader."[15] Others agreed. Hans-Robert Jauss and Stanley Fish, placing heavy emphasis on reception, argued that text could not exist without the reader.[16]

The Cambridge School Approach

Considering Dugin's transmission and its reception, the *Rezeptionsaesthetik* of the intentionalist viewpoint of the Cambridge School is germane. J. G. A. Pocock, Quentin Skinner, John Dunn, and others maintained that the intent of the author and the influence of the historical context at the time and period of the writing should drive reception.[17] Adherents of the Cambridge School, the identifier applied to Pocock, Skinner, Dunn, and others promoting an intentionalist view, hold that the author—the transmitter, within the historical context of the period of the writing, is the critical element of reception.[18] Emphasis on the transmitter is consistent with the Traditional position.[19]

The Practical Result of Dugin's Intentionalist Purpose

Strict constructionists of textual material (be they religious, artistic, political, judicial, or historical) make claims regarding the meaning of the texts based upon the original intent and meaning imbued by the author.[20] The rub, of course, lies in conflicts that arise over determining the actual intent stated or implied by the originator. In the past, appeals to authority, such as the Church, settled disputes of this nature. However, at a time in the West where an opponent's appeal to authority is often afforded little credence, various textual criticisms and more postmodern deconstruction methods are commonly applied.

There are long-standing and persistent arguments over the correctness of individual texts. Examples include accurate reception of texts depending on faithfulness to the author's original intent, contextual influences surrounding the writing, or interpretations considering the currently accepted norms of criticism. Traditionalists would argue that the intent, the original meaning imparted to the document (or other media), is paramount—the content of the text itself is consistently enduring. Considering Dugin, the Cambridge School approach should be recognized. To the Western receiver, the Social History approach

283

and Konstanz School hold sway.[21] As ambiguous as it may seem on the surface, given the stance of Traditionalists on original intent, Dugin's reception is crucial in the international security environment, not in its intentional context so much as in its reductionist interpretations.

How Dugin's transmissions, in the context of current geopolitical perceptions (with their multiple social and cultural overlays), are received is arguably of more consequence than what Dugin intends to express. In the postmodern environment, Western perception, given current geopolitical constructions, often outweighs Dugin's original intent. However, this receiver-interpreted reception is entirely in keeping with Konstanz School understandings. Despite the Traditionalist affinity to the Cambridge School priorities of authorial and textual intent, Dugin's reception derives relevance in the international environment owing to the influence of the Konstanz School. For Dugin, the Cambridge School approach should be paramount to the Western receiver—in reality, the modern, now postmodern, social- and cultural-history paradigms predominate.

The messenger, not just the message, is also a factor in reception. Sawyer commented on the diminished impact of marginalized individuals with some utility. Sawyer explained that "'valid' or 'correct' interpretations are normally those of the experts, while those of the uneducated, marginalized, anarchic or eccentric are not to be taken seriously."[22] Sawyer's comments on the diminished impact of marginalized individuals may have some utility. But there are myriad examples of rampant reception of urban myths that are relevant to understanding the power of propaganda and may argue against Sawyer's claim.[23] Dugin, it should be remembered, gained traction as a marginalized individual before his much more popular reception occurred.

The Impossibility of Presuppositionless Exegesis

All that approach the marketplace of ideas risk exposing the contents of the baggage they bring with them. Rudolf Bultmann, for example, believed that a "presuppositionless" exegesis is impossible.[24] Ironically, any presupposition that attempts an entirely objective view toward a presentation of ideas only serves to prove Bultmann's point. Reception insists on some degree of subjectivity, for the receiver's presuppositional baggage, the impossibility of unsullied transmission, interpretation, and lack of precise common cores of experience corrupt the transmitter's pure intent. Just as Dugin cannot be purely objective—for he brings all his subjective baggage along for inspection—neither can examining Dugin be a purely objective exercise.[25]

Sawyer offered an observation similar to Bultmann's:

> Given the opportunity to consider a variety of different readings of a text, we may evaluate them using aesthetic, theological, ethical, ideological, academic or other criteria, reflecting our particular hermeneutical stance.[26]

Terry Eagleton offered up an intriguing possibility.[27] Almost musing, Eagleton suggested that "most of us recognize that no reading is innocent."[28] He then characterized the realization of this recognition as "reader guilt."[29] The manifestation of this guilty awareness is "that there is no such thing as purely 'literary' response."[30] Sawyer wrote that "it seems as though, intentional or not, "texts have more than one meaning, and different meanings are largely due to differences in the reader's hermeneutical stance or horizon of expectation."[31] Eagleton's similar conclusion was that "the kind of social and historical individuals we are" impacts the transmission of the text and our reception of it.[32]

The potential receptive audience input has predictive value. Sawyer credited Fish with coining the identifier "interpretive community," and he recognized Fish's claim that texts usually have a defined readership projected before publication or distribution.[33]

To objectively arrive at predictions regarding the interpretive community, Sawyer refined several revealing questions:

- **Who is reading the text?**
- **What kind of baggage are they carrying when they come to the text—what presuppositions?**
- **What do they make of the text?**

285

- **What effect does the text have on them?**[34]

Sawyer concluded that an interpretive community determines the acceptability of ideas and actions.[35] His thoughts suggest that the extent and import of Dugin's geopolitical theology and its resulting Fourth Political Theory will be tested in the various interpretive communities throughout Europe and the rest of the Western world.

Encoding and Decoding

Cultural theorist Stuart Hall developed an Encoding-Decoding Model of communication that underscores the unpredictable nature of transmission and reception.[36] Simon During, writing an introduction to Hall's chapter, "Encoding and Decoding," in *The Cultural Studies Reader,* observed that transmissions exhibit dominance structures, implanted in the transmission process, that remain intact to some degree at the reception stage.[37] Because of this dominance structure persistence, power relationships may be intentionally or unintentionally transferred in the encoding and decoding processes.[38] The consequences of this transfer may result in the intended encoding being decoded in unintended ways resulting in unintended consequences.[39]

Hall's Encoding-Decoding Model, according to Julie Martin, "essentially states that meaning is encoded by the sender and decoded by the receiver and that these encoded meanings may be decoded to mean something else."[40] During observed, "a message can only be received at a particular stage if it is recognizable or appropriate."[41] Senders encode their messages and embed their intent into them. Receivers decode these same messages "according to their own ideals and views."[42] Often the results of this encoding and decoding lead "to miscommunication or to the receiver understanding something very different from what the sender intended."[43]

In the reception area of his Encoding-Decoding Model, Hall suggested there may be several hypothetical decoding positions. He offered three for consideration: the Dominant-Hegemonic position, the Negotiated Code (or position), and the Oppositional

286

Code position (although not stated, the alternate term "oppositional position" may be assumed).[44] Each of these possible decoding positions, except the first, is fraught with misunderstanding often encountered when language is employed—especially, cross-culturally.[45]

In the Dominant-Hegemonic position, the viewer takes the connoted meaning, from a television newscast or current affairs program, for example, and decodes the message in terms of the encoded intent.[46] Next, a majority of decoding audiences probably understand quite adequately what has been dominantly defined and professionally signified in the Negotiated Code.[47] Finally, in the Oppositional Code position, it is possible that a viewer perfectly understands both the literal and the connotative inflection imparted by discourse but decodes the message in a contrary way—in the decoder's preferred code.[48]

Other encoding-decoding perspectives are encountered in the literature of reception. Acknowledging Eco's contributions to the field of encoding and decoding, Cristinel Munteanu commented that Eco's terminological phrase, *Aberrant Decoding*, originated in a "study on semiotics regarding television."[49] Munteanu introduced an Eco-inspired classification scheme produced by John Hartley consisting of four classes or types of Aberrant Decoding stemming from people:

- **Who did not know the language (what meanings did the Greeks, and then everyone until Jean-François Champollion, ascribe to Egyptian hieroglyphics?)**
- **From future generations (what meanings did medieval Christians ascribe to Greek and Roman art?)**
- **From different belief systems (what meanings do tourists ascribe to the stained-glass windows of cathedrals such as Chartres?)**
- **From different cultures (what meanings do white people ascribe to Aboriginal art?).[50]**

Eco emphasized that Aberrant Decoding may involve "ignorance of the original codes," such "as when Achaean conquerors misinterpreted Cretan symbols."[51] He expanded the application to include when later-created codes are superimposed over earlier ones. Eco's examples were "when early Christians overlaid a Christian meaning upon a pagan symbol or ritual, or when post-romantic scholars find erotic images in what an earlier poet conceived of as philosophical allegories."[52]

Receiving Dugin is a complex process of both encoding and decoding. Neither Dugin's encoding nor Western decoding is perfectly accomplished. Aberrant Decoding may contribute to Dugin's reception issues in the West. Given the inherent imperfections, however, a realization that it is on the reception-side where the dialog with Dugin's ideas is given direction is paramount. For, it is on the reception-side that reactions must most accurately match and respond to any Dugin inspired policies to lessen the risk of unintended consequences.

Sawyer's conclusion that "we are mostly members of an interpretive community of some kind where a consensus is reached on what is acceptable, academically and ethically, and what is not," is instructive.[53] It may be paraphrased and inferred as the West is made up of an interpretive community of political, economic, academic, cultural, and religious institutions where a consensus is reached on what is acceptable, in each of these fields, and what is not. It is not just in the political capitals of the West where the extent and import of Dugin's Fourth Political Theory will be tested, but also in the various global reaches and institutions of politics and power.

The Peoria Question

The notorious trope often attributed to Groucho Marx, "but how will it play in Peoria?," has been used by comedian Jack Benny, uncountable vaudevillian, print, cinema, and television entertainers as well as political figures and commentators.[58] Initially, the question addressed the ability of a theatrical play or stage show to succeed broadly in mainstream America regardless of the success it had or had not achieved in the confined venue of New York City. So, how will Dugin play in Peoria? That is, how

288

will Dugin be received outside of the confines of politically conservative venues such as the ENR? More specifically, how will Dugin and his geopolitical theology be accepted throughout the West?

If Putin is infusing Russia's strategic future with Dugin-inspired geopolitical philosophy and metaphysics, Western reception of Russian policies embedded with Neo-Eurasianist Fourth Political Theory elements will impact the West's response to Russian actions across the entire range from near- to long-term. Using Peoria as the metaphor for the West, "how will it play in Peoria?" is the most critical question to be asked of Dugin's Fourth Political Theory from the Western geopolitical position. For it is Western reception that will determine Western response. While even the most informed and accurate interpretation of Fourth Political Theory may still result in dangerous confrontations, a misinformed and inaccurate analysis guarantees such outcomes.

Notes

1. John F. A. Sawyer, "The Role of Reception Theory, Reader-Response Criticism And/or Impact History in the Study of the Bible: Definition and Evaluation" (address, EKK Biennial Meeting, Germany, March 21-3, 2004). Cf. Sawyer, "The Role of Reception Theory, Reader-Response Criticism And/or Impact History in the Study of the Bible: Definition and Evaluation" (address, Society of Biblical Literature Meeting, San Antonio, 2004), bbibcomm.info/?page_id=183. Note: some of the verbiage in "The Role of Reception Theory" is also found (verbatim, or nearly so,) in Sawyer, "Old Testament and Its Readers," *Theology in Scotland* XII, no. 1 (2005). John F. A. Sawyer, Emeritus Head of Religious Studies, University of Newcastle-upon-Tyne.

2. Sawyer, "Role of Reception Theory."

3. Hoffer, *The True Believer,* 129.

4. Sawyer, "Role of Reception Theory."

5. Ibid.

6. Ibid.

7. Ibid.

8. Dugin, Fourth Theory, 193-97.

9. Sawyer, "Role of Reception Theory."

10. Ibid. Cf. Hans Robert Jauss, *Towards an Aesthetic of Reception*, trans. Timothy Bahti (Minneapolis: University of Minnesota Press, 1982). Konstanz is often rendered *Constance*. Hans Robert Jauss, 1921-1997.

11. Ibid. Sawyer wrote that *Rezeptionsaesthetik* "is particularly associated with the name of Hans Robert Jauss whose book *Towards an Aesthetic of Reception* appeared in 1982." Italics added.

12. Ibid.

13. Ibid.

14. Ibid. Cf. Sawyer, "Old Testament and Its Readers," 70.

15. Kathleen Connors and Sally Bayley, eds., *Eye Rhymes: Sylvia Plath's Art of the Visual* (Oxford: Oxford University Press, 2007), 60. Sylvia Plath, 1932-1963.

16. Cf. e.g., Jauss, *Aesthetic of Reception* and Stanley Fish, *Is There a Text in This Class?* (Cambridge, MA: Harvard University Press, 1982). Stanley Fish, Literary Theorist and Legal Scholar.

17. Cf. numerous works e.g., J. G. A. Pocock, "Present at the Creation: With Laslett to the Lost Worlds," *International Journal of Public Affairs* 2 (2006): 7-17, Quentin Skinner, "Meaning and Understanding in the History of Ideas," *History and Theory*, 8, (1), 3-53, and Mark Bevir, "The Contextual Approach," in *The Oxford Handbook of the History of Political Philosophy*, ed. George Klosko (Oxford: Oxford University Press, 2011), 11-23. J. G. A. Pocock, New Zealand historian of political thought. Quentin Skinner, British political historian. John Dunn, Emeritus Professor of Political Theory, King's College, Cambridge. Mark Bevir, Professor of Political Science and Director of the Center for British Studies, University of California.

18. Cf. e.g., Pocock, "Present at the Creation;" Stefan Collini, Quentin Skinner, David A. Hollinger, J. G. A. Pocock, Michael Hunter, "What Is Intellectual History?" in *What Is History...?*, ed. Juliet Gardiner (London: Macmillan Press, 1988), and Skinner, "History of Ideas," and Bevir, "The Contextual Approach."

19. Modernists depart from the stubborn Traditionalist insistence upon preserving intentional contextual consistency. Insofar as Traditionalists argue the consistent and enduring qualities of meaningful texts, The Cambridge School seems to more readily accommodate a Traditionalist

position; except that the Cambridge School does not accept the level of contextually consistent veracity claimed for Traditional transmissions.

20. Cf. e.g., Daniel A. Farber, "The Originalism Debate: A Guide for the Perplexed," *Ohio State Law Journal* 49, no. 4 (1989): 1086; "When reading a law or applying constitutional principles, strict constructionists ignore context and consider only the words on the page. The circumstances or potential result of a judicial ruling do not factor into a strict constructionist's decision-making process. They believe that legal texts carry the same meaning from the day that it is written until the day it is amended or repealed. Strict constructionists seek to understand and apply the original meaning of the legal text." Cf. study.com/academy/lesson/strict-constructionism-definition-beliefs-examples.html. Addressing U.S. Constitutional Law, but applicable to the subject here is Farber's missive that, "Originalists are committed to the view that original intent is not only relevant but authoritative, that we are in some sense obligated to follow the intent of the framers." Daniel A. Farber, Professor of Law, University of California.

21. The result of this application reveals Dugin as more Eastern than Western in presenting his Fourth Political Theory. For clues to concepts of Orientalist approaches to geopolitics, Cf. Christopher Goto-Jones, "If Not a Clash Then What? Huntington, Nishida Kitarō, and the Politics of Civilizations," *International Relations of the Asia Pacific* 2 (2002): 223-43. Christopher Goto-Jones, Dean of Humanities and Professor of Philosophy, University of Victoria.

22. Sawyer, "Role of Reception Theory." Cf. Sawyer, "Old Testament and Its Readers," 76.

23. Cf. Hoffer, *The True Believer*. Hoffer goes into some detail on the tendency to believe propaganda and the willingness to adopt unfounded rumor as truth.

24. Cf. Rudolf Bultmann, "Is Exegesis Without Presuppositions Possible?" in K. Mueller-Vollmer (ed.), *The Hermeneutics Reader,* (New York: Continuum, 1985), 246ff. Reprinted from, "Is Exegesis Without Presuppositions Possible?" in *Existence and Faith: Shorter Writings of Rudolf Bultmann*, ed. Schubert N. Ogden, trans. Schubert N. Ogden (London: Hodder and Stoughton, 1961). Rudolf Bultmann, 1884-1976.

25. Despite my attempted objectivity to systematically present Dugin, I am sure Bultmann's conclusion applies to me as well; I am, no doubt, unable to approach this study employing a "presuppositionless" exegesis.

26. Sawyer, "Role of Reception Theory." Cf. Sawyer, "Old Testament and Its Readers," 76.

27. Terence Francis Eagleton, British literary theorist and critic, Distinguished Professor of English Literature at Lancaster University.

28. Eagleton, *Literary Theory*, 89.

29. Ibid.

30. Ibid.

31. Ibid. Cf. Sawyer, "Old Testament and Its Readers," 76.

32. Ibid.

33. Sawyer, "Role of Reception Theory."

34. Ibid.

35. Ibid. Cf. Sawyer, "Old Testament and Its Readers," 76.

36. Cf. Stuart Hall, "Encoding and Decoding," in *The Cultural Studies Reader*, ed. Simon During (London: Routledge, 1993), 90-103. Stuart Hall, 1932-2014.

37. Cf. Simon During, "Editor's Introduction," Stuart Hall, "Encoding and Decoding," in *The Cultural Studies Reader*, ed. Simon During (London: Routledge, 1993), 90. Simon During, Honorary Professor, University of Melbourne.

38. During, "Editor's Introduction Encoding and Decoding," 90.

39. Hall, "Encoding and Decoding," 93ff.

40. Julie Martin, "Audiences and Reception Theory," Sociology Made Simple, 2007, sociologymadesimple.com/papers/. Julie Martin, Writer and blogger on communications issues.

41. During, "Editor's Introduction Encoding and Decoding," 90.

42. Martin, "Audiences and Reception."

43. Ibid. Cf. "Hall, Encoding and Decoding," 91. Recalling the famous Bud Abbott and Lou Costello "Who's on First?" routine is both amusing and useful. Cf. baseball-almanac.com/humor4.shtml.

44. Hall, "Encoding and Decoding," 101-03.

45. This obscuring phenomenon is demonstrated with irony in the quote often attributed to former U.S. Chairman of the Federal Reserve, Alan Greenspan: "I know you think you understand what you thought I

said but I'm not sure you realize that what you heard is not what I meant." This interesting note is attributed to Greenspan by Rupert Cornwell, Cf. "Alan Greenspan: The buck starts here," *The Independent*, April 27, 2003), citing an unspecified Capitol Hill hearing. Cf. en.wikiquote.org/wiki/Alan_Greenspan.

46. Adapted from Hall, "Encoding and Decoding," 101-3.

47. Ibid.

48. Ibid.

49. Cristinel Munteanu, "Aberrant Decoding and Its Linguistic Expression (An Attempt to Restore the Original Concept)," *Procedia - Social and Behavioral Sciences* 63 (2012): 230. Italics in original. Cristinel Munteanu, Member of the Language and Linguistics Faculty, Danubius University.

50. Munteanu, "Aberrant Decoding," 231. Here Munteanu cited John Hartley, Cf. Munteanu's footnote 3. Cf. John Hartley, *Communication, Cultural and Media Studies: The Key Concepts*, 3rd ed. (London: Routledge, 2002), 1. John Hartley, John Curtin Distinguished Professor and Professor of Cultural Science, Curtin University.

51. Ibid. Here, to reference Eco, Munteanu cites Tim O'Sullivan, John Hartley, Danny Saunders, Martin Montgomery, and John Fiske, *Key Concepts in Communication and Cultural Studies*, 2nd ed. (London: Routledge, 1994), 1.

52. Ibid. Here Munteanu is citing Eco via O'Sullivan et al, *Key Concepts*, cited above.

53. Sawyer, "Role of Reception Theory." Cf. Sawyer, "Old Testament and Its Readers," 76.

54. Cf. e.g., Barbashin and Thoburn, "Putin's Brain" and Umland, "Dugin's transformation." Some Dugin criticism may be viewed as originating outside of recognized academic venues. Cf. e.g., James Heiser, "Putin's Rasputin: the Mad Mystic who Inspired Russia's Leader," Breitbart, June 10, 2014, breitbart.com/national-security/2014/06/10/Putin-s-Rasputin-the-Mad-Mystic-Who-Inspired-Putin/. James D. Heiser, Bishop of the Evangelical Lutheran Diocese of North America, Pastor of Salem Lutheran Church, Malone, Texas.

55. Cf. Umland, "Fascist Tendencies in Russian Education," 1, for reference to Umland's labeling of Dugin as a pseudo-scholar. Also, Cf. Liverant, "The Prophet of the New Russian Empire," for contrasting praise.

56. Liverant, "The Prophet of the New Russian Empire."

57. Cf. Part 1, Chapter One, footnotes 37 and 38 herein.

58. The question is associated with American political activity; for instance, Cf. David H. Remer, "Playing in Peoria," in Letters to the Editor, *The New York Times*, November 3, 1985. Cf. Amy Groh, "The Phrase that put Peoria on the Map," Peoria Magazines.com, June 2009, peoriamagazines.com/ibi/2009/jun/phrase-put-peoria-map. Groh wrote, "Earlier this year, just one day before President Obama visited a Caterpillar plant in East Peoria, CNN Senior National Editor, Dave Schechter posted an article to the *Anderson Cooper 360° Newsroom*, which began, 'I want $1 for every time a reporter, commentator or anchor wonders aloud how President Obama and his plan to stimulate the economy are 'playing in Peoria.'" Groucho (Julius Henry) Marx, 1890-1977. Jack Benny (Benjamin Kubelsky), 1894-1974.

Chapter Two: The Expanding Range of Dugin's Reception

No Reception/No Dugin

When asking, "how does Dugin play on the political stage within Russia?," and "how will he perform in the Peoria-like venues in the West?," it is important to be mindful that both questions are largely dependent on the depth, extent, and potential of the current reception of Dugin and his Fourth Political Theory. Clover related that Dugin's audience has widened from the time of the publication of *Foundations of Geopolitics*.[1] It "sold out in four editions, and continues to be assigned as a textbook to the general staff academy and other military universities in Russia," Clover reported.[2] "There has probably not been another book published in Russia during the post-communist period which has exerted a comparable influence on Russian military, police, and statist foreign policy elites," in Dunlop's opinion.[3] In September 2008, Fred Weir wrote:

> This summer's lightning war with Georgia and the emerging political crisis in next door Ukraine are happening right on Dugin's schedule. President Dmitry Medvedev's recent foreign-policy manifesto, outlining Russia's claim to its own sphere of influence in the former Soviet Union, might have been penned by Dugin.[4]

In 2009, Umland observed that,

> In spite of Dugin's, already in the early 1990s, notable publicistic [sic] successes within the far right, the study of the ideas, entourage and activities of this non-conformist writer has, until recently, been seen as the domain of an exclusive group of students of Russian sub-culture, esotericism and occultism with a taste for the bizarre in post-Soviet society.[5]

In 2011 Natalia Morozova styled Dugin as, "the leading contemporary proponent of neo-Eurasianism."[6] Morozova wrote that Dugin "is hailed in the academic literature as the face and the leading representative of contemporary Russian geopolitics."[7] Dugin is rightly established as "heir to the classical geopolitical tradition," in Morozova's opinion.[8] "Through his translation and publishing work Dugin has been instrumental in introducing the Russian public to 'geopolitics' as a distinct and self-sufficient tradition of theorizing international relations," according to Morozova.[9]

Considering the degree of acceptance afforded Dugin and his ideas in Russia and among the ENR and other groups oriented to the political right, how those same ideas are received in the West—particularly among center- and left-leaning audiences are just beginning to be appreciated.

Dugin's Mackinderian Influence

In May 2009 Elena Ovcharenko of *Izvestia*, a state-owned newspaper, interviewed Nikolai Patrushev, Chairman of Russia's Security Council, in Moscow.[10] Clover wrote that this was nothing new; Ovcharenko had interviewed Patrushev some five times previously.[11] What was new was embedded within the overall response given by Patrushev in answer to a question regarding conflicts over natural resources. Initially, Patrushev stated that "the history of the formation, development, unification and the collapse of European and Asian countries, suggests that the political climate here is mainly determined by the interests of the world's leading nations and peoples living in these territories."[12]

Clover commented that this statement was not particularly noteworthy—what was, involved Patrushev's elaboration. Patrushev went on to offer a recital of Mackinder's Heartland Theory. He expounded on the Mackinderian idea that whoever can determine the fate of the Heartland may decide the future of the world.[13] Clover reported that Ovcharenko did not choose to follow up on Patrushev's Mackinderian observations but Kremlin watchers did.

In this Patrushev interview, a leading Russian journalist can be observed reporting on the reception given to aspects of Dugin's

Neo-Eurasianism by a member of Putin's inner circle. Clover marked the importance of this event by highlighting its considerably more significant impact compared to the rest of the interview responses. The piece caused a stir in some circles, not because of the mention of world domination by one of the most influential men in Russia, but because of the way that Mackinder, and his theory, had found his way onto his desk, Clover pointed out.[14] Calling to mind the Encoding and Decoding mentions earlier,

> Patrushev's message was classic "dog whistle" politics, communicating a message to supporters which only they could hear. "Mackinder" and "heartland" were two code words which meant very little to the uninitiated. But to those who were familiar with conservative theories of nationalism which have made dramatic inroads into Russian politics since the end of the Cold war, it meant a great deal. For them, Mackinder is like a barium meal, a visible sign of the progress of these ideas through Russia's postcommunist society, which Patrushev clearly wanted certain audiences to see.[15]

Even more telling for purposes here is Clover's pronouncement that "Patrushev's words signaled to close observers of Russian politics that a new ideology had taken hold in the Kremlin among top decision-makers: ideas which ten years before had been dismissed as completely barking mad were now mainstream."[16] Patrushev was prophetically stating the leanings of Moscow some five years before the Russian invasion of Crimea. Russian political ideology has taken on noteworthy geographical aspects—aspects that tend strongly toward Mackinderian geopolitics.

"The Putin era," Clover wrote, "has seen the emergence of this fringe strain of imperial nationalism as a shadow ideology in Russian politics."[17] Putin's "shadow ideology" is not one of Soviet-style attempts at mass mobilization characterized by propaganda and sloganeering, rather it concentrates on "consolidating an elite behind a set of understood if unspoken truths, deniably vague statements and opaque policies."[18] Putin's approach "is not the subject of booming speeches, but one of whispered codes," Clover wrote; perhaps unintentionally (or not) bringing images of esoteric aspects of Traditionalism to the fore.[19]

Marking the emergence of geopolitics into the mainstream of Russian political discourse, theory, and praxis, Clover cited Moscow bookstores as examples, writing that Dom Knigi or Biblio Globus now have entire sections devoted to geopolitics.[20] "In the State Duma, Russia's lower house of parliament, there is a geopolitics subcommittee," Clover wrote.[21] Now, "at Moscow State University," Clover continued, "there is a chair of the geopolitics department."[22]

Clover's crediting of Dugin for the emergence of current Russian geopolitical awareness was remarkable. "The man who had without a doubt put Mackinder on Patrushev's tongue was an obscure rightwing pamphleteer and ideologist named Alexander Dugin," is the way Clover put it.[23] Clover, recognizing the magnitude of Dugin's Russian reception, wrote that Dugin's "works have come into vogue following the arrival of Vladimir Putin in power in 2000."[24] "And now, thanks to Dugin," Clover stated, "the [Heartland] theory seems to have pervaded Kremlin thinking."[25] Dugin's reception among decision-makers inside Russia can now be safely assumed as fact. Clover attested to Dugin's influence in his observation that, "Mr. Patrushev's assessment of Halford Mackinder as 'one of the leading political scientists of the 20th century'" was, Clover observed, "thanks to Dugin."[26]

Putin's Reception of Dugin

Commenting on the Putin/Dugin connection, Tolstoy and McCaffray noted that Mikhail Leontiev, allegedly Putin's favorite journalist, happens to be a founding member of Dugin's own Eurasia Party.[27] They also wrote that Dugin stated, "I support Putin because he declares and fulfills the goals and ideals that are essentially mine,"[28] To the contrary, Tolstoy and McCaffray claimed it is, in fact, Putin who supports Dugin because of the pathways he creates in national and foreign policy.[29]

Tolstoy and McCaffray wrote that "there are signs that Putin believes in an international struggle that corresponds to Dugin's Neo-Eurasianist vision."[30] Additionally, they indicated that the Eurasian Economic Union (EEU) "has Dugin's intellectual fingerprints all over it."[31] Beyond this, Dugin's "crowning achievement," according to Tolstoy and McCaffray, "is to have become the spokesman for a systematic anti-liberalism that has allowed Vladimir Putin to advance not as an unprincipled tyrant but as the representative of an international philosophy whose writ stretches from the backwaters of Russia to the capitals of Europe."[32]

While Dugin's ability to directly influence Putin continues to be a matter of some debate, evidence of his indirect influence is acknowledged. Speaking specifically about Dugin's reception within circles of Russian power, Bassin questioned the evidence for Dugin's influence before going on to answer his own query:

> In Russia, you can't be a TV anchor person without official approval. Although the channels of his influence are little understood, the very fact that he directs a research centre in Moscow State University points to his status. Moreover, Dugin has always been an authority for the military. Students in military academies study by his books; some may have even been printed with the financial support of the army.[33]

Horbyk wrote that after time with the NBP and Limonov, Dugin became "one of the chief ideologists" in the Putin regime.[34] Despite his reported impact, in the public forum, Dugin appears to play down any direct connections with Putin. Indications are that Dugin does not operate within the inner sanctum as a Putin advisor. "The two men might not have ever even met," wrote Laruelle in 2015, adding that Dugin "has never bragged about having met the Russian president."[35]

Hosking wrote of the reception of Dugin's Neo-Eurasian ideas but also addressed the reliability of Putin's political consistency.

> Russian politicians usually adopt ideologies not
> because they believe in them but because they are
> useful at certain stages of their careers. Dugin
> modified Eurasianism is helpful to Putin while he
> faces conflict in Ukraine combined with western
> sanctions, and while he challenges the "unipolar"
> model of international affairs imposed by the
> US.[36]

While admitting an initial reception, Hosking doubted the staying power of Dugin's influence. He stated that, should Putin decide that Russia needs closer cooperation with the West, "to defeat Islamist terrorism or to prevent conflict getting out of hand, then the tropes of Eurasianism will fall out of his discourse."[37] Still, reflecting on the success of Dugin's *The Foundations of Geopolitics*, its reception, and continuing comments suggesting the presence of Dugin's fingerprints, one must acknowledge a growing influence of almost twenty years.

The Risk Management Lab of the New Bulgarian University also thought that Putin's reception of Dugin is observable through personal and professional linkages. "Dugin and Girkin are close collaborators," the Risk Lab reported.[38] The report went on to claim that both Dugin and Girkin "are in fact paid servants of Malofeev, the Russian oligarch and Putin associate financing a great part of the invasion in Ukraine."[39] It is not the veracity of this claim so much as its implied reception on Putin's part that deserves mention here.

Umland suggested that Dugin and Putin met, or were close enough to have done so, in December 2001 at the VI World Russian Popular Assembly.[40] The Assembly was a meeting of religious representatives, "held since 1993 under the aegis of the Russian Orthodox Church."[41] Putin was present at this event as were highly placed government officials and members of the hierarchy of the Russian Orthodox Church, including the Patriarch of Moscow and All Russias, Aleksii II.[42] Dugin's organization, Eurasia (Evraziya), "apparently sponsored a number of presentations at this congress and managed to place two of its representatives, Dugin and [Talgat] Tadzhuddin, as speakers of the main Plenary Session of the congress."[43] Based on Umland's reporting, it is possible to believe that Putin may have at least been part of the audience to hear Dugin's presentation even if they did not meet.[44]

Horbyk also expressed the opinion that Putin enjoys the cooperation of the Orthodox clergy and consciously promotes his cultish macho image. The combination of Putin's nationalism, foreign policy, support of Russia's predominant religious institution, and macho image "appeals to the far rightists," Horbyk explained.[45] Further, Horbyk implied that Dugin's Neo-Eurasian constituency and his extra-Russian connections are conscious elements of Putin's current geopolitical strategy.[46] The affectations implied by Horbyk plus his connecting Dugin to Putin's current strategy, are clear indications that Putin purposefully employs rhetoric identified with rightist populism.[47]

In 2001, Ilan Berman claimed that "the previously obscure doctrine of Eurasianism has emerged as a major force in Russian politics."[48] Berman stated that this approach to Russian foreign policy was noteworthy because it was appealing as the basis for a "renewed quest for national greatness."[49] Moreover, Berman remarked that impacts of Eurasianism "appear to have begun to animate many of President Putin's international maneuvers."[50]

Emphasizing Dugin's role in this course change from the Yeltsin days, Berman wrote that "a great deal of this newfound appeal can be attributed to Eurasianism's main ideologue— Alexandr Dugin."[51] Berman concluded that even Dugin's "checkered past" as "a former member of the radical anti-Semitic Pamyat organization," his associating with Limonov and "the racist Conservative Revolution," has not kept him from being recognized as "Russia's premier geopolitician."[52]

Berman acknowledged Putin's reception of Dugin in Eurasian matters. Dugin's influence on Putin regarding "Russia's international importance, 'Eurasian' cultural distinctness, and economic-political alliance building can clearly be felt," he said.[53] Berman noted "striking similarities" between many of Dugin's Eurasianist ideas and Putin's policy directions.[54] "Of course, Russian foreign policy is both multifaceted and multidirectional, and may well evolve along a different path over time," Berman added in his 2001 article.[55] In hindsight, nearing two decades later,

Berman's article appears to be remarkably revelatory, and Russia's Eurasianist path seems to remain constant and consistent.

Berman felt that Dugin's strategic geopolitical ideas gained traction with Putin. "a great many of President Putin's recent foreign policy initiatives appear to have been lifted directly from the strategist's playbook," said Berman, referring to Dugin's ideas.[56] An example of Dugin's influence underscores Berman's percipience. Berman's observation that "in line with Dugin's recommendations, Putin has placed great emphasis on the strengthening of the Russo-Iranian strategic partnership," is still pertinent.[57]

Alan Ingram made a point of listing Russian political and business figures that he feels Dugin has influenced and who, in turn, influence Putin. Ingram wrote that "during the Yeltsin era, figures such as Dugin were officially regarded as beyond the pale."[58] "Under Putin," Ingram conceded, "Dugin himself seized upon Putin's description of Russia as a 'Euroasiatic' entity."[59] Further, Ingram observed, "something of a rapprochement has also occurred between the Presidency and the Duma."[60] Ingram implied that Dugin's position as director of a Centre for Geopolitical Expertise within the Duma might have influenced this rapprochement, and further remarked that Dugin "is regularly quoted on the website of Gleb Pavlovksy, a controversial adviser to Putin."[61]

Portraying Dugin as a sibylline character, John Rice-Cameron noted that "as far back as the 1990s, Dugin eyed Ukraine as a target for integration into Russia."[62] Obliquely referring to Dugin, Rice-Cameron maintained that "throughout the 2000s, Eurasianists, through organizations such as the Eurasian Youth Union, fomented pro-Russian sentiment among ethnic Russians in Ukraine, ultimately laying the groundwork for the 2014 civil war.[63] Much less obliquely, Rice-Cameron wrote that in *The Fourth Political Theory*, "Dugin wrote that a 'direct military clash' with Ukraine over Crimea and Eastern Ukraine was a real possibility."[64] Rice-Cameron concluded that "by helping to build the foundation for Putin's invasion of Crimea and Ukraine's destabilization, Eurasianists scored a major victory for the Eurasian project."[65]

Dugin's Reception Outside of Russia

Regarding Dugin's reception by the ENR, Horbyk wrote that Bassin, studying connections between Putin and Eurasians, observed that "links between Russian and Eurasian radical conservatism" are long-established.[66] Recall that Dugin's initial significant reception grew from his ca. 1992 pamphlet regarding "The Great War of Continents," and has continued to grow.[67] In May 2008, Paul Goble, commenting on Eurasian issues, titled his blog post, "Aleksandr Dugin—A 'Zhirinovsky for the Intellectuals.'"[68]

"Dugin's rise," wrote Goble, "has less to do with his own thought and efforts than with his ability to reflect and articulate some of the deepest feelings of contemporary Russian nationalist thought as they have evolved since the late 1980s."[69] Goble's inclusion of this remark at the beginning of his article reveals the reception afforded in Russian circles as Dugin began to be noticed by Western observers.

Goble highlighted the contemporary Russian nationalist thought reflected by Vladimir Zhirinovsky, an advocate of an expanded Russia along Duginesque lines.[70] Ariel Cohen, a political scientist of the Fletcher School, wrote that Zhirinovsky "became an internationally recognized figure when his Liberal Democratic Party won almost a quarter of the Russian vote in parliamentary elections on December 12, 1993."[71] Cohen questioned Zhirinovsky's selection of party name as an affectation, and also criticized the title of Zhirinovsky's autobiography taken from Zhirinovsky's support of a "Final Thrust South." Cohen claimed the party name, "Liberal Democrat," is "dangerously misleading."[72] Cohen then stated that "Zhirinovsky's 1993 autobiography, *The Final Thrust South*, reveals a chauvinistic, imperialist perspective on domestic Russian politics and world affairs that is neither liberal nor democratic."[73]

Umland explained the concept behind "Russia's Final Thrust South" is contained in Zhirinovsky's assertion, "that the main source of troubles in Russia has been its southern neighbors."[74] Of particular interest regarding the reception of Dugin by Zhirinovsky and *vice versa* is Umland's interpretation of

303

Zhirinovsky's assertion that "Russia must annex not only the territories of the former Soviet Union but also Afghanistan, Iran, and Turkey."[75]

Umland listed four reasons Zhirinovsky advocates proceeding with this annexation: to strengthen its southern borders; to "pacify" bellicose nationalities of the region; to obtain access to warm seas; and, to restore its great-power status.[76] Comparisons of Zhirinovsky's ambitions with those of Dugin yield marked similarities regarding Russian/Eurasian expansion. Significantly, Dugin's reception outside of Russian Nationalist circles appears to have exceeded Zhirinovsky's.

An article by Erasmus, on a blog site of *The Economist*, asked, "who is Mr Dugin?" then responded that he is, "an exponent of 'Eurasian' geopolitical thought which dreams of a great Slavic-Turkic land empire under Moscow's command."[77] In furtherance of this dream, Dugin and "some figures on the nationalist fringe of [the] Russian Orthodox church, gave moral support to the leaders of the Russian-backed rebellion against the government of Ukraine."[78] Perhaps giving too slight a nod to Dugin's metaphysical depth while avoiding any dubious claim of purely theological endeavors, Erasmus did acknowledge Dugin's religious associations.

> Dugin sometimes describes his credo as Orthodox Eurasianiam [sic], but he is not much interested in Christian theology as such: more in Orthodoxy as a mark of distinction from the West. Among the thinkers whose guiding hand he acknowledges is Julius Evola, an Italian guru of the far right; he also draws on a "traditionalist" school of religious philosophy which sees wisdom in many ancient and elaborate faiths and loathes secular modernity.[79]

The article reported that Dugin "saw his influence soar during the early months of the conflict in eastern Ukraine in 2014."[80]

Throughout, I have presented evidence of acknowledgment from more mainstream scholars and political analysts. However, Dugin has enjoyed some measure of notoriety for a number of years, much of it emanating from the fringes of academic and political awareness. Given the entirety of his recognition already discussed, a certain amount of Dugin's reception in the United States may be safely assumed. A large measure of the recognition afforded Dugin impacting American reception grew from marginal elements but is growing in the general public, and among Russian observers and scholars.

Illustrative of the depth of Dugin's American reception is Morozova's observation, that "Dugin's highly idiosyncratic and even radical views expressed in his numerous geopolitical writings have earned him the title of Russia's most prominent and prolific geopolitician."[81] Morozova added that this reception is "mainly for confirming the worst Western fears about a wide-spread and deep-seated anti-American feeling shared by the Russian public."[82]

Reception and Reaction to Dugin

With the publication of *Foundations of Geopolitics* Dugin began to gain serious attention in Western circles, especially from Russian-focused military and political analysts. Dugin also gained early Western attention from scholars of Russian subjects studying the developing political and social policy of the then still emerging Russian Federation.

In the sphere of the Russian Federation's social policy creation and development, scholars such as Epstein, Laruelle, Poe, Rossman, Sedgwick, and Shekhovtsov, gave attention to Dugin. Outside of the more narrowly focused military and security commentators, and various esoteric and occult observers, the social and metaphysical perspective provided the West with the earliest and most comprehensive scholarly views of Dugin.

Less obvious in Western geopolitical spheres were some of the theological aspects of Dugin's reception. Even as Dugin gains Western attention, the theological elements of his geopolitical theology will likely be the least recognized facet of his works. Nevertheless, Dugin continues to garner attention in geopolitical and theological circles within Russia and beyond its borders. His geopolitical theology, espousing a Neo-Eurasian empire stretching from Dublin to Vladivostok, is becoming increasingly well known. There is substantial evidence that Putin's strategic agenda reflects distinct elements of Dugin's Neo-Eurasianism. This observation is remarkable even if Putin's strategic thinking does not rely on his direct reception of Dugin. The impact of Dugin's influence, even indirectly, may already be significant.

Dugin is a controversial player on the world stage; characterized hyperbolically as "Putin's Brain," "Putin's Rasputin," a Satanist, an apocalyptic prophet, and a neo-Nazi inhabitant of the lunatic fringe.[54] Playing to a predominately Russian audience, Dugin is noteworthy; his recognition as a player on the broader world stage is also significant and becoming more conspicuous. Given his increasing recognition, it is appropriate to inquire after Dugin's broadening contemporary influence and to speculate on his staying power.

While Umland called Dugin a "pseudo-scholar," claiming that Dugin "uses 'conservatism' as a cover for the spread of a revolutionary ultranationalist and neo-imperialist ideology," Liverant, on the other hand, describes Dugin as a "gifted and charismatic intellectual."[55] Liverant wrote of, "an undeniable connection between Dugin's politics and the regime change led by Putin."[56]

As mentioned, Dugin's status as Head of the Department of Sociology of International Relations at Moscow State University was the subject of controversy.[57] Dugin seems to exist simultaneously in an ethereal world of credibility, ridicule, political influence, and official disfavor. Dugin also dwells in a world of intertwined politics and theology to a point little appreciated in contemporary Western culture. The force of Dugin's impact must be considered both internally, in Russian geopolitical circles, and more especially as concerns this study, externally, in the corresponding Western arena.

Notes

1. Clover, "A New Eurasianism," 16.

2. Ibid.

3. Dunlop, "Aleksandr Dugin's 'Neo-Eurasian' Textbook and Dmitrii Trenin's Ambivalent Response," Harvard Ukrainian Studies XXV, nos.

1/2 (2001). Cf. Clover, "A New Eurasianism," 16-17, and Clover's footnote 1.

4. Fred Weir, "Moscow's Moves in Georgia Track a Script by Right-wing Prophet," *The Christian Science Monitor*, September 20, 2008, csmonitor.com/World/Europe/2008/0920/p01s01-woeu.html. Fred Weir, Canadian journalist living in Russia, Moscow correspondent, Christian Science Monitor.

5. Umland, "Dugin's transformation," 145. Brackets added.

6. Natalia Morozova, "The Politics of Russian Post-Soviet Identity: Geopolitics, Eurasianism, and Beyond" (PhD diss., Central European University, 2011), 137. Natalia Morozova, Instructor at the National Research University, Higher School of Economics.

7. Morozova, "Politics of Russian Identity," 30.

8. Ibid.

9. Ibid.

10. Clover, "A New Eurasianism," 13. Clover is referring to Nikolai Patrushev, "Interview With Nikolai Patrushev Secretary of Russian Federation Security Council," interview by, Elena Ovcharenko," Izvestiya Online, Moscow Edition, in Russian, May 13, 2009. Cf. Open Source Center, Foreign Broadcast Information Service Central Eurasia (FBIS SOV), May 14, 2009. Elena Ovcharenko, *Izvestiya* Managing Editor.

11. Clover, "A New Eurasianism," 13.

12. Ibid.

13. Ibid., 13-14. Clover notes that *Izvestia* published a transcript of the Patrushev/Ovcharenko conversation. In the transcript (according to Clover), Patrushev accurately paraphrased and summarized Mackinder's theory as, "Who controls eastern Europe, rules the Heartland. Who controls the Heartland, he commands the 'World Island.' Who rules the 'World Island,' he rules the world."

14. Ibid., 14.

15. Ibid. The "dog whistle" expression itself indicates a specific encoding technique where, like a high-frequency dog whistle inaudible to humans, but easily heard (decoded) by dogs, the encoded message is missed by those without the proper decoding ability.

16. Ibid.

17. Ibid.

18. Ibid.

19. Ibid.

20. Ibid., 15.

21. Ibid.

22. Ibid.

23. Ibid.

24. Ibid.

25. Ibid. Brackets added.

26. Ibid., 16.

27. Tolstoy and McCaffray, "Mind Games." Mikhail Leontiev, well-known multi-media personality in Russia. Cf. persona.rin.ru/eng/view/f/0/36727/mikhail-leontiev.

28. Ibid.

29. Ibid.

30. Ibid.

31. Ibid. The founding members of the EEU are Russia, Belarus, and Kazakhstan. The EEU has an unmistakable Eurasian unity aspect.

32. Ibid.

33. Horbyk, "The Right Model," under, An example to be followed. Here quoting Bassin.

34. Ibid.

35. Laruelle, "Scared of Putin's Shadow," Foreign Affairs Snapshot, March 25, 2015, foreignaffairs.com/articles/russian-federation/2015-03-25/scared-putins-shadow.

36. Hosking, "Theory of Russian History."

37. Ibid. Brackets added.

38. Risk Management Lab, *Hypotheses Propaganda and Forecasts*, 4. Girkin is deeply involved in the pro-Russian Ukrainian Separative Movement. Cf. e.g., 4pt.su/en/content/igor-strelkov-name-russian-myth for an example of Dugin's praise of Strelkov. Cf. Part I, Chapter One, note 35 for more on Girkin (Strelkov).

39. Ibid. Malofeev, Founder of Marshall Capital Partners. Cf. e.g., chicagotribune.com/news/nationworld/ct-dugin-trump-putin-turkey-20170203-story.html for an analysis of Malofeev's involvements—including those with Dugin. Cf. Part I, Chapter One, note 35 for more on Malofeev.

40. Umland, "Post-Soviet 'Uncivil Society' and the Rise of Aleksandr Dugin: A Case Study of the Extraparliamentary Radical Right in Contemporary Russia" (PhD diss, University of Cambridge, 2007), 127. Cf. Umland's footnote 480 where Umland credits Anastasiya V. Mitrofanova, *The Politicization of Russian Orthodoxy: Actors and Ideas. Soviet and Post-Soviet Politics & Society* (Stuttgart: ibidem, 2005), 221.

41. Umland, "Uncivil Society," 127. Cf. Umland's footnote 480.

42. Ibid.

43. Ibid. Brackets added. Talgat Tadzhuddin, Chief Mufti of Russia and Head of the Central Muslim Spiritual Directorate of Russia, 1992 to 2015.

44. Ibid., 127-28. Umland wrote that "Dugin and Tadzhuddin had the opportunity to officially present themselves on a par with a number of influential Russian figures such as Putin and Aleksii II whom they explicitly addressed in their speeches. Dugin's publishing house Arktogeya-Tsentr produced, afterwards, a small collected volume which commemorated this occasion, with a print-run of 1,000." The book included apart from texts by Putin; Aleksii II, Head of the Writers Union of Russia; Valerii Ganichev, Metropolitan of Smolensk and Kaliningrad; Kirill; Speaker of the *Verkhovna Rada* (Supreme Soviet) of the Republic of Crimea, Leonid Grach; and "pieces by various supporters of 'neo-Eurasianism,' among them several academics sympathetic to Dugin, e.g., Aleksandr Panarin."

45. Horbyk, "The Right Model," under, An example to be followed.

46. Ibid.

47. Ibid.

48. Berman, "Slouching Toward Eurasia," 1.

49. Ibid.

50. Ibid.

51. Ibid., 2.

52. Ibid.

53. Ibid., 4.

54. Ibid., 6.

55. Ibid.

56. Ibid., 4. "Recent" refers to the time of Berman's article in 2001.

57. Ibid., 5. Again, realizing that "recent" refers to the time of the Berman article.

58. Alan Ingram, "Alexander Dugin: Geopolitics and Neo-fascism in Post-Soviet Russia," *Political Geography* 20, no. 8 (2001): 1032. Alan Ingram, Associate Professor of Geography, University College London.

59. Ingram, "Geopolitics and Neo-fascism," 1032. Cf. Ingram's note: Dugin 2001; Evraziistvo: ot filosofii k politike. Nezavisimaya Gazeta, 30 May. Available at ng.ru.

60. Ibid.

61. Ibid. Cf. strana.ru.

62. John Rice-Cameron, "Eurasianism Is the New Fascism: Understanding and Confronting Russia," Stanford Politics, February 2, 2017, stanfordpolitics.org/2017/02/02/eurasianism-new-fascism/. John Rice-Cameron, son of former UN Ambassador and Obama National Security Advisor, Susan Rice, student at Stanford University when this article was published.

63. Rice-Cameron, "Eurasianism Is the New Fascism."

64. Ibid.

65. Ibid.

66. Horbyk, "The Right Model," under, Putin, a "new rightist"?

67. Barbashin and Thoburn, "Putin's Brain." Regarding confusion as to the exact title Cf. Part I, Chapter One, note 21.

68. Paul Goble, "Window on Eurasia: Aleksandr Dugin—a 'Zhirinovsky for the Intellectuals,'" WINDOWONEURASIA (blog), May 13, 2008, windowoneurasia.blogspot.com/2008/05/window-on-eurasia-aleksandr-dugin.html. Vladimir Volfovich Zhirinovsky was born Vladimir Volfovich Eidelstein in 1946. Paul Goble, Analyst, Writer, and Blogger on Russian and other geopolitical issues.

69. Goble, "Zhirinovsky for the Intellectuals." Here Goble notes Mikhail Duinov's argument in *Russkiy zhurnal* (assumed to be the 2008 issue current when Goble posted his article).

70. The more accurate statement may be that Dugin advocates an expanded Russian in very "Zhirinovskyist" terms. This chicken and egg issue is more likely the result of cross-pollination of ideas within the Eurasianist community. Who spoke first is not the primary concern here.

71. Cohen, "Zhirinovsky in His Own Words: Excerpts from The Final Thrust South," Trans. Cohen and Melana Zyla, The Heritage Foundation, February 4, 1994, heritage.org/research/reports/1994/02/zhirinovsky-in-his-own-words-excerpts-from-the-final-thrust-south.

72. Cohen, "Zhirinovsky in His Own Words."

73. Ibid. Title italics added. The title is obviously related to the Russian predilection for expansion in its Manifest Destiny assumptions.

74. Umland, "Zhirinovsky's *Last thrust to the South* and the Definition of Fascism," *Russian Politics and Law,* 46, 4, July-August 2008, 35. Italics in the original title.

75. Umland, "Zhirinovsky's Last Thrust," 35.

76. Ibid.

77. Erasmus, "Russian Anti-Liberals Love Donald Trump but It May Not Be Entirely Mutual," The Economist (blog) (The Economist, November 20, 2016), economist.com/erasmus/2016/11/20/russian-anti-liberals-love-donald-trump-but-it-may-not-be-entirely-mutual. "Erasmus" appears to be a collective pen name for an editorial community of *The Economist*. Note: Mr. is rendered Mr throughout this article.

78. Erasmus, "Russian Anti-Liberals Love Donald Trump." Brackets added.

79. Ibid., Brackets added.

80. Ibid.

81. Morozova, "Politics of Russian Identity," 30.

82. Ibid.

Chapter Three: Receiving Dugin as a Fascist

"Putinism rests on the ethics of personal enrichment," in Horbyk's mind, and Putin imbues it with "fascist elements" that are an "exploitation of the rhetoric of national renaissance, radical nationalism, aggressive foreign policy and imperialism."[1] Horbyk's opinion indicated two noteworthy elements: first, some Western commentators apply a fascist label to current Russian geopolitics. Second, given assumptions of Dugin's influence on Putin and Horbyk's inclusion of "rhetoric" that is frequently attached to Dugin in the West, Dugin is likely to be painted as a fascist along with Putin.

Regarding the first of Horbyk's elements, Ingram expressed a belief that "many writers and activists who can be argued to lie within this tradition reject the fascist label for themselves, particularly in Russia where the term is generally applicable only to the Nazi regime."[2] Regarding the second, Ingram suggested that "it is useful to consider Dugin in relation to what might be thought of as a broad fascist tradition."[3]

While Dugin may not be cast from the original Nazi mold, he "certainly makes reference to many writers (such as Schmitt and Oswald Spengler) from whom fascists draw considerable inspiration," commented Ingram.[4] Bringing to mind Dugin's mining according to the Metaphysics of Debris, "fascist themes" are among the things that Dugin "recycles," Ingram wrote.[5]

Umland also expressed a level of concern similar to that encountered in Ingram's critique of Dugin's fascist characteristics when he wrote that "Dugin is now working toward establishing his 'neo-Eurasianist' ideology as Russia's new foreign policy doctrine."[6] Umland claimed that Dugin employs "conservatism" as a term to "cover for the spread of an actually revolutionary neo-imperialist program that amounts to a blueprint for an armed confrontation with Russia's neighbours and the West."[7] Umland wrote that Dugin "openly propagated fascism in the 1990s."[8] Umland added that during this time Dugin repeatedly displayed sympathy for selected aspects of fascism and National Socialism, such as the *SS* and the *Ahnenerbe* ('Ancestral Heritage') Institute.[9]

"Fascism is a genus of political ideology whose mythic core in its various permutations is a palingenetic form of populist ultra-nationalism," as defined by Roger Griffin in 1991.[10] Despite Griffin's efforts, fascism has been separated from this definition and become a pejorative to be carelessly hurled at opponents of most any political position. George Orwell, writing in 1944, captured the issue succinctly with his observation that, "it will be seen that, as used, the word 'Fascism' is almost entirely meaningless."[11] Emphasizing his point *ad absurdum*, Orwell explained:

> In conversation, of course, it is used even more wildly than in print. I have heard it applied to farmers, shopkeepers, Social Credit, corporal punishment, fox-hunting, bull-fighting, the 1922 Committee, the 1941 Committee, Kipling, Gandhi, Chiang Kai-Shek, homosexuality, Priestley's broadcasts, Youth Hostels, astrology, women, dogs and I do not know what else.[12]

Orwell realized that "underneath all this mess there does lie a kind of buried meaning," that is useful in the present context.[13] Orwell wrote that "even the people who recklessly fling the word 'Fascist' in every direction attach at any rate an emotional significance to it."[14] "By 'Fascism,'" Orwell meant, "roughly speaking, something cruel, unscrupulous, arrogant, obscurantist, anti-liberal and anti-working-class."[15] Orwell concluded that "almost any English person would accept 'bully' as a synonym for 'Fascist,'" and found, "that is about as near to a definition as this much-abused word has come."[16] Realizing the broad and amorphous nature of fascism, Griffin redefined it as a

> revolutionary form of nationalism bent on mobilizing all 'healthy' social and political energies to resist the onslaught of 'decadence' so as to achieve the goal of national rebirth, a project that involves the regeneration (palingenesis) of both the political culture and the social and ethical culture underpinning it.[17]

313

Griffin's redefining suggestion is especially interesting because of the apparent parallels embedded in Dugin's Neo-Traditionalism, Neo-Eurasianism, and his resistance to the "decadence" of the West.

Umland has also provided definitional boundaries useful in the context of this discussion of Dugin's fascist leanings:

> In the post-Soviet discourse, the term "fascism" is equated with German National Socialism and its external trappings, such as the swastika or Roman salute. Occasionally, the propagandistic usage of the term "fascism" goes so far as to include all ideas regarded as "anti-Russian." It then, paradoxically, becomes a rhetorical instrument in xenophobic agitation campaigns of Russian ultra-nationalists.[18]

Clover saw that Dugin included in *Foundations of Geopolitics*, "thinkers associated with the far right wing, most of whom you have never heard of, some quite mad ones and not a few Nazis."[19] Analogies comparing Russia to Weimar Germany were frequent at this time. As such, Clover thought that "Dugin's book was evidence that the same dark forces radicalized by Germany's interwar collapse were on the ascent in Russia."[20] According to Clover, *The Foundations of Geopolitics* credited the country's humiliation to foreign conspiracies, its cover bore a occultish runic symbol known as the "star of chaos," and it portrayed Nazis in a favorable light.[21]

Griffin addressed contemporary fascism's postmodern inclusiveness writing that "one symptom of the extreme right's rhizomic structure is an ecumenicalism unthinkable in the 'fascist era,' expressed both in the way web-linkages exist and in cross-currents of influence detectable between diffuse currents of fascism."[22] Griffin's examples included "Universal Nazism, Christian Identity, Third Positionism" and "the New Right."[23] Referencing Dugin's occupation of a Neo-Fascist position, Griffin pointed out that the 'Eurasianism' of Arctogaia, for example, draws upon the influences of home-grown, pre-Soviet tradition of Russian ultra-nationalism; Russian dialectics of post-Soviet national Bolshevism; the French New Right; the Traditionalist Italian New Right; Third Positionism; New Age and occultist fascism; and even the punk-rock strand of 'White Noise.'[24]

Griffin commented that "in August 1998 [the Arctogaia] website paraded the name of Jonny Rotten (of the notorious anarchic punk band Sex Pistols) next to those of Alain de Benoist and Julius Evola as prophets of the new age."[25]

Suggesting Dugin's push-back to the fascist label, Umland observed that Dugin has become more cautious "and now refers to himself as an 'anti-fascist.'"[26] Ingram's position is that "if Dugin cannot be considered a fascist in the narrow historical sense of the word, he certainly inhabits a closely related ideological space, referring to the supremacy of will as well as environmental determinism."[27] Exhibiting an opinion close to Umland's, Ingram's ultimate conclusion was that "in some senses, Dugin can be considered a neo-fascist, as well as a geopolitician."[28]

Pinning the Fascist label on Dugin is not especially helpful. The muddled definition of the term reduces most any reference of fascism attached to Dugin to merely a pejorative—a meaningless exercise in name-calling. Dugin is way more complicated than simplistic labels can define. Tendencies on Dugin's part that can be examined with serious academic consideration, be it Traditionalism, Fascism, Fundamentalism, Metaphysics, or others are useful—schoolyard polemics are not.

Notes

1. Horbyk, "The Right Model," under, An example to be followed.

2. Ibid.

3. Ingram, "Geopolitics and Neo-fascism," 1033.

4. Ibid., 1034. Parentheses in original.

5. Ibid.

6. Umland, "Fascist Tendencies in Russian Education." Cf. Umland's note 27 for his references to other opinions regarding Dugin's position.

7. Ibid.

8. Umland, "'Neo-Eurasianism,' the Issue of Russian Fascism, and Post-Soviet Political Discourse," Opednews.com, June 11, 2008, under Summary, opednews.com.

9. Umland, "'Neo-Eurasianism,' the Issue of Russian Fascism," under, Aberrations of the Intelligentsia. Parentheses in original.

10. Roger Griffin, *The Nature of Fascism* (London: Pinter, 1991), 26. Roger Griffin, 1935-2021.

11. George Orwell, "What Is Fascism?," *Tribune* (London), March 24, 1944. Cf. for a reprint of this article access alexpeak.com/twr/wif/. George Orwell, 1903-1950.

12. Orwell, "What Is Fascism?"

13. Ibid.

14. Ibid.

15. Ibid.

16. Ibid.

17. Roger Griffin and Matthew Feldman, *Fascism: Critical Concepts*, vol. 1 (London: Routledge, 2004), 6. Matthew Feldman, Emeritus Professor, Teesside University, Director of the Centre for Analysis of the Radical Right.

18. Umland, "Issue of Russian Fascism," under, The Post-Soviet Conception of Fascism.

19. Clover, "A New Eurasianism," 15.

20. Ibid.

21. Ibid.

22. Griffin, *A Fascist Century*, ed. Matthew Fieldman (New York: Palgrave Macmillan, 2008), 199. Griffin explains that "if a political network has a rhizomic political structure it means that it forms a cellular, centreless, and leaderless network with ill-defined boundaries and no formal hierarchy or internal organisational structure to give it a unified direction."

23. Griffin, *A Fascist Century*, 199. Cf. e.g., Chip Berlet, "What Is the Third Position?," Political Research, December 19, 2016, politicalresearch.org/2016/12/19/what-is-the-third-position/. Berlet, former Senior Research Analyst for Political Research Associates, stated, "the Third Position—which rejects both capitalism and communism—traces its roots to the most "radical" anticapitalist wing of Hitler's Nazi Party."

24. Ibid.

25. Ibid. Cf. Griffin's note 55. Brackets added.

26. Umland, "Fascist Tendencies in Russian Education."

27. Ingram, "Geopolitics and Neo-fascism," 1034.

28. Ibid.

Conclusions

I suggest that geopolitical theology is the proper venue for studying Alexander Dugin. Among the critical points within this venue are Dugin's opinions of Liberal Democracy, and his interpretations of Traditionalism, and Eurasianism. I contend that geopolitics is part of a Clausewitzian extension, and that conflict is an extreme position on the geopolitical continuum. Dugin includes theological considerations throughout his geopolitical endeavors. Therefore, Dugin is most accurately explored via a combination of geopolitics, political theology, Traditionalism, and Eurasianism. Additionally, the level of reception of Dugin's ideas in the West will significantly affect how the West responds to Russian policy decisions. The stronger the perception of Dugin's influence, the more likely it will be that the West assumes that Dugin's goals are Russia's goals.

I looked at Dugin through observations and expressions of his commentators. Additionally, I presented the works of others who influenced Dugin and Fourth Political Theory. I followed the topical areas explored, making some comments on comparisons and contrasts to Dugin's expressed ideological thinking and presenting commentators that provide a range of opinion of Dugin and his ideas. Dugin commentators have presented his Traditionalism in comparison and contrast to Integral (Classic) Traditionalism. The consensus opinion is that Dugin is not an Integral Traditionalist. At the same time, his actively applied Neo-Traditionalism is heretical; although tainted, it is nonetheless still Traditional after a fashion. Likewise, writers and scholars—commentators all—address Dugin's Eurasianism allowing him to be correctly categorized as a Neo-Eurasianist. Additionally, more than sufficient evidence was presented to ensure a conclusion that Dugin's Neo-Eurasianism is metaphysically saturated and imperialistic.

Dugin is a severe critic of Western Liberalism. Despite the fog surrounding definitions, contemporary liberalism, with its globalist and unipolar ambitions, is Dugin's avowed enemy. Dugin can be viewed through the eyes of his various interpreters and commentators as one actively engaged in either a chaotic or a systematic and logical effort to thwart Western Liberalism and

318

promote his Fourth Political Theory as its substitute. Moreover, Dugin's hermeneutics have been shown to support his Traditional, Eurasian, and eschatological development and purposes consistent with this logic.

In a worthwhile pondering, Dugin asks a question concerning the viability of a multipolar environment resulting if his Neo-Eurasian Model were to become a reality: "how can modernity exist in the traditional world?"[1] "It is clear and evident that the tradition can survive in the modern world," but is the opposite true, Dugin asks?[2]

Contemplating the impact of Traditionalism is essential to any clear reception of Fourth Political Theory. The influence of Guénon and Evola, especially Evola, on Dugin and hence on Dugin's political theories about Eurasianism permeate his thinking. While Dugin's interpretation of Traditionalism may differ from the Integral variety, as part of Fourth Political Theory, Dugin's Neo-Traditionalism must be given due consideration.

To properly understand Dugin in his Neo-Traditional assumption, it is also necessary to grasp the relationships between fundamentalism and Traditionalism. Fundamentalism is a crucial ingredient in forming a clear idea of how Dugin develops the Neo-Traditional element of his Fourth Political Theory. Recalling the treatment of the fundamentalism/Traditionalism relationship supports viewing Dugin as a Fundamentalist. As he restricts his Fourth Political Theory to strict hermeneutical parameters and insists on the rejection of Western Liberalism and modernity, Dugin's fundamentalism is exposed.

Dugin's application of Traditionalism is not the same as Guénon's. Nevertheless, whether orthodox or heretical, Dugin's Neo-Traditionalism as an influence in contemporary Russia must be taken into account. It matters little on the cold stage of geopolitical reality if hindsight locates Dugin in history as an Integral Traditionalist, a Neo-Traditionalist, or a Traditionalist by some other name. What matters is that a more proper reception can be had by studying Dugin's Neo-Traditionalism and its place in Fourth Political Theory. Informed Western policy decisions continue to be critical as Russia continues to develop a more Eurasian persona.

Dugin is not content to be just a disciple; he must also innovate and create. Thus, Traditionalism is the earth wherein Dugin grounds his Fourth Political Theory while he raises the radical innovation of applied Neo-Traditionalism from it. Better understandings of Traditionalism, its antecedents, and its kinships allow for a better understanding of Dugin's Neo-Traditional innovation. Dugin is not merely rehashing Guénon—he is intent on building something active and radical. With his Fourth Political Theory, Dugin is attempting to occupy a place in the postmodern world. Not just that, he wishes the occupation to dominate.

Dugin believes that traditionalism (that is, traditionalism in the lowercase) opposed modernism but lost. In Dugin's view, Neo-Eurasianism, with its Neo-Traditionalist foundations, will have the strength to confront the West in this new present era. Dugin proposes opposing one postmodern reality—globalism— the evil postmodern spawn of the West, with a more potent postmodern reality—Fourth Political Theory's Tradition based Neo-Eurasianism.

Consider this example where Dugin does not hesitate to resort to esoteric metaphysical illustration, allusion, metaphor, and hyperbole in his descriptions of things Russian:

> We Russians are a blessed nation. Therefore all our manifestations—lofty and shabby, comely and terrifying—are sanctified by otherworldly senses, by rays of the otherworldly city, are washed by transcendent moisture. In the abundance of the national Grace the good and the evil are mixed, pour from one to another, and suddenly the dark lightens, whereas something white becomes a mere hell. We are as unknowable as the Absolute. We are a divine nation. Even our Crime is incomparably superior to some other's virtue.[3]

The alchemy involved in reversing the moral standard whereby crime becomes more virtuous than virtue itself speaks to Dugin's access to an incredibly esoteric toolbox indeed. The basis of Dugin's belief is certainly arguable—but the point of its elevated Russian chauvinism is not.

Separating Dugin's theologically slanted ideology from its co-joined geopolitical twin is not surgically possible. Evidence confirms that Dugin is a geopolitical theologian; his worldview cannot be adequately considered unless his geopolitical, metaphysical, and theological ideas are examined together. The subsequent hermeneutical precepts Dugin displays are derived from his overarching Hermeneutic of Geopolitical Theology. Sacred Geography/Sacred Space includes Dugin's concepts of Messianic Russia, Third Rome, Katechon, and his notion of the Collective Antichrist. His Neo-Traditionalism exposes the extent of his anti-Western manifestations.

Dugin touts a multipolar world, and Eurasia is a critical part of the model. Dugin's concept of Eurasia is based on previous models and is, hence, properly, a Neo-Eurasian development. Dugin constructs his geopolitical model using the theological and metaphysical ingredients of Neo-Traditionalism. There is no other way to correctly parse Dugin and his ideas without resorting to explanations of his particular geopolitical theology.

Dugin wants more than a Russian audience for his Neo-Eurasianist ideas. Moreover, this is readily understandable, assuming the nature of the Eurasia he envisions. For the emergence of a major regional power stretching from Dublin to Vladivostok to become more than a notional scrap in Dugin's mind, the idea must gain traction in Western Europe and Asia. Dugin is thinking much more broadly than the size and extent of current Russian borders—*Dugin is thinking empire*.

It should be remembered that Dugin is not a rank newcomer to American political dialog, where he has a history of both critique and commentary. Dugin's ideas have moved westward due in no small part to the efforts of Dugin himself. Dugin has not sprung full-grown, Athena-like; he has developed, evolved. His development is likely not over, but it is sufficiently advanced to allow this observation: what can now be seen in Dugin is the manifestation of his Neo-Traditional geopolitical theology.

If Dugin is afforded serious reception, his impact will be noticeably increased. Therefore, gaging the extent of the reception given to Dugin and his Fourth Political Theory is critical. Dugin is a force seeking traction. All indications are that he is content to be a force behind a force—a change agent affecting his desires by influence as opposed to overt leadership. Initially, he sought influence in Russia; now, he seeks it on the broader world stage.

Because Dugin not only proposes but advocates Russian expansion geopolitically as *the* Eurasian power, one of the polar powers in a multipolar world, he views a future Eurasian reality in the totality of its cultural and geopolitical manifestations. He interprets the West in a similar fashion. He argues that the West, especially the United States since the collapse of the Soviet Union, has intended to be *the* unipolar Power—the singular geopolitical superpower of the world. Conflict, even catastrophic conflict, between multipolar and unipolar competitors is a potential risk— studying how Dugin and his ideology contributes to this risk is, therefore, prudent and necessary.

Finally, Dugin sees himself as a Radical Subject and, I believe, wishes the world to see him as such. Dugin appears to believe in a participatory eschatology—the end-times can be hastened according to the applied Neo-Traditionalism version of the genre. As a Radical Subject, Dugin can be, and wishes to be, in the center of *Gottesnacht*. The express purpose for enduring such a hellish position is to hasten the end times.

If the West takes its eyes off Dugin and Russia, it risks a serious security fumble. I find myself in agreement with Tayloe's reminder that Thucydides believed that "conflict is motivated by 'fear, honor, and self-interest'—a conclusion that in the context of contemporary Russia should give all policymakers pause."[4]

Notes

1. Dugin, "The Figure of the Radical Subject," under, Part 1, Traditionalism and Sociology—The Modern and the Eternal

2. Ibid.

3. Dugin, "Dostoyevsky and the Metaphysics of St. Petersburg."

4. Tayloe, "Projecting Power in the Arctic," 11.

Selected Bibliography

Agursky, Mikhail. *The Third Rome: National Bolshevism in the USSR*. London: Westview Press, 1987.

Alston, Wallace M., and Michael Welker, eds. *Reformed Theology*. Grand Rapids, MI: Eerdmans, 2007.

Armstrong, Karen. *The Battle for God*. London: Harper Perennial, 2004.

Barbashin, Anton, and Hannah Thoburn. "Putin's Brain: Alexander Dugin and the Philosophy Behind Putin's Invasion of Crimea." Foreign Affairs, March 31, 2014. foreignaffairs.com/articles/russia-fsu/2014-03-31/putins-brain.

Barber, Benjamin. "Jihad vs. McWorld." *The Atlantic*, March 1992, 53-65.

_____. *Jihad vs. McWorld*. New York: Times Books, 1995.

Barkun, Michael. "Religious Violence and the Myth of Fundamentalism." *Totalitarian Movements and Political Religions* 4, no. 3 (2003): 55-70.

Bassin, Mark. "'Classical' Eurasianism and the Geopolitics of Russian Identity." *Ab Imperio* 2003, no. 2 (January 2003): 257-66.

_____. "Eurasianism 'Classical' and 'Neo': The Lines of Continuity." In *Beyond the Empire: Images of Russia in the Eurasian Cultural Context*, edited by Tetsuo Mochizuki, 279-96. Sapporo: Slavic Research Center, Hokkaido University, 2008.

Baudrillard, Jean. *The Illusion of the End*. Translated by Chris Turner. Stanford, CA: Stanford University Press, 1994.

Beale, Gregory K. "Eden, the Temple, and the Church's Mission in the New Creation." *Journal of the Evangelical Theological Society* 48, no. 1 (March 2005): 5–31.

Becker, Marc. "Manifest Destiny." *Encyclopedia of U.S. Military Interventions in Latin America*. Edited by Alan McPherson. Vol. 2. Santa Barbara, CA: ABC-CLIO, LLC, 2013.

Bell, Duncan. "What Is Liberalism?" *Political Theory* 42, no. 6 (November 29, 2014): 682-715.

Bendersky, Joseph W. "The Definite and the Dubious: Carl Schmitt's Influence on Conservative Political and Legal Theory in the US." *Telos* 122 (2002): 33-47.

Bendle, Mervyn F. "Putin's Rasputin." *Quadrant On-Line*. September 3, 2014. quadrant.org.au/magazine/2014/09/putins-rasputin/.

Berger, Peter L., ed. *The Desecularization of the World: Resurgent Religion and World Politics*. Grand Rapids, MI: Eerdmans, 1999.

Berman, Ilan. "Slouching Toward Eurasia." *Perspective* XII, no. 1 (2001): 1-8. bu.edu/iscip/vol12/berman.html.

Bevir, Mark. "The Contextual Approach." In *The Oxford Handbook of the History of Political Philosophy*, edited by George Klosko, 11-23. Oxford: Oxford University Press, 2011.

Blumenberg, Hans. *The Legitimacy of the Modern Age*. Translated by Robert M. Wallace. Cambridge, MA: MIT Press, 1983.

Bokenkotter, Thomas. *Church and Revolution: Catholics in the Struggle for Democracy and Social Justice*. New York: Doubleday, 1998.

Bourdin, Bernard. *The Theological-Political Origins of the Modern State: The Controversy Between James I of England and Cardinal Bellarmine*. Translated by Susan Pickford. Washington, DC: Catholic University of America Press, 2011.

Boym, Svetlana. "Conspiracy Theories and Literary Ethics: Umberto Eco, Danilo Kis and The Protocols of Zion." *Comparative Literature* 51, no. 2 (1999): 97-122.

Bradshaw, Timothy. "John Macquarrie." In *The SPCK Handbook of Anglican Theologians*, edited by Alister E. McGrath, 167–68. London: SPCK, 1998.

Brannan, David. "Violence, Terrorism and the Role of Theology: Repentant and Rebellious Christian Identity." PhD diss. University of St Andrews, 2007.

Breivik, Anders. "Anders Behring Breivik's Complete Manifesto '2083 – A European Declaration of Independence'." *Public Intelligence*. July 28, 2011. Accessed October 22, 2915. publicintelligence.net/anders-behring-breiviks-complete-manifesto-2083-a-european-declaration-of-independence/.

Brooke, Peter. "'Third Rome, Third International, Third Reich' – Alexander Dugin and the 'Fourth Political Theory.'" *The Heidegger Review*, no. 1 (July 2014). heideggerreview.org/table-of-contents-no-1/third-rome-third-international-third-reich-alexander-dugin-and-the-fourth-political-theory/.

Bruck, Arthur Moeller Van Den. *Germany's Third Empire*. London: Arktos Media, 2012.

Brzezinski, Zbigniew. *The Grand Chessboard: American Primacy and Its Geostrategic Imperatives*. New York: Basic Books, 2016.

Buckley, Peter J. "Historical Research Approaches to the Analysis of Internationalisation." *Management International Review* 56 (December 2016): 879-900.

Bultmann, Rudolf. "Is Exegesis Without Presuppositions Possible?" In *The Hermeneutics Reader*, edited by Kurt Mueller-Vollmer, 242-47. New York: Continuum, 1985.

Burge, S. R. "Angels, Ritual and Sacred Space in Islam." *Comparative Islamic Studies* 5, no. 2 (2009): 221-45.

Burke, Edmund. *Reflections on the Revolution in France: And Other Writings*. Edited by Jesse Norman. London: Alfred A. Knopf, 2015.

Cahoone, Lawrence. "Lecture Notes." In *The Modern Political Tradition: Hobbes to Habermas*. Chantilly, VA: Great Courses, 2014.

Carrère, Emmanuel. *Limonov: The Outrageous Adventures of the Radical, Soviet Poet Who Became a Bum in New York, a Sensation in France, and a Political Antihero in Russia*. Translated by John Lambert. New York: Farrar, Straus and Giroux, 2014.

Cavanaugh, William. "Messianic Nation: A Christian Theological Critique of American Exceptionalism." *University of St. Thomas Law Journal* 3, no. 2 (Fall 2005): 261-80.

Chadwick, John. *The Decipherment of Linear B*. Cambridge: Cambridge University Press, 1958.

Chan, Sylvia. *Liberalism, Democracy, and Development*. New York, NY: Cambridge University, 2002.

Chandler, A.D. "Comparative Business History." Essay. In *Enterprise and History: Essays in Honour of Charles Wilson*, edited by D. C. Coleman and P. Mathias, 473–503. Cambridge: Cambridge University Press, 1984.

Clausewitz, Carl von. *On War*. London: K. Paul, Trench, Trubner, 1918.

Clooney, Francis X. *Comparative Theology: Deep Learning across Religious Borders*. Chichester: Wiley-Blackwell, 2010.

_____. *Hindu God Christian God: How Reason Helps Break Down the Boundaries Between Religions*. Oxford: Oxford University Press, 2001.

Clover, Charles. *Black Wind, White Snow: The Rise of Russia's New Nationalism*. New Haven: Yale University Press, 2016.

_____. "Dreams of the Eurasian Heartland: The Reemergence of Geopolitics." *Foreign Affairs* 78, no. 2 (1999): 9-13.

_____. "In Moscow, a New Eurasianism." *Journal of International Security Affairs* Fall/Winter, no. 27 (2014).

Cohen, Ariel. "The Primakov Doctrine: Russia's Zero-Sum Game with the United States." *Heritage Foundation.* December 15, 1997. heritage.org/report/the-primakov-doctrine-russias-zero-sum-game-the-united-states.

_____. "Zhirinovsky in His Own Words: Excerpts from The Final Thrust South." *The Heritage Foundation.* February 4, 1994. Accessed July 25, 2017. , heritage.org/research/reports/1994/02/zhirinovsky-in-his-own-words-excerpts-from-the-final-thrust-south.

Cohn, Norman. *Pursuit of the Millennium.* London: Secker & Warburg, 1957.

Collini, Stefan, Quentin Skinner, David A. Hollinger, J. G. A. Pocock, Michael Hunter. "What Is Intellectual History?" In *What Is History...?*, edited by Juliet Gardiner, 105-19. London: Macmillan Press, 1988.

Constantakopoulou, Christy, K. Brodersen, Brodersen, C. B. Champion, A. Erskine, and S. R. Huebner. "Thalassocracy." In *the Encyclopedia of Ancient History*, edited by R. S. Bagnall, et al. Blackwell Publishing Ltd, October 26, 2012. onlinelibrary.wiley.com/doi/abs/10.1002/9781444338386.w beah04305.

Copilaş, Emanuel. "Cultural Ideal or Geopolitical Project? Eurasianism's Paradoxes." *Strategic Impact* 3, no. 2009, 65-80.

Coyer, Paul. "The Patriarch, The Pope, Ukraine, And the Disintegration of The Russian World." *Forbes*, March 20, 2016. forbes.com/sites/paulcoyer/2016/03/20/the-patriarch-the-pope-ukraine-and-the-disintegration-of-the-russian-world/#4d17a8612530.

_____. "(Un)Holy Alliance: Vladimir Putin, The Russian Orthodox Church and Russian Exceptionalism." *Forbes*, May 21, 2015. forbes.com/sites/paulcoyer/2015/05/21/unholy-alliance-vladimir-putin-and-the-russian-orthodox-church/#497ea41427d5.

Creswell, John W. *Research design: Qualitative, Quantitative, and Mixed Methods Approaches*. 4th ed. Thousand Oaks, CA: Sage, 2016.

Cresswell, Tim. *Place: An Introduction*. 2nd ed. Chichester: John Wiley and Sons, 2015.

Cutsinger, James. "An Open Letter on Tradition." *Modern Age*, Spring, 36, no. 3 (1994): 294-301.

Debord, Guy. *Society of the Spectacle*. Detroit: Black and Red, 1977.

Deleuze, Gilles. "Postscript on the Societies of Control." *October* 59 (Winter 1992): 3-7.

Deudney, Daniel H. "Geopolitics (Political Science)." In *Encyclopædia Britannica*, June 12, 2013. britannica.com/topic/geopolitics.

Diamond, Jared M. *Guns, Germs, and Steel: The Fates of Human Societies*. New York: W.W. Norton & Company, 1997.

Dible, Randolph. "The Philosophy of Mysticism: Perennialism and Constructivism." *Journal of Consciousness Exploration & Research* 1, no. 2 (March 2010): 173-83.

Dollar, George W. *A History of Fundamentalism in America*. Greenville, SC: Bob Jones University Press, 1973.

Douglas, Karen M., Robbie M. Sutton, Mitchell J. Callan, Rael J. Dawtry, and Annelie J. Harvey. "Someone Is Pulling the Strings: Hypersensitive Agency Detection and Belief in Conspiracy Theories." *Thinking & Reasoning* 22, no. 1 (2015): 57–77.

Dugin, Alexander. *Absoliutnaia Rodina*. Moscow: Arktogeia-Tsentr, 1999.

_____. "Brexit - Europe Is Falling into the Abyss." Interview by Katehon. *Katehon*. June 25, 2016. Accessed June 11, 2017. katehon.com/article/brexit-europe-falling-abyss.

_____. "Dostoyevsky and the Metaphysics of St. Petersburg." New European Conservative. August 6, 2014. neweuropeanconservative.wordpress.com/2014/08/06/dostoyevsky-and-russia-dugin/.

_____. "Eurasia Above All: Manifest of the Eurasist Movement." *Arctogaia*. Translated by M. Conserva. January 1, 2001. arctogaia.com/public/eng/Manifesto.html.

_____. "The Eurasian Idea." *Counter-Currents Publishing*. November 8, 2013. counter-currents.com/2013/11/the-eurasian-idea/.

_____. "Eurasian Idea and Postmodernism." Address, Constitutive Conference of Eurasian International Movement. Accessed June 11, 2017. 4pt.su/en/content/eurasian-idea-and-postmodernism.

_____. *Eurasian Mission: An Introduction to Neo-Eurasianism*. Leipzig: Renovamen Verlag, 2016.

_____. "The Evaporation of Fundamentals in the 'New Economy'." Evrazia. November 2001. evrazia.org/modules.php?name=News&file=print&sid=414.

_____. *The Fourth Political Theory*. Translated by Michael Millerman and Mark Sleboda. Edited by John B. Morgan. London: Arktos, 2012.

_____. "From Sacred Geography to Geopolitics." *The Fourth Political Theory*. Accessed June 12, 2017. 4pt.su/en/content/sacred-geography-geopolitics-0.

_____. "Great War of the Continents." *Open Revolt*. February 3, 2013. Accessed June 6, 2015. openrevolt.info/2013/02/03/alexander-dugin-the-great-war-of-continents/.

_____. "Ideology of the World Government." *The Fourth Political Theory*. September 28, 2012. 4pt.su/en/content/ideology-world-government.

_____. "The Indo-Europeans." *Eurasianist-Archive*. December 28, 2016. Accessed August 3, 2017. eurasianist-archive.com/2016/12/28/the-indo-europeans/.

329

_____. *Konspirologija: (Nauka o Zaverama, Tajnim Drustvima i Okultnom Ratu)*. Beograd: Brimo, 2001.

_____. "Liberal, Post-Modern Europe Is Rotting to Pieces. Strong Christian Russia Doesn't Need Her." *Russia Insider.* March 5, 2016. russia-insider.com/en/top-russian-ideologue-alexander-dugin-gives-his-take-recent-meeting-between-pope-francis-and/ri13168.

_____. "The Long Path: An Interview with Alexander Dugin." Interview by Open Revolt. *Open Revolt.* May 17, 2014. Accessed June 11, 2017. openrevolt.info/2014/05/17/alexander-dugin-interview/.

_____. "Maoism Is Too Modern for Me." *The Fourth Political Theory.* March 26, 2015. 4pt.su/en/content/maoism-too-modern-me.

_____. "The Mission of Julius Evola." *Open Revolt.* October 27, 2011. openrevolt.info/2011/10/27/the-mission-of-julius-evola/.

_____. "Moscow as an Idea." *The Fourth Political Theory.* April 9, 2018. 4pt.su/en/content/moscow-idea.

_____. *Osnovy Geopolitiki: Geopoliticheskoe Budushchee Rossii* . Moscow: Arktogeya, 1997.

_____. "Postmodern Europe Is Rotting." Interview by Rémi Tremblay. *Alternative Right.* May 21, 2015. Accessed July 24, 2016. alternative-right.blogspot.com/2015/05/an-interview-with-alexander-dugin.html.

_____. *Putin vs Putin: Vladimir Putin Viewed from the Right.* Leipzig: Renovamen Verlag, 2016.

_____. "The Radical Subject and the Metaphysics of Pain." *The Fourth Revolutionary War.* September 17, 2016, 4threvolutionarywar.wordpress.com/2016/09/17/the-radical-subject-and-the-metaphysics-of-pain-alexander-dugin/.

_____. "Russian Orthodoxy and Initiation." *The Fourth Political Theory.* Accessed June 24, 2017. 4pt.su/en/content/russian-orthodoxy-and-initiation.

————. "Russians Must Save Europe from the Liberal Elites." Interview by *Il Foglio. Geopolitica.ru*. April 25, 2017. geopolitica.ru/en/article/russians-must-save-europe-liberal-elite.

————. "Traditionalism and Esotericism in Islam." *Open Revolt*. November 16, 2011. Accessed February 01, 2018. openrevolt.info/2011/11/15/alexander-dugin-tradition-and-islam/.

————. "Traditionalism and Sociology/The Figure of the Radical Subject" (lecture, Colloquium on Evola, Curitiba, Brazil, September 2012).

————. "We Are Going to Cure You with Poison." *ARCTOGAIA* - 2001. Accessed June 16, 2017. arctogaia.com/public/eng/serpent.html.

Dunlop, John B. "Aleksandr Dugin's Foundations of Geopolitics." *Demokratizatsiya* 12, no. 1 (January 31, 2004).

————. "Aleksandr Dugin's 'Neo-Eurasian' Textbook and Dmitrii Trenin's Ambivalent Response." *Harvard Ukrainian Studies* XXV, no. 1/2 (2001): 91-127.

————. "Russia's New – and Frightening – 'Ism'." *Hoover Digest*, no. 3 (July 30, 2004). Accessed March 3, 2015. hoover.org/research/russias-new-and-frightening-ism.

Dunn, David J. "Symphonia in the Secular: An Ecclesiology for the Narthex." PhD diss., Vanderbilt University, 2011.

During, Simon. "Editor's Introduction." Introduction to *The Cultural Studies Reader*, 1-29. London: Routledge, 1993.

Durkheim, Émile. *The Division of Labour in Society*. Translated by George Simpson. New York: Free Press, 1893.

————. *Suicide*. New York: Free Press, 1951.

Eagleton, Terry. *Literary Theory: An Introduction*. Oxford: Basil Blackwell, 1983.

Eco, Umberto. "A Theory of Conspiracies." *Live Mint*, October 6, 2014. Accessed December 9, 2015,

livemint.com/Opinion/5lhODHqqZHUCqwOZcw2liL/Umb
erto-Eco--A-theory-of-conspiracies.html?facet=print.

Eliade, Mircea. *Images and Symbols: Studies in Religious Symbolism*. Translated by Philip Mairet. Princeton, NJ: Princeton University Press, 1991.

_____. *The Myth of the Eternal Return, or, Cosmos and History*. Princeton: Princeton University Press, 1954.

_____. *The Sacred and the Profane: The Nature of Religion*. New York: Harcourt, Brace and World, 1959.

Eliot, Thomas Stearns. "Tradition and the Individual Talent." In *The Sacred Wood*. New York: Alfred A. Knopf, 1921.

Emerson, Michael O., and David Hartman. "The Rise of Religious Fundamentalism." *Annual Review of Sociology* 32, no. 1 (August 11, 2006): 127-44.

Epstein, Mikhail. *The Russian Philosophy of National Spirit: Conservatism and Traditionalism*. Report. Washington: National Council for Soviet and East European Research, 1994.

Erasmus. "Russian Anti-Liberals Love Donald Trump but It May Not Be Entirely Mutual." Web log. *The Economist* (blog). November 20, 2016. economist.com/blogs/erasmus/2016/11/america-russia-and-new-right.

Evola, Julius. *The Path of Cinnabar: An Intellectual Autobiography*. Translated by Sergio Knipe. Edited by John B. Morgan. London: Arktos Media, 2010.

_____. "René Guénon & Integral Traditionalism." *Counter Currents Publishing*. June 7, 2016. counter-currents.com/2016/06/rene-guenon-and-integral-traditionalism/.

_____. *Revolt Against the Modern World*. Translated by Guido Stucco. Rochester, VT.: Inner Traditions International, 1995.

Fabbri, Renaud. "Introduction to the Perennialist School."
    Religio Perennis. Accessed June 13, 2017.
    religioperennis.org/documents/Fabbri/Perennialism.pdf.

Faber, Richard. "The Rejection of Political Theology: A Critique
    of Hans Blumenberg." *Telos* 1987, no. 72 (Summer 1987):
    173-86.

Farber, Daniel A. "The Originalism Debate: A Guide for the
    Perplexed." *Ohio State Law Journal* 49, no. 4 (1989):
    1085–1106.

Fish, Stanley. *Is There a Text in This Class?* Cambridge, MA:
    Harvard University Press, 1982.

Fishbane, Michael A. *Sacred Attunement: a Jewish Theology*.
    Chicago: University of Chicago Press, 2008.

Flint, Colin. *An Introduction to Geopolitics*. 2nd ed. New York:
    Routledge, 2011.

Foucault, Michel. *The History of Sexuality*. Vancouver: Crane
    Library at the University of British Columbia, 2009.

Freud, Sigmund. "Lecture XXXI, The Anatomy of the Mental
    Personality." In *New Introductory Lectures on
    Psychoanalysis*. London: Hogarth Press, 1933.

Fukuyama, Francis. *The End of History and the Last Man*.
    London: Hamish Hamilton, 1992.

_____. "The End of History?" *National Interest*, Summer
    1989, 1-18.

Garver, Rob. "Putin Isn't Reviving the USSR, He's Creating a
    Fascist State." *The Fiscal Times*. May 26, 2015.
    thefiscaltimes.com/2015/05/26/Putin-Isn-t-Reviving-USSR-
    He-s-Creating-Fascist-State.

Gasset, José Ortega Y. *The Revolt of the Masses*. New York:
    W.W. Norton, 1932.

Gessen, Masha. "The Weird and Instructive Story of Eduard
    Limonov.'" Review of *Limonov: The Outrageous
    Adventures of the Radical, Soviet Poet Who Became a Bum
    in New York, a Sensation in France, and a Political*

Antihero in Russia, by Emmanuel Carrère. *New York Review of Books,* May 15, 2015. nybooks.com/articles/2015/05/21/weird-and-instructive-story-eduard-limonov/.

Glaser, B.G. "Retreading research materials: The use of secondary analysis by the independent researcher." *The American Behavioral Scientist* 6 no.10. 1963: 11-14.

Goble, Paul. "Window on Eurasia: Aleksandr Dugin – a 'Zhirinovsky for the Intellectuals.'" *WINDOWONEURASIA* (blog), May 13, 2008. windowoneurasia.blogspot.com/2008/05/window-on-eurasia-aleksandr-dugin.html.

Gontier, Thierry. "Has Blumenberg: The Legitimacy of the Modern Age." *Voegelinview.* November 12, 2011. Accessed June 23, 2016. voegelinview.com/modernity-and-secularization-pt-1/.

Goto-Jones, Christopher. "If Not a Clash Then What? Huntington, Nishida Kitarō, and the Politics of Civilizations." *International Relations of the Asia Pacific* 2 (2002): 223-43.

_____. "Transcending Boundaries: Nishida Kitaro K'ang Yu-Wei, and the Politics of Unity." *Modern Asian Studies* 39, no. 4 (October 2005): 793-816.

Gould, Stephen Jay. *Full-House.* New York: Three Rivers Press, 1997.

Griffin, Roger. *A Fascist Century.* Edited by Matthew Feldman. New York: Palgrave Macmillan, 2008.

_____. *The Nature of Fascism.* London: Pinter, 1991.

_____, and Matthew Feldman. *Fascism: Critical Concepts.* Vol. 1. London: Routledge, 2004.

Grondin, Jean. *Introduction to Philosophical Hermeneutics.* New Haven, CT: Yale University Press, 1994.

Guénon, René. *The Crisis of the Modern World*. Translated by Marco Pallis, Arthur Osborne, and Richard C. Nicholson. Hillsdale, NY: Sophia Perennis, 2001.

Guénon, René. *East and West*. Translated by Martin Lings. Gent: Sophia Perennis, 2001.

_____. *The Reign of Quantity and the Signs of the times*. Translated by Walter James. Hillsdale, NY: Sophia Perennis, 2004.

_____. "What Is Meant by Tradition?" In *The Essential René Guénon: Metaphysics, Tradition, and the Crisis of Modernity*, edited by John Herlihy, 93-96. Bloomington, IN: World Wisdom, 2009.

Hakim, Catherine. *Secondary Analysis in Social Research a Guide to Data Sources and Methods with Examples*. London: G. Allen and Unwin, 1982.

Hall, Stuart. "Encoding and Decoding." In *The Cultural Studies Reader*, edited by Simon During, 90-103. London: Routledge, 1993.

Hanegraaff, Wouter J. *Esotericism and the Academy: Rejected Knowledge in Western Culture*. Cambridge: Cambridge University Press, 2013.

_____. "Will-Erich Peuckert and the Light of Nature." In *Esotericism, Religion, and Nature*, edited by Arthur Versluis, et al. East Lancing: North American Academic Press, 2009.

Hannan, Daniel. *Inventing Freedom: How the English-speaking Peoples Made the Modern World*. New York: Broadside Books, 2014.

Hanson, Richard. "A Dialogical Theism: Francis X. Clooney's Comparative Theology as a Resource for Interreligious Models of Ultimate Reality." *Journal of Inter-Religious Studies* 10, no. 10 (September 15, 2012): 61–71.

Harris, Ian. "Edmund Burke." *The Stanford Encyclopedia of Philosophy*. Edited by Edward N. Zalta. Spring 2012. plato.stanford.edu/archives/spr2012/entries/burke/.

Hassan, Ihab. "Fundamentalism and Literature." *Georgia Review*, Spring, 62, no. 1 (2008): 16-29.

Hartley, John. *Communication, Cultural and Media Studies: The Key Concepts.* 3rd ed. London: Routledge, 2002.

Havel, Václav. Address, World Economic Forum, Davos, Graubünden, February 4, 1992. vaclavhavel.cz/showtrans.php?cat=projevy&val=265_aj_pr ojevy.html&typ=HTML.

Heidegger, Martin. *Off the Beaten Path.* Edited by Julian Young and Kenneth Hayes. Translated by Julian Young and Kenneth Hayes. Cambridge: Cambridge University Press, 2002.

Hladký, Vojtěch. "From Byzantium to Italy: 'Ancient Wisdom' in Plethon and Cusanus." Edited by Paul Richard Blum. In *Georgios Gemistos Plethon: The Byzantine and the Latin Renaissance*, edited by Jozef Matula, 273-92. Olomouc: Palacke University, 2014.

Hodge, Charles. *Systematic Theology.* 1. Vol. 1. Grand Rapids, MI: Eerdmans, 1952.

_____. *Systematic Theology.* 1. Vol. 3. Grand Rapids, MI: Eerdmans, 1952.

Hoffer, Eric. *The Ordeal of Change.* New York: Harper & Row, 1967.

_____. *The Passionate State of Mind.* Cutchogue, NY: Buccaneer Books, 1996.

_____. *The True Believer: Thoughts on the Nature of Mass Movements.* New York: Harper and Row, 1951.

Hofstadter, Richard. "The Paranoid Style in American Politics." *Harpers*, November 1964, 77-86.

Horbyk, Roman. "The Right Model for the Right Europeans." *The Ukrainian Week*, February 12, 2014. ukrainianweek.com/World/101730.

Hosking, Geoffrey. "How a Theory of Russian History That Rejects the West Came to Inspire Putin's Kremlin." Review of *Black Wind, White Snow: The Rise of Russia's New Nationalism,* by Charles Clover. *Financial Times,* April 22, 2016.

Hughes, Wayne P. *Fleet Tactics and Coastal Combat.* Annapolis, Md: Naval Institute Press, 2000.

Hui-Chih Yu. "A Cross-Cultural Analysis of Symbolic Meanings of Color." *Chang Gung Journal of Humanities and Social Sciences* 7, no. 1 (April 2014): 49-74.

Huntington, Samuel P. "The Clash of Civilizations?" *Foreign Affairs* 72, no. 3 (Summer 1993): 22-49.

———. *The Clash of Civilizations and the Remaking of World Order.* New York: Simon and Schuster, 1996.

Huxley, Aldous. *The Perennial Philosophy.* London: Chatto & Windus, 1947.

Ifergan, Pini. "Cutting to the Chase: Carl Schmitt and Hans Blumenberg on Political Theology and Secularization." *New German Critique,* 111th ser., 37, no. 3 (Fall 2010): 149-71.

Inge, John. *A Christian Theology of Place.* Ashgate Publishing, 2017.

Ingram, Alan. "Alexander Dugin: Geopolitics and Neo-fascism in Post-Soviet Russia." *Political Geography* 20, no. 8 (2001): 1029-051.

James, Paul. "Emotional Ambivalence across Times and Spaces: Mapping Petrarch's Intersecting Worlds." *Exemplaria* 26, no. 1 (2014): 81-104.

Jauss, Hans Robert. *Towards an Aesthetic of Reception.* Translated by Timothy Bahti. Minneapolis: University of Minnesota Press, 1982.

Jeanrond, Werner G. *Theological Hermeneutics: Development and Significance.* New York: Crossroad, 1991.

Johnston, Melissa P. "Secondary Data Analysis: A Method of Which the Time Has Come." *Qualitative and Quantitative Methods in Libraries,* 3, no. 3 (September 2014): 619-626.

Kalberg, Stephen. "Max Weber's Types of Rationality: Cornerstones for the Analysis of Rationalization Processes in History." *American Journal of Sociology* 85, no. 5 (1980): 1145-179.

Kappeler, Andreas. *The Russian Empire: A Multi-ethnic History.* Translated by Alfred Clayton. London & New York: Routledge, 2013.

"Karl Barth's Letters 1961–1968. Edited by J. Fangmeier and H. Stoevesandt. Translated and Edited by G. W. Bromiley. Edinburgh, T. and T. Clark, and Grand Rapids, Eerdmans, 1981.

Kazami, Yudulla. "Reclaiming Tradition: An Essay on the Condition of the Possibility of Islamic Knowledge." *American Journal of Islamic Social Sciences* 15, no. 2 (1998): 97–108.

"Kennan and Containment, 1947." The U.S. State Department Office of the Historian. Accessed June 11, 2017. history.state.gov/milestones/1945-1952/kennan.

Kirkpatrick, Bill. "Play, Power, and Policy: Putting John Fiske Back into Media Policy Studies." *Fiske Matters: A Conference on John Fiske's Continuing Legacy for Cultural Studies.* Address presented at the Fiske Matters: A Conference on John Fiske's Continuing Legacy for Cultural Studies, University of Wisconsin – Madison, June 11, 2010.

Kojève, Alexandre. *Introduction to the Reading of Hegel: Lectures on the Phenomenology of the Spirit.* New York: Basic Books, 1969.

Kollmann, Nancy Shields. *The Russian Empire 1450-1801.* Oxford: Oxford University Press, 2017.

Kraye, Jill. "The Philosophy of the Italian Renaissance." Essay. In *Routledge History of Philosophy*, edited by G. H. R. Parkinson, 15-64. Vol. IV. London: Routledge, 1993.

Lakhani, M. Ali. "Understanding 'Tradition.'" Essay. In *The Timeless Relevance of Traditional Wisdom*, 3–4. Bloomington, IN: World Wisdom, 2010.

Laruelle, Marlène. *Aleksadr Dugin: A Russian Version of the European Radical Right?* Kennan Institute Occasional Papers Series #294. Washington, DC: Woodrow Wilson International Center for Scholars, 2006.

_____. "The Orient in Russian Thought at the Turn of the Century." In *Russia between East and West Scholarly Debates on Eurasianism*, edited by Dmitry Shlapentokh, 9-36. Boston: Brill, 2007.

_____. *Russian Eurasianism: An Ideology of Empire.* Washington, DC: Woodrow Wilson Center Press, 2008.

_____. "Scared of Putin's Shadow." *Foreign Affairs Snapshot*, March 25, 2015. foreignaffairs.com/articles/russian-federation/2015-03-25/scared-putins-shadow.

Laqueur, Walter. *Black Hundred: The Rise of the Extreme Right in Russia.* New York: Harper Collins, 1993.

Legenhausen, Muhammad. "Why I Am Not a Traditionalist." *Religioscope.* March 31, 2002. religioscope.com/pdf/esotrad/legenhausen.pdf.

Leithart, Peter J. "Fourth Political Theory." *First Things.* June 17, 2014. firstthings.com/blogs/leithart/2014/06/fourth-political-theory.

Lilla, Mark. *The Stillborn God: Religion, Politics, and the Modern West.* New York: Vintage Books, 2008.

Liverant, Yigal. "The Prophet of the New Russian Empire." *Azure* 35, no. Winter 2009. Accessed June 11, 2017. azure.org.il/article.php?id=483.

Lossky, Vladimir. "Theology and Mysticism in the Tradition of the Eastern Church." In *The Mystical Theology of the Eastern Church*, 7-22. Crestwood, NY: St. Vladimir's Seminary Press, 1976.

Lukacs, John. *At the End of an Age.* New Haven, CT: Yale University Press, 2003.

Lundquist, John. "The Common Temple Ideology of the Ancient Near East." In *The Temple in Antiquity: Ancient Records and Modern Perspectives*, edited by Truman G. Madsen, 53-76. Provo, UT: Religious Studies Center, Brigham Young University, 1984.

Lundquist, John M. "What Is a Temple? A Preliminary Typology." Essay. In *Temples of the Ancient World*, edited by Donald W. Parry, 83–117. Salt Lake City: Deseret Book Company, 1994.

Luven, Yvonne. *Scoping Study "Engaging Religious Fundamentalisms."* Dublin: Irish School of Ecumenics, Trinity College Dublin, 2008.

Mackinder, Halford J. *Democratic Ideals and Reality: A Study in the Politics of Reconstruction*. Washington, DC: National Defense University Press, 1996.

————. "The Geographical Pivot of History." *The Geographical Journal* 23, no. 4 (1904): 421-37.

Macquarrie, John. *God-Talk: An Examination of the Language and Logic of Theology*. London: SCM Press, 1978.

————. *Martin Heidegger*. Richmond: John Knox Press, 1968.

Malić, Branko. "Against the Gnostics: Anti-Traditional and Anti-Christian Core of Alexander Dugin's 4th Political Theory." Kali Tribune. May 9, 2015. Accessed August 3, 2015. en.kalitribune.com/against-the-gnostics-anti-traditional-and-anti-christian-core-of-alexander-dugins-4th-political-theory/.

————. "The Invisible Empire: Introduction to Alexandr Dugin's 'Foundations of Geopolitics,' Part 1." Kali Tribune, May 7, 2017. en.kalitribune.com/the-invisible-empire-introduction-to-alexander-dugins-foundations-of-geopolitics-pt-1/.

————. "The Invisible Empire: Introduction to Alexandr Dugin's 'Foundations of Geopolitics,' Part 2." Kali Tribune, July 1, 2017. en.kalitribune.com/the-invisible-empire-

introduction-to-alexander-dugins-foundations-of-
geopolitics-pt-2/.

_____. "Leviathan and Behemoth – Alexander Dugin's
Geopolitical Conspirology." Kali Tribune. December 12,
2014. en.kalitribune.com/leviathan-and-behemoth-
geopolitical-conspirology-of-alexander-dugin/.

Mantzavinos, C. "Hermeneutics." *Stanford Encyclopedia of
Philosophy.* Edited by Edward N. Zalta. June 22, 2016.
plato.stanford.edu/archives/win2016/entries/hermeneutics/.

Marsden, George M. *Reforming Fundamentalism.* Grand Rapids,
MI: Eerdmans, 1987.

Marsh, Rosalind. "The 'New Political Novel' by Right-Wing
Writers in Post-Soviet Russia." *Forum Für Osteuropäische
Ideen -Und Zeitgeschichte* 14, no. 2 (2010): 159–87.

Martin, David. *On Secularization: towards a Revised General
Theory.* Burlington, VT: Ashgate Publishing, 2005.

Martin, Julie. "Audiences and Reception Theory." *Sociology
Made Simple*, 2007. sociologymadesimple.com/papers/.

Marty, Martin E. "Too Bad We're So Relevant: The
Fundamentalism Project Projected." *Bulletin of the
American Academy of Arts and Sciences* 49, no. 6 (March
1996): 22-38.

McCormick, John P. *Carl Schmitt's Critique of Liberalism:
Against Politics as Technology.* Cambridge: Cambridge
University Press, 1997.

McCune, Rolland D. "The Self-Identity of Fundamentalism."
Detroit Baptist Seminary Journal, Spring, 1, no. 1 (1996):
9-34.

McGrath, Alister. *Christian Theology.* Oxford: Blackwell
Publishing, 2007.

Middleton, Gordon R. "Religion in Russian Geo-Political
Strategy." *Providence*, no. 9 (2017): 64–71.

Mises, Ludwig Von. *Liberalism: The Classical Tradition.* Translated by Ralph Raico. 3rd ed. San Francisco: Cobden Press, 2002.

Mitrofanova, Anastasia V. *The Politicization of Russian Orthodoxy: Actors and Ideas.* Stuttgart: Ibidem, 2005.

Mladineo, Stephen. "Introduction." Introduction to *Democratic Ideals and Reality: A Study in the Politics of Reconstruction*, by Halford Mackinder, edited by Stephen Mladineo. xvii-xii. Washington, DC: National Defense University Press, 1996.

Morgan, John B. "A Note From the Editor." In *The Fourth Political Theory*, edited by John B. Morgan, translated by Michael Millerman and Mark Sleboda, by Alexander Dugin, 7-8. London: Arktos, 2012.

Morozova, Natalia. "The Politics of Russian Post-Soviet Identity: Geopolitics, Eurasianism, and Beyond." PhD Diss., Central European University, 2011.

Mosbey, John Cody. "Churchill Was Right and Still Is." *Modern Diplomacy*, December 3, 2015. moderndiplomacy.eu/2015/12/03/churchill-was-right-about-russia-and-still-is/.

_____. "Putin, Dugin, and the Coming Wild Ride on Leviathan." *Modern Diplomacy*. March 11, 2016. moderndiplomacy.eu/index.php?option=com_k2&view=item&id=1275:putin-dugin-and-the-coming-wild-ride-on-leviathan&Itemid=480.

Moss, Vladimir. "Alexander Dugin and the Meaning of Russian History." *Vladimir Moss - Orthodox Christian Author.* Accessed April 19, 2014. orthodoxchristianbooks.com/.

Munteanu, Cristinel. "Aberrant Decoding and Its Linguistic Expression (An Attempt to Restore the Original Concept)." *Procedia - Social and Behavioral Sciences* 63 (2012): 229-41.

Nasr, Seyyed Hossein. *Knowledge and the Sacred.* Albany, NY: State University of New York Press, 1989.

Neuhaus, Richard John. "Politics and Religion: 'the Great Separation." *First Things*. January 2008

New, David S. *Christian Fundamentalism in America: A Cultural History*. Jefferson, NC: McFarland, 2012.

Newman, Saul. *Political Theology: A Critical Introduction*. Cambridge, UK: Polity, 2019.

Nietzsche, Friedrich. "Book IV: Discipline and Breeding." In *The Will to Power*, edited by W. Kaufmann, translated by W. W. Kaufmann and R. J. Hollingdale, 457-550. New York: Random House, 1968.

_____. *The Gay Science*. Edited by Walter Kaufmann. New York: Vintage, 1974.

_____. "Twilight of the Idols." Edited by Oscar Levy. In *Friedrich Nietzsche, Complete Works*. Vol. 16. New York: Russell & Russell, 1964.

Novak, David. "'God-Talk:' Review of Sacred Attunement: A Jewish Theology." *First Things,* no. 2 (February 2009): 4. firstthings.com/article/2009/02/004-god-talk.

Orwell, George. "What Is Fascism?" *Tribune* (London), March 24, 1944.

O'Sullivan, John. "Annexation." *The United States Magazine and Democratic Review* 17, no. 1 (July/August 1845): 5-10. pdcrodas.webs.ull.es/anglo/OSullivanAnnexation.pdf.

O'Sullivan, Tim, John Hartley, Danny Saunders, Martin Montgomery, and John Fiske. *Key Concepts in Communication and Cultural Studies*. 2nd ed. London: Routledge, 1994.

Parchizadeh, Reza. "The Historic Roots of Russian Expansionism in the Middle East." *American Thinker*. October 18, 2015. americanthinker.com/articles/2015/10/the_historic_roots_of _russian_expansionism_in_the_middle_east.html.

Parker, Benjamin. "Putin's Chosen People: Theories of Russian Jewish Policy, 2000-2017." Master's Thesis. University of Pennsylvania, 2017.

Parland, Thomas. *The Extreme Nationalist Threat in Russia: The Growing Influence of Western Rightist Ideas*. New York: RoutledgeCurzon, 2005.

Parsons, Talcott. *Talcott Parsons: Critical Assessments*. Edited by Peter Hamilton. London: Routledge, 1992.

Partridge, Christopher H. *New Religions: A Guide: New Religious Movements, Sects, and Alternative Spiritualities*. New York: Oxford University Press, 2004.

Pelikan, Jaroslav. *The Vindication of Tradition*. New Haven: Yale University Press, 1984.

Petrarch. "On His Own Ignorance and That of Many Others." Translated by Hans Nachod. In *The Renaissance Philosophy of Man. Edited by E. Cassirer, Paul Oskar Kristeller, John Herman Randall, in Collaboration with Hans Nachod, Etc.*, edited by Ernst Cassirer, Paul Oskar Kristeller, and John Herman Randall, 49-133. Chicago: University of Chicago Press, 1948.

Philpott, Daniel. "Political Theology and Liberal Democracy." Review of *The Stillborn God*, by Mark Lilla. *The Immanent Frame* (January 23, 2008). tif.ssrc.org/2008/01/23/political-theology-liberal-democracy/.

Plath, Sylvia. *Eye Rhymes*. Edited by Kathleen Conners and Sally Bayley. New York: Oxford University Press, 2007.

Pocock, J. G. A. "Present at the Creation: With Laslett to the Lost Worlds." *International Journal of Public Affairs* 2 (2006): 7-17.

Poe, Marshall. *Moscow, The Third Rome*. Report. Washington: National Council for Soviet and East European Research, 1997.

Popper, Karl. "The Autonomy of Sociology." In *Mill, a Collection of Critical Essays*, edited by J. B. Schneewind, 426-442. London: Palgrave Macmillian, 1968.

_____. *The Open Society and Its Enemies.* 5th ed. Princeton, NJ: Princeton University Press, 1966.

Rae, Gavin. "The Theology of Carl Schmitt's Political Theology." *Political Theology* 17, no. 6 (July 2015): 555-72.

Rashidvash, Vahid. "History of Iran: The Circumstances of Signing Golestan and Turkmanchy Treaties and Its Contents." *International Review of Social Sciences and Humanities* 3, no. 1 (March 2, 2012): 246–61.

Rawls, John. *Political Liberalism.* New York: Columbia Univ. Press, 1996.

Reardon, Bernard M. G. *Liberalism and Tradition: Aspects of Catholic Thought in Nineteenth-Century France.* Cambridge: Cambridge University Press, 2010.

Reedy, W. Jay. "The Historical Imaginary of Social Science in Post-Revolutionary France: Bonald, Saint-Simon, Comte." *History of the Human Sciences* 7, no. 1 (February 01, 1994): 1-26.

Rice-Cameron, John. "Eurasianism Is the New Fascism: Understanding and Confronting Russia." Sanford Politics. Stanford University, February 2, 2017. stanfordpolitics.org/2017/02/02/eurasianism-new-fascism/.

Riedl, Matthias. "Apocalyptic Politics – On the Permanence and Transformations of a Symbolic Complex." Paper Delivered to The John Hope Franklin Humanities Institute of Politics and Religion: A Humanities Futures Cross-Departmental Seminar, Duke University. In Proceedings of Politics and Religion: A Humanities Futures Cross-Departmental Seminar, The Franklin Humanities Institute, December 3, 2014. humanitiesfutures.org/papers/apocalyptic-politics-on-the-permanence-and-transformations-of-a-symbolic-complex/.

Rossman, Vadim. "Anti-Semitism in Eurasian Historiography: The Case of Lev Gumilev." Edited by Dmitry Shlapentokh. In *Russia between East and West Scholarly Debates on Eurasianism*, 121-88. Boston: Brill, 2007.

345

_____. *Russian Intellectual Antisemitism in the Post-Communist Era*. Lincoln, NE: University of Nebraska Press, 2002.

Rushbrook, Jonathan. "Against the Thallassocracy: Fascism and Traditionalism in Alexander Dugin's Neo-Eurasianist Philosophy." Master's thesis. University of Tartu, 2015.

Russo, Charles J. "Does the Free Exercise of Religion Have a Future in the Marketplace of Public Education in the United States?" Essay. In *International Perspectives on Education, Religion and Law*, ed. Charles J. Russo, 1–13. New York: Routledge, 2014.

Ryrie, Charles C. *Basic Theology*. Wheaton, IL: Victor Books, 1986.

Sayeed, Khalid Bin. *Western Dominance and Political Islam: Challenge and Response*. Albany, NY: State University of New York Press, 1995.

Savitskii, Petr. *Exodus to the East: Forebodings and Events: An Affirmation of the Eurasians*. Translated by Ilya Vinkovetsky. Idyllwild, CA: Schlacks, 1996.

Sawyer, John F. A. "The Old Testament and Its Readers." *Theology in Scotland* VII, no. 1 (2005): 67–79.

_____. "The Role of Reception Theory, Reader-Response Criticism And/or Impact History in the Study of the Bible: Definition and Evaluation." Address, EKK Biennial Meeting, Germany, March 21-3, 2004.

_____. "The Role of Reception Theory, Reader-Response Criticism And/or Impact History in the Study of the Bible: Definition and Evaluation." Address, Society of Biblical Literature Meeting, San Antonio, 2004.

Sazonov, Vladimir. "Russian Information Warfare against the Ukrainian State and Defense Forces." Rep. *Russian Information Warfare against the Ukrainian State and Defense Forces*. April-December. Riga: NATO Strategic Communications Center for Excellence, 2014.

Schmitt, Carl. *Dictatorship*. Oxford: Blackwell, 2010.

_____. *The Nomos of the Earth in the International Law of the Jus Publicum Europaeum*. Translated by G. L. Ulmen. New York: Telos, 2006.

_____. "Political Theology." In *Studies in Contemporary German Social Thought*, edited by Thomas McCarthy, translated by George Schwab, 5-66. Cambridge, Massachusetts: MIT Press, 1985.

Schuon, Frithjof. *In the Tracks of Buddhism*. London: Allen & Unwin, 1968.

_____. *Understanding Islam*. London: Allen & Unwin, 1963.

Schwab, George. "Introduction." In *Political Theology*, by Carl Schmitt, translated by George Schwab, x-xxvi. Cambridge, Massachusetts: MIT Press, 1985.

Sedgwick, Mark J. *Against the Modern World: Traditionalism and the Secret Intellectual History of the Twentieth Century*. New York: Oxford University Press, 2004.

_____. "Traditionalism and Art - and Perhaps More than Art." *Traditionalists*. June 18, 2010. traditionalistblog.blogspot.ie/2010/06/traditionalism-and-art-and-perhaps-more.html.

Shekhovtsov, Anton. "Aleksandr Dugin's Neo-Eurasianism: The New Right à La Russe." *Religion Compas* 3, no. 4 (2009): 697-716.

_____, and Andreas Umland. "Is Aleksandr Dugin a Traditionalist? 'Neo-Eurasianism' and Perennial Philosophy." *The Russian Review* 68, no. 4 (2009): 662-78.

Sheldrake, Philip. *Spaces for the Sacred: Place, Memory, and Identity*. Baltimore: Johns Hopkins University Press, 2001.

Shenfield, Stephen D. *Russian Fascism: Traditions, Tendencies, Movements*. Armonk, NY: M.E. Sharpe, 2001.

Shils, Edward Albert. *The Constitution of Society*. Chicago: University of Chicago Press, 1982.

_____. "Tradition, Ecology, and Institution in the History of Sociology." *Daedalus*, The Making of Modern Science: Biographical Studies, 99, no. 4 (Fall 1970): 760-825.

Shiraev, Eric. *Russian Government and Politics, 2nd Ed.* London: Palgrave MacMillan, 2013.

Shklar, Judith N. "The Liberalism of Fear." In *Political Thought and Political Thinkers*, edited by Stanley Hoffmann, 3-20. Chicago: University of Chicago Press, 1998.

Shlapentokh, Dmitry. "Introduction: Eurasianism and Soviet/Post-Soviet Studies." In *Russia between East and West Scholarly Debates on Eurasianism*, edited by Dmitry Shlapentokh, 1-7. Boston: Brill, 2007.

_____. *Russian Elite Image of Iran: From the Late Soviet Era to the Present*. Carlisle: Strategic Studies Institute, Army War College, 2009. ssi.armywarcollege.edu/pdffiles/PUB936.pdf.

Shnirelman, Victor. "Alexander Dugin: Between Eschatology, Esotericism, and Conspiracy Theory." Essay. In *Handbook of Conspiracy Theory and Contemporary Religion*, edited by Asbjørn Dyrendal, David G. Robertson, and Egil Asprem, 443–60. Leiden: Brill, 2018.

Sigalet, Geoffrey. "Eric Voegelin: Political Theology in a New Key." *Voegelinview*, April 28, 2014. voegelinview.com/political-theology-new-key.

Simmins, Geoffrey. *Sacred Spaces and Sacred Places*. Saarbrücken: VDM Verlag, 2009.

Skinner, Quentin. "Meaning and Understanding in the History of Ideas." *History and Theory* 8, no. 1 (1969): 3-53.

Soral, Alain, Alexander Dugin, and Sergio Knipe. "Why We Should Read Alexander Dugin." Foreword, translated by Alain Soral. In *The Fourth Political Theory*, edited by John B. Morgan, translated by Michael Millerman and Mark Selboda, 9–10. London: Arktos Media, 2012.

Spencer, Herbert. *The Man Versus the State*. Indianapolis: Liberty Fund, 1969.

Sproul, R. C. *Everyone's a Theologian: An Introduction to Systematic Theology*. Orlando, FL: Reformation Trust, 2014.

_____. *Foundations: An Overview of Systematic Theology*. Stanford, FL: Ligonier Ministries, 1999.

Spykman, Nicholas John. *The Geography of the Peace*. Edited by Helen R. Nicholl. Hamden, CT: Archon Books, 1969.

Stackhouse, John G. "Putting God in God's Place: Does Theology Belong in the University?" *Studies in Religion/Sciences Religieuses* 45, no. 3 (2016): 377–96.

Stoner, James R., Jr., Stanley Hauerwas, Paul J. Griffiths, and David B. Hart. "Theology as Knowledge: A Symposium." *First Things*, no. May (2006): 21-27. Accessed January 14, 2014. firstthings.com/article/2006/05/theology-as-knowledge.

Thackara, W.T. S. "The Perennial Philosophy." *Sunrise Magazine*, April/May 1984.

The Future of World Religions: Population Growth Projections, 2010 - 2050. Report. April 2, 2015. Pew Research Center, 2015.

Tolstoy, Audrey, and Edmund McCaffray. "Mind Games: Alexander Dugin and Russia's War of Ideas." *World Affairs* 177, no. 6 (2015): 25-30.

Tönnies, Ferdinand. *Tönnies: Community and Civil Society*. Edited by Jose Harris. Translated by Jose Harris and Margaret Hollis. Cambridge: Cambridge University Press, 2001.

Toynbee, Arnold. *Turkey: A past and a Future*. Middletown, De: CreateSpace Independent Publishing Platform, 2015.

Tremblay, Rémi. "An Interview with Alexander Dugin: Against Universalism." *Affirmative Right*, May 21, 2015. affirmativeright.blogspot.com/2015/05/an-interview-with-alexander-dugin.html.

_____. "Thoughts of Dugin's 'Eurasian Mission.'"
Alternative Right. May 7, 2015. alternative-
right.blogspot.com/2015/05/thoughts-on-dugins-eurasian-
mission_7.html.

Trubetzkoy, Nikolai. "Europe and Mankind." In *The Legacy of
Genghis Khan and Other Essays on Russia's Identity*, edited
by A. Liberman. Ann Arbor: Michigan Slavic Publications,
1991.

_____. "Pan-Eurasian Nationalism." In *The Legacy of
Genghis Khan and Other Essays on Russia's Identity*, edited
by A. Liberman. Ann Arbor: Michigan Slavic Publications,
1991.

_____. *Principles of Phonology*. Berkeley, CA: University of
California Press, 1969.

_____. "The Russian Problem." In *The Legacy of Genghis
Khan and Other Essays on Russia's Identity*, edited by A.
Liberman. Ann Arbor: Michigan Slavic Publications, 1991.

Tsygankov, Andrei P. "Mastering Space in Eurasia: Russia's
Geopolitical Thinking after the Soviet Break-up."
Communist and Post-Communist Studies 36, no. 1 (2003):
101-27.

Umland, Andreas. "Aleksandr Dugin's Transformation from a
Lunatic Fringe Figure into a Mainstream Political Publicist,
1980 – 1998: A Case Study in the Rise of Late and Post-
Soviet Russian Fascism." *Journal of Eurasian Studies* 1, no.
2 (May 21, 2010): 144-52. Accessed April 18, 2015.

_____. "Fascist Tendencies in Russian Higher Education:
The Rise of Aleksandr Dugin and the Faculty of Sociology
of Moscow State University." *Demokratizatsiya: The
Journal of Post-Soviet Democratization* 1, no. Spring
(2011): 1-5.

_____. "Post-Soviet 'Uncivil Society' and the Rise of
Aleksandr Dugin a Case Study of the Extraparliamentary
Radical Right in Contemporary Russia." PhD diss.,
University of Cambridge, 2007.

_____. "Zhirinovsky's "Last Thrust to the South" and the Definition of Fascism." *Russian Politics and Law* 46, no. 4 (July/August 2008): 31-46.

Valodia, Deon. "Glossary of Terms Used by Frithjof Schuon." *Sophia Perennis*. Accessed June 15, 2017. sophia-perennis.com/Glossary%20Schuon%20Revised.pdf.

Vandervelde, George. "The Grammar of Grace: Karl Rahner as a Watershed in Contemporary Theology." *Theological Studies* 49, no. 3 (September 1, 1988): 445-59.

Versluis, Arthur. "Carl Schmitt, Modernity, and the Secret Roads Inward." *Telos*, no. 148 (Fall 2009): 28-38.

Voegelin, Eric. *The New Science of Politics*. Chicago: University of Chicago Press, 1987.

_____. "The Political Religions." In *Modernity Without Restraint, The Collected Works of Eric Voegelin*. 19-73. Columbia: University of Missouri Press, 2000.

Weber, Max. "Politics as a Vocation." In *Essays in Sociology*, edited by Hans H. Gerth and C. Wright Mills, translated by Hans H. Gerth and C. Wright Mills, 77-128. New York: Oxford University Press, 1946.

_____. "Science as a Vocation." In *Essays in Sociology*, edited by Hans H. Gerth and C. Wright Mills, translated by Hans H. Gerth and C. Wright Mills, 129-56. New York: Oxford University Press, 1946.

Weintraub, Jeff. *Handout #7: Reading Edmund Burke: Edmund Burke – Community, Authority, Tradition, and Conservatism*. 2012. Lecture Notes for PPE 475-302, University of Pennsylvania, Philadelphia. Accessed June 4, 2015. academia.edu/3884831/Edmund_Burke_Community_authority_tradition_and_conservatism.

Weir, Fred. "Moscow's Moves in Georgia Track a Script by Rightwing Prophet." *The Christian Science Monitor* (Boston), September 20, 2008.

Wiederkehr, Stephan. "Eurasianism as a Reaction to Pan-Turkism." In *Russia between East and West Scholarly Debates on Eurasianism*, edited by Dmitrij Shlapentokh, 39-57. Boston: Brill, 2007.

Wike, Richard, Katie Simmons, Bruce Stokes, and Janell Fedderolf. *Globally, Broad Support for Representative and Direct Democracy*. Report. Pew Research Center, 2017.

Willis, Cecil L. "Durkheim's Concept of Anomie: Some Observations." *Sociological Inquiry* 52, no. 2 (1982): 106-13.

Wood, Andrew. "Cold War II?" *The American Interest*, July 18, 2018. the-american-interest.com/2018/07/18/cold-war-ii/.

Wyllie, Robert. "Against Schmitt's Political Theology, Prometheus or Pandora? Hans Blumenberg and Walter Benjamin as Political Theologians." *Telos Scope*. July 30, 2013. Accessed June 20, 2016. telospress.com/against-schmitts-political-theology-prometheus-or-pandora-hans-blumenberg-and-walter-benjamin-as-political-theologians/.

Østbø, Jardar. *The New Third Rome Readings of a Russian Nationalist Myth*. Stuttgart: Ibidem, 2016.

Index

Antrim · 94, 113
Apocalypse · iv, 222, 223, 224, 225
apocalyptic · 8, 54, 192, 197, 207, 222, 223, 224, 225, 226, 228, 260, 306, 345
Apocalypticism · 162, 223
Apollo · 36
apostasy · 198, 199, 203, 219
Aquinas · 177
Arctic · 74, 93, 94, 113, 114, 148, 149, 150, 151, 152, 153, 154, 155, 156, 157, 322
Arctic Circle · 113
Arctic Institute · 149, 155
Arctic Ocean · 74, 148, 151
Arctic Region · 154
Arctic Zone · 148, 154
Arctogaia · 4, 155, 219, 315, 329
Arktogeya · 3, 16, 69, 216, 309, 330
Arktos · 17, 279, 325, 329, 332, 342, 348
Armageddon · 224, 225, 260
Armstrong · 250, 254, 255, 256, 258, 323
Arthurian Narrative · 36
Aryanist · 2
Aryiana Vaeijao · 135
Asahara · 225
asharitas · 188
Asia · 70, 74, 75, 76, 86, 95, 100, 105, 106, 124, 127, 131, 152, 153, 193, 202, 291, 321, 334
Åslund · 111
Atheism · 170, 173, 222
Atlantic Ocean · 128, 138
Atlantic Zone · 126, 127, 140
Atlanticist · 78, 80, 223
Atlantis · iii, 81, 84, 134, 137, 139, 145, 146, 270
Atlantism · 128, 130, 140
Atomism · 25, 26, 188, 212
Aum Shinrikyō · 224, 225
Australian National University · 149
axes of power · 133
axis mundi · 133

B

Baev · 149
Baigent · 62
Bakunin · 158
Baltics · 88, 96
Bannon · 56, 64
Baptism of the 'Rus · 195
Baraclough · 218
Barbashin · 3, 4, 14, 15, 293, 310, 323
Barkun · 249, 255, 256, 258, 323
Barth · 159, 175, 338
Barthold · 86
Bassin · 4, 16, 80, 84, 86, 87, 89, 97, 101, 102, 104, 110, 111, 115, 117, 118, 119, 129, 299, 303, 308, 323
Beale · 213, 323

354

355

California · 32, 110, 196, 244, 290, 291, 350
Cambridge School · 283, 284, 290
Campbell · 244
Canon Law · 7
Capitalism · ii, 40, 41, 42, 43, 51, 59, 205, 261, 317
Capitalist · 60
cardinal points · 132, 133, 192, 193
Carnegie · 115, 148, 154
carpe diem · 134
Carrère · 14, 326, 334
Cartesian · 29, 36, 187
Cartesianism · 187
catastrophe theories · 232
Catechon (see Katechon) · 199, 203, 218
Cathar(s) · 37, 58
Catholic · 12, 21, 38, 176, 177, 186, 198, 199, 216, 220, 268, 324, 345
Catholicism · 8, 12, 38, 39, 58, 216
Cavanaugh · 197, 216, 326
Center for Circumpolar Security Studies · 149
Center for Geopolitical Expertise · 3
Center for Special Meta-Strategic Studies · 3
Central Muslim Spiritual Directorate of Russia · 309
Chadwick · 47, 61, 326
Chair of Peter · 198
Champollion · 287
Charlemagne · 36, 111

Chartres · 287
Chauvinism · 74, 173, 321
Chechen · 140
Chiang Kai-Shek · 313
Chilingarov · 93, 113
China · 127, 129, 177
Chinese · 101, 135, 194, 197, 214
Christ · 11, 19, 34, 38, 42, 159, 199, 207, 211, 220, 223
Christian · vii, 4, 6, 7, 8, 9, 10, 19, 21, 33, 34, 35, 51, 86, 95, 111, 159, 163, 167, 168, 175, 185, 192, 193, 197, 202, 203, 205, 206, 209, 210, 212, 214, 216, 218, 220, 221, 230, 233, 238, 249, 250, 251, 252, 253, 255, 256, 257, 262, 263, 267, 288, 304, 307, 314, 325, 326, 330, 337, 340, 341, 342, 343, 351
Christianity · i, 6, 7, 8, 10, 11, 13, 18, 37, 38, 58, 132, 168, 198, 199, 202, 204, 205, 217, 219, 227, 241, 255, 256, 259, 260, 266, 270
Christian Identity · 209, 210
Church and State · 11, 20, 21, 159
Churchill · 124, 129, 342
Cicero · 243
civil religion · 6, 187, 188
civil religious · 168
civilizational struggle · 198
Clarke · 59

eschatological · 8, 20, 36, 54, 187, 196, 205, 212, 220, 221, 222, 223, 224, 226, 227, 260, 319

Eschatology · 63, 162, 204, 223, 224, 226

Esoteric · i, 2, 6, 7, 8, 10, 14, 23, 29, 36, 37, 40, 41, 48, 66, 81, 137, 142, 185, 187, 188, 205, 214, 225, 233, 234, 235, 259, 266, 268, 277, 298, 305, 320

Esotericism · 4, 7, 30, 66, 232, 235, 268, 295

Eurasia · iv, xiii, xv, 1, 16, 39, 64, 70, 71, 72, 74, 76, 80, 82, 84, 86, 88, 93, 95, 96, 98, 99, 101, 102, 103, 106, 108, 111, 112, 114, 115, 121, 122, 123, 124, 125, 126, 129, 130, 131, 138, 139, 145, 170, 195, 197, 199, 203, 205, 206, 208, 209, 212, 223, 259,260, 272, 276, 278, 279, 298, 300, 307, 309, 310, 321, 324, 329, 334, 350

Eurasian · iii, xii, xiii, xv, 4, 12, 15, 18, 19, 20, 34, 36, 52, 53, 56, 62, 63, 66, 69, 71, 72, 74, 77, 84, 86, 87, 88, 89, 92, 93, 95, 96, 97, 98, 99, 100, 101, 102, 103, 104, 105, 106, 107, 108, 109, 110, 111, 114, 115, 116, 118, 120, 121, 122, 123, 124, 125, 126, 127, 128, 129, 130, 131, 132, 133, 140, 142, 143, 146, 147, 154, 162, 172, 186, 191, 194, 195, 208, 212, 213, 215, 216, 219, 221, 223, 227, 240, 248, 259, 273, 274, 299, 301, 302, 303, 304, 305, 306, 308, 319, 321, 322, 323, 326, 329, 331, 345, 350

Eurasianist · 2

Eurasian Economic Union · 299

Eurasian Youth Movement · 4

Eurasian Youth Union · 302

Eurasianism · ii, iii, v, xv, 18, 31, 73, 77, 79, 80, 82, 83, 84, 86, 87, 88, 89, 95, 97, 98, 99, 100, 103, 104, 105, 106, 107, 108, 109, 110, 111, 115, 116, 117, 118, 119, 120, 121, 124, 125, 128, 129, 131, 132, 140, 146, 147, 160, 170, 172, 175, 184, 243, 251, 252,260, 271, 273, 274, 275, 279, 281, 296, 297, 300, 301, 306, 307, 309, 310, 314, 315, 316, 318, 319, 320, 323, 327, 329, 339, 342, 345, 347, 348, 352

Eurasianist(s) · vii, viii, 67, 70, 73, 77, 89, 91, 95, 97, 98, 100, 103, 104, 105, 106, 108, 109, 111, 119, 128, 147, 172, 209, 253, 259, 263, 273, 289, 299,

301, 302, 311, 312, 318, 321, 329, 346

Eurasians · 52, 77, 84, 100, 303, 346

Euro-Africa Zone · 127

Europe · xv, 20, 36, 46, 55, 70, 71, 72, 74, 75, 76, 80, 82, 84, 87, 89, 91, 98, 100, 101, 102, 106, 107, 112, 117, 124, 128, 131, 140, 152, 153, 174, 177, 193, 196, 218, 243, 252, 254, 263, 278, 286, 299, 307, 321, 328, 330, 331, 350

European · xii, xv, 4, 14, 16, 19, 23, 25, 31, 54, 74, 75, 79, 80, 85, 86, 91, 92, 93, 95, 98, 100, 101, 102, 117, 127, 128, 130, 148, 165, 167, 189, 197, 209, 215, 217, 228, 229, 243, 257, 263, 268, 275, 278, 296, 307, 325, 329, 332, 339, 342, 344

European New Right (see ENR) · 4, 85, 263, 278

European Rationalist Utopians · 189

Evgeniia Debrianskaia · 14

Evola · v, 30, 35, 45, 141, 147, 173, 188, 231, 234, 241, 242, 243, 244, 248, 260, 261, 262, 263, 264, 265, 267, 271, 272, 273, 276, 277, 278, 304, 315, 319, 330, 331, 332

Evrazia · 59, 63, 329

Evraziiskoe obozrenie · 25

Evraziiskoe vtorzhenie · 25

Evraziya · 4, 16, 300

exegesis · 209, 210, 254, 284, 291

Exoteric · 7, 9, 266

Expert Commission on Norwegian Security and Defence Policy · 148, 154, 155

F

Fabbri · 234, 236, 239, 242, 246, 247, 272, 278, 333

Faber · 166, 179, 333

Fahey · 113

family resemblance · 255

Far North · 148

Farber · 291, 333

Fascism · 13, 15, 45, 82, 119, 172, 173, 182, 275, 310, 311, 312, 313, 314, 315, 316, 317, 334, 337, 343, 345, 346, 347, 350, 351

Fascist · vi, 4, 17, 58, 182, 257, 293, 312, 313, 314, 315, 316, 317, 333, 334, 350

Feldman · 316, 334

Fenghi · 15

Ferguson · 84

Fifth Directorate · 176

Filofei of Pskov · 200

Final Thrust South · 303

Finis Mundi · 5

First Principles · 238

Griffiths · 177, 349
Grigorova · 77
Groh · 294
Grondin · 183, 210, 334
Groznyy · 92
Guaita · 245
Guelph · 20
Guénon · 6, 7, 35, 40, 41, 45, 66, 68, 143, 188, 207, 221, 230, 231, 233, 234, 236, 237, 239, 240, 242, 243, 244, 245, 246, 247, 248, 260, 261, 262, 263, 264, 265, 267, 268, 269, 270, 271, 272, 273, 274, 275, 277, 278, 279, 319, 332, 335
Guenonism · 8
Guenonists · 265
Gulf War · 205
Gumilev · 18, 87, 98, 99, 100, 103, 104, 107, 111, 116, 117, 118, 119, 132, 345
Gumilyov National University · 87
Gurdjieff · 35
Gurganus · 96, 115, 202, 217

H

Halewood · 75
Hall · 286, 292, 293, 335
Hanegraaff · 232, 233, 241, 242, 245, 335
Hansen · 229
Hanson · 158, 168, 175, 180, 335

Harakas · 20
Harris · 170, 171, 181, 335, 349
Hart · 177, 349
Hartley · 214, 287, 293, 336, 343
Hartman · 249, 250, 255, 256, 332
Harvard · 116, 181, 215, 243, 290, 306, 331, 333
Hasidic · 258
Hasidim · 52
Hassan · 250, 256, 336
Hauerwas · 177, 349
Haushofer · 67
Heartland · 69, 70, 71, 73, 74, 76, 88, 114, 147, 296, 298, 307, 326
Heavenly Jerusalem · 228
Hebrew · 11, 192, 230
Heidegger · i, 26, 27, 28, 29, 30, 33, 34, 35, 68, 210, 246, 269, 276, 325, 336
Heiser · 293
Heraclitus · 32
heresy(ies) · 38, 58, 167, 200, 270, 271, 272
heretical · 249, 270, 271, 272, 273, 278, 318, 319
heretics · 10, 271
Heritage Foundation · 120, 311, 327
Hermeneutic of Geopolitical Theology · 184, 185, 321
Hermeneutic of Political Theology · 183

I

265, 272, 276, 303, 313, 318, 330, 331, 344

Liberal Democracy · vii, xvi, 47, 220, 265, 272, 318, 344

Liberal Democratic Party · 303

Liberalism · xv, 21, 22, 27, 39, 53, 78, 82, 83, 167, 169, 173, 178, 182, 187, 190, 211, 222, 223, 250, 257, 265, 272, 299, 318, 324, 326, 341, 342, 345, 348

Licinius · 227

Lifton · 225, 228

Limonka · 3, 15

Limonov · 2, 3, 14, 299, 301, 326, 333

Lincoln · 31, 62, 214, 346

Linear B · 61, 326

Lings · 279, 335

Liverant · 87, 110, 111, 293, 294, 306, 339

Locke · 170

Logos · 32, 135

Lossky · 10, 19, 20, 339

Lucifer · 211

Luddism · 226

Luddite · 225

Lundquist · 193, 214, 340

Luther · 242, 270

Luven · 250, 256, 340

M

machine-of-state · 165

Mackinder · 67, 70, 71, 72, 73, 74, 75, 122, 129, 151, 296, 297, 298, 307, 340, 342

Mackinderian · vi, 150, 151, 296, 297

Macquarrie · 33, 176, 325, 340

magic · 40, 59, 66, 233, 267

Magical Materialism · 36, 38, 39

Mahan · 67, 70, 75, 150, 151

Mahanian · 150, 151

Maimonides · 160

Malić · 46, 60, 61, 68, 176, 340

Malofeev · 5, 17, 300, 309

Mamleyev · 263

Man of Lawlessness · 203, 219

Man of Sin · 208

Manichaean · 81, 254

Manicheaen · 85

Manifest Destiny · iv, xiii, 1, 88, 131, 149, 184, 185, 195, 196, 197, 215, 274, 279, 311, 324

Mantzavinos · 184, 210, 211, 341

Marsden · 249, 253, 255, 258, 341

Marsh · 241, 341

Martin · 21, 242, 245, 250, 256, 279, 286, 292, 293, 335, 336, 341, 343

Martinism · 245

Martinist · 245

Marty · 250, 254, 256, 258, 341

Marx · 42, 288, 294

Mladineo · 71, 72, 75, 76, 342

modern · xvi, 6, 25, 26, 30, 33, 41, 43, 66, 109, 112, 137, 140, 141, 146, 161, 164, 165, 166, 167, 178, 195, 207, 220, 223, 226, 227, 232, 239, 247, 251, 262, 265, 268, 270, 273, 279, 284, 319, 330

Modern · xv, xvi, 31, 32, 41, 59, 137, 143, 146, 167, 170, 176, 178, 179, 180, 211, 212, 213, 214, 220, 228, 234, 243, 244, 246, 248, 256, 274, 275, 276, 277, 278, 322, 324, 326, 328, 330, 332, 334, 335, 339, 340, 342, 347, 348

Modernism · iv, 33, 184, 188, 226, 233, 249, 251, 253, 259, 264, 267, 268, 269, 270, 271, 320

Modernist(s) · 257, 290

Modernity · v, xv, 25, 26, 27, 29, 30, 49, 82, 109, 165, 166, 167, 168, 171, 174, 178, 179, 181, 182, 188, 205, 206, 207, 223, 228, 239, 240, 246, 247, 254, 259, 261, 265, 267, 270, 271, 276, 277, 278, 304, 319, 334, 335, 351

Mölder · 114

mole · 42, 43

monarchical · 165, 167, 171

Mondialism · 222, 224, 266

Mondmensch · 134

Mongols · 95, 135, 150

Monotheism · 168

monotheistic · 39, 166, 167

Montgomery · 293, 343

Morgan · 17, 32, 33, 75, 85, 104, 119, 147, 162, 176, 227, 329, 332, 342, 348

Morgan-Owen · 75

Morning Star · 187

Morozova · 296, 305, 307, 311, 342

Mosbey · 211, 226, 342

Moscow · 1, 4, 5, 8, 9, 10, 16, 17, 31, 63, 68, 69, 76, 90, 96, 97, 105, 114, 115, 121, 146, 148, 149, 155, 198, 199, 201, 202, 203, 206, 212, 213, 215, 216, 217, 276, 278, 296, 297, 298, 299, 300, 304, 306, 307, 327, 328, 330, 344, 350, 351

Moscow State University · 4, 5, 17, 298, 299, 306, 350

Moses · 43, 138

Moshiah · 205, 206, 219, 222

Moss · 9, 10, 19, 20, 189, 207, 212, 220, 221, 223, 224, 227, 342

Mount Olympus · 138

Mount Sinai · 138

multipolar · xii, xiii, xv, 6, 56, 82, 87, 105, 108, 120, 123, 125, 126, 127, 128, 141, 149, 174, 253, 270, 319, 321, 322

multipolarity · 105, 140

Munteanu · 287, 293, 342
Murrah Federal Building · 225
Muscovy · 195, 215
Muslim · 98, 309
Muslims · 10, 99, 195
Mutti · 263
Müür · 114
mystery of grace · 208, 221
mystic · 235
mystical · 2, 8, 10, 11, 36, 41, 50, 64, 89, 159, 187, 192, 193, 202, 208, 245, 263
Mysticism · 10, 19, 20, 235, 242, 328, 339

N

Nasr · 234, 243, 247, 277, 342
National Bolshevik Party · 2
national psychology · 201
National Socialism · 58, 252, 312
National Socialist · 172, 252, 257
Nationalism · 50, 74, 100, 103, 105, 111, 190, 297, 301, 312, 313, 315
Nationalist School · 153, 154
Native American(s) · 132, 191, 192
NATO · xv, 114, 120, 150, 346
Natural Law · 226

Nature · 142, 181, 190, 233, 241, 256, 316, 332, 334, 335, 336
Nazi(s) · 4, 150, 252, 306, 312, 314, 317
NBP · 2, 3, 299
Negotiated Code · 286, 287
Nelson · 21
Neo-Eurasianism · 95, 98, 104, 105, 106, 109, 273, 318, 320
Neoplatonism · 111
Neo-Traditional · 267, 319
Neo-Traditionalism · 32, 174, 184, 234, 260, 261, 262, 264, 265, 267, 270, 276, 318, 319, 320
Neo-Traditionalist · 264, 271, 319
Netherlands · 140
New (David)· 257, 343
New Age · 14, 265, 315
New Grange · 191
New Right · 315, 347
New Testament · 7, 190, 192, 214, 224
New University · 263
New World Order · xvii, 50, 52, 53, 54, 55, 56, 57, 78, 205, 220, 223
New York (City) · 14, 288, 333
Newman · 158, 159, 164, 174, 175, 178, 207, 221, 343
Nicholas I · 218
Nicon · 219, 220
Nightingale of the General Staff · 276

371

199, 200, 203, 218, 219,
250, 254, 260, 267, 269,
270, 271, 272, 304, 309,
330, 342
orthopraxis · 7, 254, 270
Orwell · 313, 316, 343

Ø

Østbø · 112, 352

O

O'Sullivan · 196, 215, 293,
343
Ottomans · 90, 91, 198
Outer Crescent · 72
Ovcharenko · 296, 307

P

Pacific Zone · 127
pagan · 7, 10, 134, 288
Pamyat · 4, 301
Panarin · 309
Panslav · 201
Pantheism · 245
Pan-Turkism · 77, 116, 117,
118, 352
Papava · 74, 76, 96, 114
Papocaesarism · 20, 169
Paracelsus · 233, 242
Paradise · 38, 39, 42, 52,
193
paranoia · 46, 54, 55, 56
paranoid · 53, 54, 55, 56,
64, 336

Parchizadeh · 90, 91, 96,
111, 112, 114, 343
Parker · 52, 63, 344
Parland · 3, 15, 344
Parsons · 174, 182, 344
Partridge · 228, 344
Passionarnost (also
Passionarost) · 100, 117
patriarch · 8, 12, 142, 202,
214, 215, 216, 217, 218,
219, 220, 300, 327
Patriarchy · 199, 207
Patrushev, · 296, 307
Paul · xiv, 131, 142, 149,
154, 157, 177, 195, 199,
203, 208, 237, 242, 276,
303, 310, 326, 327, 334,
336, 337, 344, 349
Pavlovksy · 302
Pax Americana · 125
Péladan · 245
Pelikan · 235, 240, 245,
248, 250, 344
People's National-Patriotic
Orthodox Christian
Movement · *See* Pamyat
Peoria · vi, 288, 289, 294,
295
Perennial Christianity · 6
Perennial Philosophy · 232,
242, 275, 337, 347, 349
Perennialism · 230, 231,
233, 234, 241, 242, 243,
269, 328, 333
Perennialist · 231, 233, 235,
242, 246, 247, 262, 268,
272, 278, 333
Perlwitz · 113
Peter I · 91, 92, 112, 207

373

344, 345, 348, 349, 350, 352

Russia-Central Asia Zone · 127

Russian Empire · 74, 90, 92, 93, 94, 101, 103, 110, 111, 112, 113, 114, 128, 293, 294, 338, 339

Russian Federation · 105, 115, 120, 127, 128, 148, 154, 305, 307

Russian foreign policy · 97, 149, 301

Russian Messianism · 201

Russian Nationalism · 169, 190, 212

Russian Orthodox · 11, 198, 262, 300

Russian Revolution · 102, 107, 207

Russkiy Mir · 114

Russo · ix, 21, 90, 302, 346

Ryrie · 175, 346

S

Saadia · 160

Sacred Architecture · 7

Sacred Determinism · 29

Sacred Emperor · 37

Sacred Geography · iii, iv, xvi, 29, 34, 57, 66, 68, 80, 81, 82, 84, 88, 89, 133, 134, 137, 139, 141, 190, 195, 131, 132, 133, 137, 141, 142, 143, 144, 145, 146, 147, 160, 162, 183, 184, 185, 189, 190, 191, 193, 194, 195, 213, 214, 321, 329

Sacred Geography/Sacred Space. · iii, iv, xii, xvi, 80, 84, 131, 132, 133, 142, 143, 183, 184, 185, 189, 190, 191, 192, 193, 195, 321, 325

Sacred Geometry · 133, 142

Sacred Imperialism · 37, 58

Sacred Poles · 133

Sakha Republic · 154

Salafism · 188

Salafist · 188

San Francisco State University · 115

sarin gas · 224

Satan · 42, 43, 187, 206, 211, 219, 227

Satie · 245

Saunders · 293, 343

Savenko · *See* Limonov

Savitskii · 77, 116, 346, *See* Savitsky

Savitsky · 74, 77, 87, 98, 99, 100, 103, 110

Sawyer · 280, 281, 282, 284, 285, 288, 289, 290, 291, 292, 293, 346

Sazonov · 114, 346

Schechter · 294

schism · 9, 198

Schmitt · iv, 6, 13, 17, 32, 49, 160, 161, 162, 164, 165, 166, 167, 168, 176, 178, 179, 180, 185, 186, 188, 203, 206, 207, 211, 212, 216, 218, 220, 221, 251, 252, 253, 257, 259,

274, 312, 324, 337, 341, 345, 346, 347, 351, 352

Schuon · 234, 240, 243, 244, 245, 247, 265, 347, 351

Schwab · 17, 211, 347

science · 15, 66, 140, 162, 177, 242, 256, 257, 267, 290, 293

Scientism · 39, 40

Scripture · 35, 182, 210, 211, 237

Scruton · 84

sea-power · 70, 85, 137, 145

Second Rome · 11, 198, 203

Second Theory · 172

secular · xiii, 1, 52, 109, 133, 138, 140, 151, 162, 163, 164, 166, 179, 187, 188, 225, 249, 250, 268, 304

Secularism · 162, 163, 176

secularization · 21, 49, 165, 166, 178, 179, 185, 274, 334, 337, 341

Secularization Theorem · 165, 166, 178, 185

Secularization Theory · 178

secularized · 161, 165, 166, 178, 198, 222, 224

Sedgewick (see Sedgwick)

Sedgwick · 14, 35, 64, 234, 235, 236, 243, 244, 245, 246, 248, 276, 305, 347

Sein · 27, 28, 29

Seitz · 60

Sekatski (see Sekatsky)

Sekatsky · 172, 182

Separation of Church and State · 12, 21

Separation of Powers · 47, 170

Separatism · 253, 254

Seredonin · 88, 89

Sermon on the Mount · 138, 146

Serpent(s) · ii, 42, 43, 57, 60, 211, 227, 331

Sex Pistols · 315

Shekhovtsov · 25, 31, 227, 264, 267, 271, 272, 273, 274, 275, 276, 278, 305, 347

Sheldrake · 133, 143, 189, 212, 215, 347

Shenfield · 13, 80, 84, 263, 275, 347

Shiite(s) · 12

Shils · 174, 182, 190, 347

Shiraev · 88, 111, 348

Shiva · 225

Shlapentokh · 18, 77, 87, 106, 110, 111, 116, 120, 339, 345, 348, 352

Shnirelman · 52, 62, 63, 348

Shōkō Asahara · 225

Shtyrov · 154

Siberia · 92, 105

Sigalet · 180, 348

Siira · 75

Simmins · 132, 142, 191, 192, 193, 213, 348

Sinai · 138

Skinner · 283, 290, 327, 348

381

384

Wyllie · 166, 179, 352

X

xenophobia · 173, 226
xenophobic · 314

Y

Yale University · 15, 210,
245, 326, 334, 339, 344
Yamal-Nenets Autonomous
Region · 154
Yang · 194, 214
yedinoverie · *See* Old
Believer
Yeltsin · 105, 205, 301, 302
Yin · 194, 214

Young · 33, 154, 157, 214,
336, 340
Yuriev · 217

Z

Zarathustra · See
Zoroaster
Zavtra · 25, 63
Zhirinovsky · 303, 310,
311, 327, 334, 351
Ziegler · 261, 274
Zoroaster · 233, 242
Zoroastrian · 135, 233
Zwischen · 29
Zyuganov · 98, 104, 105,
115

www.ingramcontent.com/pod-product-compliance
Lightning Source LLC
Chambersburg PA
CBHW070051030426
42335CB00016B/1851